PRIVATE PARTIES IN EUROPEAN COMMUNITY LAW

Challenging Community Measures

Private Parties in European Community Law

Challenging Community Measures

ALBERTINA ALBORS-LLORENS
Licenciada en Derecho (Valencia)
LL.M. (London)
Ph.D. (Cantab)

CLARENDON PRESS · OXFORD
1996

Oxford University Press, Walton Street, Oxford OX2 6DP
Oxford New York
Athens Auckland Bangkok Bombay
Calcutta Cape Town Dar es Salaam Delhi
Florence Hong Kong Istanbul Karachi
Kuala Lumpur Madras Madrid Melbourne
Mexico City Nairobi Paris Singapore
Taipei Tokyo Toronto
and associated companies in
Berlin Ibadan

Oxford is a trade mark of Oxford University Press

Published in the United States
by Oxford University Press Inc., New York

British Library Cataloguing in Publication Data
Data available

Library of Congress Cataloging in Publication Data
Albors-Llorens, Albertina.
Private parties in European Community law: challenging Community measures / Albertina Albors-Llorens.
p. cm.
Includes bibliographical references.
1. Extraordinary remedies—European Union countries. 2. Popular actions—European Union countries. 3. Judical review of administrative acts—European Union countries.
KJE5461.A947 1996
347.4′077—dc20
[344.077] 96–10666
ISBN 0–19–826080–6

1 3 5 7 9 10 8 6 4 2

Typeset by Vera A. Keep, Cheltenham
Printed in Great Britain
on acid-free paper by
Bookcraft Ltd., Midsomer Norton, Avon

Στόν Παντελῆ καί στόν Ἀλέξανδρο,
μέ ἀγάπη καί εὐγνωμοσύνη

Preface

A. SCOPE OF THIS BOOK

This book focuses on the study of the rights of private parties to challenge European Community measures. The Community legislative process is still characterized by a certain lack of democracy, even after the Maastricht amendments to the European Community Treaties. It is therefore of the utmost importance to ensure the appropriate functioning of a system of judicial review of Community acts. Private parties have been granted access to this system by means of two direct actions (the action for annulment and the action for a failure to act) and one indirect action (the plea of illegality). In addition to these remedies, there are two other methods that may be used to challenge a Community act (preliminary rulings on validity and action for damages).

This book is divided in two main parts. They follow a chapter that introduces the subject of the book and places it in its immediate context.

The first part deals in detail with annulment proceedings, which occupy a central position in the system of judicial review. The action for annulment was conceived specifically as the direct means of challenging Community measures and was endowed with all the advantages of a direct action. In the case of natural and legal persons, however, the drafters of the EC Treaty attached draconian conditions of *locus standi* to this remedy, and it fell to the European Court of Justice to interpret and apply these conditions by way of its case law. Academic writers hae found it rather difficult to discern a consistent trend in the Court's approach to the *locus standi* issue. It appears clear, however, that the Court has followed a very restrictive approach and many actions hae been dismissed as inadmissible. In this book,the case law is systematized and it is shown how the case law in certain areas (anti-dumping, competition, and state aids) and even in the area of general management of the market has evolved towards more lenient standards in its treatment of the issue of the *locus standi* of natural and legal persons.

The second part of the book deals with the alternative means that may be used by private parties in order to obtain the review of a Community measure. If a non-privileged applicant is not able, owing to lack of *locus standi*, to bring annulment proceedings before the European Court of Justice to review allegedly illegal Community acts, that does not matter if the system of remedies provided by the Community Treaties offers an alternative route to obtaining that review. The object of this second part is to consider those means of redress in the light of the underlying question whether they guarantee a satisfactory alternative for a natural or legal person unable to bring annulment proceedings as a consequence of the admissibility conditions attached to Article 173 proceedings.

B. PRELIMINARY NOTES

This book is based on the revised texts (incorporating the Maastricht amendments) of the European Community Treaties. *Before* the Maastricht amendments to the EEC Treaty, the legal provision that contained the *locus standi* eonditions imposed on private parties in the framework of annulment proceedings was Article 173(2) EEC Treaty. The relevant provision *after* the Maastricht amendments is Article 173(4) EC Treaty, which reads in identical terms. In this book reference sometimes is made to Article 173(2) EEC Treaty in order to avoid confusion, given that the European Court of Justice refers to this provision in all the case law studied.

Council Decision 93/350[1] has transferred to the Court of First Instance jurisdiction to deal with all actions brought by private parties. The Decision entered into force on 1 August 1993 (for anti-dumping cases, on 15 March 1994). This book has taken into consideration the case law of the European Court on annulment proceedings and on alternative means of review, and the case law of the Court of First Instance to date.

The law is stated as at 1 June 1995.

My greatest debt is to Ms Eleanor Sharpston, who supervised my Ph.D Thesis, on which this book is based. She has been both guide and friend to me. All errors remain entirely my own.

Mrs Thirza Hope and Miss María Paz Aparisi have given me great encouragement. Miss Rosemary Graham has, with great patience, helped me to copy-edit this book.

My thanks also go to Mr Richard Hart of Oxford University Press for his kindness to me during the time of preparation of this book.

I am very grateful to my family for their constant support.

A. Albors-Llorens
September 1995

[1] [1993] OJ L144/21.

Contents

PART TWO—ALTERNATIVE MEANS OF REVIEW

Table of Cases

European Court of Justice

numerical list

ALPHABETICAL LIST

OPINIONS

Court of First Instance of the European Communities

NUMERICAL LIST

ALPHABETICAL LIST

Courts of the Member States

BELGIAN COURTS

FRENCH COURTS

GERMAN COURTS

ENGLISH COURTS

IRISH COURTS

SCOTTISH COURTS

SPANISH COURTS

OTHER COURTS

UNITED STATES COURTS

EUROPEAN COMMISSION OF HUMAN RIGHTS

Table of Legislation

Treaties

EC Treaty

EEC TREATY

ECSC TREATY

EURATOM TREATY

GENERAL AGREEMENT ON TARIFFS AND TRADE (GATT)

MAASTRICT TREATY

SINGLE EUROPEAN ACT

REGULATIONS

Directives

Decisions

council decisions

Commission Decisions

general decisions

competition decisions

anti-dumping decisions

National Legislation

BELGIUM

ENGLAND

GERMANY

GREECE

IRELAND

ITALY

NETHERLANDS

PORTUGAL

SCOTLAND

SPAIN

European Courts

Court of First Instance

European Court of Justice

Abbreviations

AC	*Appeal Cases*
AS	*Act of Sederunt*
BOE	*Boletín Oficial del Estado Español*
BVerwGE	*Entscheidungen des Bundesverwaltungsgerichts*
BYIL	*British Yearbook of International Law*
CDE	*Cahiérs de Droit Européen*
CFI	*Court of First Instance of the European Communities*
CH	*Chancery*
CJCEE	*Cour de Justice des Communautés Européennes*
CLJ	*Cambridge Law Journal*
CMLR	*Common Market Law Reports*
CMLRev	*Common Market Law Review*
EAGGF	*European Agricultural Guidance and Guarantee Fund*
EC	*European Community*
EC	*Treaty European Community Treaty*
EEC	*Treaty European Economic Community Treaty*
ECHR	*European Commission of Human Rights*
ECJ	*European Court of Justice*
ECSC	*European Coal and Steel Community*
ECR	*European Court Reports*
EFG	*Entscheidungen der Finanzgerichte*
ELRev	*European Law Review*
EURATOM	*European Atomic Energy Community*
Fordham Int. L.J.	*Fordham International Law Journal*
GATT	*General Agreement on Tariffs and Trade*
ICLQ	*International Comparative Law Quarterly*
ILRM	*Irish Law Reports Monthly*
IR	*Irish Reports*
JDI	*Journal du Droit International*
JO	*Journal Officiel des Communautés Européennes*
JWTL	*Journal of World Trade Law*
KB	*King's Bench*
LGDJ	*Librairie General de Droit et Jurisprudence*
LGR	*Local Government Reports*
LIEI	*Legal Issues of European Integration*
Northwestern U.L.R.	*Northwestern University Law Review*

OJ	*Official Journal of the European Communities*
OJ Eng. Sp. Ed.	*Official Journal of the European Communities, English Special Edition*
QB	*Queen's Bench*
RCJB	*Revue Critique de Jurisprudence Belge*
RDIDC	*Revue du Droit International et de Droit Comparé*
RDR	*Revue de Droit Rural*
Rec.	*Recueil de la Jurisprudence de la Cour de Justice des Communautés Européennes et du Tribunal de Première Instance*
Rec. Arr. Av. Con. d'État.	*Recueil des Arrêts et Avis du Conseil d'État* (Belgium)
Rec. Con. d'État	*Recueil des Arrêts du Conseil d'État* (France)
R. Esp. D. Int.	*Revista Española de Derecho Internacional*
Rev. Dr. Pub.	*Revue du Droit Public et de la Science Politique*
RMC	*Revue du Marché Commun*
RSC	*Rules of the Supreme Court* (England)
RSCts	*Rules of the Superior Courts* (Ireland)
RTDE	*Revue Trimestrielle de Droit Européen*
SEA	*Single European Act*
SLT	*Scotts Law Times*
South. Cal. L. R.	*South California Law Review*
Texas Int. L. J.	*Texas International Law Journal*
Univ. Cinc. L. R.	*University of Cincinnati Law Review*
Univ. Det. L. J.	*University of Detroit Law Journal*
US	*United States Supreme Court Reports*
Vir. Int. L. J.	*Virginia International Law Journal*
VwGO	*Verwaltungsgerichtsordnung*
YEL	*Yearbook of European Law*

1

Private Parties and Judicial Review of Community Action

1.1 Judicial Review in the European Communities

After several failed attempts by the European States to achieve some form of unity following the end of the Second World War, the signing of the Treaty of Paris in 1951 laid the foundation stone of a European Community. This Treaty established the European Coal and Steel Community,[1] which sought a form of sectorial integration by the pooling of French and German coal and steel resources and those of any other countries wishing to participate. The idea was endorsed with enthusiasm by other European States, and a few years later, further developments took place with the signing of the Treaty of Rome, which established the European Atomic Energy Community,[2] again seeking sectorial integration, and the European Economic Community,[3] which had the more far-reaching aim of general economic integration.

These three Treaties created a structure hitherto unknown and called by many 'supranational': the European Communities. They brought with them a new legal order which, although linked with International Law, had revolutionary features.

In the first place, the European Communities Treaties provided for a set of independent institutions vested with powers irreversibly transferred to them by the Member States, which in their turn were required to accept a limitation on their sovereignty in certain fields.[4]

In the second place, the subjects of this new legal order are not only the Member States but also their nationals. As the Court emphasized in *Van Gend en Loos* v. *Nederlandse Administratie der Belastingen*, 'this view is confirmed by the preamble of the Treaty, which refers not only to Governments but to peoples'.[5]

[1] The Treaty establishing the European Coal and Steel Community will hereafter be referred to as the ECSC Treaty.

[2] The Treaty establishing the European Atomic Energy Community will hereafter be referred to as the Euratom Treaty.

[3] The Maastricht Treaty has replaced the term 'European Economic Community' for the European Community (Title II, Art. G of the Treaty). The Treaty establishing the European Economic Community (the EEC Treaty) will hereafter be referred to as the EC Treaty.

[4] See Case 26/62 *Van Gend en Loos* v. *Nederlandse Administratie der Belastingen* [1963] ECR 1 at 12. Also Case 6/64 *Costa* v. *Enel* [1964] ECR 585 at 593, [1964] ECR 585 at 593.

[5] Case 26/62, n. 4 above, 12.

The institutions of the European Communities have been entrusted with the task of supervising the process of European integration. These bodies are the Commission, the Council, the European Parliament, the Court of Justice, and the Court of Auditors,[6] which, by exercising their functions within the limits of powers attributed to them by the founding Treaties, contribute to the growth of the European Community legal order.

The Commission and the Council have power to pass legislation to implement and develop the objectives and principles contained in the Treaties. In the case of the European Community of Coal and Steel, the Commission—originally known as High Authority—is the main legislative body. In the case of the European Atomic Energy Community and the European Community, the Council represents the major decision-making power, leaving to the Commission the role of initiating the legislative process and of implementing Council decisions by means of delegated powers.

The European Parliament performs a role quite different from that of the national parliaments. Under the original Treaties its powers in the legislative process were minimal and mainly of a consultative nature. This led to general concern for the lack of democracy in the European arena. The Council (the representative of national governments' interests) and the Commission (the guardian of Community interests) performed both legislative and executive functions when neither body had been directly elected by the nationals of the Member States. As a consequence, the participation of the Parliament in the adoption of legislation was increased with the introduction, by the Single European Act, of the co-operation procedure.[7] The Maastricht Treaty has effectively enlarged the legislative powers of the European Parliament by giving it the right of veto in some areas of legislation.[8] In spite of these much-welcomed reforms, the position of the European Parliament is quite substantially weaker in relation to the national parliaments, which are the main legislators in the Member States. This creates a situation where there is much less control over the executive activity of the Community and less participation of the European Parliament in the legislative process than is the case in a typical Member State.[9]

[6] Art. 4 EC Treaty, Art. 7 ECSC Treaty, and Art. 3 Euratom Treaty, all as amended by the Maastricht Treaty.

[7] Art. 6 and 7 of the Single European Act (SEA). According to some authors, the co-operation procedure did not bring about a very significant change in the position of the European Parliament. Thus T. C. Hartley, *The Foundations of European Community Law* (3rd edn., Oxford, 1994), 43. Other authors believe that in order for the European Parliament to intervene effectively in the EC law-making through this procedure, it needs the support of the Commission and of at least one of the Member States. Thus S. Weatherill and P. Beaumont, *EC Law* (London, 1993), 102.

[8] Art. 189(b) EC Treaty.

[9] There are areas where the Council may adopt legislation without consulting the European Parliament. See S. Weatherill and P. Beaumont, n. 7 above, 796–7.

All these institutions must act in a way that respects the rule of law, which is one of the pillars of the Community,[10] as it is of the Member States. The rule of law implies that the European institutions are bound in the performance of their functions by the Constitutional Charter of the European Communities, i.e. by the Treaties and their subsequent amendments, their Annexes and Protocols, and the Treaties of Accession of new Member States. They are also bound by the general principles of law as developed by the case law of the European Court,[11] and by the international agreements concluded by the Community.[12] In particular, given the democratic deficit present in the EC and the feeble powers of the Parliament, it was of the utmost importance to ensure that the legislative and administrative measures adopted by the Commission and the Council—which form the body of the so-called 'secondary Community legislation'—complied with the guidelines of superior legal norms.

A form of control had therefore to be devised. A 'guardian of the legality' had to be created in order to make sure that, in the performance of their functions, the EC institutions respected the rule of law.

In the majority of the Member States, two types of control exist to limit the action of the executive: on the one hand there is the political control exerted by the national parliaments and on the other there is the judicial control exerted by the courts. In the European Community, the supervisory role of the Parliament is very limited.[13] The main burden thus rests upon the European Court of Justice, an independent judicial body entrusted by the Treaties with the task of upholding the rule of law in the Community. Thus, Article 164 of the EC Treaty[14] reads: 'The Court of Justice shall

[10] The ECJ has acknowledged this principle through its case law. Thus, in Case 294/83 *Parti Ecologiste 'Les Verts'* v. *European Parliament* [1986] ECR 1339 at point 23, the Court said: 'It must be first emphasised in this regard that the European Economic Community is a Community based on the rule of law. '

[11] The European Court has developed in its jurisprudence a consistent body of general principles of law that all secondary legislation must respect. Respect for fundamental human rights (Case 4/73 *Nold* v. *Commission* [1974] ECR 491 at point 13); principle of proportionality (Case 18/57 *Nold* v. *Commission* [1959] ECR 41 at 52); legitimate expectations (Case 112/77 *Töpfer* v. *Commission* [1978] ECR 1019 at points 18–20); legal certainty (Case 169/80 *Administration des Douanes* v. *SA Gondrand Frères* [1981] ECR 1931 at point 17); equality (Case 106/83 *Sermide SpA* v. *Cassa Conguaglio Zucchero* [1984] ECR 4209 at point 28), and right to a fair hearing (Case 17/74 *Transocean Marine Paint Association* v. *Commission* [1974] ECR 1063 at point 15) are some of these principles.

[12] Thus, Joined Cases 21–24/72 *International Fruit Company* v. *Produktschap voor Groenten en Fruit* [1972] ECR 1219 at points 5–6 and *Opinion 1/75*, (*Local Cost Standard*) [1975] ECR 1355 at 1360–1.

[13] The most powerful weapon of the Parliament is to pass a motion of censure on the Commission in accordance with Art. 144 EC Treaty, but so far there have been only 5 (unsuccessful) attempts to pass such a motion.

[14] See also Art. 31 ECSC Treaty and Art. 136 Euratom Treaty.

ensure that in the interpretation and application of this Treaty the law is observed.'[15]

In *Parti Ecologiste 'Les Verts'* v. *European Parliament*, the Court said that the Community is based on the rule of law inasmuch as

[N]either its Member States nor its institutions can avoid a review of the question whether the measures adopted by them are in conformity with the basic constitutional charter, the Treaty. In particular, in Articles 173 and 184, on the one hand, and in Article 177, on the other, the Treaty established a complete system of legal remedies and procedures designed to permit the Court of Justice to review the legality of measures adopted by the institutions.[16]

Therefore the European Court not only ensures the uniform interpretation of EC law and upholds the Community rights of EC nationals against their Member States, but also carries out the task of ensuring that the EC institutions act within the limits of legality.[17]

The term 'judicial review' has so far been avoided. The reason for this is that, in the majority of the Member States, there is a clear-cut distinction between the review of the constitutionality of the laws and the judicial review of administrative acts.

With the exception of the United Kingdom all the Member States have written constitutions. In some States it is possible to obtain a judicial decision on the conformity of the national laws with the constitution,[18] which is normally decided by a special court.[19] In other Member States,

[15] See also Case C–2/88 Imm. *Zwartveld* [1990] ECR 1–3365 at point 16, where the Court explained that 'The EEC Treaty established the Court of Justice as a judicial body responsible for securing compliance with the law by the Member States and the Community's institutions.'

[16] Case 294/83, n. 10 above, at point 23. See also *Zwartveld* n. 15 above, at point 16.

[17] This duty to uphold the rule of law implies that the Court should interpret liberally the provisions of the Treaty concerning judicial protection in order to create a system that ensures protection without any gaps. The Court widely acknowledged this principle of the case law concerning preliminary rulings, through which the principles of direct effect and supremacy have developed, producing a more comprehensive system of judicial protection (see 182 below). However, in the case of annulment proceedings before the Court, and especially in the case law concerning the access of private parties to such remedy, the case law of the Court has been fairly restrictive in spite of the general mandate contained in Art. 164 and affirmations of the Court like the one given in Case 25/62 *Plaumann* v. *Commission* [1963] ECR 95 at 107: '[P]rovisions of the Treaty regarding the right of interested parties to bring an action must not be interpreted restrictively'. (See below Ch. 3, n. 94.)

[18] This is the case in Belgium (Art. 107*ter* of Belgian Constitution and implementing Act of 28 June 1981), Germany (Arts. 20(3) and 93 of the German Constitution), Greece (Art. 100 of the Greek Constitution), Ireland (Arts. 26 and 34 of the Irish Constitution), Italy (Art. 134 of the Italian Constitution), Portugal (Art. 281 of the Portuguese Constitution and Act 28/82 of 15 Nov. 1982 as amended by Act 143/85 of 26 Nov. 1985 and 85/89 of 7 Sept. 1989), and Spain (Art. 161 of the Spanish Constitution and *Ley Orgánica del Tribunal Constitucional* of 3 Oct. 1979).

[19] Thus, the Belgian Court of Arbitration, the German Federal Constitutional Court, the Greek Highest Special Court, the Irish Supreme and High Courts, and the Italian, Portuguese, and Spanish Constitutional Courts.

there is prior control of the constitutionality of the laws.[20] Finally, in some of the Member States the possibility of challenging legislative acts is altogether excluded.[21] Even in those countries where legislative acts cannot be subject to review, the presence of parliaments with strong legislative powers and formed by representatives directly elected by the nationals of the State ensures to a great extent the protection of their interests.

In all the Member States it is possible to challenge administrative acts. In some Member States there is a system of separate administrative courts endowed with jurisdiction in administrative matters. This system was first set up in France and in due course adopted in Belgium, Germany, Holland, Greece, Italy, Luxembourg, Portugal, and Spain. In other Member States like the United Kingdom, Denmark, and Ireland, the jurisdiction to decide such matters rests with the ordinary courts. For all these States the term 'judicial review' refers mainly to the courts' supervision of the action of public bodies to prevent them from enjoying absolute power.

In the European Communities the situation is quite different. The clear distinction between laws and administrative acts does not exist, due partly to the confusion of legislative and executive powers in the Council and the Commission. For instance, Article 189(1) EC Treaty succinctly declares that:

> In order to carry out their tasks *and in accordance with the provisions of this Treaty, the European Parliament acting jointly with the Council*, the Council and the Commission shall make regulations and issue directives, take decisions, make recommendations or deliver opinions.[22]

Thus, this formula does not specify which of these acts are of a legislative nature and which are of an administrative nature. Generally speaking, regulations are normally identified as 'Community laws'. Undeniably, some of them are real 'EC laws' but others clearly resemble general administrative acts.[23] Even decisions, which by definition are

[20] This control is exercised by the French *Conseil Constitutionnel*. The procedure regulated in Art. 228 EC Treaty, whereby the European Court may give a preliminary opinion on the compatibility of an international agreement with the EC Treaty before the former enters into force echoes the previous control of the constitutionality of laws as it appears in the French legal system.

[21] This is the case in the U.K. (by virtue of the principle of sovereignty of the Parliament), Luxembourg—M. Sheridan, J. Cameron, and J. Toulin, *EC Legal Systems: An Introductory Guide* (London, 1992), 3 (section on Luxembourg)—and The Netherlands (Art. 120 of the Dutch Constitution). In Denmark there is no constitutional provision guaranteeing the review of the conformity of ordinary laws with the Constitution. However, a jurisprudential trend has developed admitting the existence of such a control in some special cases (L. Favoreu, and J. A. Jolowicz, *Le Contrôle Juridictionnel des Lois* (Paris, 1985), 241). The Court of Appeal and the Supreme Court are considered by academic writers in general to be the competent bodies—M. Sheridan, J. Cameron, J. Toulmin, 3 (section on Denmark).

[22] The italicized words represent the Maastricht amendments.

[23] See 107 below.

individual administrative acts, can sometimes have a very general scope of application, especially in the case of decisions addressed to the Member States.

This confusion has resulted in the same remedies being used to assess the 'constitutionality' of legislative measures and the legality of administrative acts, whereas in the Member States there are separate remedies to control the conformity of laws with the constitution and to protect nationals against any illegal action by the Executive, as explained above.[24]

What is unquestionable is that in the Community it is necessary to have a system of judicial control over the acts enacted by the Council, the Commission, and other Community institutions. This system will be referred to from now on as a system of judicial review—bearing in mind the peculiarities of the EC legal order—that will cover both legislative and administrative acts. This system of judicial review is all the more important on account of the limited powers of the Parliament to intervene in the legislative process and the absence of a real supervisory role for this institution in respect of the Community's executive function.

There are two important areas that deserve attention in this system of judicial review: the avenues of review provided by the European Community Treaties and the position of private parties in the context of EC law.

1.2 Avenues of Judicial Review

The European Community Treaties established a system of judicial review whereby the European Court could control the legality of the acts of the Commission and the Council.[25] In this system of review, two direct actions and one indirect one were provided.

The two direct means of redress are the action for annulment and the

[24] See 4 above. This situation could give rise to conflict for various reasons. In the first place the grounds of illegality alleged in the national Member States by private parties when challenging administrative acts are substantially different from the grounds alleged to control the constitutionality of laws. In the second place the *locus standi* conditions imposed on private parties who wish to challenge both types of acts are very different, in individual national legal systems (see 30–1 below). In the EC Treaty the two situations merge into one which makes it very difficult to draw comparisons with the situation in national legal systems. The common approach amongst academics has been to draw comparisons between the national administrative law systems and annulment proceedings on account of the peculiarities of the Community legislative process. Thus, M. Fromont, 'L'influence du Droit français et du Droit allemand sur les Conditions de Recevabilité du Recours en Annulation devant la Cour de Justice des Communautés Européennes' [1966] 2 *RTDE* 47.

[25] The Maastricht Treaty has extended this possibility to acts adopted jointly by the Council and the European Parliament, acts of the European Central Bank (other than recommendations and opinions), and to acts of the European Parliament intended to produce legal effects *vis-à-vis* third parties. (Art. 173(1) EC Treaty, see 18 below.)

action for a failure to act. The action for annulment[26] occupies a central position in the system of judicial review and has its origins in annulment proceedings against illegal administrative action, as known to the legal systems of all the Member States. This recourse allows the applicant to attack directly the allegedly illegal Community act. As it is the core of the system of judicial review, the action for annulment will receive ample consideration throughout this work. The action for a failure to act[27] is aimed at challenging unlawful omissions of the Community institutions and represents the logical complement to the action of annulment.

The plea of illegality[28] is an indirect action, permitting applicants to invoke the illegality of the general measure that constitutes the legal basis of an individual measure at issue in proceedings before the European Court.

In addition to this system, specifically designed to assess the legality of Community measures, there are two other remedies not intended for this purpose but through which consideration of the legality of a certain Community act may be undertaken by the Court: these are preliminary rulings on the validity of the acts of the institutions[29] and actions for damages.[30]

The action for annulment, the plea of illegality, the action for a failure to act, and the action for damages adopt the form of a contentious procedure, whereas the system of preliminary rulings is a non-contentious procedure based upon the principle of co-operation between national courts and the European Court of Justice, where the initiative to review lies with the national courts and not with the parties in the national proceedings.

1.3 Private Parties and European Community Law

It has already been noted[31] that one of the revolutionary features of the Community legal system is the fact that private parties, as well as the Member States, are subject to EC law.[32] Thus, EC law has gone beyond the boundaries of International Law to produce a direct impact on the rights

[26] Art. 33 ECSC Treaty, Art. 173 EC Treaty, and Art. 146 Euratom Treaty.

[27] Art. 35 ECSC Treaty, Art. 175 EC Treaty, and Art. 148 Euratom Treaty.

[28] Art. 36 ECSC Treaty, Art. 184 EC Treaty, and Art. 156 Euratom Treaty.

[29] Art. 41 ECSC Treaty, Art. 177(1)b EC Treaty, and Art. 150(1)b Euratom Treaty.

[30] Art. 40 ECSC Treaty, Arts. 178, 215(2), and 215(3) EC Treaty and Arts. 151 and 188 Euratom Treaty.

[31] See above, 1.

[32] P. W. Gormley, 'The Procedural Status of the Individual before Supranational Judicial Tribunals' (1963–5) 41–42 *Univ. of Det. LJ* 405, 409; M. R. Angulo and F. G. Dawson, 'Access by Natural and Legal Persons to the Court of Justice of the European Communities' (1967) 36 *Univ. of Cinc. LR* 583, 583.

and obligations of Community nationals. Accordingly, it was only fair that natural and legal persons should be able to obtain a review not only of acts of the Member States[33] in contravention of EC law but also of acts of Community institutions that could be illegal or disproportionately harmful to their interests.[34]

The European Community Treaties granted private parties[35] direct access to the European Court of Justice in a move described by one author as a 'bold new experiment in transnational justice'.[36] In this way, private parties could not only bring proceedings before the national courts to enforce their rights under EC law against national governments ,but they could also have access to the European Court of Justice to challenge the legality of decisions made by the Commission and the Council. As a result of the jurisprudential effort of the Court and the Maastricht amendments, this possibility has been extended to decisions adopted by the European Parliament and intended to produce legal effects *vis-à-vis* third parties, to decisions adopted jointly by the Parliament and the Council, and to decisions of the European Central Bank.[37] Accordingly, private parties may obtain a review of the legality of secondary EC legislation through annulment proceedings, or by means of the exception of illegality, or by the review of unlawful omissions by the Commission, Council, or European Parliament. However, in the EC and Euratom Treaties such possibilities have been severely limited in the context of the action for annulment due to the draconian *locus standi* conditions attached to this action which is in theory the main channel of judicial review open to individuals. These restrictions are one of the main concerns of this work in so far as they represent an important hindrance to access by natural and legal persons to the European Court in contrast to the privileged position of the Member States and the Community Institutions. As Gormley commented, 'the individual is a subject of Community Law though he does not possess a status equal to the Member States'.[38]

[33] Private parties cannot bring a direct action against Member States before the ECJ. Only the Commission (Art. 169 EC Treaty) or another Member State (Art. 171 EC Treaty) may bring such an action. Despite this, the system of preliminary rulings has allowed private parties to obtain a review of illegal action by the Member States. See for instance Case 31/74 *Galli* [1975] ECR 47 at 66.

[34] In this respect, see A. G. Toth, 'The Individual and European Law' (1975) 24 *ICLQ* 659, 670.

[35] The concept of private parties varies according to the Treaties. In the context of the ECSC Treaty, its provisions refer normally to undertakings (as defined by Art. 80 ECSC Treaty) and associations of undertakings (as defined by Art. 48 ECSC Treaty), whereas in the context of the EC and Euratom Treaties the concept of private parties enlarges to comprise the general formula of 'natural or legal persons'.

[36] K. A. Parkinson, 'Admissibility of Direct Actions by Natural or Legal Persons in the European Court of Justice: Judicial Distinctions between Decisions and Regulations' (1989) 24 *Texas Int. LJ* 433.

[37] Art. 173 EC Treaty as amended by the Maastricht Treaty (see 15 below).

[38] N. 32 above, 410.

Since EC law can penetrate and directly affect the sphere of interests of EC law can penetrate and directly affect the sphere of interests of EC nationals—natural persons, undertakings, companies, associations of consumers and users, etc.—they have to be provided with adequate means of redress before the European Court (or the Court of First Instance) to protect such interests. This is all the more important when most of the law-making in the Community lies in the hands of the Commission and the Council, and the powers of the Parliament are still weak. In the course of this work it will be seen how the *locus standi* conditions imposed by the EC and Euratom Treaties in annulment proceedings, together with the severe interpretation practised by the European Court, have reduced that the access of private parties to this means of redress to very specific circumstances. Natural and legal persons may have recourse to alternative means, namely the system of preliminary references, the plea of illegality, the action for a failure to act, and the action for damages,[39] but a detailed examination of this possibility shows that in some cases they do not provide as satisfactory an option as annulment proceedings can offer.[40]

1.4 Courts before which a Challenge may be Made. The Role of the Court of First Instance

In the original scheme of the Treaties, private parties, like Member States and Community institutions, could bring direct actions (an action for annulment, an action for a failure to act, and an action for damages) before the European Court. As far as the indirect means of review are concerned, the plea of illegality could be invoked—given its nature as an incidental and subsidiary method of review[41]—in the course of proceedings brought before the European Court[42] under some other provision of the Treaty; in the case of preliminary rulings on validity, it is only for the national court and not for the parties to request a review of the validity of a Community act.[43] Although actions brought before the European Court of Justice have no suspensory effect, the European Court had jurisdiction to grant interim relief in conjunction with direct actions,[44] provided that some conditions were fulfilled.[45] In the case of preliminary rulings on validity, the non-

[39] See 6–7 above. [40] See 177 ff. below. [41] See 198 below.

[42] Albeit not clear from the wording of Art. 184 EC Treaty, the Court has explained in its decision in Joined Cases 31 and 33/62 *Wöhrmann* v. *Commission* [1962] ECR 501 at 506–7 that proceedings had to be pending before the ECJ.

[43] Frequently, private parties will initiate proceedings before the national courts against national measures taken in implementation of a Community act, with the hope that the national court will refer a question on the validity of a Community measure to the ECJ. See 000 below.

[44] Thus see Arts. 185 and 186 EC Treaty, Art. 39 ECSC Treaty, and Arts. 157 and 158 Euratom Treaty.

[45] Thus, Art. 83 of the ECJ Rules of Procedure provides that an application for interim

contentious nature of this system, based on the principle of co-operation between national courts and the European Court determined that interim relief could only be sought before the national court.[46] In effect, the judgment of the Court in *Zuckerfabrik Süderdithmarschen* v. *Hauptzollamt Itzehoe*[47] has established the principle that a national court may suspend the enforcement of a national measure based on a Community measure if three conditions are fulfilled: the first is that the national court entertains serious doubt as to the lawfulness of the Community measure and refers the question of its validity to the European Court under Article 177.[48]

This scheme has changed with the creation of the Court of First Instance and the transfer of jurisdiction that has taken place as a result.

The European Court of Justice began to struggle in the wake of the great number of cases that had reached its Registry since the mid-1970s. As a consequence of the continuous growth of European Community law and the accession of new Member States, the Court was finding it almost impossible to cope with the increasing number of proceedings.[49] The Single European Act incorporated Article 168(a) into the EC Treaty thereby providing for the creation of a Court of First Instance by a decision of the Council.[50] In furtherance of this provision, the Council enacted Decision 88/591 establishing the Court of First Instance.[51] Article 3 of that Decision conferred jurisdiction on the Court of First Instance to deal with (a) staff cases; (b) actions brought by undertakings or associations of undertaking pursuant to Articles 33(2) and 35 ECSC Treaty against individual acts relating to the application of the ECSC Treaty provisions on levies, production controls, price regulations, or competition issued by the Commission; (c) actions brought by natural and legal persons pursuant to Articles 173(2) and 175(3) EEC Treaty against decisions adopted in the area of competition proceedings; and (d) damage claims related to the actions described in

measures 'shall state the subject-matter of the proceedings, the circumstances giving rise to urgency and the pleas of fact and law establishing a prima facie case for the interim measures applied for'.

[46] Given that, the ECJ has never been asked to grant interim relief in references for a preliminary ruling; as P. Oliver explained, 'were the Court to grant interim relief on a reference for a preliminary ruling, this would no doubt be seen as an interference with the powers of the national courts' ('Interim Measures: Some Recent Developments' (1992) 29 *CMLRev.* 7, 10). See also K. P. Lasok, *European Court of Justice: Practice and Procedure* (London, 1994), 234 and E. V. E. Sharpston, *Interim and Substantive Relief in Claims under Community Law* (London, 1993), 113.

[47] Joined Cases C-143/88 and C-92/89 [1991] ECR 1-415.

[48] *Ibid.* at point 33.

[49] Thus, the average length of time needed for the ECJ to deliver a judgment in a direct action rose from 9 months in 1975 to 24 in 1988. See T. Millett, *The Court of First Instance of the European Communities* (London, 1990), 2.

[50] See also Art. 32(d) ECSC Treaty and Art. 140(a) Euratom Treaty.

[51] Council Decision 88/591 [1988] OJ L319/1; corrected version [1989] OJ C 214/1. For a complete survey of the historical background to the enactment of this Decision see T. Kennedy, 'The Essential Minimum: The Establishment of the Court of First Instance' (1989) 14 *ELRev.* 7, 7–21.

(a), (b), and (c). The European Court retained jurisdiction to deal with actions brought by Member States and Community institutions and to give preliminary rulings. Furthermore, Article 4 of the Decision makes applicable to the Court of First Instance Article 184 EC Treaty, Article 36(3) ECSC Treaty, and Article 156 Euratom Treaty, i.e., the possibility to plead the exception of illegality in proceedings before the Court; it also gives the Court of First Instance jurisdiction to grant interim relief.[52]

In the field of direct actions brought by private parties, therefore, the Court of First Instance acquired jurisdiction only to deal with cases that involved decisions adopted in the area of competition law.[53] In contrast, it did not have jurisdiction to deal with cases arising from measures adopted in the area of general management of the market and those adopted in the course of state aids or anti-dumping proceedings. The European Court of Justice, in its formal proposals submitted before the adoption of Decision 88/591, had suggested that the actions brought by natural and legal persons under Articles 173 and 175, relating to anti-dumping and anti-subsidy matters, should be allocated to the Court of First Instance.[54] In the years preceding the establishment of the Court of First Instance, the case-load of the European Court of Justice concerning anti-dumping measures had greatly increased. Those cases involve facts of great complexity requiring a vast amount of time and resources for proper review. The European Court of Justice felt that the transfer to the Court of First Instance of actions brought by private applicants in those areas would ease its task. The European Parliament also produced a favourable Opinion[55] on the European Court proposals. The Commission[56] and France, however, opposed the transfer of jurisdiction in matters relating to anti-dumping and subsidies.[57] The Council Decision tried to compromise on the opposing views of the Court and the European Parliament on the one hand and those of the Commission and France on the other. Thus, Article 3 of the Decision provided that after the Court of First Instance had been functioning for two years, the Council would re-examine the proposal of the European Court to give the Court of First Instance jurisdiction in the specified actions. Two years elapsed without further action being taken.

[52] In this respect, see Art. 104(2) of the CFI Rules of Procedure, which makes the grant of interim relief dependent on the same conditions as before the European Court (see n. 45 above).

[53] See 77 below.

[54] Thus see 'The Proposal for a European Court of First Instance' (1987) 12 *ELRev.* 77.

[55] European Parliament, Session Doc. Series A, Doc. A 2–107/88. Report drawn up on behalf of the Committee on Legal Affairs and Citizens Rights on the proposal for a Council decision establishing a Court of First Instance submitted by the Court of Justice.

[56] Opinion of the Commission adopted on 20 July 1988. Commission Doc. Series SEC(88)366 final.

[57] See T. Kennedy, 'The Essential Minimum: The Establishment of a Court of First Instance', n. 51 above, 20; T. Millett, n. 49 above, 32; and R. Joliet and W. Vogel, 'Le Tribunal de Première Instance des Communautés Européennes' [1984] *RMC* 423, 428.

In the years that followed, the Court of First Instance itself suggested that all proceedings—and not only those brought by natural or legal persons—arising from dumping practices or subsidies should be dealt with by the Court of First Instance.[58]

A recent Decision of the Council, Decision 93/350,[59] amended Decision 88/591[60] and extended the jurisdiction of the Court of First Instance. In accordance with Article 1 of that Decision, Article 3 of Decision 88/591 was amended so that the Court of First Instance now has jurisdiction to deal with: (a) staff cases; (b) all actions brought by undertakings or associations of undertakings (1) pursuant to Articles 33(2) and 35 ECSC Treaty, (2) for damages, and (3) concerning arbitration clauses; (c) all actions brought by natural and legal persons (1) pursuant to Articles 173(2) and 175(3) EEC Treaty, (2) for damages, and (3) concerning arbitration clauses; and (d) all actions brought by private parties under (1) Articles 146(2) and 148(3) Euratom Treaty, (2) for damages, and (3) concerning arbitration clauses.

The Decision entered into force on 1 August 1993.[61] The Court of First Instance now has jurisdiction to deal with *all* annulment actions, *all* actions for a failure to act, and *all* actions for damages brought by private parties.[62] In actions relating to anti-dumping and anti-subsidy measures, the Council established that the Decision would enter into force 'on a date that the Council shall fix by unanimous decision'[63] instead of on 1 August 1993, when all the other provisions of that Decision entered into force. Accordingly, the Council, by Decision 94/149 of 7 March 1994,[64] established that, in relation to the specified actions, Decision 93/350 entered into force on 15 March 1994.

The European Court of Justice retains exclusive competence to give preliminary rulings. The research undertaken in this work has had as its basis the case law of the European Court of Justice and the case law of the Court of First Instance that has been decided so far.

[58] See the paper published by the CFI on 3 Dec. 1990, 'Reflections on the Future Development of the Community Judicial System' (1991) 16 *ELRev.* 175, 184.

[59] Council Dec. 93/350 of 8 June 1993 [1993] OJ L144/21.

[60] See n. 51 above.

[61] The Council, however, made a reservation in relation to actions relating to measures adopted in the course of anti-dumping proceedings. For those actions, the entry into force of Dec. 93/350 was deferred to a later date. Dec. 94/149 of 7 Mar. 1994 [1994] OJ L66/29 established that, in relation to these actions, Dec. 93/350 entered into force on 15 Mar. 1994.

[62] The CFUI will also be competent to rule on exceptions of illegality that may arise in the course of those actions and to grant interim relief (Art. 1(3) of Dec. 93/350).

[63] Art. 3 of the Dec. (see n. 59 above).

[64] [1994] OJ L66/29.

PART I

The Action for Annulment

2

The Action for Annulment in the EC Treaty: An Overview

2.1 The Treaty Provisions

The action for annulment is regulated by Article 173 EC Treaty, which reads as follows:

The Court of Justice shall review the legality *of acts adopted jointly by the European Parliament and the Council*, of acts of the Council, of the Commission *and of the ECB*, other than recommendations and opinions, *and of acts of the European Parliament intended to produce legal effects vis-à-vis third parties.*

It shall for this purpose have jurisdiction in actions brought by a Member State, the Council or the Commission on grounds of lack of competence, infringement of an essential procedural requirement, infringement of this Treaty or of any rule of law relating to its application, or misuse of powers.

The Court shall have jurisdiction under the same conditions in actions brought by the European Parliament and by the ECB for the purpose of protecting their prerogatives..

Any natural or legal person may, under the same conditions, institute proceedings against a decision addressed to that person or against a decision which, although in the form of a regulation or a decision addressed to another person, is of direct and individual concern to the former.

The proceedings provided for in this Article shall be instituted within two months of the publication of the measure, or of its notification to the plaintiff, or in the absence thereof, on the day on which it came to the knowledge of the latter as the case may be.[1]

[1] The italicized words represent the Maastricht amendments. Note that Art. 146 Euratom Treaty is almost identical to Art. 173 EC Treaty. The ECSC Treaty provides that annulment proceedings may be brought by a Member State or by the Council against a decision or recommendation of the Commission, on the same grounds as those described in Art. 173 EC Treaty (Art. 33(1) ECSC Treaty). The Maastricht Treaty has added that the European Parliament may also bring annulment proceedings under the same conditions for the purpose of protecting its prerogatives (Art. 33(4) ECSC Treaty). Undertakings and associations of undertakings may bring annulment proceedings against decisions and recommendations concerning them which are individual in character, or against general decisions or recommendations which they consider to involve a misuse of powers (Art. 33(2) ECSC Treaty). Art. 38 ECSC Treaty grants jurisdiction to the Court to annul binding acts of the Parliament or of the Council when the applicant is a Member State or the Commission, but only on the grounds of lack of competence or infringement of an essential procedural requirement. Undertakings and associations of undertakings do not have a right of action under this provision (in this respect see Case 78/85 *Group of European Right* v. *European Parliament* [1986] ECR 1753 at point 10). The time-limit for bringing annulment proceedings is one month from notification or publication of the act, as the case may be.

Three aspects of this legal provision will be considered here: i.e. first the existence of limited grounds to allege the illegality of an EC act; secondly, the existence of rigid time-limits for the submission of an application of annulment; and, finally, the different admissibility conditions imposed on the various applicants. The first two aspects are common to all applicants.

The grounds of illegality were, admittedly, inspired by French administrative law.[2] They are: lack of competence, infringement of an essential procedural requirement, infringement of the Treaty or of any rule of law relating to its application, or misuse of powers. With the exception of the ground of infringement of the Treaty or of any rule of law relating to its application, a ground which bears resemblance to the ones used in the national legal systems to control the constitutionality of laws, the other three grounds appear in the French *recours pour excès du pouvoir*, which is the core of the system of judicial review of administrative action.

With regard to the time-limit imposed on the applicants for bringing annulment proceedings, Article 173 EC Treaty and Article 80 of the Rules of Procedure impose a period of two months[3] from the publication of the measure, or of its notification to the plaintiff, or (in the absence thereof) of the day on which it came to the knowledge of the latter. The reason for this strict time-limit is the wish to strike a balance between the principle of legal certainty and the principles of legality and of adequate protection of individual interests.[4] In other words, it is accepted that an illegal measure should be repealed but such a possibility is not open indefinitely as other subjects may have placed reliance on an apparently legal measure.

As far as the third aspect is concerned, the existence of three groups of applicants is immediately evident.

The Commission, the Council, and the Member States together constitute the category of *privileged applicants*[5] since they may challenge any binding act of the EC Institutions without having to satisfy any further admissibility conditions.

The European Parliament and the European Central Bank are *semi-privileged applicants*[6] in so far as they may also challenge any reviewable EC measure, but they may only act in defence of their prerogatives.

[2] In this respect, see the Report of the French delegation on the Treaty and the preamble of the German Act authorising the ratification of the Treaty. Also the Opinion of Lagrange A.G. in Case 3/54 *Assider* v. *High Authority* [1954–56] ECR 63 at 75.

[3] This time-limit operates unless *force majeur* has prevented the applicant(s) from complying with it.

[4] In this respect see Joined Cases 42 and 49/59 *SNUPAT* v. *High Authority* [1961] ECR 53 at 87, where the Court said: 'The principle of legal certainty, important as it may be, cannot be applied in an absolute manner, but its application must be combined with that of the principle of legality. The question of which of those principles should prevail in each particular case depends upon a comparison of the public interest with the private interest in question.'

[5] Art. 173(2) EC Treaty (formerly Art. 173(1) EEC Treaty).

[6] Art. 173(3) EC Treaty (new addition by the Maastricht Treaty).

Natural and legal persons constitute the class of *non-privileged applicants*.[7] In view of the wording of the Treaty, when these subjects are not the addressees of the contested measure, they are not only restricted as to the kind of act they may challenge—i.e. decisions—but they must also show that the contested measures affect them in a particular way that singles them out from the rest of the persons affected.

There is one feature common to the two last categories, which is the fact that both semi-privileged and non-privileged applicants need to fulfil some *locus standi* conditions.

The notion of *locus standi* or 'standing' is common to the administrative systems of the Member States and it is defined as 'A position from which one may validly make a legal claim or seek to enforce a right or duty . . . [O]ne is said to have standing when one's arguments on the merits of a case are able to be heard by an adjudicator'.[8] In other words, 'standing' means the right to be heard by a court or tribunal. For some authors[9] there is a distinction between the need for a special capacity in the applicant to sue—defined by the French term *qualité* or the German term *Prozeßführungsbefugnis*—and the existence of an interest to sue—defined by the French term *intérêt à agir* and the German term *Rechtsschutzinteresse*. It is commonly accepted that the notion of *locus standi* embraces these two notions.

To have *locus standi* 'a person who brings legal proceedings must have some interest in the subject-matter of the litigation'.[10] The concept of standing finds a place in all the continental legal systems and its existence has a double purpose: to prevent the courts from being flooded with unnecessary litigation and to ensure that the efficacy in the administration of justice is not hindered by continuous challenges to the measures in force.[11] The degree of interest that the applicants have to prove varies in the different Member States and ranges from simple harm to an interest of the applicants—as in France—to the infringement of a subjective public right—as in Germany.

[7] Art. 173(4) EC Treaty (formerly Art. 173(2) EEC Treaty).

[8] B. A. Garner, *A Dictionary of Modern Legal Usage* (Oxford, 1987), 515.

[9] Thus P. Van Dijk, *Judicial Review of Governmental Action and the Requirement of an Interest to Sue* (Alphen aan den Rijn, 1980), 18 ff.

[10] D. Foulkes, *Administrative Law* (7th edn., London, 1990), 342.

[11] As P. Andersen suggested, 'The decisive viewpoint [must] be however, that the comparatively more costly judicial machinery should be set in motion only when the matter is of some significance important to the individual' [1925] *Ugeskrift for Retsvaesen* ('A Weekly Law Journal') B 244. Very clear also were the words of Lord Ardwall in *Swanson* v. *Manson* ([1907] SLT 737, 738) where he explained the logic behind the *locus standi* requirements: 'The grounds for this rule are (1) that the law courts of the country are not instituted for the purpose of dealing with academic questions of law, but for settling disputes where any of the lieges has a real interest to have a question determined which involves his pecuniary rights or his status and (2) that no person is entitled to subject another to the trouble and expense of litigation unless he has some real interest to enforce or protect'.

In the context of annulment proceedings before the European Court there is a clear distinction between a group of applicants—*privileged applicants*—that always enjoy standing, and two other categories—*semi-privileged* and non-privileged applicants—that have to surmount some *locus standi* conditions before their actions for annulment are declared admissible.

From what has been said, it would appear that Article 173 EC Treaty embodies two different types of control over the legality of EC acts. On the one hand, it could be said that the second paragraph of this provision represents an objective control over the legality of EC measures inasmuch as the applicants do not have to satisfy any requirement about standing. That does not mean that the Member States or the Community institutions do not have an interest in the declaration of nullity of a measure. On the contrary, in most of the cases a privileged applicant will not be acting philanthropically but out of interest in the annulment of a measure. Therefore what really happens is that any subjective reasons for the application are disregarded by the Court. On the other hand, the third and fourth paragraphs of Article 173 regulate a form of subjective control, since the applicants may only allege the illegality of Community measures in so far as the latter have harmed their prerogatives or rights.[12] In this case, therefore, the subjective element is not disregarded by the Court but taken into consideration, and unless this is satisfactory, a non-privileged applicant will not obtain a decision on the merits of its case.

The position of these applicants will be briefly examined in this Chapter. As a preliminary, however, it is important to devote some attention to the question of which acts may be subject to judicial review in annulment proceedings.

2.2 Acts Susceptible to Review

The text of Article 173(1) EC Treaty indicates that the acts that may be subject to annulment proceedings are: acts adopted jointly by the European Parliament and the Council, acts of the Council, of the Commission, and of the *European Central Bank*, other than recommendations and opinions, and *acts of the European Parliament intended to produce legal effects vis-à-vis third parties.*[13]

As far as the acts of the Council and the Commission are concerned, the

[12] Thus P. Cane pointed out 'The existence of the requirement of standing indicates that the law's primary concern is not as such to control Governmental activity, but rather to control it at the suit of the persons affected by it in a particular way' (*An Introduction to Administrative Law* (2nd edn., Oxford, 1992), 44).

[13] The italicized words represent the Maastricht amendments of Art. 173(1) EC Treaty.

immediate provision to look at is Article 189 EC Treaty.[14] This legal provision enumerates the measures open to the Council and the Commission. Five types of acts are contemplated there: regulations, directives, decisions, recommendations, and opinions. From these acts the common feature of regulations, directives, and decisions is their binding character, i.e. the fact that they produce legal effects. Therefore it could be said that reviewable acts would be those intended to produce legal effects.[15] At this stage, two questions arise: whether the enumeration contained in Article 189 is exhaustive, and when it is that an act produces legal effects. As to the first question, the Court made it clear in *Commission* v. *Council*[16] that the protection of the rule of law in the Community required that the concept of reviewable act encompassed all measures intended to produce legal effects adopted by the institutions and therefore it went beyond the limited categories listed in Article 189 EC Treaty.[17] As to the second question, the Court made it clear in *Société Anonyme Cimentières CBR* v. *Commission* that a measure produced legal effects because 'it affected the interests of the undertakings by bringing about a distinct change in their legal position'.[18] As Hartley explained, a measure has legal force when 'it produces a change in somebody's rights and obligations'.[19] The Court has produced a consistent body of case law to determine the nature of acts at issue in annulment proceedings and has admitted the reviewability of acts not contained in the formula of Article 189 EC Treaty provided that they produced legal effects, regardless of the formal appearance of such acts.[20]

It has been said that Article 189 EC Treaty presents *recommendations and opinions* as devoid of legal effect and, as such, Article 173 excludes their reviewability. It is thought, however, that the case law of the Court shows a different picture that could have a great impact in the field of

[14] See 5 above.

[15] Privileged and semi-privileged applicants are able to challenge regs., dirs., and decs. In the case of non-privileged applicants, the Treaty seems to exclude the possibility of challenging acts intended to produce general effects. See 26 below.

[16] Case 22/70 [1971] ECR 263. This case is also known as the *ERTA* case.

[17] The Court said:

> '[39] . . . Article 173 treats as acts open to review by the Court all measures adopted by the Institutions which are intended to have legal force.
>
> [40] The objective of this review is to ensure, as required by Article 164, observance of the law in the interpretation and application of the Treaty.
>
> [41] It would be inconsistent with this objective to interpret the conditions under which the action is admissible so restrictively as to limit the availability of this procedure merely to the categories of measures referred to by Article 189.'

[18] Joined Cases 8–11/66 [1967] ECR 75 at 91.

[19] T. C. Hartley, *The Foundations of European Community Law* (3rd edn., Oxford, 1994), 344.

[20] Thus, in Case 54/65 *Compagnie des Forges de Châtillon* v. *High Authority* [1966] ECR 185 at 195, the Court said: 'A decision must in fact appear as a measure emanating from the component authority, intended to produce legal effects and constituting the culmination of a procedure within that authority whereby the latter gives its final ruling in a form from which its nature can be identified.'

judicial review. In *Grimaldi* v. *Fonds des Maladies Profesionnelles*[21] the Court was asked whether a recommendation concerning the adoption of a European schedule of occupational diseases was a legally binding act and whether it could confer rights on individuals upon which they could rely before the national courts. The Court started by saying that recommendations are non-binding acts and, as such, they cannot create rights for individuals.[22] Having said that, the Court nevertheless explained that recommendations cannot be regarded as having no legal effect and that 'national courts were bound to take those recommendations into consideration when deciding disputes submitted before them'.[23] Effectively, it is thought that the Court gave legal effects to a recommendation, obeying considerations of *effet utile*. A similar move had been effected in *Saarland* v. *Minister for Industry*[24] in relation to an opinion. This line of case law is a clear example of the role of the Court as a true re-drafter of the Treaty (in this case of Article 189).[25] Therefore, if it is now possible for recommendations and opinions to produce legal effects, there is no reason to exclude them from being reviewable under Article 173. Although in *Grimaldi*[26] the Court repeated that recommendations are excluded from the scope of Article 173, it is only logical that, if the Court has decided to recognize their binding effects, the next step should be the determination of their reviewability.

In the case of *international agreements* concluded by the Community, it could be thought that, because they produce legal effects, they are included in the category of reviewable acts.[27] The Court did not face such a situation for many years and only ruled the impossibility of challenging the Acts of Accession,[28] which is understandable given the constitutional rank of these instruments. Only recently, in *France* v. *Commission*[29] the Court declared that an Agreement between the Commission and the United States regarding the application of their competition laws was reviewable.[30]

[21] Case 322/88 [1989] ECR 4407.
[22] *Ibid.*, at point 16.
[23] *Ibid.*, at point 19.
[24] Case 187/87 [1988] ECR 5013.
[25] This approach is rather different from the reluctance shown by the Court to alter the wording of Art. 173(2) EEC Treaty, see Ch. 3, n. 94 below.
[26] Case 322/88, see n. 21 above, at point 8.
[27] Academic writers were divided on this point. R. Kovar thought that such a possibility would be excluded, given that annulment proceedings refer to unilateral acts of the Council and the Commission, whilst international treaties are bilateral or multilateral. Moreover, the other Contracting Parties are not subject to the jurisdiction of the European Court. ('Les Accords Liant les Communautés Européennes et L'ordre Juridique Communautaire: A Propos d'une Jurisprudence Récente de la Cour de Justice' [1974] *RMC* 345, 357). Other authors like Schemers and Waelbroeck believed that the hypothetical possibility exists if the Treaty itself is not considered but the act whereby the Council approves the Treaty (H. G. Schermers and D. Waelbroeck, *Judicial Protection in the European Communities* (5th edn., Deventer, 1992), 181).
[28] Joined Cases 31 and 35/86 *Laisa* v. *Council* [1988] ECR 2285 at point 18.
[29] Case C-327/91 [1994] ECR 1-3641.
[30] The Court explained that the action of the French Republic had to be understood as directed against the act whereby the Commission concluded the Agreement (*ibid.*, at point 17).

The Maastricht Treaty has established the creation of a European System of Central Banks and a *European Central Bank* to pursue the objectives of economic and monetary policy contemplated by the EC Treaty.[31] The European Central Bank has the power to make regulations and take decisions for the performance of its functions[32] which are reviewable under Article 173(1). This body may also produce recommendations and opinions which are theoretically non-binding, but in view of the developments explained above[33] it is suggested that these acts could also be subject to judicial review.

As far as the acts of the *European Parliament* are concerned, not all of them are open to review, but only the ones adopted jointly with the Council and those intended to produce legal effects *vis-à-vis* third parties. The reviewability of acts adopted together with the Council is a reflection of the new powers of the Parliament in the legislative process according to the new conciliation and veto procedure.[34] The second category is the result of a development in case law. The original version of the Treaties did not cover acts of the Parliament at all. This was quite logical, as this institution was only meant to have consultative powers. Later on the powers of the Parliament were increased through the signing of the Budgetary Treaties and the Single European Act. Subsequently, in *Parti Ecologiste 'Les Verts'* v. *European Parliament*,[35] the Court recognized that 'an interpretation of Article 173 of the Treaty which excluded measures adopted by the European Parliament from those which could be contested would lead to a result contrary both to the spirit of the Treaty as expressed in Article 164 and to its system'.[36] This was a clear example of a very liberal interpretation by the Court even against the wording of a Treaty provision, in order to uphold the rule of law in the EC.[37] The Court concluded that acts of the European Parliament intended to produce legal effects *vis-à-vis* third parties could be the object of review.

2.3 Privileged Applicants

The Commission, the Council, and the Member States form the category of privileged applicants to whom the Treaty grants unlimited capacity to bring an action under Article 173.[38] Not only can they challenge any

[31] Art. 4(a) EC Treaty, inserted by the Maastricht Treaty.

[32] Art. 108(a) EC Treaty, inserted by the Maastricht Treaty.

[33] See 20 above.

[34] Art, 189(b) EC Treaty, inserted by the Maastricht Treaty.

[35] Case 294/83 [1986] ECR 1339.

[36] *Ibid.*, at point 25.

[37] The standpoint of the ECJ was repeated in Case 221/86R *Group of European Right* v. *European Parliament* [1986] ECR 2969 at point 10.

[38] For the unlimited capacity of the Council and the Commission, see Case 45/86 *Commisson* v. *Council* [1987] ECR 1493 at point 3. For the Member States see Case 41/83 *Italy* v.

reviewable act enacted by the EC institutions, but they do not have to prove beforehand that their interests have been affected by the contested measures.

The Council and the Commission are presumed to be concerned with any act of the Community. In other words, each of these institutions is invested with a 'public interest' in the legality of any act issued by another EC institution.[39] The tasks that the Commission and the Council have to perform, in accordance with Articles 145 and 155 EC Treaty respectively, could not be carried out unless these institutions were granted such a wide right of action.

It is surprising that the Parliament was not included amongst those privileged applicants if the principle of equality of the institutions is taken into account.[40] It has been said[41] that the position of this institution is substantially weaker than that of the national parliaments and that the Community legislative process is vitiated in some instances by lack of democracy and aggravated by the 'confusion' rather than the distribution of powers amongst the EC institutions. To confer upon the European Parliament an unlimited right of action would effectively increase its chances of exerting control over the acts of the other institutions. Instead of this, and after the evolution in case law described later[42] and the modifications inserted by the Maastricht Treaty, the Parliament has gained only the status of *semi-privileged applicant*.

In the case of the Member States, the explanation lies in the supranational nature of the European Community and the care shown by the authors of the Treaty not to undermine the position of the Member States, which are always reluctant to relinquish any area, however small, of their sphere of influence. The European Community works on the basis of a political compromise amongst the Member States and cannot survive without their backing. By being able to contest any binding act of the EC without any *locus standi* limitations, the Member States which effected irreversible transfers of sovereignty to the EC retained powerful means of surveillance and control over the exercise of legislative and executive power in the EC.

Commission [1085] ECR 873 at point 30, and Case 166/78 *Italy* v. *Council* [1979] ECR 2575 at point 6.

[39] This notion of 'public interest' bears resemblance to figures present in the legal systems of the Member States, such as the Crown in England.

[40] Thus, Art. 4 EC Treaty, when enumerating the Community institutions, does not establish any hierarchy amongst them but rather gives them equal status.

[41] See 2 above.

[42] See 23–6 below.

2.4 Semi-privileged Applicants

This category comprises the European Parliament and the European Central Bank. They are referred to as semi-privileged applicants[43] in so far as (unlike non-privileged applicants) they may challenge any reviewable act enacted by the Community institutions but they have to show a certain interest in bringing annulment proceedings (which distinguishes them from privileged applicants): they have to act in defence of their prerogatives. The term has been chosen, moreover, in so far as the European Court has expressly excluded the European Parliament from the circle of non-privileged applicants[44] and from the circle of privileged applicants.[45]

The Maastricht Treaty has granted the European Central Bank this status straight away, whereas in the case of the European Parliament the new wording given to Article 173 by the Maastricht Treaty is the result of a long struggle by the Parliament and of a conflicting judicial approach adopted by the European Court of Justice. The European Central Bank has been assigned by the Maastricht Treaty very important functions in the field of monetary policy[46] and it is thought that the reason a right of action has been directly conferred on it is the drafters' determination not to see the difficult experience of the Parliament repeated.

The European Parliament was not given the right of action to bring annulment proceedings under the original version of the EC Treaty. However, in one author's view a fairly liberal judicial trend was already paving the way for the final attribution of *légitimation active* to the European Parliament.[47]

It is thought that against this background, and especially due to the recognition of the reviewability of the acts of the Parliament, it could reasonably be expected that the Parliament would be granted a right of action. It would be quite unfair that the Parliament could have its acts challenged by the other institutions or by private parties and that it could

[43] Using the term of K. St. Clair Bradley in 'The Variable Evolution of the Standing of the European Parliament in Proceedings Before the Court of Justice' (1988) 8 *YEL* 27, 56.

[44] Case 302/87 *European Parliament* v. *Council* [1988] ECR 5615 at point 10.

[45] Case C–70/88 *European Parliament* v. *Council* [1990] ECR 1–2041 at point 24.

[46] See Title VI, Ch. 2, Arts. 105 ff. of the EC Treaty as amended by the Maastricht Treaty.

[47] G. Bebr, 'The Standing of the European Parliament in the Community System of Legal Remedies: A Thorny Jurisprudential Development' (1990) 10 *YEL* 171. This evolution comprised three major landmark steps: the establishment of the right of the Parliament to intervene in proceedings under Art. 173 (Case 138/79 *Roquette Frères* v. *Council* [1980] ECR 3333 at point 21); the recognition of the possibility of instituting an action for a failure to act (Case 13/83 *European Parliament* v. *Council* [1985] ECR 1513 at point 17) and finally the determination of the reviewability of acts of the European Parliament with legal effects *vis-à-vis* third parties (see 21 above). All these steps pointed in the direction of a higher degree of participation of the Parliament in the system of judicial control over the action of the Community Institutions.

not enjoy, in return, the right to bring annulment proceedings. Unfortunately the first reaction of the Court to this problem was rather discouraging.

In *European Parliament* v. *Council*[48] (otherwise known as the *Comitology* case) the Council failed to consult the European Parliament again after it had modified a Commission proposal for the adoption of measures laying down the procedures for the exercise of implementing powers conferred on the Commission. The Parliament brought an action for the annulment of the final decision adopted by the Council.

The Parliament expressed its view, based on the principle of equality amongst the Community Institutions,[49] that if the Parliament enjoyed *légitimation passive*, it ought to have the right to challenge acts of the other institutions. The Court rejected this contention, adhering to the principle that such a result could not be inferred from the provisions of the Treaty.[50] At first sight, it would seem that the Court somehow withdrew from its long-established approach of respect for the rule of law even if, on some occasions, the wording of the Treaty had to be modified to some extent.[51] The standpoint of the Court was the object of fierce criticism.[52]

The decision of the *Comitology* case was rather unfortunate but, to do full justice to the Court, it has to be said that it did try to show that in any case the prerogatives of the Parliament could be protected by a combination of its powers of control over the Commission (mainly the motion of censure), its powers of intervention in the legislative process, and its right to bring an action for a failure to act and to intervene in annulment proceedings. The Court also emphasized that the Commission had a duty under Article 155 to protect the Parliament's prerogatives and that Member States or even private parties (under Article 177, 173, or 184 EC Treaty) could act as 'defenders' of the Parliament.[53] In other words, the Court did not concede that there was a gap in the system of judicial protection and seemed to understand that there were alternative options rather than a right of action under Article 173 to protect the Parliament, both in a preventive and in a curative manner against illegal action by the other Community Institutions.[54]

[48] Case 302/87, n. 44 above.

[49] *Ibid.*, at point 19.

[50] In this respect see the case law relating to the *locus standi* of private parties, where the Court expressed similar arguments to justify the restricted access of private parties to annulment proceedings. Thus, Case 40/64 *Sgarlata* v. *Commission* [1965] ECR 215 at 227.

[51] See *Parti Ecologiste 'Les Verts'* v. *European Parliament*, n. 35 above. In the case law in preliminary rulings, these instances multiply (see 182 below).

[52] Thus J. Weiler, 'Pride and Prejudice: *EP* v. *Council*' (1989) 14 *ELRev.* 334, 343 ff.; G. Bebr, n. 47 above, 192 and K. St. Clair Bradley, n. 43 above, 54.

[53] Case 302/87, n. 44 above, at point 27.

[54] The approach of the Court in this instance bears parallels in two respects with the interpretation of *locus standi* conditions adopted by the Court in many annulment actions brought by private parties: the fear of altering the wording of a Treaty provision (see Ch. 3, n.

Fortunately, a subsequent judgment of the Court gave new insight in respect of this point and completely reversed the position of the Court in a bold move that represented, not only the restoration of the former liberal approach, but also a true modification of the letter of the Treaty in an effort to fill any gaps in the system of judicial review. This was effected in *European Parliament* v. *Council*[55] (otherwise known as the *Tchernobyl* case). In that case, the Parliament disagreed on the legal basis chosen by the Council for enacting a regulation laying down the maximum permitted level of radioactive contamination of foodstuffs and feeding stuffs. The Council had chosen Article 31 Euratom Treaty where the Parliament only had to be consulted, instead of Article 100(a) EC Treaty, which comes under the co-operation procedure. In this case, the Court found that none of the alternative solutions that it had proposed in *Comitology* were applicable here. The Commission had itself chosen the contested legal basis and therefore it could not be expected to bring an action,[56] an action for a failure to act could not be brought, as the measure had already been adopted,[57] and the possibility of a preliminary ruling or an annulment action was uncertain.[58] The Court concluded that these alternative means could not guarantee in all cases that all acts of the Council and the Commission could be reviewed, and reached the conclusion that the Parliament needed to have a right of action, since the absence of such a right in Article 173 was a procedural gap: 'it could not prevail over the fundamental interest in the maintenance and observance of the institutional balance laid down in the Treaties establishing the European Communities'.[59]

The Court decided that the Parliament should enjoy a limited right of action for the protection of its prerogatives—thus reversing the position taken in the *Comitology* judgment.[60]

This judgment is a landmark case, but it could still be said that the position attained by the Parliament is not satisfactory. It is believed that the Parliament ought to have a general right of action against all measures adopted by the Council and the Commission. Only in this fashion would the Parliament—in those instances where it has not effectively intervened in the legislative process—have a powerful means of control over the action of the other institutions.

This judgment is of the utmost importance in so far as the European Court upheld the rule of law despite the wording of the Treaty.[61] It will be

94 below) and the finding of alternative routes to achieve a similar result to the one that would have been achieved through annulment proceedings (see 186, n. 55 below).

[55] Case C–70/88, n. 45 above. [56] *Ibid.*, at point 6. [57] *Ibid.*, at point 17.
[58] *Ibid.*, at point 18. [59] *Ibid.*, at point 26. [60] *Ibid.*, at point 27.

[61] The standpoint of the Court has been confirmed in two later judgments. Thus see Case C–295/90 *European Parliament* v. *Council* [1992] ECR I–4193 at point 10, where the Parliament brought proceedings for the annulment of a dir. relating to the rights of residence of students because the Council chose as a legal basis Article 235 EC Treaty instead of Article 7 EEC

seen later on that the Court has been the main moving force in the development of the principles contained in the Treaty, and has played a very creative role, specially through its preliminary rulings.[62] In the area of annulment proceedings the Court has shown more caution in amending or expanding the letter of the Treaty to widen the access of private parties to the Court. In the case of the Parliament, the Court showed restraint in the *Comitology* judgment, now dismissed as an early aberration, but fortunately it has finally opted for a much more satisfactory, even if not ideal, and fair solution. This evolution of the *locus standi* of the Parliament shows that the Court is ready to uphold a comprehensive system of judicial protection. The case law concerning the *locus standi* of private parties has evolved towards a greater degree of leniency, as will be shown in the course of this work.

2.5 Non-privileged Applicants

Article 173 EC Treaty limits the right of action of natural and legal persons in two ways: first in the kinds of act they may challenge, and secondly by means of severe *locus standi* requirements. As regards the types of act susceptible to challenge, the wording of this legal provision indicates that only decisions[63]—either addressed to the applicant or to another person(s) or even disguised as regulations—are challengeable by individuals. In relation to the *locus standi* requirements, Article 173 EC Treaty specifies that the prospective applicant needs to be either in the position of addressee of the measure, or, if the decision is in the form of a regulation or of a decision addressed to another person, he needs to show that he is in a very special position regarding the contested measure by satisfying the tests of direct and individual concern.

Two immediate problems arise from these admissibility conditions:

1. As far as the *acts susceptible of challenge* are concerned, Article 173

Treaty. Also see Case C–65/90 *European Parliament* v. *Council* [1992] ECR I–4593 at point 13, where the Parliament sought the annulment of a Council reg. laying down the conditions under which non-resident carriers may operate national road haulage services within a Member State. The facts in this later case are very similar to the ones at issue in the *Comitology* judgment in so far as the Council failed to reconsult the Parliament after substantially amending the Commission proposal. In both cases the measures at issue were annulled. At the moment there is another case pending before the Court (Case C–360/93 *European Parliament* v. *Council*) concerning the annulment of a Council dec. relating to an agreement between the EC and the United States on government procurement. The Parliament alleges that the Council used the wrong legal basis by using Art. 113 instead of Arts. 57, 66 and 100 EC Treaty that allow a greater intervention of the Parliament in the legislative procedure.

[62] See 181 below.

[63] But see 150–2 below, where it is shown that, despite the wording of Art. 173(2) EEC Treaty, in some cases regs. may be challenged by private parties who may be directly and individually concerned about one or some of their provisions.

EC Treaty admits of the possibility that a decision could appear disguised as a regulation, in which case it would be challengeable in spite of its appearance.[64] However, neither Article 173 nor Article 189 EC Treaty provided a test to ascertain the true legal nature of the measures at issue in each case and, particularly, a test to distinguish 'true regulations' from disguised decisions. It was therefore left to the European Court to elaborate such a test, which will hereafter be referred to as *test of legal nature*.[65] This test is of great importance in that the line drawn between regulations and decisions defines the extent to which private parties enjoy legal protection.[66] In the case of measures in the form of decisions, the Court has never inquired whether they could be, in reality, 'disguised' regulations[67] and has always accepted that was their real nature.

2. As far as *locus standi* conditions are concerned, if the measure at issue is a decision addressed to the applicant, no further problems arise. If that decision is addressed to a third party, the applicant will have to satisfy the tests of direct and individual concern. If the decision appears in the form of a regulation, the applicant will have to show that he is directly and individually concerned and he will have to surmount the further additional hurdle of showing that it is really a decision.[68] None of the relevant tests were specified in the Treaty, and therefore it was for the European Court to give them meaning.

An enormous task was left to the European Court. The Court found itself dealing with novel notions and had to try to strike a balance between the need for effective administration within the EC (not hindered by an avalanche of applications) and the need to respect the principle of legality and judicial protection for EC nationals.

The admissibility conditions imposed on private parties wishing to bring annulment proceedings are one of the main concerns of this work. The test of legal nature, although not strictly a *locus standi* condition, is so closely

[64] This provision has the object, as the European Court has repeatedly observed, '[of] prevent[ing] the Community Institutions from being in a position, merely by choosing the form of a regulation, to exclude an application by an individual' Case 101/76 *KHS* v. *Council and Commission* [1977] ECR 797 at point 6; Case 162/78 *Wagner* v. *Commission* [1979] ECR 3467 at point 16; and Joined Cases 789 and 790/79 *Calpak* v. *Commission* [1980] ECR 1949 at point 6.

[65] See 112 ff. below.

[66] Albeit there are instances in the case law where the Court has decided the *locus standi* of the applicants on the basis solely of the tests of direct and individual concern, and has thus ignored the test of legal nature (see 103 below).

[67] See T. C. Hartley, n. 19 above, 375. In Case 25/62 *Plaumann* v. *Commission* [1963] ECR 95, at 98, the Commission tried to persuade the Court that a decision addressed to a Member State is of a general nature and therefore ought to be excluded from annulment actions brought by private parties. The Court fortunately rejected this argument (see 46 below), otherwise a major limitation would have been established to the right of action of natural and legal persons.

[68] But see n. 66 above, and 102 below, on the existence of two divergent lines of case law on this point.

related to the problem of *locus standi* that it will be studied together with these requirements. In the following chapters, a study of these admissibility requirements will be undertaken and therefore the scene has only been set in outline here.

3

The Locus Standi *of Non-Privileged Applicants to Challenge Measures in the Form of Decisions*

The object of this Chapter is to study the position of natural and legal persons who are non-addressees and who wish to obtain the annulment of a decision of the Council or the Commission,[1] and, in particular, to ascertain the meaning of the terms 'direct and individual concern'. These notions were not defined in the Treaty, and therefore it was for the European Court to make them meaningful through its case law. As a consequence, the core of this Chapter will be the study of such development in case law. First, however, we will survey briefly the *locus standi* conditions attached to the actions to obtain the review of the legality of administrative acts in the various Member States and those attached to annulment proceedings under the ECSC Treaty.[2] Although it is true that the influence of the national legal systems must not be overestimated,[3] given the autonomy of the Community legal system, it is also undeniable that they serve as a very helpful guide to the interpretation of the *ratio legis* underlying the EC Treaty. This point is proved in many instances where, especially through the Opinions of the Advocates General, the comparative approach has been used to clarify the meaning of terms contained in Treaty provisions.[4] Sometimes the Court itself has expressly admitted the validity of this method of interpretation.[5] As for the ECSC Treaty, although it is

[1] Since the Maastricht Treaty, this possibility has been extended to decs. adopted jointly by the Council and the Parliament, decs. of the Parliament intended to produce legal effects *vis-à-vis* third parties (Case 294/83 *Parti Ecologiste 'Les Verts'* v. *European Parliament* [1986] ECR 1339) and decs. of the European Central Bank. See Art. 173(1) EC Treaty, and 15 above.

[2] It must be recalled here that the *locus standi* conditions imposed on private parties by Art. 146 Euratom Treaty are almost identical to those of Art. 173 EC Treaty.

[3] Roemer A.G. in his Opinion in Case 1/64 *Glucoseries Réunies* v. *Commission* [1964] ECR 413 at 420 said: 'The Treaty is not meant to be a copy of any particular national system; its structure is too idiosyncratic for that purpose and to a large extent it has no parallel in national law'. J. Peters also pointed out that 'It is not advisable to rely too much on the systems of the Member States, as it is possible for the EEC to have instituted its own system and not having followed national systems' ('Annotations on *Alfred Toepfer* v. *Commission*' (1965–6) 3 *CMLRev.* 233, 239).

[4] e.g. the Opinion of Lagrange A.G. in Case 3/54 *Assider* v. *High Authority* [1954–6] ECR 63 at 73 ff. on the notion of 'misuse of powers'. See also the Opinion of Roemer A. G. in *Glucoseries Réunies* n. 3 above, at 420 on the notion of 'direct interest'.

[5] Joined Cases 7/56 and 3–7/57 *Algera* v. *Common Assembly* [1957–8] ECR 39 at 55–6.

the most immediate precedent of the EC Treaty, the solutions reached in its context have to be used with caution as there are profound differences between the scope and character of the two Treaties.[6]

3.1 The *Locus Standi* of Private Parties under the National Legal Systems in Actions to Review the Legality of Administrative Action

It has already been explained[7] that under EC law—unlike the national legal systems—there is not a clear-cut distinction between legislative and administrative acts. This is a problem that complicates any comparative study of the systems of judicial review of the Member States and of the Community, especially in the case of measures of general application, i.e. regulations, which do not fall squarely into one or other category.[8] In the Member States, there are different remedies to control the constitutionality of the laws and the legality of administrative action.[9] The right of action is very different in these remedies.

On the one hand, in the case of legislative measures, natural and legal persons may only challenge them in very special cases (if at all), generally when they believe that the measure in issue has violated some rights safeguarded by national constitutions.[10] Thus, the right of action of private parties is quite restricted, but it must not be forgotten that in the Member States laws are enacted by parliaments that directly express the voice of the people and thus have a key role in the legislative process, unlike the European Parliament, whose role in the legislative process is still limited even after the Maastricht amendments.

On the other hand, in all Member States private parties may challenge administrative acts and, in general, enjoy a wide right of action. In this sense there are three preliminary points worth noting which are common to all the Community national legal systems. In the first place, it is generally accepted in all Member States that the addressees of an administrative act are automatically allowed to challenge such a measure as a logical reflection of the principle of protection of individuals against the Executive. In the second place, in all Member States it is possible to challenge individual administrative acts addressed to a third-party non-addressee, provided that certain *locus standi* conditions have been satisfied. As far as general administrative measures are concerned, the only Member

[6] Thus, it must not be forgotten that, whereas the ECSC Treaty was aimed at achieving some sectorial integration (Art. 2 ECSC Treaty), the EEC Treaty sought a general economic integration (Art. 2 EC Treaty).

[7] See 5 above. [8] See 110–12 below. [9] See 4 above.

[10] e.g. Art. 107*ter*(2) of the Belgian Constitution, Art. 93(4)a of the German Basic Law, or Art. 161(b) of the Spanish Constitution.

States where these are not challengeable by natural or legal persons are Germany[11] and Luxembourg.[12] In the third place, the possibility of an *actio popularis* only admitted in very exceptional circumstances.[13]

The following sections consider the *locus standi* requirements attached to actions used to challenge the legality of administrative acts in the different Member States. Particular attention will be paid to the French and German systems, which are regarded by academic writers[14] as having had significant influence on the shaping of annulment proceedings under the EC Treaty. The coverage of each system is rather uneven, as it depended both on the availability of material and on linguistic accessibility.

Under Belgian law, the *contentieux objectif* aims to control the legality of administrative acts, as opposed to the *contentieux subjectif*, which seeks to obtain the recognition of a right. A potential applicant wishing to contest an administrative act does not have to demonstrate a violation of one of his rights:[15] it is enough for the applicant to demonstrate the injury of one of his interests. Such an interest has to be *personal*, i.e. the applicant must show that he is in a different position from that of the community at large,[16] and *direct*, in so far as the applicant must show that he is or will be immediately affected. In the case of general administrative acts, the requirements are the same, and Belgian case law has been fairly liberal and has allowed members of large categories to challenge such acts, provided that an individual and direct interest is demonstrated.[17]

[11] M. Fromont, 'L'Influence du Droit français et du Droit allemand sur les Conditions de Recevabilité du Recours en Annulation devant la Court de Justice des Communautés Européennes' [1966] *RTDE* 47, 49. Also C. Debbasch, *Administration et Administrés en Europe* (Paris, 1984), 83. However this is not a pacific view, as P. van Dijk has pointed out (*Judicial Review of Governmental Action and the Requirement of an Interest to Sue* (Alphen aan den Rijn, 1980), 156) since there is a doctrinal debate amongst German lawyers in which some of them understand that a teleological interpretation of Art. 19(4) of the German Constitution would grant protection to individuals against unlawful action by the Federal Government and the governments of the *Länder* in all cases, whether the acts were general or individual in nature. Strangely enough, the German courts have not yet solved this dilemma.

[12] F. Welter, 'La Protection juridictionelle du Particulier contre le Pouvoir exécutif au Luxembourg' in H. Mosler (ed.), *Gerichtsschutz gegen die Exekutive* (Köln, 1969) ii, 709.

[13] This would be the case, for instance, under Belgian law for electoral matters as regulated by Art. 19 of the *Code éléctoral*, or under Portuguese law for the remedy against acts resulting from the deliberation of local authorities, which is open to all taxpayers, or under Spanish law for the remedy against decisions of local authorities in town-planning law (Art. 235 of *Ley del Suelo*).

[14] Thus M. Fromont, n. 11 above, 47.

[15] Art. 19 of the *Lois Coordoneés du Conseil d'Etat* provides that an application may be submitted by '*toute partie justifiant d'une lésion ou d'un intérêt*'.

[16] Thus, for instance, the shopkeepers that ran souvenir businesses next to a tourist spot in Waterloo could challenge an authorization given to a third party to install a speaking guide in that location (*Grauwels et consorts*, 11.221, 7 May 1965. Rec. Arr. Av. Cons. d'Etat 465). Although the applicants formed a large group of people they had a defined interest different from that of the community at large.

[17] Thus *Baert* and *Mahy*, 13.123 and 13124, 19 Sept. 1968. Rec. Arr. Av. Cons. d'Etat 681.

Under French law, the *recours pour excès de pouvoir* is aimed at controlling the legality of administrative acts. French administrative proceedings have a markedly objective character in so far as their purpose is to control the legality of an act independently of the protection of individual interests. As a consequence, private parties have a wide right of action to challenge administrative acts, but they still have to indicate a certain interest—*intérêt à agir*—in the annulment of a measure, otherwise their intervention would be an *actio popularis*.[18] Under French administrative law it is not necessary for the applicant to indicate the violation of a right.[19] The notion of 'interest' is mainly an empirical one that the French courts have constructed, depending on the facts of each individual case.[20] In the nineteenth century 'a private and individual interest'[21] was required. Today, as Auby and Dragó point out,[22] it is not necessary to show such an individualized interest, and actions brought by applicants forming part of a wide category of people are admitted. The best summary of the situation is found in the words of *commissaire du gouvernement* Moset,[23] who explained that there are two conditions that must be met: first, a certain degree of harm must occur or have occurred to the interests of the applicants from the contested measure, and secondly, the applicant's interest must be to a certain degree individualized or, in other words, separate from that of the community at large. As regards the first point, the interest at issue may be a legally protected interest or a factual interest.[24] As far as the degree of individual-

[18] Thus, the applicants need to prove an interest different from that of the community at large. See G. Braibant, *Le Droit Administratif Français* (2nd edn., Paris, 1988), 507; B. Pacteau, *Contentieux Administratif* (Paris, 1985), 123; R. Chapus, *Droit du Contentieux Administratif* (3rd edn., Paris, 1991), 300. See also the conclusions of M. Chenot in *Gicquel* 10 Feb. 1950, Rec. Cons. d'Etat, 100.

[19] *Syndicat des Marchands de Carreau du Temple*, 17 Jan. 1954, Rec. Cons. d'Etat, 55.

[20] M. Chenot explained in his conclusions in *Gicquel* (n. 18 above, 101) that it was very difficult to give a coherent picture of the logic behind the determination of this notion by the French administrative courts.

[21] Conclusions of M. Robert in *Académie des Beaux-Arts* (21 July 1864, Rec. Cons. d'Etat, 687), where he said that what was required was '*un intérêt individuel et privé ayant à un degré quelconque ce caractère privatif et personnel qui apparaît au plus haut point dans le droit de propriété*'.

[22] J. M. Auby and R. Dragó, *Traité des Recours en Matière Administrative* (Paris, 1992), 235.

[23] '*La reconnaissance d'un intérêt ouvrant le recours pour excès de pouvoir est subordonnée par votre jurisprudence à une double condition. Il faut que la décision attaquée lèse le requérant matériellement ou moralement, qu'elle ait pour lui des conséquences fâcheuses sur l'un ou l'autre plan. Mais il faut aussi que ces conséquences fâcheuses atteignent le requérant en qualité, à un titre particulier, en tant qu'appartenant une catégorie, definie et limitée,—i.e. usager d'un service, habitant d'un quartier, contribuable d'une collectivité locale—et non comme un membre quelconque de la nation tout entière—simple citoyen, contribuable de l'Etat, etc.*' Conclusions of M. Moset in *Association Générale des Administrateurs Civils* (26 Oct. 1956, Rec. Cons. d'Etat 391). Also [1956] *Rev. Dr. Pub.* 1309 at 1311.

[24] Thus in *Barrau* (13 June 1952, Rec. Cons. d'Etat 309) the decision by a municipal council to sell the fodder produced by a meadow to the charitable board of a community was challenged by M. Barrau. The applicant was granted standing in so far as he had been harvesting the fodder produced by the meadow for several years previously.

ization is concerned the case law of the *Conseil d'Etat* is fairly liberal in so far as all the persons affected by a general administrative act (*règlement*) are entitled to bring annulment proceedings. Thus the users of a public service could challenge a regulation concerning the organization of that service.[25] In the same way a regulation prohibiting the practice of usury in Indo-China was challengeable by any person able to enter into contract and with residence in that country.[26] The *locus standi* requirements could also be described as requiring the presence of a *direct* and *individual* interest. It can be concluded, therefore, that the admissibility barrier is relatively easy to overcome for private parties in French annulment proceedings.

The German legal system of judicial review has markedly subjective character in so far as the control of the legality of administrative acts operates for the purpose of protecting the interests of private parties. This creates a string of limitations in the right of action of individuals. It has been noted earlier that, under German law, natural and legal persons can only contest the validity of individual acts.[27] Moreover, Article 19(4) of the German Basic Law contains a guarantee only against illegal action by the Executive for persons whose rights have been violated.[28] These rights must be subjective public rights, i.e. rights accruing from the relationship between the state and the citizen. As Bühler explained, an act of the Executive

[25] *Meyet*, 19 Dec. 1979, Rec. Cons. d'Etat 475.

[26] *Daffeleuf*, 28 May 1943, Rec. Cons. d'Etat 135.

[27] See 31 above.

[28] This legal provision reads: '*Wird jemand durch die öffentliche Gewalt in seinen Rechten verletzt, so steht ihm der Rechtsweg offen*' ('Should any person's right be violated by a public authority, recourse to the court shall be open to him'—as translated by A. Blaustein and G. H. Flanz in *Constitutions of the Countries of the World* (New York, London, Rome, 1971), vi, sect. on Germany, 89). In the same way, Art. 42(2) of the VwGO requires an infringement of the applicant's rights; the applicant must be '*in seinen Rechten verletzt*'. This finds a reflection in the case law. For instance, the tenant of an apartment could challenge the decision addressed to the landlord authorizing him to raise the rent (BVerwGE 1, n°44, 23 Apr. 1954, II C 50.53, 104). On the other hand, the owner of a driving school could not attack a decision preventing him from using a certain area to conduct driving tests (BVerwGE 39, n°61, 25 Feb. 1972, VII C 20.71, 345). This admissibility test recalls the early American rules on *locus standi*. Thus, in *Frost* v. *Corporation Commission of the State of Oklahoma*, 278 US 515 at 519 (1928), it was held that a company having a franchise to operate a cotton gin could resort to a court to restraint the illegal operation of a competing cotton gin under a void permit, upon the ground that it was an injurious invasion of the company's property rights. See also *Philadelphia Co.* v. *Stimson*, 233 US 605 at 619 (1911). In *Alabama Power Co.* v. *Ickes* 302 US 464 at 479 (1938), a distributor of electricity under a franchise was not given the right to challenge a programme of public grants whereby a municipality would construct its own electricity plant. It was held that the applicant had not sustained a direct injury, which was defined as 'a wrong which directly results in the violation of a legal right'. In *Tennessee Electric Power Co.* v. *Tennessee Valley Authority*, 306 US 118 at 137 (1939), such a right invaded had to be 'one of property, one arising out of contract, one protected against tortious invasion or one found in a statute that confers a privilege'.

that violates a legal rule would also violate a subjective public right if the legal rule:

has been enacted to favour certain persons or group of persons, to gratify their individual interests and not only in the general interests and has been enacted in the interests of these persons such that they can invoke it, and thus can elicit a certain behaviour on the part of the administrative authorities.[29]

These were very restrictive *locus standi* conditions for private parties. Fortunately, and thanks to evolution in case law, these conditions have been made more lenient,[30] and from the infringement of a subjective public right as a condition for *locus standi*, the courts imposed the more magnanimous form of 'legally protected interest', which is still a more restrictive concept than the notion of *intérêt à agir* in French administrative law. In other words, in German administrative law there has to be a connection between an interest to sue and a legally protected interest, whereas in French law this nexus need not necessarily exist, since a factual interest of the applicant is also admitted. This *legal interest* needs to be both *direct* and *susceptible of individualization*.

Under Italian law private parties need to show an interest in order to challenge the validity of administrative action.[31] Such an interest has to be *direct* and *personal*,[32] but this does not exclude the right of individuals belonging to a wide category of people provided that they are affected by the measure in question.[33]

Under Luxembourg law, private parties have the right to contest only individual administrative acts.[34] In order to exercise such right of action a *direct* and *individual* interest is required.[35]

[29] O. Bühler, *Die subjektiven öffentlichen Rechte und ihr Schutz in der Verwaltungsrechtsprechung* (Berlin, 1914), 21, translation by P. van Dijk, n. 11 above, 178.

[30] BVerwGE 37, n°47, 17 Feb. 1971, VC. 68.69, 243. Also BVerwGE 30, n°37, 30 Aug. 1968, VII. C 122.66, 191 where a company engaged in marketing wines was granted standing for the challenge of subsidies allocated to its competitors. In American law, a similar evolution occurred. See E. Stein and J. Vining, 'Citizen Access to Judicial Review of Administrative Action in a Transnational and Federal Context' in F. G. Jacobs (ed.), *European Law and the Individual* (Amsterdam, New York, Oxford), 128. Thus, in *Association of Data Processing Service Organisations* v. *Camp*, 397 US 150 (1970), a group of data-processing service organizations was declared to have standing to challenge a regulation of the Comptroller of the Currency establishing that national banks could make data-processing services available to bank customers and to other banks. The American Supreme Court found that a plaintiff would have standing (1) if the challenged measure had caused him an 'injury of fact, economic or otherwise', and (2) if the 'interest sought to be protected by the complaint is arguably within the zone of interest to be protected or regulated by the statute or constitutional guarantees in question' (187–8). In this sense, see also *Barlow* v. *Collins*, 397 US 159 at 203 (1970), and *Anglo Tours* v. *Camp*, 397 US 315 at 333 (1970).

[31] S. 3 of the Act of 20 Mar. 1865 and S. 5 of the Act of 3 Mar. 1934.

[32] G. Zanobini, *Corso di Diritto Amministrativo* (6th edn., Milan, 1950), iv, 48.

[33] In this respect see 'The Concept of Interest in Administrative Litigation' in *Eighth Colloquium of the Councils of State and the Supreme Courts of Justice of Member States of the European Community* (Copenhagen, 1982), 105.

[34] See 31 above.

[35] N. 33 above, 140.

Under Dutch law a purely factual interest is needed to pursue an action against an administrative act, but it has to be *direct* and to a certain extent *individualized*.[36]

In Danish law the interest must be *direct* and to some extent *individualized*.[37]

Under English law an evolution in the *locus standi* rules took place. Prior to 1977, there were different rules for the different remedies,[38] but on the whole they were quite limiting rules. In 1977, a single procedure was instituted for all kinds of remedies and, logically, a uniform rule of *locus standi* was established. Thus, Order 53 rule 3(7)[39] now provides that 'the Court shall not grant leave unless it considers that the applicant has a sufficient interest in the matter to which the application relates'.

The principles underlying this provision were developed in *R.* v. *Inland Revenue Commissioners, ex parte National Federation of Self-Employed and Small Business Ltd.*[40] In this case, a federation representing small businesses sought to challenge an agreement whereby the Inland Revenue granted an amnesty on tax evasion to some Fleet Street employees. The applicants believed that such an agreement was in stark contrast to the attitude adopted by the tax authorities in former instances. The question of the standing of the applicants arose. In the first place, it was necessary to define a 'sufficient interest'. In the words of Lord Fraser of Tullybelton:

A direct financial or legal interest is now not required and the requirement of a legal specific interest laid down in *Reg.* v. *Lewisham Union Guardians* [1897] 1QB 488 is no longer applicable. There is also general agreement that a mere busybody does not have a sufficient interest. The difficulty is between those extremes, to distinguish between the desire of the busybody to interfere in other people's affairs and the interest of the persons affected by or having a reasonable concern with the matter to which the application relates. In the present case, the matter is an alleged failure by the appellants to perform the duty imposed upon them by statute.[41]

[36] *Ibid.* 141.

[36] *Ibid.* 143.

[38] In the case of private law remedies, namely, injunction and declaration, the *locus standi* rules were more severe. An injunction normally required the violation of a legal right of the applicant (*Boyce* v. *Paddington BC* [1930] 1 Ch. 109), although in some cases, a special interest was deemed to be sufficient (*Lee* v. *Enfield Borough Council* (1967) 66 LGR 195). Likewise, for declaration, a legal right of the applicant ought to be at issue. In the case of the prerogative remedies, more liberal rules of *locus standi* applied, but they were still not uniform. In the case of certiorari, it was necessary that the applicant had sustained a 'particular grievance' (*R.* v. *Thames Magistrates Court, ex parte Greenbaum* (1957) 55 LGR 129). For mandamus there had to have been a violation of a specific legal right (*R.* v. *Lewisham Union Guardians* [1897] 1 QB 498). In some instances, though, mandamus was granted on the basis that the applicants had a 'sufficient interest' (*R.* v. *Manchester Corporation* [1911] 1 KB 560).

[39] RSC 1993; Supreme Court Act 1981 (c.54), S. 31(3).

[40] [1982] AC 617 (HL).

[41] *Ibid.* 646.

In the second place, it was established that the question of standing cannot be isolated from the merits of the case in all instances.[42] Wade explains that the examination of the applicants' standing must be made in a two-stage process. The first step is to turn away hopeless applicants. The second is to examine whether the applicant has 'a strong enough case on the merits, judged in relation to his own on the concern with it'.[43] The novel aspect of the second stage is that it is more a test on the merits and it would mean that, even in those cases where an applicant may have an insufficient interest, he still may be allowed to pursue it.[44] In the case at issue, it was decided unanimously that the applicant had failed to show that a breach of duty serious enough had taken place; had the applicants shown such a breach, they might have been granted standing. As Wade said: 'However remote the applicant's interest, even if he is merely one taxpayer objecting to the assessment of another, he may still succeed, if he shows a clear case of default or abuse. The law will now focus upon public policy rather than private interest.'[45]

The conclusion to be drawn from this overview of the English legal system is that, at present, a direct personal interest will be required[46] but that, in some circumstances, applicants with a general or public interest will be granted standing when there has been a breach, or failure to carry out statutory or public duties, by the authorities involved.

Under Scottish law, there were always uniform rules of *locus standi* even though there were different procedures for the different remedies. In 1985, by Act of Sederunt, a new procedure was created, namely the application for judicial review.[47] The new Rule of the Supreme Court 260B superseded the various procedures by a single one, i.e. the petition for judicial review, but it did not introduce a major development of the rules of *locus standi*, as these were already uniform (unlike the situation in England and Ireland). The law of Scotland provides that a potential litigant has always to qualify

[42] 'There may be simple cases in which it can be seen at the earliest stage that the person applying for judicial review has no interest at all, or no sufficient interest to support the application: then it would be quite correct at the threshold to refuse him leave to apply . . . But in other cases, this will not be so . . . In other words, the question of sufficient interest cannot, in such cases, be considered in the abstract, or as an isolated point: it must be taken together with the legal and factual context' (*per* Lord Wilbeforce at 630). See also Lord Roskill at 656.

[43] H. W. R. Wade, *Administrative Law* (6th edn., Oxford, 1988), 703.

[44] This point is of great importance, in that some decisions of the ECJ show that the question of standing is not entirely separate from the substance of a case. In this sense see *Parti Ecologiste 'Les Verts'* v. *European Parliament*, n. 1 above, and Case 11/82 *Piraiki-Patraiki* [1985] ECR 207. See also the differences on this point with Scottish and Irish law (see 38 below).

[45] *Ibid.* See also Sir Jack I. H. Jacob (gen. ed.), *The Supreme Court Practice* (London, 1993), i, 847.

[46] Such interest need not be legal, but it may be a factual interest. For a list of situations where the applicants were held to have a 'sufficient interest' see C. B. Lewis, *Judicial Remedies in Public Law* (London, 1992), 271–2.

[47] Act of Sederunt (Rules of Court Amendment No 2) (Judicial Review) 1985, SI 1985/500 inserting Ch. IV, s. 14, Application for Judicial Review, RC 260 B.

title and interest.[48] The title to sue implies that 'the person must be a party (using the word in its widest sense) to some legal relation which gives him some right which the person against whom he raises the action either infringes or denies'.[49] The requirement of an interest to sue was qualified by Lord Clyde in *Scottish Old People's Welfare Council, Petitioners* by saying that the 'interest must be such as to be seen as material or sufficient. The pursuit of an academic issue would not suffice, nor would an attempt to seek a general pronouncement of law on facts which were hypothetical. There must be a real issue.'[50]

The problem that arose was that in administrative law it is not difficult to find instances where the applicants have an interest to sue but none of their rights are at issue.[51] Thus, in *Wilson* v. *Independent Broadcasting Authority*,[52] three individuals petitioned the court to interdict the Independent Broadcasting Authority from broadcasting four party political programmes, and especially one on the eve of a referendum. The applicants were in favour of a 'no' and alleged that three of the programmes were aimed to secure a 'yes' in the election and that the last programme was unduly influential. They argued that the broadcasting authority was in breach of its statutory duty under section 2(2) of the Independent Broadcasting Act 1973.[53] Lord Ross explained that 'In Scotland, I see no reason in principle why an individual should not sue in order to prevent a breach by a public body of a duty owed by that public body to the public.'[54]

The question of title received a very broad construction, in that the duty of public authorities to act within the law was interpreted as a right of the members of the community. By these means a very wide interpretation of *locus standi* conditions appears.

Under Irish law, Order 84 rule 10(r) of the Rules of the Superior Courts[55] states that leave to apply for judicial review shall not be granted unless the applicant has a 'sufficient interest in the matter to which the application relates'. In earlier instances, applicants were treated with great severity, as they had to show that a legal right or a legally protected interest had been threatened by the measure in question.[56]

[48] *D. & J. Nicol* v. *Trustees of the Harbour of Dundee* (1914) 2 SLT 418 at 420, *per* Lord Dunedin.

[49] *Ibid.* 421.

[50] [1987] SLT 179 at 186.

[51] See Sir Thomas Smith and R. Black (gen. eds.), *The Laws of Scotland*, Stair Memorial Encyclopaedia, i, para. 308.

[52] [1979] SLT 279.

[53] This provision reads: '[I]t shall be the duty of the Authority . . . (b) to ensure that the programmes broadcast by the Authority in each area maintain a high general standard in all respects, and in particular in respect of their content and quality and a proper balance and wide range in the subject matter.'

[54] See n. 52 above, 282.

[55] RSCts. 1986.

[56] As the case was in English law, the private-law remedies—declaration and injunction—had stricter rules and the applicants had to prove that a legal right was impaired (*Weir* v. *Fermanagh* [1913] 1 IR 193). In the case of public law remedies, the rules for certiorari and prohibition

The principles contained in the new Order were developed in *Cahill* v. *Sutton*,[57] where it was said that '[an applicant] must show that the impact of the impugned law on his personal situation discloses an injury or prejudice which he has either suffered or is in imminent danger of suffering.'[58] This judgment has been confirmed by subsequent case law.[59] Under Irish law, a direct interest, whether legal or factual, is required.

There is an important point of divergence between English law on the one hand and Scottish and Irish law on the other. Under English law, the *Fleet Street* case[60] suggested that in some cases the applicants' interest has to be determined in the light of whether they have or have not a strong case on the merits. Under Scottish law[61] and under Irish law[62] the question of standing is independent and preliminary to the analysis of the substance of a case.

Under Greek law, natural and legal persons must show an interest that needs to be direct and individual in order to control the legality of administrative acts.[63]

In the Portuguese legal system likewise, a direct and individual interest[64] is required of private parties in order to bring annulment proceedings against administrative acts.

In Spain, in the nineteenth century the right of action of private parties against administrative measures was only admitted in those instances where the applicant had suffered a violation of one of his rights.[65] Several subsequent laws began to reduce the severity of these *locus standi* conditions,[66] and finally the law on administrative jurisdiction[67] established that a potential applicant only needed to show a *direct* interest to be granted *locus standi* in annulment proceedings against an administrative act. The Spanish Supreme Court has interpreted this to mean that an applicant has a direct interest whenever a benefit accrues to him by the annulment of the

were theoretically more lenient, whereas for mandamus they were stricter *(R. (I.U.D.W.C.)* v. *Rathmines UDC* [1928] IR 260). In truth, however, in the cases of certiorari and prohibition relief was only granted when the applicant was the 'person aggrieved': *The State (Toft)* v. *Galway Corporation* [1981] ILRM 439.

[57] [1980] IR 269.

[58] *Per* Henchy J at 284.

[59] *The State (King)* v. *Minister of Justice* [1984] IR 169.

[60] N. 40 above.

[61] See *Scottish Old People's Welfare Council, Petitioners*, n. 50 above, *per* Lord Clyde at 187.

[62] See G. Hogan and D. Morgan, *Administrative Law in Ireland* (2nd edn., London, 1991), 613.

[63] s. 47 of Act 170/973 on the Council of State.

[64] Thus M. Caetano, 'La Protection juridictionelle du Particulier contre le Pouvoir Exécutif au Portugal', n. 12 above, ii, 893.

[65] s. 1 of *Ley de Santamaría de Paredes* of 1888 provided that the right of action of natural and legal persons was limited to cases where the administrative act in question had violated a right previously vested in the applicant by a low, reg., or other provision.

[66] s. 253 of the *Estatuto Municipal* of 1924 and s. 233b of the *Ley Municipal* of 1935.

[67] *Ley Reguladora de la Jurisdicción Contencioso-Administrativa* of 27 Dec. 1956 (BOE 363, 28 Dec. 1956).

contested act or a prejudice results from its maintenance.[68] Subsequently, with the enactment of the Spanish Constitution of 1978, a further step forward was taken by Article 24(1), which guarantees the judicial protection of all 'rights and legitimate interests'. According to the case law of the Spanish Constitutional Court, the notion of 'legitimate interest' is wider than the one of 'direct interest',[69] and therefore the constitutional term takes precedence over the former 'direct interest' required of private litigants. In consequence, a very liberal concept of *locus standi* emerges from the present system of Spanish administrative law. A very interesting evolution has also taken place in the domain of challenge to general administrative acts. Article 18(1)b of the Act on administrative jurisidiction[70] conferred such a right on only some public entities. This restriction was seen by the Constitutional Court as contradicting the mandate contained in Article 24(1) of the Constitution which guarantees an overall system of judicial protection, and, as such, the restriction has been understood as being overridden by the constitutional provision.[71]

From the study of these national legal systems, several common features can be extracted in the field of *locus standi*. In the first place, the applicant will be granted standing if he or she shows an interest in the annulment of the measure that in general must be of an *individualized* character—i.e. different from that of the Community at large—and *direct*, in the sense that the act may cause or be likely to cause some harm to the applicant. Under German law, such an interest must be legally protected, unlike the situation in the other Member States, where a factual interest could also suffice. In the second place, the courts of the Member State seem also to coincide in treating the notion of interest as an empirical one, in the sense that it is constructed on a case-by-case basis.[72] Thirdly, another common feature that can be observed is an evolution in the practice regarding the severity of the *locus standi* conditions attached to actions to review the legality of administrative action. In France, Ireland, England, Spain, or even in Germany, the right of action of natural and legal persons has been progressively extended as a consequence of the development of the principles of respect for the rule of law and the need for adequate judicial protection of individual interests against the action of the Executive. Applicants no longer have to show the violation of a right in order to be

[68] Dec. of the Sup. Ct. (*Tribunal Supremo*) of 19 Dec. 1968 [1968]. Repertorio de Jurisprudencia Aranzadi, 5805.

[69] Dec. of the Const. Ct. (*Tribunal Constitucional*) 60/1982 of 11 Oct. 1982.

[70] N. 67 above.

[71] Dec. of the Const. Ct. (*Tribunal Constitucional*) 160/1985 of 28 Nov. 1985.

[72] See conclusions of M. Chenot in *Giquel* (n. 18 above, 100); *R.* v. *Inland Revenue Commissioners, ex parte National Federation of Self-employed and Small Businesses Ltd.*, (n. 40 above, at 646, *per* Lord Fraser of Tullybelton; *Scottish Old People's Welfare Council, Petitioners*, n. 50 above, at 187, *per* Lord Clyde.

granted *locus standi*; the proof that one of their interests is affected is sufficient. Under European Community law, the wording of Article 173 does not make use of the concept of 'interest', but of 'concern' which seems to be a narrower term. Such concern must be *direct* and *individual*, which recalls the expressions used in the national legal systems in relation to the interest to sue. It will be seen later on that the European Court has interpreted the notion of 'concern' as very close to the notion of 'interest' in case law concerning the ECSC Treaty,[73] whereas it has interpreted the notion of 'direct and individual concern' under the EC Treaty in a fashion that recalls the early standing requirements contained in the national legal systems, and especially in German administrative law.[74] It is noted that a further point of connection between *locus standi* under the EC Treaty and the national legal systems is the existence of an evolution in the case law, both of the national courts and of the European Court, towards a more lenient view of the right of action of private parties.[75]

3.2 The *Locus Standi* of Non-privileged Applicants in Annulment Proceedings under the ECSC Treaty

Article 33 ECSC Treaty makes a distinction between *privileged applicants* (Member States and Council),[76] *semi-privileged applicants* (European Parliament), and *non-privileged applicants* (undertakings and associations of undertakings). Non-privileged applicants are able to challenge the legality of individual decisions and recommendations 'concerning them' and of general decisions and recommendations which 'they consider to involve a misuse of powers affecting them'. Therefore the system provided by this Treaty is more liberal than that of the EC Treaty in two aspects: i.e. first, private parties have a limited right of action against general measures,[77] and, secondly, the requirement of 'concern' seems more lenient than the formula under the EC Treaty of 'direct and individual concern'.

In relation to individual acts, Article 33 ECSC Treaty provides that non-privileged applicants may challenge such acts 'concerning them'. This expression was defined by the case law of the European Court, which followed a very liberal trend. Thus, in *Groupement des Industries Sidérurgi-*

[73] See 41–2 below.

[74] This parallel with the German administrative law system was first pointed out by M. Fromont (n. 11 above, 63). See also E. Stein and J. Vining, 'Citizen Access to Judicial Review of Administrative Action in a Transnational and Federal Context' in F. G. Jacobs (ed.), *European Law and the Individual* (Amsterdam, New York, Oxford, 1976), 125.

[75] This point is particularly clear in the case law concerning the right to challenge regulations. See 150–2 below.

[76] The Commission may bring an action for annulment against the European Parliament or the Council, but on limited grounds. See 15 above.

[77] See 15 above.

ques Luxembourgeoises v. *High Authority*[78] the Court made clear that this formula did not mean that the decision had to be addressed to the applicant, it being sufficient that the decision concerned him. In *Nold* v. *High Authority*,[79] where the applicant was one of the undertakings affected by a trading regulation, the Court explained that the requirement of 'concern' meant that the decision 'directly affected the position of the applicant'.[80] This appeared very clearly in *Chambre Syndicale de la Sidérurgie de l'Est de la France* v. *High Authority*,[81] where the existence of a competitive relationship between the applicants and the addressees of the decision was thought to be sufficient to prove that the former were likely to be affected by the contested measure, and therefore they enjoyed *locus standi*.[82] In *De Gezamenlijke Steenkolenmijnen in Limburg* v. *High Authority*[83] the European Court declared that for an application for annulment to be admissible it is enough that 'the applicant claims that the decision concerns it and supports its claim by an appropriate statement explaining the *interest* which it has in having the decision declared void'.[84]

It follows from these instances that the Court adopted a very liberal interpretation of the standing requirements in the context of the ECSC Treaty, and in the end a concept very close to the notion of 'interest' as present in the French system of administrative law arose.[85] However, the position adopted by the drafters of the EC Treaty was deliberately more restrictive than the one adopted in the ECSC Treaty,[86] and the liberal case law of the Court in the framework of this latter Treaty was not adopted. In

[78] Joined Cases 7 and 9/54 [1954–6] ECR 175 at 192.

[79] Case 18/57 [1959] ECR 41.

[80] *Ibid.* 51. In the same way Lagrange A.G. in his Opinion in Joined Cases 36–38 and 40/59 *Geitling* v. *High Authority* [1960] ECR 423 at 449, emphasized that what the ECJ required was the existence of a direct interest on the part of the applicant.

[81] Joined Cases 24 and 34/58 [1960] ECR 281.

[82] *Ibid.* 292. This decision is in stark contrast to Joined Cases 10 and 18/68 *Eridania* v. *Commission* [1969] ECR 459, decided under the EC Treaty, where the existence of a competitive relationship of the applicant with the addressee of a decision was declared not to be sufficient to grant him *locus standi*. See 50 below. Recent decisions of the CFI in competition and state aids cases however, suggest that the existence of a competitive relationship between the applicants and the addressees (or beneficiaries) of a measure may influence the *locus standi* of the applicants (see 75 ff., below).

[83] Case 30/59 [1961] ECR 1.

[84] Ibid. 16, emphasis added.

[85] See 00–0 above.

[86] Thus, in Joined Cases 16–17/62 *Confédération Nationale des Producteurs de Fruits et Légumes* v. *Council* [1962] ECR 471 at 482, the ECJ admitted this fact. The Advocates General of the Court also acknowledged this view: Lagrange A.G. in *De Gezamenlijke Steenkolenmijnen in Limburg* v. *High Authority*, n. 83 above, at 30; Mayras A. G. in Case 43/72 *Merkur* v. *Commission* [1973] ECR 1055 at 1078; and Lagrange A.G. in *Confédération Nationale*, at 486. Academic opinion also points in this direction. See P. Gormley, 'The Procedural Status of the Individual before Supranational Judicial Tribunals' (1963–5) 41–42 *Univ. Detr. LJ* 422; J. Boulois and R. M. Chevallier, *Grands Arrêts de la Cour de Justice des Communautés Européennes* (Paris, 1974), 122, and C. Harding, 'The Private Interest in Challenging Community Action' (1980) 5 *ELRev.* 354. For a dissenting view see D. Weinhardt, *Die Klagebefugnis des Konkurrenten* (Göttingen, 1973), 171–2.

the context of the EC Treaty, the notion of 'direct and individual concern' was not, in the case law of the Court, conceived as equivalent to 'interest' but rather as equivalent to the existence of damage to a right of the applicant.[87] It has been stated that there are great differences between the two Treaties, especially in relation to their scope of application.[88] It could well be that the drafters of the EC Treaty were fearful that granting wide access to private parties[89] would open the floodgates of litigation before the European Court and diminish the efficacy of Community law by posing a constant threat to the legality of Community measures. This would correspond to the ancient concern underlying the very concept of *locus standi*. The European Court bore this in mind and acted accordingly by refusing to adopt the same liberal trend that it had adopted under the provisions of the ECSC Treaty.[90] This is quite understandable, but it is equally important to observe that, in a Community whose measures produce a direct impact on the interests of natural and legal persons and Member States alike, and where the legislative process is still vitiated by a substantial lack of democracy, the reasons stated above do not provide a full justification, especially when alternative means of redress are not always available.[91]

3.3 The Challenge of Decisions by Non-addressees under the EC Treaty. General Area of Case Law: The Tests of Direct and Individual Concern

As already pointed out, the drafting of Article 173(2) EEC Treaty is more restrictive than that of Article 33 ECSC Treaty.[92] Some hope remained, though, that the European Court would adopt a liberal interpretation of that legal provision. After all, the notion of 'direct and individual concern'

[87] See 54 below. [88] See 29 above.

[89] It is also important to remember that the concept of private parties under the EC Treaty is wider than under the ECSC Treaty (see 8 above, n. 35).

[90] For a comprehensive survey of the reasons that may have driven the ECJ to adopt a severe interpretation of the *locus standi* requirements contained in Art. 173(2) EEC Treaty see E. Stein and J. Vining, n. 74 above, 122–5 and H. Rasmussen, 'Why is Article 173 interpreted against Private Plaintiffs?' (1980) 5 *ELRev*. 112. This latter author put forward a very attractive theory by saying that the reason underlying the ECJ's approach is a deliberate move to deviate the bulk of individual applications to proceedings before the national courts (see 187–8 below). Other authors believed that the ECJ did not pursue a consistent policy; thus L. Neville Brown and F. G. Jacobs explained that the Court was 'anxious, on the one hand, to allow individuals or companies an opportunity to seek annulment of acts of the Council or the Commission, yet on the other fearful of finding itself overwhelmed by a flood of such suits' (*The Court of Justice of the European Communities* (London, 1983), 97.

[91] See 185 ff., below.

[92] Even after the Maastricht Treaty amendments, the wording of Art. 173(2) EEC Treaty (now Art. 173(4) EC Treaty) has remained unchanged.

was not defined in the Treaty, and the Court certainly had the option of construing it in a flexible manner. Unfortunately, this was not the case, and the Court—possibly for the reasons given above[93]—chose to adopt a rigid interpretation of these *locus standi* conditions, preferring to adhere to the literal wording of Article 173(2) EEC Treaty. This approach was manifest in the early case law,[94] and was carried out, even against the recommendations of the Advocates General[95] and despite the Court's own statements in favour of an overall system of judicial protection.[96] However, it is one of the arguments of this work that the Court's attitude to the *locus standi* problem has slowly moved towards a more liberal interpretation that has facilitated the access of private parties to annulment proceedings.[97] This will be demonstrated in the context of the challenge of decisions[98] and of regulations.[99] In any case, the caution of the Court in this area and its reluctance to alter the wording of Article 173(2) EEC Treaty[100] is in contrast with the creative role that it played in Article 177 EC Treaty[101] and the interpretation followed by the European Court in other

[93] See 42 above.

[94] Thus in Joined Cases 16 and 17/62 *Confédération Nationale des Producteurs des Fruits et Légumes* v. *Council,* n. 86 above, at 478, the ECJ, while acknowledging that the system under the EEC Treaty was more restrictive than the one in the ECSC Treaty, said that 'it would not be appropriate for the Court to pronounce on the merits of this system which appears from the text under examination'. Likewise in Case 40/64 *Sgarlata* v. *Commission* [1965] ECR 215 at 227, when the ECJ was confronted with the applicant's argument that a restrictive interpretation of Art. 173 would deprive him of all means of protection, it replied that those considerations 'cannot be allowed to override the clearly restrictive wording of Art. 173, which it is the Court's task to apply'. In later instances, however, the Court chose a more flexible stand favouring the considerations of an overall system of judicial protection. See Case 294/83 *Parti Ecologiste 'Les Verts'* v. *European Parliament*, n. 1 above, at point 23.

[95] See the Opinions of Roemer A.G. in Case 6/68 *Zuckerfabrik Watenstedt* v. *Council* [1968] ECR 409 at 421, and in Joined Cases 10 and 18/68 *Eridania* v. *Commission*, n. 82 above, 492–3); Opinion of Warner A.G. in Case 162/78 *Wagner* v. *Commission* [1979] ECR 3467 at 3494 and Opinion of VerLoren van Themaat A.G. in Case 45/81 *Moksel* v. *Commission* [1982] ECR 1129 at 1152.

[96] Thus, in Case 25/62 *Plaumann* v. *Commission* [1963] ECR 95 at 107, the ECJ said that 'provisions of the Treaty regarding the right of interested parties to bring an action must not be interpreted restrictively'.

[97] A good indication of this trend is the proposals made by the ECJ in its 'Suggestions on European Union' ([1975] Bull. EC, supp. 9/75 18), where it advocated a system wherein the rights of the individual ought to be protected. In its view, the safeguarding of these rights requires that 'acts of subordinate legislation are open to challenge by private parties having a direct interest as is the case in the legal systems of several of the Member States'.

[98] See 60 ff. below. See also instances decided in the field of competition (see 81 ff. below) and state aids proceedings (see 90 ff. below).

[99] See 150–2 below. See also anti-dumping cases, 152 ff. below.

[100] At 31 Dec. 1990, of 383 actions of annulment brought by natural or legal persons, as many as 105 had been declared inadmissible. Source: Offprint from the *XXIV General Report on the Activities of the European Communities* (Luxembourg, 1990), 449.

[101] See 181 below.

instances.[102] This attitude of the Court has been the object of considerable criticism.[103] In the case of regulations, the main obstacle to the admissibility of individual applications has been the test of legal nature. In the case of decisions, the main obstacle has been the test of individual concern, as will be seen throughout this Chapter. In the subsequent sections a study of the case law of the Court is undertaken, with two main purposes. In the first place it is sought to ascertain the meaning of the notion of 'direct and individual concern'. In the second it is shown that, despite the overall restrictive interpretation of these requirements by the Court, a certain degree of liberalization has been achieved in some specific areas—competition proceedings and state aids—and in some isolated instances in the area of general case law.[104] The area of general case law will be studied first. The case law concerning competition and state aids proceedings will be dealt with in a separate section, given the Court's different approach to the *locus standi* conditions.[105]

[102] In some cases the ECJ has truly 're-drafted', through its interpretation, provisions both of the EC Treaty and of secondary legislation. An example of the first class is Joined cases 267–269/81 *Amministrazione delle Finanze dello Stato* v. *SPI* [1983] ECR 801, where the ECJ established that the provisions of the GATT could be interpreted by the Court in the course of a preliminary reference despite the wording of Art. 177 EEC Treaty which does not provide for such a possibility. An example of the second is the decision in Case 67/79 *Fellinger* v. *Bundesanstalt für Arbeit* [1980] ECR 4535 at 545, where the Court adopted an interpretation *a sensu contrario* of Art. 68(1) of Reg. 1408/71, on the application of social security schemes to employed persons and their families moving within the Community, obeying considerations of *effet utile* and respect for the principles of free movement of workers. In Case 44/81 *Germany* v. *Commission* [1982] ECR 1875, the ECJ followed a very liberal interpretation of the number of remedies available under Community law. In that case, the German Government had brought an action to obtain a payment from the Commission that was due under a Commission dec. and that the institution concerned refused to make on the ground that the requests were not submitted within the period of 18 months laid down by the original dec. In its judgment, the ECJ explained that 'there is no provision in the EEC Treaty entitling a person in favour of whom an institution has entered unilaterally into a financial commitment to bring before the Court an action for payment against that institution' (point 6). However, it held that 'It follows that whilst the EEC Treaty makes no provision for an action of the type brought by the applicants, this cannot be regarded as a lacuna which must be filled in order to ensure that persons concerned have effective protection of their rights' (consideration 7). This argument could be used *a sensu contrario*, to formulate the proposition that had it been a lacuna in the system of judicial protection, the ECJ would have filled it by creating a remedy not contemplated in the EC Treaty.

[103] Thus A. Barav, 'Direct and Individual Concern: An almost Insurmountable Barrier to the Admissibility of Individual Appeals to the European Court' (1974) 11 *CMLRev.* 191, 191–2; A. G. Toth, 'The Individual and European Law' (1975) 24 *ICLQ* 659, 678; L. Neville Brown and F. G. Jacobs, n. 90 above, 97, and H. Rasmussen, n. 90 above, 114. Other authors adopted an intermediate solution, claiming that the ECJ had no other option given the strict drafting of Art. 173(2) EEC Treaty (see M. Waelbroeck, J. V. Louis, D. Vignes, J. L. Dewost, and G. Vandersanden, *Le Droit de la Communauté Economique Européenne* (Brussels, 1983), x, 121). It is argued that this latter standpoint is hardly defensible if the judicial approach of the Court in other instances is taken into account (see n. 102 above).

[104] Case 294/83 *Parti Ecologiste 'Les Verts'* v. *European Parliament*, n. 1 above, points 35–7; Case 294/81 *Control Data* v. *Commission* [1983] ECR 911, and Case C–354/89 *Schiocchet* v. *Commission* [1991] ECR I–1775. See 60–2 below.

[105] See 75 ff. below.

3.3.1 THE TEST OF INDIVIDUAL CONCERN

The concept of 'individual concern' was described by Bebr[106] as 'one of the thorniest problems of judicial review'. The present section considers the case law on the concept of individual concern in the area of decisions adopted in the area of general management of the market.[107]

Most of the cases decided concern decisions addressed to Member States.[108] For the purpose of this study, two main groups of instances have been identified. On the one hand, it may be said that a general trend emerges from the majority of the decisions given by the Court and by the Court of First Instance, i.e. that an applicant is individually concerned when the decision at issue has affected his individual rights under Community law. This will be the subject of the first subsection. On the other, it is thought that there have been special cases where the test of individual concern has been constructed in a different way as a consequence of a more liberal interpretation by the Court of Article 173(2) EEC Treaty. This will be the subject of study in the second subsection.

3.3.1.1 The Case Law on Individual Concern: The General Trend

The great majority of instances concern the challenge by private parties of decisions enacted by the Commission and addressed to a Member State in the field of customs duties, authorization for protective measures, or within the framework of the Common Agricultural Policy.

The first case where the analysis of the notion arose was *Plaumann* v. *Commission*.[109] The case involved a Commission decision addressed to Germany, whereby the Commission refused to authorize Germany to suspend the collection of a customs duty of 13 per cent—as set out in the Common Customs Tariff—on the importation of fresh clementines from non-member countries and to apply instead a 10 per cent duty as set out in the German Customs Tariff. Plaumann, a German importer, sought the annulment of this decision.

The Commission disputed the admissibility of the application on various

[106] G. Bebr, *Development of Judicial Control in the European Communities* (The Hague, Boston, Mass., London, 1981), 65.

[107] In the case law concerning regs., the ECJ constructed the test of individual concern in identical terms. See 112 below, n. 60.

[108] The instances concerning decisions addressed to private parties belong mainly to the area of competition proceedings (see 75 ff. below). In the area of general case law only Joined Cases 10 and 18/68 *Eridania* v. *Commission*, see n. 82 above; Case 294/83 *Parti Ecologiste 'Les Verts'* v. *European Parliament*, n. 1 above, and some instances involving contractual relations entered into by the Community, concerned the challenge of decs. addressed to private parties. See 59–60 below.

[109] Case 25/62, n. 96 above.

grounds, two of which were particularly interesting. In the first place, the Commission believed that, since the decision was addressed to a Member State, the State could not be considered as 'another person' within the meaning of Article 173(2) EEC Treaty.[110] Secondly, the Commission thought that the decision was not of individual concern to the applicant.[111] The applicant, on the other hand, thought that he was indeed individually concerned, in that a lower duty would increase the volume of sales. In other words, *Plaumann* was relying on the notion of interest that, in national legal systems, suffices to grant standing.[112]

The Court began its judgment in a very liberal way, by ruling that the expression 'another person' contained in Article 173(2) EEC Treaty could encompass a Member State and pronouncing itself in favour of a liberal interpretation of the provisions concerning judicial protection of private parties.[113] It then went on to define the meaning of individual concern by saying:

> Persons other than those to whom a decision is addressed may only claim to be individually concerned if that decision affects them by reason of *certain attributes which are peculiar to them* or by reason *of circumstances in which they are differentiated from all other persons* and by virtue of these factors distinguishes them individually just as in the case of the person addressed.[114]

The Court further said:

> In the present case the applicant is affected by the disputed Decision as an importer of clementines, that is to say, by reason of a commercial activity which may at any time be practised by any person and is not therefore such as to distinguish the applicant in relation to the contested Decision as in the case of the addressee.[115]

Two observations may be made about this judgment. In the first place, it defined 'individual concern': that an applicant must be individualized from all other persons to such a degree as to turn him into a sort of *de facto* addressee. The question that arises is: which are those peculiar attributes or differentiating circumstances? The Court did not explain. It was clear, though, that a mere factual interest in the annulment of the measure, like that of *Plaumann*, was not sufficient. Further, it is somewhat surprising that the Court began its judgment in a very liberal fashion, favouring a

110 Case 25/62, 99.

111 *Ibid.* 100.

112 See 30 ff. above.

113 See 43, n. 96 above.

114 Case 25/62, see n. 96 above, at 107, emphasis added.

115 *Ibid.* The idea that the mere capacity of an applicant as a trader, importer, or exporter does not suffice to render it individually concerned by a Community measure has been consistently repeated in the case law involving decs. (Case 34/88 *Coopérative Agricole de l'Anjou et du Poitou (Cevap)* v. *Council* [1988] ECR 6265 at point 15; Case 206/87 *Lefebvre Frère et Sœur* v. *Commission* [1989] ECR 275 at point 14); and regs. (Case 26/86 *Deutz und Geldermann* v. *Council* [1987] ECR 941 at point 12).

wide interpretation of the provisions regulating the right of action of private parties, and yet, when the time came to define what individual concern meant, the Court did so in the narrowest terms possible.[116]

In *Glucoseries Réunies* v. *Commission*[117] the Commission had issued a decision authorizing France to levy countervailing charges on the importation of glucose originating in other Member States. The applicant, a Belgian exporter of glucose to France, maintained that the decision was illegal and thought himself individually concerned because he was one of the Community's leading manufacturers of this product and because he was the only Belgian exporter of glucose to France.

The Court concluded that the decision affected all exports from the Common Market—excepting Italy which did not export any glucose—and therefore the attributes of the applicant[118] did not suffice to make him 'directly and individually concerned'.[119]

In *Getreide-Import Gesellschaft* v. *Commission*,[120] the facts at issue could suggest that there was a considerable degree of individualization in the applicant's position. Article 17(2) of Regulation 19 of the Council[121] established that the rates of levy for the importation of cereals had to be based on the c.i.f. prices fixed by the Commission. The Commission determined by decision of 25 June 1964 those prices which were to be in force until the 26 June 1964. *Getreide*, an importer of cereals and fodder of all kinds, was the only one which applied for an import licence on 25 June. This company believed that it was individually concerned by the decision, due to this highly distinctive circumstance.

The Advocate General, Mr Gand, thought, on the contrary, that the applicant was not individually concerned as, at the time when the decision was enacted, it was not possible to determine the strength of the category of entities to which it was to apply. Mr Gand anticipated the idea of a 'closed category' as the notion underlying the concept of 'individual concern'. A closed category is, according to one author,[122] 'one the membership of which is fixed and determined at the time the measure comes into force', or, the same thing, one whose membership cannot be enlarged after the measure is issued. The applicant belonged to an open category, given

[116] Perhaps the reason the Court admitted so readily that the expression 'another person' in Art. 173(2) EEC Treaty could encompass a Member State was the fact that it was aware that the majority of case law on admissibility of actions against decs. addressed to third parties would concern decs. addressed to Member States. If private parties had been denied the right to attack such decs., a very significant limitation on the judicial protection of natural and legal persons would have been imposed.

[117] Case 1/64, see n. 3 above.

[118] Compare this judgment with Case 294/81 *Control Data* v. *Commission*, n. 104 above.

[119] Case 1/64, n. 3 above, at 417.

[120] Case 38/64 [1965] ECR 203.

[121] JO 933/62 of 20 Apr. 1962.

[122] T. C. Hartley, *The Foundations of European Community Law* (3rd edn., Oxford, 1994) 367.

that, at the time when the decision was issued, it affected 'both actual and potential importers, if only in so far as the price fixed might deter them from applying for a licence'.[123] The fact that the applicant was individualized, after the decision came into force, by reason of his particular conduct —the company's application for a licence—seemed irrelevant.

The Court (clearly following the suggestions of its Advocate General) dismissed the application as inadmissible by saying that the applicant was not individual concerned, since the 'purely fortuitous fact' that only the applicant had applied for a licence during the period of enforcement of the measure was not sufficient to differentiate the company from the other importers.[124]

Toepfer v. *Commission*[125] provided the first case where an applicant was found to be individually concerned. The case arose as a result of a mistake made by the Commission, when it established the prices for cereals which were subsequently used to determine the import levy to be applied to them. The Commission had failed to take into account the new harvest and fixed a price for maize at 1 October that reduced the levy to nil. Knowing this, fourteen importers applied for import licences for large quantities of maize. The German Government, in its concern about this situation, suspended the issue of all import licences, making use of the safeguard measures provided in Article 22(1) of Regulation 19.[126] The use of these measures, however, required the approval of the Commission. The Commission fixed a new price on 2 October and, by decision of 3 October, retrospectively authorized Germany to apply the safeguard measures from 1 October. The authorization was valid until 4 October inclusive. The category of people affected by the Commission decision was partially closed (the traders that had applied for licences between 1 October and 3 October) and partially open (the traders that might have wished to apply for licences during the remaining period that the authorization covered, i.e. until 4 October). The applicants belonged to the first of these groups and brought annulment proceedings against this authorization.

The Court, in its judgment, dealt first with the test of direct concern[127] and, finding it met, went on to deal with the notion of individual concern. The Court found the applicants individually concerned. Three considerations seem to stand out from the Court's judgment. In the first place, the Court observed that, since the Commission had raised the price from 2 October, the only persons really affected by the measure were those who applied for a licence on 1 October (who would have to pay an increased rate of levy as a result of the decision).[128] In the second place, this last

[123] Case 38/64, n. 120 above, 213.

[124] Case 38/64, n. 120 above, 208.

[125] Joined Cases 106 and 107/63 [1965] ECR 405.

[126] See n. 121 above.

[127] See 65 below.

[128] Joined Cases 106–107/63, n. 125 above, at 411. It is believed that there is a slight error in the text of the judgment. Both in the French version ([1965] Rec. 526 at 533) and in the

group of traders had become fixed and ascertainable when the Commission adopted the contested decision.[129] Finally, the Court pointed out that the Commission was in a position to know whom the decision was going to affect.[130] This seems a very stringent test to define the right of action of private parties. As Kovar[131] has pointed out, it would seem that, without expressly admitting it, the Court was aiming to cover those situations where, although a decision is addressed to a third party, in truth it is intended to regulate the situation of the applicant. This could explain why the Court emphasized that the contested decision in reality, *only* affected the group of traders that applied for licences on 1 October. In other words, the aim of Article 173(2) EEC Treaty is to protect private applicants against situations of misuse of power.[132] It would be quite unfair if the European institutions could escape judicial control by addressing a decision to a third party when really they had intended to affect the situation of a particular group of people who would be real 'co-addressees' of the measure.

In *Eridania* v. *Commission*[133] the Commission issued three decisions whereby it granted aid from the European Agricultural Guidance and Guarantee Fund (EAGGF) to certain sugar refineries established in Italy. The addressees of the decision were the Italian Government and the prospective beneficiaries. The applicants, certain undertakings in the sugar industry in competition with the beneficiaries of the aid, requested the annulment of the decision of the Commission. The Advocate General (Mr Roemer) recalled that, both in national legal systems and in the context of the ECSC Treaty,[134] undertakings had suffered an interference in their

English translation ([1965] ECR 405 at 411), the ECJ said that the contested decision had been issued on 4 October, when in the description of the facts (Rec. at 528; ECR at 407), in the Opinion of the A.G. (Rec. at 537; ECR at 416) and in the *dispositif* of the judgment (Rec. at 536; ECR at 415) the decision is said to have been enacted on 3 October. This point is not devoid of importance, if the facts of the case are taken into account.

[129] *Ibid.* 411 (ECR). [130] *Ibid.*

[131] R. Kovar, 'Chronique de la Jurisprudence de la Court de Justice des Communautés Européennes' (1966) 93 *JDI* 707, 712.

[132] But other authors like L. Goffini believed that the judgment emphasized that Art. 173(2) was contemplating true *locus standi* conditions, and that was the reason the term 'interests' was used in the judgment ('Jurisprudence. Affaires Jointes 106 et 107/63' [1966] *CDE* 72, 91). The reactions to the judgment were varied. Some authors, like J. Peters, acknowledged that the stand taken by the Court in these cases was quite restrictive. However he believed that 'it is perhaps now not the time for too bold judgements, impeding possibly the already laborious development of the Community, by rendering doubtful the force of decisions having a general effect and by that perhaps risking new attempts to restrict access to the Court by clearer and even more restrictive texts'. ('Annotations on the *Toepfer* case' (1965–6) 3 *CMLRev.* 233, 240). Others, like N. Catalano, criticized the restrictive approach of the Court and argued that a private party could suffer irreparable damage by an unlawful decision, a result that ought to be prevented at any cost ('Ancora Sulla Tutela Giurisdizionale degli Exportatori di Prodotti Agricoli' [1965] 4 *Il Foro Italiano* 124).

[133] Joined Cases 10 and 18/68, n. 82 above.

[134] *Ibid.* 491. See also 41 above and n. 30 above.

legally protected interests when aid was granted to competitors, and therefore they ought to be able to bring proceedings for the annulment of the decision in question. In spite of this, a full Court dismissed these arguments. The Court said: 'The mere fact that a measure may exercise an influence on the competitive relationships existing on the market cannot suffice to allow any trader in any competitive relationship whatever with the addressee of the measure to be regarded as directly and individually concerned by that measure.'[135]

The *Plaumann* case showed that a mere factual interest on the part of the applicants would not suffice to grant them individual concern. The *Eridania* case went further and appeared as particularly restrictive, in that it is clear that a private party suffers a particular harm to its interests when aid is granted to its competitor.[136]

In *Bock* v. *Commission*,[137] the Court found another instance where the applicant was declared to be individually concerned. *Bock* was a German undertaking which imported from a Dutch company a consignment of Chinese mushrooms, which were already in free circulation in the Netherlands. The applicant submitted his application for an import licence, which he lodged with the corresponding German office. The German authorities told the applicant that they were going to ask the Commission for the application of Article 115(1) EEC Treaty and that they intended to reject his application as soon as the Commission granted authorization to apply the safeguard measures required (with retroactive effect). The Commission enacted a decision authorizing the protective measures in relation both to pending licences and to future ones. Therefore the decision affected a category of people that was partially closed (traders who had already submitted applications for licences) and partially open (the potential importers). *Bock*, who was the only member of the first group, challenged the provision of the Commission decision that authorized the protective measures with retroactive character. The Court acknowledged that *Bock* was individually concerned by the aforesaid provision on the basis that: (a) the applicant formed part of a closed category, and (b) the Commission was in a position to be aware of his existence and of the fact that the provision was going to affect him alone.[138]

[135] Joined Cases 10 and 18/68, n. 82 above, at point 7.

[136] However, the ECJ changed its standpoint in later cases. See Case C–354/89 *Schiocchet* v. *Commission*, n. 4 above and 61 below). In the area of contracts awarded by the Commission, see case law on actions brought by unsuccessful tenderers (see 59–60 below). In the areas of competition (Case 43/85 *Ancides* v. *Commission* [1987] ECR 3131, see 86 below) and state aids proceedings (Case 169/84 *COFAZ* v. *Commission* [1986] ECR 391), private applicants were readily granted *locus standi* to challenge decisions favouring their competitors. See 90–4 below.

[137] Case 62/70 [1971] ECR 897.

[138] *Ibid.*, at point 10 of the judgment. The approach of the ECJ was identical to the one followed in Joined Cases 106–107/63 *Toepfer* v. *Commission*, n,. 125 above.

At this point, and with two examples of the circumstances that could determine the existence of individual concern, it would seem appropriate to consider the main conceptions of academic writers on the notion of individual concern.

On the one hand, a group of authors[139] believes that, in order to be individually concerned, an applicant ought to belong to a closed category. The measure would need to apply, either wholly or in part, exclusively to a group of people that cannot be enlarged after the measure enters into force and to which the applicants belong.[140] The determination of individual concern would be made with reference exclusively to objective parameters. It would seem that, for these authors, the consideration given by the Community institution to the situation of the applicants in issuing the contested measure would not be important.

On the other hand, another group of authors[141] explains that the notion of individual concern involves the participation of elements of two kinds: in the first place, elements of an objective nature, i.e. the limitation of the persons affected and the possibility of individualizing them, and, secondly, elements of a subjective nature, i.e. the fact that the EC institution took into account the situation of the applicants as one of the elements affecting the adoption of the measure.[142] This is an even more restrictive view, in that it requires not only that the applicants be members of a closed category, but also that the institution concerned enact the measure thinking of the situation of the applicants, even though it addresses the decision to a third party.[143]

[139] T. C. Hartley, n. 122 above, 367; H. G. Schermers and D. Waelbroeck, *Judicial Protection in the European Communities* (5th edn., Deventer, 1992), 241; S. Weatherill and P. Beaumont, *EC Law* (London, 1993), 206; A. G. Toth, *Legal Protection of Individuals in the European Community* (Amsterdam, New York, Oxford, 1978), ii, 68 and *The Oxford Encyclopedia of European Community Law* (Oxford, 1991), 297; D. Wyatt and A. Dashwood, *European Community Law* (3rd edn., London, 1993), 126;. and J. Steiner, *Textbook on EEC Law* (2nd edn., London, 1990), 296.

[140] The applicants would then be given standing to challenge either a provision in the dec. or the whole measure, as the case may be. It is not enough if the applicant belongs to a small group that could be more or less ascertained before the measure is taken. Thus, see Case 231/82 *Spijker Kwasten* v. *Commission* [1983] ECR 2559, where the applicant was the only importer of the product subjected to protective measures and he was not regarded as individually concerned. The important characteristic of a closed category is the fact that nobody may become part of it after the measure enters into force; in other words, it contains a certain element of retroactivity.

[141] M. Waelbroeck, 'Le Recours en Annulation' [1971] *RCJB* 513, 533. See also G. Vandersanden and A. Barav, *Contentieux Communautaire* (Brussels, 1977), 173.

[142] Thus, M. Waelbroeck, n. 141 above, 533, said '*il faut un lien de causalité entre la connaissance que l'institution a de la situation du requérant et la mesure adoptée*'.

[143] In later cases, however, it has been shown that this subjective element is not necessary in order to ascertain the existence of individual concern—see Case 11/82 *Piraiki-Patraiki* v. *Commission*, n. 44 above and 54 below, where individual concern was not recognized (e.g. Case 231/82 *Spijker* v. *Commission*, n. 140 above). The only cases where such an element is always present is where the whole measure affects in its entirety a closed category of people, both in the case of decs. (Case 92/78 *Simmenthal* v. *Commission* [1979] ECR 777) and of regs. (Joined Cases 41–44/70 *International Fruit Company* v. *Commission* [1971] ECR 411).

The concept of individual concern seeks to set the applicant apart from other people affected by a particular measure. In the national legal systems, the applicants need to show an individual interest in the annulment of an administrative measure.[144] The national courts, excepting the German courts,[145] interpreted this requirement fairly liberally, and held that such interest exists even if the applicant is a member of a large category of people equally affected, provided that the group is distinguished from the community at large, i.e. by reason of a commercial activity,[146] especially when it intends to challenge individual administrative acts. Under EC law, however, a further degree of individualization is required. An applicant not only needs to be distinguished from the community at large but also from the group of people generally affected by the contested measure. Such a degree of individualization, according to the case law of the Court, only arises (in those cases where decisions at issue affect both open and closed categories[147]) where the applicants had applications or transactions pending when the decision at issue was adopted which were affected by such a decision. In other words, an applicant would be individually concerned by a measure when its individual rights under EC law were affected as a result of the decision enacted.[148]

The whole process could be described as follows. It would be necessary for the applicants to have acted prior to the enactment of the measure, placing reliance on a valid Community measure. Both in *Toepfer* and in *Bock*, the applicants applied for import licences relying on EC measures in force. By reason of their conduct—their application for a licence—they were distinguished from all potential importers. In accordance with a normal course of events, *Toepfer* would have obtained import licences at a zero rate of levy and *Bock* would freely have imported a consignment of mushrooms. At that point, however, the contested decisions were enacted, affecting the benefits that those traders expected in good faith. Those decisions did not merely affect the interests of *Toepfer* and *Bock* but their individual rights under Community law. Accordingly, the applicants were individually concerned.

The notion of individual concern appears as an admissibility condition that has the purpose of ensuring that private parties, whose individual rights under EC law are affected by an ulterior measure, have the chance to put forward their submissions in favour of the annulment of the deci-

[144] See 30–40 above. [145] See 33–4 above.

[146] See the examples provided by the case law of the national courts (see 31 ff. above).

[147] For those cases where the decs. at issue affect exclusively closed categories, see 57–60 below.

[148] This standpoint builds on the views put forward by M. Fromont, n. 11 above, 63. See also E. Stein and J. Vining, n . 74 above, 121, who spoke of the necessity that the Community decision violated the 'vested rights' of the applicants. In the present work that view is developed by providing further evidence from recent case law in the context both of decs. and regs.

sion.[149] The test of individual concern would be, to a certain extent, a kind of procedural equivalent to the substantive general principle of protection of legitimate expectations.

This line of reasoning is strongly reminiscent of the initial approach to *locus standi*, taken by French, German, English, Irish, and Spanish Courts,[150] according to which only applicants showing a violation of one of their rights would enjoy *locus standi*. Moreover, this reasoning would accord with the intention of the drafters of the European Community treaties, who obviously wanted to curb a wide access of private litigants to annulment proceedings.

The question arises how this standpoint differs from the arguments put forward by the two groups of authors mentioned above.[151] In the first place, and in relation to the first group of authors,[152] their views and the one presented in this work complement each other. The fact that the applicants belong to a category of people fixed and ascertained will almost invariably be a safe indicator that they are individually concerned by a subsequent Community measure that affects their position.[153] In fact, the division of the case law into blocks carried out in this work revolves around the question whether the applicants belong to an open or closed category.[154] It is argued, however, that a further question has always to be posed, i.e. whether the applicants held some individual rights under EC law, by reason of their belonging to the closed category.[155] Almost certainly that will be so, but the case law has shown that it is not *always* the case;[156]

[149] However, two authors (R. Kovar and A. Barav, 'Variations Nouvelles sur un Thème Ancien: Les Conditions de Recevabilité du Recours en Annulation dans la CEE' [1976] *CDE* 73, 93) took the view that an applicant is individually concerned when his interests and not his rights are injured by an EC measure. They found support in the statement of the ECJ in *Plaumann* (n. 96 above, and accompanying text), where the Court made reference to factual and not legal situations to ascertain when an individual could be individually concerned.

[150] See 30–40 above.

[151] See nn. 139 and 141 above.

[152] See n. 139 above and accompanying text.

[153] This is so for cases involving decs. and regs. adopted in the area of general management of the market. In cases concerning competition (see 81 below), state aids (see 90 below), and anti-dumping measures (see 155 below), different considerations apply.

[154] See 124 and 138 below.

[155] It is thought that the ECJ has pointed out this fact. Thus, in Case 97/85 *Deutsche Lebensmittelwerke* v. *Commission* [1987] ECR 2265 at point 21, a group of German producers of margarine wanted to challenge a Commission dec., addressed to Germany, promoting the sale of butter. The Court denied that the applicants were individually concerned, since the decision 'did not apply to a closed circle of persons who were known at the time of its adoption *and whose rights* the Commission intended to regulate (emphasis added).

[156] Thus, in a very recent case involving the annulment of a reg., the CFI spelt out this point in very clear terms by saying: 'In the present case the Court considers that *those importers . . . constituted a closed group of persons* identifiable at that moment. However . . . *that circumstance is not in itself sufficient for the regulation in question to be of individual concern to those traders*' (emphasis added) (Case T–489/93 *Unifruit Hellas* v. *Commission* [1994] ECR II–1201 at consideration 25). In another case involving the annulment of a reg. (Case 64/69 *La Compagnie Française Commerciale et Financière* v. *Commission* [1970] ECR 221), the applicants belonged to a closed category and nevertheless it is suggested that they were not individually

hence the importance of the distinction drawn in this work . In the second place, and in relation to the views of the second group of authors,[157] it is thought not to be necessary for the institution concerned to take account of the situation of the applicants. Otherwise, as indeed happened in one instance,[158] the defendant institution could allege, as an objection to the admissibility of the action, that it did not know of the situation of the applicants when it enacted the measure.

To summarize, it is believed that *locus standi* is granted to the applicants only in those instances where their individual rights are directly affected by decisions adopted in the area of general management of the market. In the area of competition and state aids proceedings,[159] the Court truly relaxed the *locus standi* requirements by allowing applicants whose *legally protected interests* have been affected to bring annulment proceedings.[160]

Piraiki-Patraiki v. *Commission*[161] offers further confirmation of the points made above. The applicants were a group of Greek cotton undertakings who brought an action to obtain the annulment of a Commission decision, whereby France was allowed to limit imports of cotton yarn from Greece. The decision contained a provision authorizing France to apply protective measures to pending contracts. Some of the applicants had already entered into contracts to export cotton yarn which were going to be carried out during the period in force of the decision in question. The decision had been applied in pursuance of Article 130 of the Act of Accession of Greece to the EC. Under this provision, any Member State was empowered to ask for an authorization to take protective measures against Greece in special cases where serious difficulties were affecting a particular economic sector. However, such measures were also to be exceptional and, so, priority was to be given to 'such measures as will least disturb the functioning of the market'.[162]

It is argued that the category of people affected was partially open—the traders that would enter into contracts in the future—and partially closed—the traders that had entered into contracts when the decision was adopted. Two authors[163] believed that the decision affected an open category of people, because it equally affected traders who could enter into contracts in the future and those who had already entered into contracts

concerned (see 120 below), in that they did not hold any individual rights under EC law. In the case law concerning competition and state aids decs., it could be argued that some applicants belonged to closed categories by reason for their conduct before the dec. was issued (e.g. submission of a complaint) . In those cases, however, the fact that the applicants belonged to a closed category gave them only some rights of a procedural nature (see n. 334 below) and not individual substantive rights.

[157] See n. 141 above and accompanying text.
[158] Case 11/82 *Piraiki-Patraiki* v. *Commission*, n. 44 above.
[159] See 75 ff. below.
[160] *Ibid.*
[161] Case 11/82, n. 44 above.
[162] Art. 130(3) Act of Greek Accession.
[163] See S. Weatherill and P. Beaumont, n. 139 above, 207.

when the Commission reached the decision. It is thought, however, that the second group of applicants belonged to a closed category in that they were in a different position from the rest of the traders: they had already signed the contracts, they had possibly made arrangements for the contracts to be performed and, as a result of the decision, they were going to suffer immediate consequences, i.e. contractual penalties, for failing to export the amounts promised. They belonged to the fixed class of traders that had entered into contracts and there was a provision in the decision that exclusively affected their situation.[164] Furthermore, there were indications in the judgment that the applicants were regarded as members of a closed category.[165]

The Commission argued in its submissions[166] that it had not been aware of the number of contracts concluded prior to the enactment of the measure. Unlike the situation in *Toepfer* and *Bock*, where there were suggestions of a certain misuse of powers, in this instance the Commission was completely unaware of those transactions which, in any case, belonged to the realm of private law. This is a very important point, because, according to some authors,[167] unless the Commission had enacted the measure after taking into consideration the situation of the applicants, they could not have been individually concerned by it.

The Court, however, when dealing with this argument, expressly acknowledged that the submissions on the substance of the case were closely linked at this point to the question of admissibility.[168] The Court looked at the provision in the Act of Accession and concluded that the Commission:

> [M]ust take into account the situation in the Member State with regard to which the protective measure is requested. In particular, in so far as the circumstances of the case permit, the Commission must enquire into the negative effects which its decision might have on the economy of that Member State, as well as on the undertakings concerned. In that connection, it must also consider, insofar as possible, the contracts which those undertakings, relying on the continuation of free trade within the Community, have already entered into and whose execution will be wholly or partially prevented by the decision authorising the protective measure.[169]

[164] It is noteworthy that, although the applicants asked for the annulment of the whole decision, they were only given *locus standi* to challenge the decision in so far as it affected their situation.

[165] The Court said: 'It follows that the undertakings which were party to the contracts meeting that description must be considered as individually concerned for the purpose of the admissibility of this action, as members of a limited class of traders identified or identifiable by the Commission, and by reason of those contracts particularly affected by the decision at issue' (Case 11/82, n. 44 above, at point 31).

[166] *Ibid.* 232.

[167] See n. 44 above.

[168] Case 11/82, n. 44 above at point 21. In this sense, it seems important to recall the situation in English law in the *Fleet Street Casuals* case (see 35 above), where it was clear that in some cases consideration of the substance influences the question whether the applicants enjoy *locus standi*. See also Case 294/83 *Parti Ecologiste 'Les Verts'* v. *European Parliament*, n. 1 above).

[169] Case 11/82, n. 4 above, at point 28.

In the Court's view, then, the Commission had a duty to observe the provisions of the Act of Accession; this duty consisted partly in considering the effects of the protective measures on contracts entered into by undertakings prior to the adoption of the measure. The Commission had failed to fulfil such duty and therefore it could not allege that it did not know of the existence of such contracts as an objection to the admissibility of the action.[170] The Court thus finally acknowledged that the traders that had entered into contracts were individually concerned.[171]

The basis of the recognition of individual concern in this case could be explained as follows. The successful applicants had entered into a course of conduct—the signing of contracts—that distinguished them from other Greek undertakings. By reason of that conduct, they were members of a closed category and they were in a special position: they were entitled to a certain degree of protection, afforded by the Act of Accession to individuals in that particular situation before any safeguard measures were taken.[172] This case presents a situation slightly different from that of the applicants in *Toepfer* and in *Bock*. In *Piraiki-Patraiki*, the transactions pending at the time the measure was enacted were governed by private law, and the applicants did not have a right similar to the securing of a licence, but they did have an individual right granted to them by the Act of Accession. The Commission, when enacting the measure in question, failed to take into account the special position of the applicants; in other words, it affected their rights under the Act of Accession, and owing to that fact the applicants should have been able to find protection against the illegal action of the Commission. In other words, the duty of the Commission under the Act of Accession was construed as a right of the applicants.[173] The line of reasoning of the Court in this case accords in particular with that followed in earlier stages by German courts when judging the *locus standi* of private parties.[174]

For the authors mentioned above[175] who believed that the applicants

[170] Case 11/82, n. 4 above, at point 31.

[171] The Court had explained earlier in the judgment that it could not find any individualizing circumstances in the case of the group of traders that had not entered into contracts prior to the enactment of the dec.

[172] In this respect, see the judgments of the ECJ in Case C–152/88 *Sofrimport* v. *Commission* [1990] ECR I–2477, discussed below at 147 and the judgment of the CFI in Case T–489/93 *Unifruit Hellas* v. *Commission*, n. 156 above.

[173] In this sense, see the interesting parallel with the question of title under Scottish Law at 36–7 above.

[174] See 33–4 above. P. van Dijk explained, n. 11 above, 179, that 'a judicial remedy against unlawful administrative action is awarded to a private person, only in those cases in which the legal rule violated by the administration is at the same time intended to protect the individual interests of a defined group of people'. In the present case, it could be said that the provision in the Act of Accession intended to protect the interests of a defined group of people and the Commission failed to fulfil the duty to consider them.

[175] See n. 163 above.

belonged to an open category, this case was an isolated instance where the Court adopted a more liberal view of the *locus standi* requirements contained in Article 173(2) EEC Treaty.[176] It is thought, however, that this case indicates a continuity of the line followed so far by the case law, and that it has marked strong differences from those cases where the Court has deliberately relaxed the requirements of Article 173, as will be explained below.[177]

So far, two kinds of cases have been studied: first, cases where the applicants belonged to open categories, either large[178] or small.[179] In none of those cases were the applicants individually concerned. Secondly, we have looked at cases where the applicants belonged to closed categories but the decisions at issue also affected open categories of traders.[180] In these cases the applicants were individually concerned.[181]

Finally, reference must be made to cases where the decisions at issue affected exclusively the closed categories to which the applicants belonged. These cases unveiled the clearest examples of measures affecting the rights of a fixed group of people. The decisions at issue decided, so to speak, the fate of the situation of each of the members of that group. These were the cases where the subjective element already referred to[182] was always present, since the Commission took a group of people that it individualized and enacted a decision that affected only them. There was a causal link between the situation of the applicants and the measure taken by the Commission.[183] More than a decision addressed to a third party, the measure at issue was a bundle of individual decisions addressed to each one of the members of that group. In all these cases, the applicants were individually and directly concerned by the decisions in issue. Several examples may be furnished in this respect.

[176] See S. Weatherill and P. Beaumont, n. 139 above, 206. [177] See 60 ff. below.

[178] Thus see Case 25/62 *Plaumann* v. *Commission*, n. 86 above; Case 1/64 *Glucoseries Réunies* v. *Commission*, n. 3 above; Case 38/64 *Getreide-Import* v. *Commission*, n. 120 above; Joined Cases 10 and 18/68 *Eridania* v. *Commission*, n. 82 above; Case 97/85 *Deutsche Lebensmittelwerke* v. *Commission*, n. 155 above. See also Case 206/87 *Lefébvre* v. *Commission* [1989] ECR 275, Case 191/88 *Co-frutta* v. *Commission* [1989] ECR 793, and the recent ECJ judgments in Joined Cases C–429/92 and C–25/93 *Association Bananière Camerounaise (Assobacam)* v. *Commission*, judgment of 12 July 1993 and Case C–6/92 *Federmineraria* v. *Commission*, judgment of 7 Dec. 1993.

[179] Thus see Case 231/82 *Spijker* v. *Commission*, n. 140 above.

[180] See Joined Cases 106–107/63 *Toepfer* v. *Commission*, n. 125 above; Case 62/70 *Bock* v. *Commission*, n. 137 above, and Case 11/82 *Piraiki-Patraiki* v. *Commission*, n. 44 above.

[181] On direct concern, see 63 below.

[182] See n. 141 above and accompanying text.

[183] In the case of decs. it is easy to ascertain the existence of this causal link, given that decs. are acts of an individual nature; the Commission first individualizes a group of private parties and then takes a dec. that affects the position of those parties. In the case of regs., since they are measures of general application which aim to regulate an objective situation in the market, it is much more difficult to ascertain the existence of a causal link between the measure and the situation of the applicants (see 122 below). In the latter situation, if the causal link is proved to exist, the measure ceases to be a reg. and becomes a dec.

In *Simmenthal* v. *Commission*[184] the applicant brought proceedings against a Commission decision addressed to the Member States, fixing the minimum selling price for frozen beef put up for sale by the intervention agencies. The Commission had fixed these prices *after* considering all the tenders that the national intervention agencies had received. The applicant had submitted to the Italian intervention agency a tender at a price lower than the one established by the Commission, and, as a result, its application was implicitly rejected. The Court held that the applicant was individually concerned, the decisive element being the fact that the Commission had first considered all the individual tenders, including the applicant's, and *then* it had fixed a price on the basis of them.[185] The Commission decision was therefore a bundle of individual decisions addressed to each one of the tenderers.

In *Schoellershammer* v. *Commission*[186] a German undertaking brought annulment proceedings against a decision addressed to Germany, whereby the Commission established that in the applicant's case a certain repayment of import duties was not justified. The Commission did not object to the admissibility of the action and the matter was not discussed by the Court.[187] It is clear that the decision was enacted to deal exclusively with the situation of the applicant.[188]

A similar situation arose in *Asociación Profesional de Empresarios de Pesca Comunitarios (APESCO)* v. *Commission.*[189] In Annex IX of the Act of Accession of Spain and Portugal there is a list of 300 vessels that may fish in Community waters; of these, only 150 are authorized to fish at any one time. APESCO was a Spanish association of fishing entrepreneurs whose members appeared in the list annexed to the Act of Accession. The

[184] Case 92/78 [1979] ECR 777.

[185] Ibid., at point 24. There is a great similarity between this case and Joined Cases 41–44/70 International Fruit Company v. Commission [1971] ECR 411. See 000 below.

[186] Case 283/82 [1983] ECR 4219.

[187] Mancini A.G. believed that it was clear that Schoellershammer was individually concerned because the dec. referred to the particular situation in which it found itself and presupposed that the Commission knew of it (ibid. 4228).

[188] In Case C–304/89 *Oliveira* v. *Commission* [1991] ECR I–2283, a similar situation arose. In this case, the Commission addressed two decs. to the Portuguese Government, which reduced the assistance which the European Social Fund had originally granted for two training projects submitted on behalf of the applicant. The Commission did not dispute the admissibility of the action (ibid. I–2287) and the matter was not discussed by the ECJ. See also Case C–291/89 *Interhotel* v. *Commission* [1991] ECR I–2257, involving very similar facts. In a recent case, Case C–135/92 *Fiskarno* v. *Commission* [1994] ECR I–2885, the Commission had sent a letter to the Swedish Ambassador to the EC, relating to an infringement committed by a vessel owned by the applicant. The Commission disputed the admissibility of the action on the ground that the dec. was addressed to Sweden. The ECJ declared the action admissible, given that, although the dec. was addressed to the Swedish Government, it was clear that the intention was to impose a penalty on the applicant (at points 24–6 of the judgment). See also Case T–478/93 *Wafer Zoo* v. *Commission*, judgment of the CFI of 18 May 1995, not yet reported. See also 60 below.

[189] Case 207/86 [1988] ECR 2151.

Spanish Government submitted periodical lists that the Commission approved. APESCO brought an action for a declaration that a Commission decision approving the periodical lists of vessels that were authorized to fish during the month of July 1986 (which excluded some members of APESCO) was void. The Commission argued that APESCO could only represent the owners of vessels appearing in the periodical list. The Court considered that *all* the applicants were individually concerned, in that 'the periodical list either allocates or refuses by implication to each of the 300 vessels identified on the basic list the *right* to fish in the waters of the previous Community of Ten [emphasis added]'.[190] In this case, yet again the decision was in truth a bundle of decisions addressed to the applicants.

In the area of contractual relations entered into by the Community there are some cases where the Commission awarded a contract to a company to perform certain work or to supply the EC with temporary staff after considering several tenders. The Court allowed unsuccessful tenderers to challenge the Commission decisions of award.[191] In theory, such decisions were addressed to a third party, and therefore the issue of admissibility could have arisen. The Commission did not dispute the admissibility of the actions and the Court did not consider it either. The observations of the Advocate General were, however, very useful. Thus, in *Pellegrini* v. *Commission*,[192] Mr Mayras pointed out that unsuccessful tenderers had 'a *legitimate interest*'[193] in the procedure which entitled them to challenge the final decision. In *Agence Européenne d'Interims* v. *Commission*,[194] Mr Reischl[195] considered the issue of admissibility and explained that the decision at issue was of direct and individual concern to the unsuccessful tenderers, given that, once the Commission accepts a tender, all the others are implicitly rejected.

The Court of First Instance has followed the guidelines laid down by the case law of the European Court of Justice. It has so far decided two cases concerning decisions affecting exclusively closed categories. Thus, in *Consorzio Gruppo di Azione Locale 'Murgia Messapica'* v. *Commission*,[196] the applicants had submitted a project for assistance, within the framework of a Community initiative for rural development, to the competent Italian authorities, which in their turn presented the project to the Commission. The Commission addressed a decision to Italy whereby it allocated the

[190] *Ibid.*, at point 12.

[191] See Case 23/76 *Pellegrini* v. *Commission* [1976] ECR 1807 and Case 56/77 *Agence Européenne d'Interims* v. *Commission* [1978] ECR 2215.

[192] Case 23/76, n. 191 above, 1829.

[193] Emphasis added. This wording recalls the pronouncements of the ECJ on *locus standi* in the area of cases concerning competition proceedings. See n. 332 below and accompanying text.

[194] Case 56/77, n. 191 above.

[195] *Ibid.* 2240.

[196] Case T–465/93 [1994] ECR II–361.

funds to another applicant for aid. The Court of First Instance declared that *Murgia Messapica* was directly and individually concerned by the Commission's decision, in that the effect of the latter was to exclude their project from Community assistance.[197] In *Wafer Zoo* v. *Commission*,[198] a similar situation arose. The applicants were Italian agricultural producers who submitted an application for Community aid. The Commission addressed a decision to Italy, explicitly excluding aid for the applicant's project. The issue of admissibility was not even discussed and the applicants went on successfully to challenge the decision, which was declared illegal by the Court of First Instance. Although the decision was addressed to Italy, it was clear that it was adopted in relation to the applicant's project.[199]

3.3.1.2 The Case Law on Individual Concern: Special Cases

As explained above, a general trend emerges from the majority of cases that have arisen before the European Court where *locus standi* of private parties has been an issue, namely that a prospective applicant will be individually concerned by a decision addressed to a third party when its individual rights have been affected by that decision. There are some instances, however, where *locus standi* has been recognized having regard to different considerations. These cases are exceptions to the general rule, and it is submitted that they respond to a liberalization in the Court's interpretation of the *locus standi* requirements contained in Article 173(2) EEC Treaty, and more specifically of the test of individual concern. However, it has also been observed that those cases involved highly coloured facts. In two cases,[200] the applicants were greatly individualized and had triggered the adoption of the measures in question. In another instance,[201] there were no such special individualizing circumstances but overriding constraints arose from the substance of the case.

In *Control Data* v. *Commission*,[202] the applicant, a Belgian subsidiary of an American company that manufactured a certain type of computer (CD–Cyber 170–720 and Cyber 170175), was given standing to challenge a Commission decision addressed to the Member States, establishing that such computers could not be considered as 'educational and scientific material', and therefore they could not be imported duty-free into the

[197] Case T–465/93, n. 196 above, at point 26.

[198] Case T–478/93, judgment of 18 May 1995, not yet reported.

[199] See n. 188 above and accompanying text.

[200] Case C–354/89 *Schiocchet* v. *Commission*, n. 104 above; Case 294/81 *Control Data* v. *Commission*, n. 104 above.

[201] Case 294/83 *Parti Ecologiste 'Les Verts'* v. *European Parliament*, n. 1 above and 62 below.

[202] Case 294/81, n. 104 above.

Community. The Commission objected to the admissibility of the application on two grounds:[203] (a) it should have been the parent company which brought proceedings, and (b) the applicant did not belong to a closed category. The Court considered only the first of these arguments and concluded that the applicant was individually concerned because: (a) it was a wholly-owned subsidiary of Control Data;[204] (b) it was the sole importer into Belgium of the product in question;[205] and (c) its application led to the adoption of the decision at issue.[206] The issue of direct concern did not receive separate consideration. The Court noted that, in the circumstances, to require the parent company to bring the action would have been an 'excessive degree of formalism'.[207] The ruling of the Court seems particularly liberal in that it did not discuss whether the applicant belonged to a closed category (which it did not), and in that the grounds (b) and (c) above had been expressly rejected in other cases.[208]

Schiocchet v. *Commission*[209] involved a dispute between Luxembourg and France on the establishment of a special regular passenger service between these two States. The dispute was referred to the Commission, which enacted a decision addressed to these two Member States, granting a company (Frisch) the right to operate such services. The applicant in this case was the direct competitor of Frisch and so far the only one operating such services.

The issue of admissibility was not discussed, given that the Commission acknowledged that the applicant was directly and individually concerned[210] by the decision. The Court accepted these submissions and went straight to the substance of the case. The ruling seems fairly liberal in that in a former case, *Eridania* v. *Commission*,[211] the Court refused to grant *locus standi* to an applicant which was in competition with the addressees of the measure. However, two qualifications to this statement are necessary. In the first place, the relationship between Schiocchet and Frisch was of direct competition, whereas Eridania was one of a large group of competitors. In the second place, the Commission enacted the decision in *Schiocchet* in response to the dispute between France and Luxembourg on the one hand and Schiocchet and Frisch on the other,[212] after having heard the views of

[203] *Ibid.* 919. [204] *Ibid.*, at point 10. [205] *Ibid.*

[206] *Ibid.* This element appeared also in an anti-dumping case, Case 264/82 *Timex* v. *Council and Commission* [1985] ECR 849, see 163 below. [207] *Ibid.*

[208] In Case 1/64 *Glucoseries Réunies*, n. 3 above, the ECJ regarded as unimportant the fact that the applicant was the sole importer of glucose into Belgium. Likewise, in Case 231/82 *Spijker* v. *Commission*, n. 140 above, there was proof that the dec. at issue had been enacted as a result of the particular situation of the applicant and the Court refused to consider the applicant individually concerned.

[209] Case C-354/89, n. 104 above.

[210] See also the Opinion of Jacobs A.G. at 1786. [211] See 49–50 above.

[212] This is very clear from the preamble to the dec. at issue where *Schiocchet* is mentioned on several occasions (Commission Dec. 89/524/EEC of 7 Sept. 1989 [1989] OJ L272/18).

all the four parties involved.[213] All these elements show that, if this case appears as representative of a more liberal trend in the interpretation of *locus standi* requirements, very special circumstances no doubt influenced its outcome.

Finally, *Parti Ecologiste 'Les Verts'* v. *European Parliament*[214] is a case in a class of its own. The European Parliament enacted a decision whereby it decided to allocate money to political parties that were going to participate in the forthcoming elections. The decision allocated the bulk of funds to parties already present, thus discriminating against parties that were newcomers to the elections. A political party belonging to the latter category brought an action against the decision. The Parliament acknowledged that, as the case law on admissibility stood, the applicants did not have a chance to enjoy *locus standi*, but only a liberal interpretation of Article 173(2) EEC Treaty would overcome such a barrier. The Court conceded that it was dealing with a unique situation and that it was most unlikely that the favoured parties would bring an action against the measure when such a measure 'would give rise to inequality in the protection afforded by the Court to the various grouping competing in the same elections'.[215] The Court also found the applicants directly concerned.[216] On these grounds the Court granted *locus standi* to the applicants. In this case a true evolution in the *locus standi* conditions occurred.[217] The applicants had not provided evidence of any conduct that could distinguish them or give them any rights. The considerations of the substance influenced the position of the Court, since otherwise a flagrant case of lack of judicial protection would have arisen.[218]

[213] Commission Dec. 89/524, n. 212 above. It must be noted here that procedural involvement of the applicants in the elaboration of the contested decs. has been viewed as a very important element in the determination of the *locus standi* of private parties in the context of competition and state aids proceedings (see 75 ff. below) and anti-dumping proceedings (see 152 ff. below).

[214] Case 294/83, n. 1 above.

[215] *Ibid.*, at point 36.

[216] See 74 below.

[217] Thus V. Constantinesco and S. Denys spoke of a 'jurisprudential revolution' ('Note on "Les Verts v. European Parliament" ' [1987] *Recueil Dalloz Sirey* Jur. 79, 81). Others, like R. Kovar, were more cautious and preferred to take the view that the ruling should be confined to the framework of the unique circumstances that surrounded the case ('Observations sur la Cour de Justice, 23 avril 1986, Aff. 294/83, *Parti Ecologiste "Les Verts" c./P.E.*' [1987] *CDE* 300, 327).

[218] As J. P. Jacqué explained ('Notes sur CJCE, 23 avril 1986, *Parti Ecologiste "Les Verts" c./ Parlement Européen*' (1986) 22 *RTDE* 491, 506), it was the principle of non-discrimination that propelled the admissibility of the action so that the applicants could challenge the inequality of the measure at issue. This author concluded that the outcome of such a decision was that, despite the overall restrictions contained in Art. 173(2) EEC Treaty, a private applicant victim of a discrimination should try to bring annulment proceedings, even if it is a member of an open category.

3.3.2 THE TEST OF DIRECT CONCERN

The test of direct concern represents the second hurdle that private applicants (non-addressees) need to overcome before their action for annulment is deemed admissible. This section will be devoted to the study of this admissibility condition. By way of introduction it is necessary to note that some authors interpret this notion according to whether or not the implementation of the decision in question requires the exercise of discretion by the addressee.[219] It is submitted that such an interpretation is limited to the cases where the addressee of the measure is a Member State,[220] while it does not cover situations where the addressees of the decisions are other private parties. It will be argued that, in defining direct concern, the primary emphasis should be placed upon the existence of a direct causal relationship between the decision at issue and damage or harm inflicted on the rights of the applicants.[221] Such a feature is common to successful applicants in actions in the context of decisions addressed to Member States and in the context of decisions addressed to other private parties. This approach also recalls a line of continuity in the cases concerning competition and state aids proceedings, as described below.[222] The conclusion drawn from the case law is that the notion of individual concern implies that individual rights held by the applicants under Community law have been affected by the decision at issue. The notion of direct concern creates an additional requirement, namely that it is necessary that such a decision be the direct cause of the damage suffered. The case law has been divided into two subsections: (a) cases concerning decisions addressed to

[219] Thus, H. G. Schermers and D. Waelbroeck, n. 139 above, 241, say that 'The Court of Justice interprets direct concern to mean that the addressee is left no latitude of discretion, i.e. that the decision affects the applicant without the addressee being necessitated to take any decision himself.' See also S. Weatherill and P. Beaumont, n. 139 above, 210; A. G. Toth, *The Oxford Encyclopedia of EC Law*, n. 139 above, 164–5, and J. Steiner, n. 139 above, 293.

[220] And even in those cases, there are instances where the addressee enjoys some discretion, and yet a third party is directly concerned by the measure at issue (see 67 below); conversely there are cases where there is complete lack of discretion on the part of the addressee and yet a non-addressee has not been declared directly concerned by the dec. in question (see 70–2 below).

[221] This idea builds on the views expressed by L. Goffin on the *Toepfer* case ('*On peut donc parfaiment défendre l'opinion que l'acte concerne le requérant dès qu'il y a relation causale entre l'intérêt lésé et l'acte attaqué*') (n. 132 above, 78). T. C. Hartley, n. 122 above, 366 and 383–7, also expressed the idea that the notion of direct concern related to the existence of a 'direct link of cause and effect between the act and its impact on the applicant'. Gand, A.G. in his Opinion in Case 69/69 *Alcan* v. *Commission* [1970] ECR 385 at 397, said that for a person to be directly concerned there must be a 'direct relationship of cause and effect between the measure and its possible effects on the person in question'.

[222] e.g. Case 26/76 *Metro* v. *Commission* [1977] ECR 1875; see 81 below; Case 169/84 *COFAZ* v. *Commission*, n. 136 above and 90 below, and Case C–198/91 *Cook* v. *Commission*, judgment of 19 May 1993.

Member States, and (b) cases concerning decisions addressed to other private parties. The cases concerning competition and state aids proceedings will be the object of separate consideration.[223]

3.3.2.1 Case Law in Relation to Decisions Addressed to Member States

In the early cases, the Court considered first the test of individual concern and, when finding that it was not fulfilled, dismissed the actions as inadmissible without giving any consideration to the test of direct concern. Thus, in *Plaumann* v. *Commission*,[224] the Court expressed a preference to deal first with the test of individual concern.[225] The question arises why the Court made this choice when, even in the wording of Article 173, individual concern is mentioned in second place. It is believed that this approach could reflect the fact that the test of individual concern is more difficult to satisfy than the test of direct concern, and therefore the Court sought to consider it first, especially in cases where the action was inadmissible, in order to comply with requirements of procedural expediency. A strong supporting argument is that, in cases where the actions were declared admissible, the Court changed its approach and considered direct concern first.[226]

In these early cases, where the Court remains silent on the question of direct concern, it is worth examining the Opinions of the Advocates General. They gave the word 'direct' the most logical construction, i.e. as meaning 'without intermediary'. This concept, applied in the context of Article 173(2) EEC Treaty (now Article 173(4) EC Treaty) and particularly to decisions addressed to Member States, implied that an applicant would be directly concerned by a Community decision when the measure did not leave any room for discretion to its addressee, i.e. to the Member State.

In *Plaumann* v. *Commission*,[227] the Commission had refused to authorize Germany to suspend the collection of the customs duty set out in the Common Customs Tariff. Mr Roemer suggested that in those cases where a Community institution grants authorization to a Member State to pursue a particular course of action, a third party could never be directly concerned, because 'only when the Member State avails itself of the author-

[223] See 75 ff. below.

[224] Case 25/62, n. 96 above.

[225] The ECJ said: 'It is appropriate in the first place to examine whether the second requirement of admissibility is fulfilled; if the applicant is not individually concerned by the decision, it becomes unnecessary to enquire whether he is directly concerned' (Case 25/62, n. 96 above, at 107). A very similar statement was made by the Court in Case 1/64 *Glucoseries Réunies* v. *Commission*, n. 3 above, at 417. In Case 38/64 *Getreide-Import* v. *Commission*, n. 120 above, the test of direct concern was not even mentioned and the Court only dealt with the question whether the applicants were individually concerned.

[226] See Joined Cases 106–107/63 *Toepfer* v. *Commission*, n. 125 above, Case 62/70 *Bock* v. *Commission*, n. 137 above, and Case 11/82 *Piraiki-Patraiki*, n. 44 above.

[227] Case 25/62, n. 96 above. For a description of the facts, see 45 above.

isation, which is left to its discretion, are the legal effects created for the individual'.[228] In the case of a refusal of authorization, the Advocate General reached the same conclusion, by saying that ultimately it was the decision of the Member State to pursue further action before the Court or to accept the decision of the Commission .

In *Glucoseries Réunies* v. *Commission*,[229] Mr Roemer expressed a similar view. This case concerned a decision authorizing France to take protective measures. Mr Roemer believed that the decision was not of direct concern to the applicants because the Member State addressee had the choice of whether or not to use the authorization,[230] even if this was a rather remote possibility. He provided several examples to support his affirmation:

> [T]here may be changes in the political intention of the Member States, because of a better understanding of the situation, because of a change in the composition of the political decision-making organs or in the economic situations, because of obstacles raised by national law or because the Commission has made its authorisation subject to conditions which discourage the Member States from using or making full use of the authorisation.[231]

A different situation arose in *Getreide-Import Gesellschaft* v. *Commission*.[232] In that case, the Commission addressed a decision to Germany wherein it established the rates of levy for imports of cereals and fodders. Subsequently, the German Government took two measures of implementation which nevertheless were 'purely technical'. The Commission itself recognized that the applicant was directly concerned, as the Member State was left no measure of discretion. Advocate General Gand suggested that, although the Member State had adopted the measures after the Commission decision had been enacted , in reality it did not exercise any discretion, whereas in *Plaumann* and in *Glucoseries Réunies* the addressees had, albeit theoretically, some degree of discretion.[233] In this case it was very clear that the addressee did not enjoy any discretion. In other cases, however, this concept poses greater difficulty. In general terms it could be said that a Member State has a degree of discretion when its intervention has the power to guide the Community measure in one direction or in another. In other words, the Member State enjoys discretion when it has the power to turn the scales.

Toepfer v. *Commission*[234] was the first case in which an applicant was found to be directly concerned by a Community decision. In this case, a Commission decision validating protective measures already taken by the German Government was at issue. The Commission had to decide whether the measures ought to be retained, amended, or abolished. Mr Roemer,

[228] *Ibid.* 115.
[229] Case 1/64, n. 3 above. For a description of the facts, see 47 above.
[230] *Ibid.* 421.
[231] *Ibid.*
[232] Case 38/64, n. 120 above. For a description of the facts, see 47 above.
[233] *Ibid.* 210.
[234] Joined Cases 106–107/63, n. 125 above. For a description of the facts, see 48 above.

following his approach in earlier cases, concluded that the Commission had only validated the safeguard measures and that the German authorities were always free to revoke the measures already taken and, therefore, the applicants could not be directly concerned.[235] The Court took a different approach, and spelt out how, in the event that the Commission decided to amend or abolish the national measures, the decision would come into force immediately and would be of direct concern to the parties subjected to it. On this basis, the Court found the applicants directly concerned: 'It would be illogical to say that a decision to retain protective measures had a different effect, as the latter type of decision does not merely give approval to such measures but renders them valid.'[236]

In *Eridania* v. *Commission*,[237] the decisions at issue were addressed partly to the Italian Government and partly to three Italian refineries which were recipients of aid from the EAGGF. Eridania, a competitor of the addressees, sought the annulment of the decision. When considering the admissibility of the action, the Court only analysed the measure in so far as it was addressed to the Italian Government. The Court believed that the applicants were not directly concerned by the decision. Despite the fact that the surrounding circumstances, i.e. the Italian Government had itself recommended which undertakings ought to be granted the aid and it had committed itself financially, showed this Member State's clear intention to favour the recipients of the aid, the Court seemed to accept that the Italian Government still enjoyed a degree of discretion that prevented the applicants being directly concerned by the Commission decision.[238]

In *Alcan* v. *Commission*,[239] three Belgian undertakings challenged a decision of the Commission addressed to the Belgian Government, whereby the Community institution refused to grant a quota of unwrought aluminium imports at a reduced rate of duty. The Court followed the line inaugurated in *Plaumann* by Advocate General Roemer and reached the conclusion that 'a decision taken by the Commission in pursuance of the provisions quoted above, has thus no effect other than to create a power in favour of the Member States concerned and does not confer any rights on possible beneficiaries of any measures to be taken subsequently by the said States.[240]

[235] Joined Cases 106–107/63, n. 125 above, 418.
[236] *Ibid.* 411.
[237] Joined Cases 10 and 18/68, n. 82 above. For a description of the facts see 49 above.
[238] *Ibid.*, at point 11. On the other hand, Roemer A.G. understood the problem from the point of view of the renunciation of the exercise of discretion effected by the Italian Government. For Mr Roemer, the fact that the Italian Government had recommended the undertakings to the Commission and had contributed financially to the aid meant that it had given up its discretionary powers, and that once the Commission decision was issued, an immediate negative effect would be created for the applicant. In consequence, he concluded that *Eridania* was directly concerned (*ibid.* 493). Most probably, Mr Roemer changed the approach that he had followed in earlier cases after the Court's judgment in *Toepfer* (see 65–6 above).
[239] Case 69/69 [1970] ECR 385.
[240] *Ibid.*, at point 8.

The *Alcan* case seemed to assert the view that the degree of discretion bestowed upon the Member State addressee was a very important indicator of the presence of direct concern. The Belgian Government would have had the choice to use or not to use the authorization if it had been granted by the Commission, and therefore the applicants would be directly concerned only by the Member State's decision. Accordingly, the action was dismissed as inadmissible.

In *Bock* v. *Commission*,[241] the Commission had authorized Germany to take protective measures. The Commission put forward the familiar argument, which had succeeded in *Alcan*, that the Member State could choose either to use or not to use the authorization. Advocate General Dutheillet de Lamothe highlighted the circumstance that the German Government had made clear prior to the enactment of the decision in question, that it was only waiting for the Commission decision to reject the applications for import licences. The Advocate General argued that 'it would betray excessive formalism to accept that in fact the said provision was not of direct concern to the Bock company'.[242] The Court picked up this point in its judgment and followed the views of Mr Dutheillet de Lamothe by acknowledging that the previous declaration of intention of the German Government sufficed to explain that, once the Commission decision was enacted, no exercise of discretion was left to the Member State.[243]

In *Bock* the Court took a definite step forward and gave a more liberal construction to the concept of direct concern.[244] This conclusion becomes very clear if this ruling is compared with the one in *Alcan*. In *Alcan*, the Commission *refused* to grant an authorization to Belgium. In *Bock*, on the other hand, the Commission *authorized* Germany to take protective measures. As Mr Gand pointed out in his Opinion in the first of these cases, decisions of authorization and decisions of refusal were 'two forms—positive and negative—of the exercise of the same power by the Commission'.[245] In *Alcan* the Court argued that a power in favour only of the

[241] Case 62/70, n. 137 above. For a description of the facts, see 50 above.

[242] *Ibid.* 915. These words of the A.G. found an echo in later judgments, as in Case 294/81 *Control Data* v. *Commission*, n. 104 above, at point 10, and in Case 11/82 *Piraiki-Patraiki* v. *Commission*, n. 44 above, at point 9, where the ECJ decided not to apply the traditional interpretation of the *locus standi* conditions, in that such application would have amounted to an 'excessive formalism' (Case 294/81, n. 104 above, and accompanying text) or to an 'entirely theoretical' possibility (Case 11/82, n. 44 above, and 69 below) and to look instead at the circumstances surrounding the particular cases. The difficulty, of course, arises in defining the situations in which the Court would decide to take that approach. There is no uniform answer to this question in the case law and it has to be solved on a case-by-case basis.

[243] Case 62/70, n. 137 above, at point 7.

[244] Although according to some authors, this case was an exception to the general trend of the case law. See R. Joliet, *Le Droit Institutionnel des Communautés Européennes* (Liège, 1981), 89.

[245] Case 69/69, n. 239 above, at 393.

Member State would have been created if the permission had been granted. In the same fashion, it could be argued that in *Bock*, the German Government still enjoyed a degree of choice and could decide not to use the authorization.[246] In consequence, the same result ought to have been achieved. Yet, whereas in *Alcan* the applicants were declared not to be directly concerned, the opposite conclusion was reached in *Bock*. Why were the outcomes of the two cases different?

Hartley's view[247] is that one of the reasons for such a different approach could be that in *Alcan*, the Belgian Government was acting in defence of the interests of the applicant, and therefore there was hope that the Member State would bring annulment proceedings 'on behalf' of the applicant.[248] In *Bock*, on the other hand, the German Government was acting against the applicant company. This argument, however, does not explain other instances. A similar situation had arisen in *Glucoseries Réunies*,[249] where the Member State addressee was also acting against the interests of the applicants. In that case, the issue of direct concern was not discussed by the Court, but the view of the Advocate General[250] was that the applicants were not directly concerned, given the degree of discretion enjoyed by the addressee. Moreover, it can never be completely certain that the Member State in question *will* bring annulment proceedings no matter how likely it is that it may do so. It is believed that the only plausible explanation for the ruling in *Bock* is that the Court advanced a step towards a more liberal construction of the test of direct concern.

The most striking feature in the case law so far is the evolution in the approach of the Court towards a greater degree of flexibility. It is suggested that the Opinions of the Advocates General in the early cases,[251] and the rulings of the Court in *Alcan* and *Eridania*, supported the view that an applicant would be directly concerned by a decision addressed to a Member State if the addressee had *complete lack of discretion* in the implementation of the measure. However, the first step towards a more liberal construction of this concept was effected in *Toepfer*,[252] and then completed in *Bock*. After the ruling in *Bock*, even if the Member State addressee

[246] In this sense, see the remarks made by Roemer A.G. in Case 1/64 *Glucoseries Réunies* v. *Commission*, n. 3 above, at 421.

[247] T. C. Hartley, n. 122 above, 386.

[248] In this sense, see the judgment of the ECJ in Case 282/85 *Comité de Développement et de Promotion du Textile et de l'Habillement (DEFI)* v. *Commission* [1986] ECR 2469. For a description of the judgment see 95 below. Decided in the area of state aids proceedings, it offers support to this view. In that case, the Court, when declaring the inadmissibility of the action brought by the applicants, regarded as a very important factor the fact that the French Government had already brought an action for the annulment of the decision in question (point 19 of the judgment).

[249] Case 1/64, n. 1 above.

[250] See 65 above.

[251] See 64–5 above.

[252] The ruling in *Toepfer* has already been welcomed by one author (J. Peters, n. 132 above, at 242) as more liberal since the ECJ did not take into account 'the competence of the Member State to revoke the measure'. Theoretically, a degree of discretion still existed.

enjoyed a certain degree of discretion, a natural or legal person could be directly concerned if the Member State had expressly declared beforehand how the discretion would be used in the event that the authorization was granted.[253] But what would happen if the Member State did not make an express declaration of intention? Could the applicants still be directly concerned? The ruling of the Court in *Eridania* seemed to point out in the negative. However, this approach changed with the decision of the Court in *Piraiki-Patraiki*.[254]

In *Piraiki-Patraiki*,[255] the Commission decision at issue authorized France to impose a system of quotas on the importation of cotton yarn from Greece. The Commission and the French Republic based their submissions on the argument used by the Court in *Alcan*,[256] that, even if the authorization was granted, the French Government had the choice whether or not to use or not to use it.[257] The Court took a different view and, whilst acknowledging that national implementing measures were necessary,[258] it said: 'that fact does not in itself prevent the decision from being of direct concern to the applicants, if other factors justify the conclusion that they have a direct interest in bringing the action'.[259]

The Court then looked at these 'other factors' which were two: the fact that France was already applying a very restrictive system of licences for imports of cotton yarn from Greece and the fact that the system requested by France to be authorized by the Commission was more restrictive than the one finally adopted.[260] The Court decided that in those circumstances the possibility that the Member State addressee would not use the authorization was 'entirely theoretical'[261] and that the applicants were directly concerned.[262]

It can be concluded that these cases confirmed the ruling in *Bock*, and, what is more, it went a step further. The French Republic had not made an express declaration about how its discretion was going to be used, but it

[253] The authors mentioned above (see n. 219 above) share the view that *Bock* brought a degree of liberalization to the case law. Thus, see S. Weatherill and P. Beaumont, n. 139 above, 211, and A. G. Toth, n. 219 above, 165. In this context, the views of H. W. Daig have great interest. He explained that the notion of direct concern presents a formal and a substantive aspect. Formally, a measure is of direct concern for an applicant if it does not require further implementation by the addressee. Substantially, it is of direct concern even when implementation is needed, provided that it is possible to foresee with a high degree of probability in what way the measure is going to be implemented. ('Zum Kalgerecht von Privatpersonen nacht Art 173 Abs.2 EWG–146 Abs 2 EGA–Vertrag' in *Festschrift für Otto Riese* (Karlsruhe, 1964), 204–5). P. van Dijk, n. 11 above, 302 ff., built on this view and explained the evolution of the case law by saying that the ECJ started with a very formalistic attitude in the early judgments, but in *Toepfer* and in *Bock*, the substantive criterion was adopted. See also the arguments of the applicants in Case 231/82 *Spijker Kwasten* v. *Commission* n. 140 above, at 2564.

[254] Case 11/82, n. 44 above.

[255] *Ibid.* For a description of the facts, see 54 above.

[256] Case 69/69, n. 239 above.

[257] Case 11/82, n. 44 above, at 231.

[258] *Ibid.*, at point 7.

[259] *Ibid.*

[260] *Ibid.*, at point 8.

[261] *Ibid.*, at point 9.

[262] See the observations already made on *Bock* (see 67 ff. above).

was clear from the attendant circumstances how the Member State was going to act. In conclusion it could be said that a third party non-addressee may be directly concerned by a decision even if the Member State addressee enjoys some discretion, when it is clear, either from the declaration of the latter or from the circumstances of the adoption of the decision, how the discretion will be used.

From what has been explained so far, and despite the existence of some more liberal rulings, like the ones in *Toepfer*, *Bock*, or *Piraiki-Patriaki*, it would seem that the test of direct concern revolves around the question whether the application of the decision in question depends on the exercise of discretion by the addressee.[263] It is suggested, though, that three flaws appear if this standpoint is taken. First, as explained earlier, it is difficult to obtain a precise definition of discretion. Secondly, it does not explain why, in some examples of the case law, the Member State addressee did not enjoy any discretion in the implementation of the Community decisions, yet private applicants were declared not to be directly concerned.[264] Thirdly, it does not give a good explanation for the issue of direct concern in the case of actions against decisions addressed to other natural or legal persons.[265] It is therefore suggested that the presence or absence of a causal link may be a better test.

In relation to the first point, it would be clear that at opposite ends of the spectrum there are cases like *Getreide-Import*[266] (where it was clear the Member State addressee did not enjoy any discretion) and *Piraiki-Patraiki*[267] (where it was clear that the Member State did have an ample margin of discretion), but in between it is easy to imagine cases where it is not so clear whether the Member State enjoys discretion or not.

In relation to the second of the points made, it is certainly true that in many cases where there was total absence of discretion for the Member State addressee, private applicants were directly concerned.[268] However,

[263] The case law on direct concern in the case of regs. also points in the same direction. See 112 below, n. 60.

[264] Joined Cases 89 and 91/96 *L'Etoile Commerciale and Comptoir National Technique Agricole (CNTA)* v. *Commission* [1987] ECR 3005 and Case 126/83 *STS* v. *Commission* [1984] ECR 2769.

[265] Although some authors like A. G. Toth, n. 219 above, 165, believed that the criteria for ascertaining direct concern are the same. Even the ECJ itself, in Case 294/83 *Parti Ecologiste 'Les Verts'* v. *European Parliament*, n. 1 above, at point 31, took this same view. Other writers, like G. Bebr, n. 106 above, 82, pointed out the inadequacy of transposing the same parameters of absence or presence of discretion.

[266] Case 38/64, n. 3 above.

[267] Case 11/82, n. 44 above.

[268] The clearest example which illustrates this proposition is Case 92/78 *Simmenthal* v. *Commission*, n. 184 above. This case was described earlier as one where the decision concerned affected on the whole a closed category of people, i.e. all the traders that had submitted tenders to the national intervention agencies. The dec. reached by the Commission directly 'decided' the fate of each application, and the Italian Government enjoyed no discretion whatsoever in its implementation (*ibid.*, at points 22, 26, 28–30). The same result would apply to Case 207/86 *APESCO* v. *Commission*, n. 189 above.

there are two examples in the case law where the issue of direct concern was judged according to parameters different from the discretion given to the Member State addressee. Those cases can be explained only by reference to the presence or absence of a causal link in establishing whether the applicants were directly concerned.[269]

L'Etoile Commerciale and Comptoir National Technique Agricole (CNTA) v. *Commission*[270] was a case that arose in the framework of the system of subsidies set up as part of the common organization of the market in oils and fats.[271] The applicants had applied for a subsidy from the EAGGF to the French body in charge of the operation of those subsidies, namely the *Société interprofesionnelle des oléagineux* (SIDO). SIDO agreed to pay the subsidy but made its payment conditional upon the lodging of a security guaranteeing the repayment of such an amount if the EAGGF gave a negative decision on the eligibility for the subsidies. The Commission, when clearing the accounts, addressed a decision to France refusing to recognize the amount of the subsidy chargeable to the EAGGF. CNTA, one of the undertakings affected by this decision, brought annulment proceedings against the Commission decision. The action was dismissed as inadmissible by the European Court, owing to lack of direct concern.

In this case, SIDO did not enjoy any discretion in the implementation of the Commission decision; once the Commission refused to recognize the subsidies, the national authorities could not do anything to restore them. The Court explained that

> It is true that in this case the Commission, addressed to the French Republic, not to recognise the subsidies as chargeable to the EAGGF prompted the SIDO to recover those amounts. However, *that was not a direct consequence of the contested decision itself but derived from the fact that SIDO had made the definitive grant of subsidies conditional upon their finally being charged to the EAGG.*[272]

The Court concluded that the decision did not affect the legal situation of the applicants.[273] The damage to their situation arose as a consequence

[269] The same conclusions apply in cases concerning competition and state aids proceedings. In cases involving competition proceedings, the issue of direct concern was never discussed separately from the issue of individual concern (see 75 ff. below), but it is also clear that it is not related to the degree of discretion given to the addressee. In the area of cases relating to state aids proceedings, the commonest situation is where a natural or legal person challenges a decision benefiting a competitor. In these cases the issue of direct concern has been related to the existence of a prejudice to the interests of the applicant as a consequence of the enactment of the contested decision. See Case 169/84 *COFAZ* v. *Commission*, n. 136 above, at points 15 and 30.

[270] Joined Cases 89 and 91/86, n. 264 above.

[271] This system was set up by Art. 27 of Reg. 136/66, JO 3025/66.

[272] Joined Cases 89 and 91/86, n. 264 above, at point 13, emphasis added.

[273] *Ibid.*, at point 14.

of the course of action taken beforehand by the national authorities and not as a consequence of the Commission decision.[274] Therefore the notion of direct concern was not associated in this case with the absence or presence of discretion granted to the Member State but with the lack or existence of a causal relationship between the decision at issue and the damage inflicted upon their interests.

STS v. *Commission*[275] is another example of the same line of thought. The national authorities of the ACP countries had awarded a series of contracts for the performance of public works to the French undertaking Télespace. The Commission issued a decision addressed to the national authorities, approving the contracts and limiting itself to establishing that the conditions for Community financing were met. The applicant, an unsuccessful tenderer, challenged the Commission's decision.

The Advocate General, Mr VerLoren Van Themaat, explained that it was not the approval of the Commission but 'the prior placing and signing of the contracts by the competent authorities of the ACP States concerned that had direct consequences for the applicant'.[276]

The Court followed the opinion of its Advocate General. In the first place,[277] it explained that the Commission's decision was limited to establishing whether the conditions for Community financing were met, and that this institution could not interfere in the allocation of the contracts, which was within the sphere of competence of national authorities. In the second place, the Court concluded that the applicants were not directly concerned because they 'have legal relations only with the ACP State which is responsible for the contract, and the measures adopted by the representatives of the Commission cannot substitute in relation to them a Community decision for the decision of the ACP State, which has the sole power to conclude and sign that contract'.[278]

This is another clear instance where the issue of direct concern did not relate to the discretion granted to the Member State. The applicant was not directly concerned because a causal link did not exist between the Commission decision and the damage caused to its interest.

Finally, and in relation to the third of the points raised above,[279] it is clear that in cases involving decisions addressed to private parties, the notion of direct concern cannot be based on the absence of discretion bestowed on the addressee. A private party addressee does not enjoy 'discretion' in the same sense that a Member State does. Under EC law, the Member States are the main co-operators with the Community institutions in the application of Community law; they are not merely recipients of

[274] Thus, both the A.G., Mr Da Cruz Vilaça, in his Opinion, at 3017, and the ECJ itself, at point 14, believed that the undertakings affected by the contested decision could effectively be protected by means of remedies available in the national courts.

[275] Case 126/83, n. 264 above.

[276] *Ibid.* 2786.

[277] *Ibid.*, at point 16.

[278] *Ibid.*, at point 18.

[279] See 70 above.

Community law but they carry out an important role in the implementation of EC secondary legislation. In order to fulfil this task they have, more or less, a wide margin of discretion which they exercise in one direction or another, depending on a series of economic or political factors. The decisions addressed to them are, in many cases, of great generality and very often incorporate a wide choice as to their application. Conceivably, a Member State that is granted an authorization to apply protective measures may decide not to use them after all.[280] Private parties, on the other hand, are mere subjects of the EC legal order. They do not have a choice in the implementation of decisions in the same way as the Member States. If a decision favours their position (i.e. by granting them an aid), it is unlikely that they will refuse to accept its benefits, or, to use the terminology of the Court in other cases, it would probably be an 'excessive degree of formalism' to defend this view. It cannot be said that the prejudice sustained by other parties (i.e. a competitor) would be caused by the decision of the addressee to accept the aid. The clearest examples which explain this argument arise in the area of contractual relations entered into by the Community[281] and in the area of competition proceedings.[282]

Given that all the cases reviewed in this section can be explained on the basis of the presence or absence of a causal link, it could be said that what is really central to the notion of direct concern is the existence of a direct relationship of causality between the Community decision and the damage suffered by the applicant. In other words, the *raison d'être* of this *locus standi* condition is to ensure that the prejudice sustained by the applicants derives directly from the Community decision. The purpose of drawing attention to the discretion granted to the addressee (in the case of decisions addressed to Member States) is to ensure that the chain of causation is not broken by the intervention of an intermediary whose choice may direct in one way or another the course of the Community decision.[283] In this sense, this criterion is very useful, but, as has been seen above, not infallible. On the one hand there have been instances where the decisions at issue left a measure of discretion to the Member State addressee, and yet the applicants were directly concerned by them.[284] On the other hand there have been cases where the decisions did not leave any discretion to the Member

[280] In this respect see the conclusions of Roemer A.G. in Case 1/64 *Glucoseries Réunies*, n. 3 above (see n. 231 above and accompanying text).

[281] See 75 below.

[282] See 81 ff. below.

[283] In some decisions of the ECJ, this is especially clear, e.g. in Case 222/83 *Municipality of Differdange and others* v. *Commission* [1984] ECR 2889, where the Court decided that a Commission dec. addressed to a Member State and requiring, in return for the right to grant aids, the adoption of measures to reduce production capacity in an industrial sector 'left to the national authorities and undertakings concerned such a margin of discretion with regard to the manner of its implementation . . . that the decision cannot be regarded as being of direct and individual concern to the municipalities' (*ibid.*, at point 12).

[284] See 67–70 above.

State in respect of their application and yet private applicants were not directly concerned.[285] It is submitted that it would be wise not to limit the issue of direct concern to the discretion bestowed on the addressee of the measure, given that in some instances such an equivalence would be fallacious. It would be easier to see, first, whether the prejudice that the prospective applicant has suffered has been directly caused by the Community decision. Such an approach will also allow for an understanding of the situation in cases involving decisions addressed to other private parties and decisions in the area of state aids proceedings.[286]

3.3.2.2 Case Law in Relation to Decisions Addressed to Private Parties

Only a few cases have been decided in the general area of case law where the issue of direct concern arose in the context of decisions addressed to private parties. Unfortunately these cases did not provide any degree of clarification on this point, and the ruling of the Court simply transposed the criteria applied in the context of decisions addressed to Member States.

In *Parti Ecologiste 'Les Verts'* v. *European Parliament*,[287] the applicants were members of a political party that had challenged a decision addressed to political parties already represented in the European Parliament. Surprisingly enough, the Court in this context used the 'lack of discretion' argument.[288] The Court explained:

> It must be pointed out that the contested measures are of direct concern to the applicant's association. They constitute a complete set of rules which are sufficient in themselves and which require no implementing provisions, since the calculation of the share of the approbation to be granted to each of the political groupings concerned is automatic and leaves no room for discretion.[289]

With due respect for the Court it is suggested that in the case of decisions addressed to private parties it is quite impossible to talk about implementation or the discretion granted to the addressee as illustrated above.[290] It is thought (and this argument finds support in the cases that have been decided in the area of competition proceedings[291]) that the

[285] See 71–2 above.

[286] See 88 below. In cases concerning state aids proceedings, where all contested decs. were addressed to Member States, the issue of discretion bestowed on the addressee did not appear at all.

[287] Case 294/83, see n. 1 above.

[288] As J. P. Jacqué observed (n. 218 above, 505) the Court simply transposed its case law in the field of discussion addressed to Member States to the field of decisions addressed to private parties.

[289] Case 294/83, n. 1 above, at point 31.

[290] See 72–3 above.

[291] As pointed out above (see n. 269 above), in the cases concerning competition proceedings, the tests of direct and individual concern were always treated as one, so there was no explicit indication of the criterion followed by the Court to determine direct concern. It is clear in that context, however, that the issue did not relate to the fact that the addressee enjoyed a degree of [illegible]tion but to the existence of a certain negative effect on the interests of the applicants [illegible]d from the decision at issue.

requirement of direct concern reflects the concern of the drafters of the Treaty that the Community measure at issue be the direct cause of damage to the interests of the private applicant.

The only other instances in the case law of decisions addressed to private parties were those involving the award of contracts by the Commission to successful tenderers.[292] In these instances, as explained above, the issue of admissibility did not arise, given that the Commission always accepted that the applicants had *locus standi*. In the view of the Advocates General, unsuccessful tenderers could challenge the Commission decision of award because the acceptance of one tender implied the rejection of the others. It is thus clear that the existence of discretion on the part of the addressee was not considered.

3.4 The *Locus Standi* of Private Parties to Challenge Decisions Enacted in the Area of Competition and State Aids Proceedings

In this section, the case law of the European Court on the *locus standi* of private parties who wish to challenge decisions reached in the area of competition and state aids proceedings will be discussed. The reason for this separate consideration is the different and more liberal approach of the European Court in the interpretation of the admissibility conditions contained in Article 173(4) EC Treaty in relation to such cases.[293] One author,[294] in an attempt to rationalize the approach of the Court, used the new term of *quasi-judicial determinations* to define the measures taken in the course of competition, state aids, and anti-dumping proceedings. According to this writer in those cases 'the Community Institution adopting the act is bound by clear rules and the final determination depends largely on the question of fact',[295] in contrast to measures taken in the area of customs duties, protective measures, or the common agricultural policy, which are largely discretionary decisions.

There are great similarities in the approach of the Court to the question of the *locus standi* of natural and legal persons to challenge decisions in the areas of anti-dumping, competition, and state aids proceedings.[296] However, for methodological reasons, the case law in anti-dumping proceedings

[292] See 59.

[293] This is the unanimous view of academic writers. Thus, see T. C. Hartley, n. 122 above, 383; J. Dinnage, 'Locus Standi and Article 173 EEC Treaty; the effect of Metro-SB-Groß-märkte v. Commission' (1979) 4 *ELRev*. 15, 19 ff.; S. Weatherill and P. Beaumont, n. 139 above, 207 and A. G. Toth, n. 219 above, 289–99.

[294] T. C. Hartley, n. 122 above, 378–83.

[295] *Ibid*. 369.

[296] These areas are contemplated in the same section of the Treaty (Title V, Part Three Arts. 85–94 EC Treaty).

will be dealt with in the next chapter,[297] due to the fact that most of the instances concern the challenge of measures in the form of regulations. In the present Chapter, attention will focus on cases decided in the field of competition and state aids proceedings, where the measure challenged is always a decision. However, it is first important to describe briefly the special features characterizing these proceedings.

3.4.1 BACKGROUND TO COMPETITION PROCEEDINGS

3.4.1.1 General Remarks

In accordance with Article 3(g) of the EC Treaty,[298] one of the activities of the Community is to achieve a system 'ensuring that competition in the internal market is not distorted' in order to fulfil the aims of the European Community, as provided in Article 2 EC Treaty. A system of free competition benefits both enterprises that continually try to improve their efficiency[299] and consumers, who may purchase goods and services under conditions that are uniform throughout the Common Market. The guidelines for the establishment of a competition policy are contained in Articles 85 and 86 EC Treaty. Article 85 renders invalid agreements and concerted practices that aim to restrict competition, whereas Article 86 prohibits abuses of dominant position. In this context, it must be stated that competition law is to a certain extent a hybrid discipline. On the one hand, it has elements of public law. Thus it is in the public interest that competition in the Common Market is not distorted. On the other hand, it has an impact on private interests. Thus (for instance), if an agreement is found to be incompatible with the rules on competition, the immediate consequence is its nullity, and private parties involved in it will have to face civil claims for damages and/or an injunction. The enforcement authority in the field of competition is the Commission, whereas the Council, the European Parliament, and the Member States play a more limited role in this area.

The Council, under Article 87 EC Treaty is responsible for adopting measures for the enforcement of Articles 85 to 86 EC Treaty.[300]

[297] See 152 ff. below. [298] This legal provision corresponds to Art. 3(f) EEC Treaty.

[299] In this respect see the *IX Report on Competition Policy* (1979), 9.

[300] Thus, amongst others, the Council enacted Reg. 17 (JO 204/62 of 21 Feb. 1962; [1959–62] OJ.Spec. Ed., 87; Reg. 2988/74 in relation to the limitation periods in proceedings and the enforcement of sanctions ([1974] OJ.L319/1), and Reg. 19/65 on the application of Art. 85(3) to certain categories of agreement and concerted practices (JO 533/65 of 6 Mar. 1965; [1965–66] OJ.Spec. Ed., 35). The Commission then enacts detailed provisions. Thus, Reg. 27 of the Commission, concerning the form and content of applications and notifications (JO 1118/62 of 10 May 1962; [1959–62] OJ.Spec. Ed. 132) and Reg. 99/63 on hearings provided by Arts. 19(2) and 19(3) of Reg. 17 of the Council (JO 2268/63 of 20 Aug. 1963; [1963–64] OJ. Spec. Ed. 47 were enacted on the basis of Reg. 17. In the same way, Reg. 19/65 of the Council was the basis for the Commission enacting the block exemption regulations like e.g. Reg. 1984/83 on exclusive distribution agreements ([1983] OJ L173/5—explanatory Notice [1984] OJ L101/2).

The Commission plays the central role in these proceedings, inasmuch as it conducts the investigations of alleged infringements, imposes fines, and grants exemptions under Article 85(3) EC Treaty.

Likewise, the national authorities participate in these proceedings by virtue of Article 9(3) of Regulation 17,[301] which gives them competence to enforce Articles 85(1) and 86 EC Treaty as long as the Commission 'has not initiated any procedure'. The Member States also collaborate with the Commission through the Advisory Committee on Restrictive Practices and Monopolies.

Finally, the European Parliament also exerts a degree of influence in the field of competition proceedings through three main channels: first, through the Resolution that it annually adopts on the Commission's *Report on Competition Policy*; secondly, through the questions it poses to the Commission,[302] and, finally, through its participation in the legislative process for any new Council Regulations.

Initially, the European Court of Justice had jurisdiction to deal with annulment actions brought by private parties against measures adopted in the context of competition proceedings. However, jurisdiction to deal with these actions has been transferred to the Court of First Instance[303] as from 31 October 1989.[304] An appeal to the European Court on points of law was provided.[305]

From a glance at the case law in annulment proceedings brought by private parties in this area, several points emerge clearly: first the contested measures were always measures in the form of decisions.[306] Secondly, they were always Commission decisions—given the key role played by this institution, as explained earlier—and they were always addressed to private parties.[307] In state aids cases, decisions were always addressed to Member States, as in the general case law studied hitherto.[308]

301 See n. 300 above.

302 During 1992, the Parliament submitted 141 written questions and 66 oral questions to the Commission (*XXIInd Report on Competition Policy* (1992), 296 at point 540).

303 Art. 3(1)c of Council Dec. 88/591 [1988] OJ L319/1, corrected version [1989] OJ C215/1. See 00 above.

304 *Ibid.*, Art. 13 of the Decision.

305 Arts. 49–54 of the Statute of the ECJ and Arts. 110–123 of the Rules of Procedure.

306 In most cases the Council Regs. (see n. 300 above) provide that the Commission shall enact a decision (i.e. Art. 3(1) of Reg. 17, see n. 300 above).

307 Following the views of L. Ritter, D. Braun, and F. Rawlinson (*EEC Competition Law. A Practitioner's Guide* (Deventer, 1991), 699-700) the decisions susceptible of review are: decisions imposing fines, cease and desist orders, decisions granting, withdrawing, and reviewing exemptions, negative clearances, and discovery and investigation orders. The Court has followed in this field the non-formalistic approach that has prevailed in its case law when deciding whether an act is a decision or not (see 19 above) and has termed as decisions letters of the Commission withdrawing immunity from fines (e.g. Joined Cases 8–11/66 *Société Anonyme Cimentières CBR* v. *Commission* [1967] ECR 75), rejecting complaints, refusing to grant an interim order, or refusing to disclose confidential documents. However, decisions opening a formal investigation are not susceptible of review under Art. 173 (see Case 60/81 *IBM* v. *Commission* [1981] ECR 2639).

308 The only exceptions in the area of general case law were *Parti Ecologiste 'Les Verts'* v.

In proceedings under Article 173 EC Treaty, the simplest situation arises when addressees of the decision at issue decide to bring an action for annulment.[309] In these cases no problems concerning *locus standi* arise. *Locus standi* again becomes an issue, however, in those cases where annulment proceedings are brought by non-addressees. However, and contrary to the situation in the general area of case law, the Commission rarely objected to the admissibility of the actions.[310] In this context the most common situation is that in which actions for annulment are brought by complainants,[311] or competitors who object to a benefit conferred on the addressee, i.e. an exemption under Article 85(3) EC Treaty from the prohibition contained in Article 85(1) Treaty.[312] To understand the position of these applicants, it is necessary first to describe the role that third parties play in the administrative process leading to the adoption of the contested decision. Unlike the general area of case law (concerning customs duties, protective measures, etc.), third parties play a significant role in this process from the moment the Commission recognizes them as 'interested parties'. As a consequence of this position, they enjoy a series of procedural guarantees regulated in the basic regulations.[313] It is suggested that this particular circumstance has a great influence on the ensuing

European Parliament (Case 294/83, n. 1 above); Joined Cases 10 and 18/68 *Eridania* v. *Commission*, see n. 82 above, and cases involving contractual awards (see 59 above).

[309] The addressees may be either individual undertakings (Case 77/77 *Benzine en Petroleum Handelsmaatschappij* v. *Commission* [1978] ECR 1513; Case 210/81 *Demo-Studio Schmidt* v. *Commission* [1983] ECR 3045) or associations of undertakings (Case 71/74 *Frubo* v . *Commission* [1975] ECR 563). The addressee of a decision would be entitled to challenge it when this measure alters its legal position, causing a prejudice to its interests. The CFI decided that the addressee of a decision of the Commission granting negative clearance to a series of regs., decs., and circulars issued by the former could not challenge such an act because it neither modified its legal position nor conveyed any negative consequences for the applicant, and was, in any event, the result that the applicants had pursued. (Case T–138/89 *Nederlandse Bankiersvereniging en Nederlandse Vereniging van Banken* v. *Commission* [1992] ECR I–2181, at point 32).

[310] This seems to be a circumstance not devoid of importance. In the area of general case law, the Commission normally objected to the admissibility of actions brought by private applicants. However, in Case C–354/89 *Schiocchet* v. *Commission*, see n. 104 above, the Commission had not put forward any submissions against the admissibility of actions and the action was declared admissible. In cases involving decisions adopted in the context of competition proceedings, the Commission did not raise objections to the admissibility of the actions in *Metro* v. *Commission*—hereafter referred to as the *First Metro* case (Case 26/76 *Metro* v. *Commission* [1977] ECR 1875); Case 75/84 *Metro* v. *Commission*—hereafter referred to as the *Second Metro* case [1986] ECR 3021 at 3032—or in Case 43/85 *Ancides* v. *Commission*, n. 136 above. In all these cases the applications were declared admissible. Only in Case T–138/89 *Nederlandse Bankiersvereniging en Nederlandse Vereniging van Banken* v. *Commission*, n. 309 above, did the Commission object to the admissibility of an action brought by a third party, but the CFI dismissed the application on other grounds without considering this issue. The same conclusions apply to the case law on state aids where, in some instance, no objections were raised by the Commission; see nn. 396, 410, and 425 below.

[311] *First Metro* case, Case 26/76, see n. 310 above.

[312] e.g. Case 43/85 *Ancides* v. *Commission*, n. 136 above.

[313] See n. 300 above.

finding that they are directly and individually concerned by the decision if they decide to bring annulment proceedings against it. For this reason, the following section examines the position of third parties in competition proceedings.

3.4.1.2 The Role of Third Parties in Competition Proceedings

It is tempting to understand EC competition law in terms of the relationship between the Commission and an undertaking or group of undertakings that may have entered into an agreement or concerted practice that distorts competition or that may have abused its dominant position in the market or that will benefit from an exemption from the rules of Article 85 EC Treaty. In all these instances, the public interest would be affected, but it is also undeniable that the interests of certain third parties would be particularly affected. For example, a direct competitor will be particularly affected if a dominant undertaking practises predatory price cutting and will be especially interested that the Commission should open an investigation and find that such dominant undertaking is liable under Article 86 EC Treaty. Again, an undertaking may be unhappy that an exemption from the rules of Article 85 EC Treaty has been granted to a direct competitor. Conversely, a natural or legal person may have an interest in the Commission's not finding a violation of the rules contained in Article 85 EC Treaty in an agreement between two other countries on the basis that it is engaged with one of the parties under investigation in a similar agreement. In any of the situations described, both the third party and the community at large have an interest in the annulment proceedings. The importance of the position of these third parties is reflected in the fact that their position is foreseen and protected in the basic regulations.[314]

In the first place, Article 3(2)b of Regulation 17[315] entitles 'any natural or legal person who claims a legitimate interest' to complain to the Commission and to request a decision that an undertaking or association of undertakings is acting in violation of Articles 85 to 86 EC Treaty. The Court has not yet defined what *legitimate interest* means, but there is a non-contentious view that a 'reasonable direct and practical interest in the outcome of the complaint would be sufficient'.[316] According to one

[314] In the area of general case law there are no legislative measures regulating the position of third parties in the adoption of the measures at issue, mainly due to the fact of the great margin of discretion enjoyed by Community institutions. However, there were instances in the case law where the involvement of the applicants in the procedure leading to the adoption of the decision was an important factor in determining their *locus standi*. See Case 294/81 *Control-Data* v. *Commission*, n. 104 above, and Case C–354/89 *Schiocchet* v. *Commission*, n. 104 above).

[315] See n. 300 above.

[316] See J. Temple Lang, 'The Position of Third Parties in EEC Competition cases' (1978) 3 *ELRev.* 177, 179. See also Art. 37 of the Protocol on the Statute of the Court of Justice and Art. 93 of the Rules of Procedure. Practically speaking, the Commission has recognized the

author,[317] it is clear that a complainant would normally have an interest, since 'it is a rule of logic that nobody would go to the trouble and expense of complaining unless there were a prospect of obtaining some practical utility'. These complaints or private initiatives constitute a valuable source of information that helps the Commission to trace possible violations of the principles of free competition that govern the common market .

In the second place, Regulation 17[318] protects the position of third parties that show a *sufficient interest* by granting them the right to be heard in the proceedings.[319] Within this category it is not difficult to imagine that associations of traders and consumers, as well as complainants, may be interested in the result of certain proceedings. In those cases where the Commission intends to give a negative clearance, it has to publish a summary of the application or notification and invite all the interested third parties to submit their observations.[320]

Regulation 99/63[321] develops the principles contained in Regulation 17. On the one hand, it contains a series of procedural guarantees conferred on complainants with the purpose of protecting their legitimate interest.[322] Thus, under Article 6 of the Regulation, the Commission must inform the complainant if it decides that it does not have enough evidence to reach a decision, and it must also fix a time-limit for the submission of further comments.[323] On the other hand, it regulates the conditions for the right of a hearing available to interested third parties.[324]

It seems thus clear from this overview that whenever a private party has a *legitimate* or *sufficient* interest in the outcome of the proceedings, it is granted a series of procedural guarantees described in the basic competition legislation in order to ensure that its interests are taken into consideration by the Community Institution enacting the decision. In order to enjoy such procedural advantages it is often necessary that the natural or legal person takes the first step of becoming actively involved in the procedure, either

legitimate interest of a trade association that complained that an undertaking had refused to supply it (Commission Dec. of 14 Dec. 1984, *John Deere* [1984] OJ L35/58), or of complainant undertakings that supplied products to companies involved in an anti-competitive agreement (Commission Dec. of 20 Dec. 1977, *The Distillers Co. Ltd* [1978] OJ L50/16), or of a party which was refused entry to an undertaking distribution network (*First Metro* case, Case 26/76, n. 310 above).

[317] See F. Mancini, 'Access to Justice. Individual Undertakings and EEC Anti-trust Law: Problems and Pitfalls' (1988) 12 *Fordham Int. LJ* 189, 189.

[318] See n. 300 above.

[319] *Ibid.*, Art. 19(2) of the Reg.

[320] *Ibid.*, Art. 19(3) of the Reg.

[321] See n. 300 above.

[322] The 5th preamble to the Reg. expressly acknowledges this fact.

[323] In this respect see *Transocean Marine Paint Association* v. *Commission* (Case 17/74 [1974] ECR 1063, at point 15), where the Court said that 'this Regulation applies the general rule that a person whose interest is perceptibly affected by a decision taken by a public authority must be given the opportunity to make his point of view known'.

[324] Thus, Arts. 5, 7, and 8 of the Reg. The 4th Preamble to the Reg. expressly sets out its purpose of protecting the right to a hearing of parties showing a sufficient interest.

by submitting a complaint to the Commission or by applying to be heard.[325] Once the Commission recognizes that the private party has a *legitimate* or *sufficient* interest, the latter will become entitled to a series of procedural rights. Once the decision is enacted, some of these third parties may wish to bring annulment proceedings. The case law in the area shows that they are very likely to have *locus standi* to challenge the measure.

3.4.2 JUDICIAL REVIEW OF DECISIONS ADOPTED IN THE COURSE OF COMPETITION PROCEEDINGS

The following section will be divided into two parts: the first of them will deal with the case law of the European Court of Justice, whereas the second will deal with the case law of the Court of First Instance.

3.4.2.1 The Case Law of the European Court of Justice

Metro v. *Commission*[326] was the first case in which the *locus standi* of non-addressees was discussed. The facts of that case may be summarized as follows: Metro was a self-service wholesaler which had complained to the Commission under Article 3(2)b of Regulation 17[327] that SABA, a German manufacturer of electronic audio equipment, had refused to include *Metro* in its distribution network . *Metro* believed that the conditions of the SABA distribution system were objectionable and precluded it from becoming a distributor. The Commission investigated the complaint and found it unjustified. In spite of that, it asked *Metro* to forward some comments in accordance with Article 6 of Regulation 99/63. As a result, the Commission asked SABA to amend some conditions of its distribution system. SABA proceeded to do so and the Commission issued a decision declaring that the system did not infringe Article 85 EC Treaty. *Metro* brought annulment proceedings against this decision and, since it was not the addressee of the measure, the issue of *locus standi* arose.

The Advocate General (Mr Reischl) perceived this case as presenting special features. For him the applicant was directly concerned, given that the decision had produced direct effects on its situation.[328] The issue of individual concern presented more complications. Mr Reischl believed that *Metro* did not belong to a closed category.[329] Therefore, if the pattern that

[325] See, however, the recent case law of the CFI (86–8 below).

[326] Case 26/76, n. 310 above.

[327] See n. 300 above. See also 79 above, on the position of complainants.

[328] Case 26/76, n. 310 above, at 1922. In this respect see the observations presented on the notion of direct concern as related to the existence of a causal relationship between the decision at issue and the negative effects suffered by the applicants (see 63 ff. above).

[329] Mr Reischl believed that anyone, at any time, could wish to join SABA distribution system (see n. 310 above, at 1921).

the Court had followed to determine individual concern in other cases was also followed in this case, the applicant could not be individually concerned. For Mr Reischl it was clear that the applicant had a *legitimate interest* in the outcome of the proceedings: it had lodged a complaint, it had taken active part in the proceedings, and it had been specially informed of the reasons that guided the final decision of the Commission. On these grounds, he concluded that *Metro* was individually concerned. [330]

The judgment on the admissibility of the application was rather terse. The Court acknowledged first that the Commission's decision was adopted as a result of *Metro*'s complaint.[331] Then the Court said:

It is in the interest of a satisfactory administration of justice and of the proper application of Articles 85–86 that natural or legal persons who are entitled pursuant to Article 3(2)b of Regulation N° 17, to request the Commission to find an infringement of Articles 85 and 86 should be able, if their request is not complied with either wholly or in part, to institute proceedings to protect their legitimate interests. [332]

The Court clearly adopted a more lenient approach to the issue of *locus standi* of non-privileged applicants.[333] In the first place the Court did not link the notion of individual concern to the traditional 'closed category' argument present in the area of general case law,[334] but to the existence of

[330] Case 26/76, n. 310 above, at 1923.

[331] *Ibid.*, at point 13. The fact that a decision has been adopted as a result of particular conduct pursued by the applicant has exerted influence on the final determination of its *locus standi* even in cases in the area of general case law (see Case 294/81 *Control Data* v. *Commission,* n. 104 above, and observations on this case, 60–1 above) and certainly in the area of anti-dumping proceedings (see Case 264/82 *Timex* v. *Council and Commission*, n. 206 above).

[332] Case 26/76, n. 310 above, at point 14.

[333] This view is shared by the academic writers. Thus, see T. C. Hartley, '*Locus Standi* in Actions under Article 173 EEC Treaty. *Metro-SB-Großmärkte* v. *Commission* (1978) 3 *ELRev.* 209, 212 and J. Dinnage, n. 293 above, 32.

[334] The intervener (SABA), on the other hand, based its submissions on the fact that Metro did not belong to a closed category. Some academic writers maintain that Metro did not belong to a closed category in so far as the decision affected anyone who wished to enter in SABA distribution network and who did not comply with the conditions set out by the distribution agreement (see T. C. Hartley, n. 122 above, 379, and S. Weatherill and P. Beaumont, n. 139 above, 208. See also the Opinion of Reischl, A.G., n. 329 above, and accompanying text). It could be said, however, that by reason of having complained, Metro belonged to a fixed category of people that could not be enlarged after the decision entered into force. This view was first put forward by J. Dinnage (n. 293 above, 32). It is suggested that the difference between this case and those decided in the general area of case law is that in the case of Metro the membership of a closed category did not confer on the applicants any individual rights under Community law other than of a procedural nature. In cases in the general area of case law, as for instance *Piraiki-Patraiki* (Case 11/82, n. 44 above), the applicants had engaged in conduct (export agreements) to which special rights had been attached (thus they were entitled to a certain degree of protection conferred by the Act of Accession before any protective measures were taken). On the other hand, Metro, as complainant, only acquired rights of a procedural nature. For similar conclusions in the area of anti-dumping cases, see 161 below.

a legitimate interest on the part of the applicant, proved by the facts that it had complained and that the Commission had initiated proceedings following the complaint. It is suggested that the Court's reasoning may have been as follows. From the moment that Metro complained and the complaint was considered by the Commission, this institution acknowledged that the applicant did have a legitimate interest in the outcome of the proceedings. Once the Commission reached a decision, it was only logical that, if the result was adverse to the complainants, they should be able to bring annulment proceedings for the annulment of such a decision in order to protect their legitimate interest.[335] The applicant was, therefore, singled out from the remainder of the undertakings affected because it lodged a complaint and, as a consequence, it participated in the proceedings leading to the adoption of the decision in question. After all, the Commission obtained great help from the complainant undertaking, which submitted very useful information throughout the length of the proceedings and incurred great expense and trouble in doing so. It would be rather unfair if it could not challenge a final decision detrimental to its interests.

The Court thus adopted a position that accorded with the dictates of logic and 'of a satisfactory administration of justice and of the proper application of Articles 85–86 EC Treaty'.[336] This was a very welcome move.[337]

The test of direct concern was not even considered by the Court, but it is

[335] It would have been most unlikely that SABA, the addressee of that favourable decision, would have brought annulment proceedings (in this respect, see the Opinion of Reischl A.G. at 1921). The result would have been that Metro was left without legal protection. Recently, the CFI has expressly declared that a decision granting negative clearance cannot be challenged by its addressees (see Case T–138/89, n. 310 above). In the same judgment, the CFI declared that a third party with a legitimate interest may challenge such a decision (*ibid.*, at point 32).

[336] *First Metro Case* (Case 26/76, n. 310 above, at point 14). For one author (A. Frignani, 'Observations sur la Cour de Justice, 25 Octobre 1977, Aff. 26/76, *Metro*' [1978] *CDE* 440, 468) there were great similarities between the approach of the Court in this case and the American case law on *locus standi*.

[337] In the field of actions for failure to act, however, complainants enjoy a less privileged position. Whereas in Cases 142, 156/84 *BAT & Reynolds* v. *Commission* [1987] ECR 4487, the Court held that complainants may attack a decision rejecting the complaint, in Case 125/78 *Gema* v. *Commission* [1979] ECR 3173, at point 18, the Court concluded that if the Commission does not take a final decision on a complaint, the complainant does not have the power to compel the Commission to reach a final decision as regards the existence or non-existence of the alleged infringement. Similarly, in Case T–3/90 *Prodifarma* v. *Commission* [1991] ECR II–1, the CFI decided that a complainant cannot force the Commission to take a final decision to withdraw the immunity from fines provided by Art. 15(6) of Reg. 17. In Joined Cases T–24/90 and T–88/80 *Automec* v. *Commission* [1992] 5 CMLR 431, the Court concluded that the Commission could not be forced to conduct an investigation, and had the right to give different priority to the complaints it received. This line of case law proves that the Commission could, by refusing to take final decisions or to conduct investigations, effectively diminish the opportunities of access by interested third parties to judicial review of unlawful omissions. For some authors, like R. Whish, *Competition Law* (3rd edn., London, 1993), 313, such an approach is justified, given the limited resources of the Community institution, which could not allow it to consider every complaint in depth.

clear that in this context the criterion of the presence or absence of discretion bestowed on the addressee, which seem to underlie the reasoning of the Court in many rulings in the general area of case law, does not work here. Rather, there was clearly a direct causal link between the decision at issue and the negative effects produced in the legal situation of the applicant.[338]

The question that arose after the *First Metro* case was whether only complainants would be entitled to bring proceedings. In a subsequent case where a decision was addressed to a company belonging to a group of companies, incorporated under the law of a Member State, it was held that the decision directly and individually concerned another company within that group which co-ordinated the production and sale of its projects within the Common Market, because the content of the decision fell 'within the province of activities for which the applicant [was] responsible'.[339] From this case, it emerges that co-subsidiaries that have not complained may also have *locus standi*. Although in this case a third party was given standing to challenge a decision addressed to another company, its results have to be treated with caution, for the Court has always shown a more lenient attitude to applicants that are subsidiaries of the same company than the addressees.[340] The question that remained after these cases was whether a third-party undertaking that did not complain, and that was not a subsidiary or co-subsidiary of the addressees, could be entitled to bring annulment proceedings.

An answer was provided with the ruling of the Court in the *Second Metro* case,[341] which involved a set of facts quite similar to those involved in the *First Metro* case.[342] A few years later, after the ruling of the Court in this latter case, SABA adopted new terms for the agreements that constituted its distribution system which were basically the same as those constituting the old system, apart from certain changes in relation to the procedure for the admission of specialist distributors. SABA applied to the Commission so that the agreements comprising the distribution system could be exempted from the application of Article 85(1) EC Treaty. The Commission adopted a decision granting SABA the requested exemption. Metro brought annulment proceedings against this decision.

338 In this respect see A. Frignani (n. 336 above, 467). See also the Commission submissions in Case 169/84 *COFAZ* v. *Commission*, n. 136 above and 90 ff. below, in the context of state aids and the Court judgment in that case.

339 Joined Cases 228 and 229/82 *Ford of Europe and Ford Werke* v. *Commission* [1984] ECR 1129, at point 13.

340 In this respect see the Opinion of Sir Gordon Slynn A.G. (at 1167) and the observations of K. Hendry 'Ford Sheds further Light on the Commission's Power to grant Interim Measures' (1984) 9 *ELRev.* 344, 346), in the sense that this case appears to be a sequel to the *Japanese Ball Bearing* cases (Joined Cases 113 and 118–121/77 [1979] ECR 1205), which are discussed later in this work (see 158 below).

341 Case 75/84, n. 310 above.

342 Case 26/76, n. 310 above.

The situation presented in this instance differed from the one in the *First Metro* case in that here Metro had not submitted a complaint that triggered the Commission investigation. For the intervener, SABA, this was an important point, which was at the core of its objections to the admissibility of the action.[343]

The Court declared that the applicant had *locus standi*. The Court did not treat separately the issues of direct and individual concern but it was clear from its judgment that again it only gave importance to the circumstances that could single out Metro from the rest of the undertakings affected, or, in other words, the question whether it was individually concerned. This element was ascertained by the Court on the basis of two kinds of elements: in the first place, a factual element, that Metro had been refused entry to SABA's distribution system;[344] in the second place, two legal elements: the facts that the applicant had submitted observations according to Article 19(3) of Regulation 17, or, the same thing, that it had become procedurally involved in the adoption of the measure[345]—which requires that parties have a *sufficient interest*—and that the Commission had acknowledged such an interest by more or les replying to the comments made by the applicant and rejecting one by one the objections set out by Metro in its letter.[346]

The two *Metro* cases show an innovation, in that the applicants do not need to prove that their individual rights under EC law have been affected by the decision in question, but only have to show that they have a legitimate or sufficient interest recognized in the administrative proceedings leading to the adoption of the contested decision. The recognition of *locus standi* is the corollary of the recognition of an interest of the applicants that has to be protected. The Court in these cases shifted from its traditional approach to a more liberal view. The applicant must have become procedurally involved in the adoption of the measure, either by submitting a complaint or by submitting observations. Thus in the *First Metro* case the applicant was a complainant, whose position was recognized and protected in the basis regulations. The *Second Metro* case, whilst confirming this view—Metro had submitted observations in pursuance of

[343] Case 75/84, n. 310 above at 3032.

[344] *Ibid.*, at point 21. In the general area of case law, factual considerations were never taken into account when deciding the *locus standi* of private applicants. This is so, with the exception of those cases where the Court adopted a more liberal construction of the *locus standi* requirements. See Case 294/81 *Control-Data* v. *Commission*, n. 104 above and Case 294/83 *Parti Ecologiste 'Les Verts'* v. *European Parliament*, n. 1 above. In competition proceedings, the *Second Metro* case was the first indication in this direction. In anti-dumping proceedings, Case 264/82 *Timex* v. *Commission and Council*, n. 206 above, had been the first case where factual considerations were taken into account. See also the judgment of the Court in Case C–358/89 *Extramet* v. *Commission* [1991] ECR I–2501, see 167 below.

[345] Case 75/84, n. 310 above, at point 22.

[346] *Ibid.*

Article 19(3) of Regulation 17—seems also to demonstrate that factual considerations may be important.

The position was confirmed by *Ancides* v. *Commission*.[347] In that case, an association of undertakings in the Italian dental products market objected to a Commission decision granting an Article 85(3) EC Treaty exemption to a decision issued by *Ancides*' competitor, UNIDINI, that set out the rules governing a series of exhibitions of dental materials. The issue of admissibility was not even discussed by the Court. *Ancides* had submitted its observations in accordance with Article 19(3) of Regulation 17.

3.4.2.2 The Case Law of the Court of First Instance

The case law of the Court of First Instance has not only confirmed the line followed by the European Court of Justice[348] but has also shown interesting developments, mainly in the area of merger control.

In *Zunis Holding* v. *Commission*,[349] the Court of First Instance declared that minority shareholders were not individually concerned by a Commission decision declaring that a concentration between an Italian bank and an insurance company did not fall within the scope of the Merger Regulation.[350] It could be thought, *a sensu contrario*, that, had the applicants represented a bigger proportion of the social capital, they could have been individually concerned.

The two *Air France* cases[351] show yet again a move of the Court of First Instance towards a more liberal interpretation of the question of *locus standi*. In the first of them,[352] the Commission enacted a decision addressed to British Airways, in which it declared that the proposed concentration between British Airways and Dan Air was not considered to be of a Community dimension as one of the quantitative thresholds fixed by the Merger Regulation[353] had not been reached. In consequence, the Commission declared itself incompetent to assess the concentration under the terms of the Regulation. Air France, the direct competitor of British Airways, brought annulment proceedings against the Commission decision. The Commission objected to the admissibility of the action and, in particular, contended that the mere fact that the applicant was a competitor did not

[347] Case 43/85, n. 136 above.

[348] In Case T-138/89 *Nederlandse Bankiersvereniging en Nederlandse Vereniging van Banken* v. *Commission*, n. 310 above, at points 31–34, the Court reiterated that a third party possessing a legitimate interest within the meaning of Art. 19(3) of Reg. 17 has the *locus standi* to bring proceedings for the annulment of a Commission decision.

[349] Case T-83/92, judgment of 28 Oct. 1993.

[350] Regulation 4064/89 [1990] OJ L257/14.

[351] Cases T-3/93 and T-2/93 *Société Anonyme è Participation Ouvrière Compagnie Nationale Air France* v. *Commission* [1994] ECR II-121 and [1994] ECR II-323.

[352] Case T-3/93, see n. 351 above.

[353] See n. 350 above.

suffice to make it directly and individually concerned.[354] The Court of First Instance, however, declared the action admissible. In relation to the issue of direct concern, the Court held that it was clear that the applicant would be deprived of the procedural advantages contemplated in the Merger Regulation, which it would have enjoyed, had the Commission initiated the procedure to assess the compatibility of the merger with the Common Market.[355] In relation to individual concern, the Court concluded that the British Airways–Dan Air merger reinforced the competitive position of British Airways on routes also operated by Air France, and therefore that the competitive position of the applicant was weakened as a consequence of the concentration.[356] On this basis, the applicant was individually concerned. The basis for declaring Air France individually and directly concerned was its position as a competitor of the addressee, and the damage caused to its interests as a consequence of the decision.[357] In competition proceedings so far, it seems that in order to be granted *locus standi*, potential applicants need to have participated in the procedure of the adoption of the contested decision,[358] either by submitting a complaint,[359] or by submitting observations. In the presence case, the Court declared admissible an action for annulment brought by a private applicant, not on the basis of its participation in the procedure of the adoption of the contested decision, but on the basis of the effect of the measure on its position in the market. Therefore this ruling liberalizes the interpretation of the *locus standi* conditions imposed on private applicants.

In the second of the *Air France* cases,[360] Air France brought an action under Article 173 EC Treaty for the annulment of a Commission decision that found that the concentration between British Airways and TAT did not raise serious doubts as to its compatibility with the Common Market. In this case, the applicants had taken part in the administrative procedure leading to the adoption of the decision. The Court concluded that Air France was individually concerned by the decisions not only on the basis of its participation in the administrative procedure[361] but also gave consideration to the effects of the decision on the applicant and in particular

[354] Case T–3/93, see n. 351 above, at point 73.

[355] Case T–3/93, n. 351 above, at point 81. See also Case C–198/91 *Cook* v. *Commission*, n. 222 above, and 98 below, for a discussion of the judgment.

[356] Case T–3/93, n. 351 above, at point 82.

[357] It seems that the Court's approach is a very sound one, especially if it is borne in mind that Art. 10(1) of the Merger Reg. compels the Commission to reach a decision within a month of the notification of the proposed merger. In general, a degree of secrecy pervades this preliminary investigation, and the rights of interested third parties are not protected. Under these conditions, to make *locus standi* dependent on procedural involvement would have been a very restrictive approach. See the great similarities between this case and Case C–198/91 *Cook* v. *Commission*, n. 222 above and 98–100 below.

[358] See 85 above.

[359] *First Metro* case (Case 26/76, n. 310 above).

[360] Case T–2/93, n. 351 above.

[361] *Ibid.*, at point 44.

at the applicant's position in the market would be seriously :onsequence of the decision.[362] The question of direct concern considered.

t cases have had as background a Commission decision which : the Nestlé-Perrier concentration (*Mineral waters*) was compatible with the Common Market.[363] Both cases[364] involved actions brought by workers' representatives who believed that serious damage could be caused to the employees of Perrier in the first case and of Vittel and Pierval in the second.[365] The Commission had argued that some of the applicants had not participated in the administrative proceedings and therefore they could not be individually concerned. In both cases the Court ruled that all applicants were individually concerned, given that the Merger Regulation protects the right of workers' representatives to be heard. In effect, Article 18 of the Merger Regulation[366] protects the right to be heard of the undertakings concerned,[367] and of natural and legal persons who show a sufficient interest, 'especially members of the administrative or management bodies of the undertakings concerned or the recognised representatives of their employees'.[368] Therefore, although some of the applicants had not become involved in the procedure leading to the adoption of the contested measure, the Court found that they were individually concerned since they held a legally protected interest. The Court did not believe, however, that the applicants were directly concerned, given that the decision did not in any way undermine the rights of the workers' representatives or the rights of the companies' employees.

It appears, therefore, from the case law of the Court of First Instance that participation in the administrative procedure leading to the adoption of the contested decision is not the only element to justify the presence of *locus standi*: factual elements and the existence of a legally protected interest may also play a part.

3.4.3 STATE AIDS PROCEEDINGS

Articles 92 to 94 EC Treaty constitute a set of rules that aims to control certain aids granted by Member States that distort or threaten to distort

[362] In this case Air France would have had to give up all its interests in TAT (Case T–2/93, n. 351 above, at points 45–46). The consideration given by the Court to factual elements has appeared sporadically in decisions of the ECJ. See the *Second Metro* case (Case 75/84, n. 310 above) and Case 264/82 *Timex* v. *Council and Commission*, n. 206 above, and Case C–358/89 *Extramet* v. *Council* [1991] ECR I–2501.

[363] Dec. of 22 July 1992 [1992] OJ L356/1.

[364] Case T–96/92 *Comité Central de la Société Générale des Grandes Sources* v. *Commission*, judgment of 27 Apr. 1995, not yet reported, and Case T–12/93 *Comité Central d'Entreprise de la Société Anonyme Vittel* v. *Commission*, judgement of 27 Apr. 1995, not yet reported.

[365] One of the conditions imposed on Nestlé by the decision was that it had to sell the Pierval make and spring. Pierval had a collective agreement with Vittel.

[366] Reg. 4064/89, see n. 350 above.

[367] *Ibid.*, Art. 18(1).

[368] *Ibid.*, Art. 18(4).

competition by favouring certain undertakings or the production of certain goods.[369] This area of Community law is intimately related to the Treaty provisions on competition and to the provisions on the free movement of goods. It would be illogical to eliminate quantitative restrictions and customs duties without contemplating the problem of a domestic market flooded with products from other Member States with a clear competitive advantage as a result of the export subsidies they had been granted.

State aids that distort competition are prohibited under Article 92(1) Ec Treaty. Some aids are expressly declared compatible with the Common Market under Article 92(2), whilst Article 92(3) provides for a series of cases where the EC authorities enjoy discretion to declare particular categories of aids compatible with the Common Market. Article 93(2) EC Treaty regulates the procedure to be followed in order to ascertain whether an existing aid is compatible with the Common Market. In the case of a new aid, Article 93(3) obliges the Member State that intends to grant an aid to notify the Commission in advance of the date of implementation in order to enable the Commission to conduct a preliminary examination of the compatibility of the aid with he principles of the Single Market. The Commission may either reach a favourable decision or, if it is in doubt as to the compatibility of the aid with the Common Market, initiate the procedure set out in Article 93(2). The procedure contemplated in Article 93(2) EC Treaty covers, on the one hand, the abolition or modification of aids found incompatible with the Common Market and, on the other, the definitive approval of those that are compatible. Such a procedure is used also to assess the compatibility of existing aids with the Single Market. Article 94 EC Treaty, as amended by the Maastricht Treaty, entrusts the Council—after consultation with the European Parliament—with making appropriate regulations for the application of Articles 92 and 93 EC Treaty.

In the course of state aids proceedings, there are three main types of decisions enacted by the Commission that may be the object of an application for judicial review by natural or legal persons. These decisions are: (a) Commission decisions authorizing the grant of an aid; (b) Commission decisions refusing to authorize an aid; (c) Commission decisions declaring the *prima facie* compatibility of an aid with the common market.[370] The case law in these areas will now be examined.

[369] See C. Quinley, 'The Notion of State Aid in the EEC' (1988) 13 *ELRev.* 242; D. Wyatt and A. Dashwood, n. 139 above, 519–46, and D. Schina, *State Aids under the EEC Treaty* (Oxford, 1987).

[370] See Case C–198/91 *Cook* v. *Commission*, n. 222 above, and 98 below. In those cases where the Commission reaches the conclusion that an aid is *prima facie* incompatible with the Common Market, that decision would not be challengeable in that it would simply be paving the way for a final decision taking in proceedings under Art. 93(2) EC Treaty.

3.4.4 JUDICIAL REVIEW OF DECISIONS ADOPTED IN THE COURSE OF PROCEEDINGS UNDER ARTICLE 93(2) EC TREATY

Under this heading, two main types of cases will be studied: those concerning the challenge of Commission decisions authorizing an aid and those concerning Commission decisions declaring the incompatibility of an aid with the Common Market. The addressee of these decisions is always a Member State, but private parties may have a very strong interest in seeing such decisions quashed. In the first of these cases, the third parties are mainly competitors of the addressees who have benefited from the aid. In the second case, potential recipients of the aid, and associations defending their interests, constitute the third-party group. In these areas the Court has produced a progressively more liberal case law leading to a more tolerant understanding of the admissibility conditions imposed on private parties. The approach of the Court to the question of the *locus standi* of these private parties will be illustrated in this section.

In relation to the first group of cases, i.e. the one concerning Commission decisions declaring the compatibility of an aid with the Common Market, it is very unlikely that the Member State addressee, or the undertaking that receives or could receive the aid, would bring proceedings for its annulment.[371] The commonest situation that arises is where a competitor of the favoured undertaking decides to apply for the review of the decision.

This issue first arose in *Compagnie française de l'Azote (COFAZ)* v. *Commission*.[372] The facts of this case can be summarized as follows. The French Trade Association of Nitrate Fertilizers complained to the Commission, on behalf of the applicants, against the application by the Netherlands of a preferential tariff system for Dutch producers of nitrate fertilizers for the supply of natural gas intended for the manufacture of ammonia. The Commission initiated proceedings under Article 93(2) EC Treaty and gave notice of its decision in the Official Journal, inviting interested parties to submit their observations in accordance with the above-mentioned legal provision. The applicants availed themselves of this opportunity and submitted their observations, setting out their objections to the system of natural gas tariffs established by the Dutch gas board (GASUNIE). As a result of this series of events, GASUNIE decided to amend its tariff structure and the Commission, satisfied by this decision, decided to terminate the procedure under Article 93(2) EC Treaty.

[371] Of course, nothing prevents another Member State which objects to the grant of an aid bringing proceedings under Art. 173(1) EEC Treaty (now Art. 173(2) EC Treaty). See Case 84/82 *Germany* v. *Commission* [1984] ECR 1451.

[372] Case 169/84, n. 136 above.

The Commission objected to the admissibility of the action, on the ground that the applicants were not directly and individually concerned. For the Commission, the fact that the applicants had participated in the procedure leading to the adoption of the decision could not endow them with the status of complainants in the sense of Article 3(2)(b) of Council Regulation 17.[373] Moreover, the Commission believed that the fact that COFAZ was competing with the undertakings in receipt of the aid did not constitute a circumstance that could enable them to claim that the decision affected its position in the market, and therefore the applicant was not directly concerned.[374]

The main difference between this case and those in the context of competition proceedings and anti-dumping proceedings is that, in the area of state aids proceedings, there are no basic regulations concerning the procedural rights of interested third parties. This circumstance was very much the basis of the Commission's submissions. The only provision made for these natural and legal persons is the one contained in Article 93(2) EC Treaty, according to which the Commission must serve notice to concerned parties[375] so that they may submit their observations.

The Court delivered a judgment that extended the possibilities of access to judicial review by private parties and constituted one of the landmark cases in the slow march of the Court towards a more flexible consideration of the *locus standi* of natural and legal persons. The Court began by tackling the question of individual concern and recalled how, in cases that had arisen in the area of competition and anti-dumping proceedings, where a regulation had given third parties procedural advantages (thus acknowledging their legitimate interests), such parties were able to institute proceedings to protect their interests.[376] In particular, the Court emphasized the importance of the participation of the applicant undertakings in the proceedings leading to the adoption of the measure as a factor leading to the ultimate recognition of their entitlement to bring annulment proceedings.[377] The Court then extended this line of reasoning to the present case

[373] In this respect see the considerations on the role of complainants and the implications in the field of judicial review, 79–81 above.

[374] It is a very important point that, in this area of case law, the nexus between the test of direct concern and the criterion of absence or presence of discretion has vanished, and the real test is the existence of a causal link between the decision at issue and the injury suffered by the applicants. This approach appeared in the very early cases, both in the submissions of the parties involved, as in the present instance, and in the judgments of the Court.

[375] In Case 323/82 *Intermills* v. *Commission*[1984] ECR 3809, at point 16, the Court established that 'concerned parties' within the meaning of Art. 93(2) EC Treaty are not only undertakings receiving an aid but also 'the persons, undertakings and associations whose interests might be affected by the grant of the aid, in particular competing undertakings and trade associations'.

[376] Case 169/84, n. 136 above, at point 23.

[377] *Ibid.*, at point 24. In particular the Court referred to Case 264/82 *Timex* v. *Council and Commission*, n. 206 above, a case decided in the framework of anti-dumping proceedings and which will be discussed later (see 163 below).

by saying: '[t]he same conclusions apply to undertakings which have played a comparable role in the procedure referred to in Article 93 of the EEC Treaty, provided, however, that their position in the market is significantly affected by the aid.'[378]

The Court therefore abandoned any trace of its traditional approach to the test of individual concern. The applicants did not have any individual rights under Community law and there were no basic regulations that granted them procedural guarantees. Two elements carried weight for the Court; the role played by the applicants in the procedure and the impact of the decision on the applicant's position in the market.[379] In relation to the first point, the Court was satisfied by the fact that COFAZ had submitted a complaint and made observations under Article 93(2) EC Treaty. The involvement of the applicants in the procedure as a factor leading to an ultimate recognition of *locus standi* had already appeared in the context of anti-dumping proceedings[380] and in competition proceedings.[381] In relation to the second point, the Court found that the applicants had adduced pertinent reasons to show that the Commission's decision could adversely affect their legitimate interest 'by seriously jeopardising their position on the market in question'.[382] The Court decided therefore that the applicants were individually concerned. It is important to observe that the Court gave weight to the effect that the measure could have on the applicant. In other words, a factual consideration was taken into account in order to determine the standing of the applicants. Factual considerations do play a role in ascertaining the standing of potential applicants in some national legal

[378] Case 264/82, n. 377 above, at point 25.

[379] It is interesting to recall that this second element did not carry weight in the considerations of the Court in cases decided in the general area of case law. Thus, in Joined Cases 10 and 18/68 *Eridania* v. *Commission*, n. 82 above and accompanying text, the ECJ did not consider at all the effect of the decision on the applicants, who were in competition with the recipients of the aid, and limited itself to declaring that the existence of a competitive relationship with the addressee is not a sufficiently important element to make the applicant individually concerned. One point that needs to be stressed, however, is that in the area of general case law there is no intervention of private parties in the elaboration of measures, which is one of the main elements of distinction between these cases and those decided in the area of competition, state aids, and anti-dumping proceedings. In the area of competition proceedings, for instance, competitors of the addressees of the decision who had participated in the proceedings leading to the adoption of that measure were granted *locus standi* in subsequent annulment proceedings. See Case 43/85 *Ancides* v. *Commission*, n. 136 above, and observations submitted on the judgment, 86 above.

[380] See Cases 239, 275/82 *Allied Corporation* v. *Council and Commission* [1984] ECR 1005 and Case 264/82 *Timex* v. *Council and Commission*, n. 206 above.

[381] Thus, see *First Metro* case (Case 26/76, n. 310 above) and *Second Metro* case (Case 75/84, n. 310 above).

[382] VerLoren Van Themaat A.G. was more precise in his Opinion (Case 169/84, n. 136 above, at 406) and explained that this requirement meant that a substantial proportion of the sales of the applicants 'are in direct competition with a substantial proportion of the sales of undertakings . . . favoured by the measure to which the Commission's contested decision relates'.

systems[383] but in the case law of the European Court, in annulment proceedings, they had only appeared rarely.[384] In the present judgment the Court combined both elements and brought a substantial degree of flexibility to the definition of the test of individual concern within the framework of state aids.[385]

The test of direct concern received briefer consideration. The Court decided that there was a causal relationship between the decision at issue and the harmful effects on the interests of the applicants.[386] Although the addressee of the decision was a Member State, the criterion of the presence or absence of discretion was not used by the Court.[387]

A further development has taken place with a recent case. In *Landbouwschap* v. *Commission*,[388] the Landbouwschap, a Dutch body governed by public law which has as its object the promotion of the interests of Dutch agricultural producers, brought proceedings for the annulment of a Commission decision that had declared void a system of aid projected by the Dutch Government and that appeared in a statute containing general provisions for environmental protection compatible with the Common Market . The Court by order declared the action inadmissible on the ground that the system of aid benefited exclusively a group of big enterprises with whom the applicant and the undertakings it represented were not in competition.[389] The applicant was therefore not individual concerned. Furthermore, its interests were not affected by the maintenance of the contested decision[390] and consequently it was not directly concerned. The Court said nothing about whether or not the Landbowschap had been

[383] See for instance the French legal system, 32–3 above.

[384] See *Second Metro* case in the field of competition (Case 75/84, n. 310 above, and 84–5 above) and *Timex* v. *Council and Commission* in the area of anti-dumping (Case 264/82, n. 206 above, and 163 below).

[385] For D. Schina, n. 369 above, 162, the fact that COFAZ had complained was of a paramount importance for the decision about *locus standi*, to the point that it is not clear whether, in the absence of this circumstance, the same ruling would have been obtained. In the same vein, VerLoren Van Themaat A.G. in his Opinion stressed the importance of this element at 407. When these views were formulated, there were no examples in the case law that could show otherwise. Presently, and in the light of recent judgments of the ECJ, like the one in Case C–295/92 *Landbouwschap* v. *Commission* [1992] ECR I–5003 and the one of the CFI in Case T–435/93 *ASPEC* v. *Commission* of 27 Apr. 1995, not yet reported, it could be inferred that the fact that the applicants were in competition with the beneficiaries of the aid—provided that significant damage had resulted or would result to their interests as a consequence of the contested decision—could suffice to determine their individual concern. The same result seems to emerge from Case C–198/91 *Cook* v. *Commission*, see n. 222 above, and for a discussion on the judgment, 98–100 below.

[386] Case 169/84, n. 136 above, at point 30.

[387] In this respect see the considerations underlying the notion of direct concern, as presented earlier (73 above).

[388] Case C–295/92, n. 385 above.

[389] *Ibid.*, at point 12.

[390] *Ibid.*, at point 13.

involved in the procedure. It seemed likely that it had not been involved.[391] Although this particular case culminated with the declaration of inadmissibility of the application presented by the Landbouwschap, it could be inferred *a sensu contrario* that, had the applicant been in competition with the beneficiaries of the aid, it might well have been individually concerned by the decision.[392]

In effect, a significant step in this direction has taken place with a recent decision of the Court of First Instance. In *Association of Sorbitol Producers within the EC (ASPEC) and others* v. *Commission*,[393] the applicants, producers of sorbitol and starch in the Community, brought annulment proceedings against a Commission decision terminating the procedure under Article 93(2) EC Treaty and declaring the compatibility with the Common Market of an investment aid granted by the Italian authorities to their competitors. In that case, the applicants had submitted observations to the Commission, but the Commission had not taken them into account. The Court explained that this element should not deprive the applicants of the chance of being individually concerned,[394] and went on to examine whether their position in the market had been seriously affected as a result of the decision. The Court concluded, in view of the limited number of producers of sorbitol and of the significant increase that would follow in the production capacity of their competitors as a consequence of the aid, that the applicants were individually concerned. In consequence, the Court granted *locus standi* to the applicants on the basis of the devastating effects that the grant of aid would have on them and not on the basis of procedural involvement. The decision was annulled by the Court on the merits.

The second group of cases concerns those situations where the Commission declares an aid incompatible with the Common Market. In this case, it is clear that the Member State addressee of the decision may bring proceedings for its annulment. In the case of non-privileged applicants, the case law of the European Court has repeatedly admitted that potential beneficiaries of an aid may bring an action for annulment. Thus, in *Philip*

[391] Case C–295/92, n. 385 above. In this respect see the very active procedural role that this body took in Joined Cases 67–68 and 70/85 *Van der Kooy* v. *Commission* [1988] ECR 219. For a discussion of the judgment, see 96 below.

[392] Thus this case could be linked to the recent decision of the Court in Case C–198/91 *Cook* v. *Commission*, n. 222 above, and 98–100 below, where the crucial factor taken into account by the Court was the position of the applicants as competitors with the beneficiary of the measure, and not its procedural involvement.

[393] Case T–435/93, judgment of the CFI of 27 Apr. 1995, not yet reported. See also Case T–442/93 *Association des Amidonneries de Céréales de la CEE (AAC)* v. *Commission*, judgment of the CFI of 27 Apr. 1995, not yet reported.

[394] The reasoning of the Court appears to be very sound in that, otherwise, the Commission could, by not taking into consideration the observations presented by potential applicants for judicial review in the course of the administrative phase of a decision, effectively diminish their right to challenge resulting Community measures.

Morris v. *Commission*,[395] the defendant institution itself did not object to the admissibility of an action brought by the potential recipient of an aid that was intended to increase its production capacity.[396] The Court did not discuss the admissibility issue and, in the cases that followed, such actions were admitted without further discussion.[397]

Other non-privileged applicants that may be interested in challenging this type of decision are associations formed for the protection of the interests of undertakings that are generally affected by the refusal of the Commission to authorize a certain aid. In this field two contradictory rulings were given by the Court. In *Comité de développement et de promotion du textile et de l'habillement (DEFI)* v. *Commission*,[398] the Commission decision at issue declared the aid to undertakings in the textile and clothing sector in France provided in two French Decrees was incompatible with the Common Market. The decision was addressed to France and the latter brought annulment proceedings under Article 173(1) EEC Treaty.[399] DEFI, an association for the promotion of the clothing sector, also brought annulment proceedings. The Court rejected the action brought by DEFI as inadmissible on the ground that the Court had repeatedly held in its case law that an association set up to represent the collective interests of the traders does not have a right of action.[400] The Court did not consider at all

[395] Case 730/79 [1980] ECR 2671.

[396] *Ibid.* 2675. In relation to the importance of the fact that the Commission did not raise objections, see n. 310 above.

[397] Thus, the rulings of the Court in Case 323/82 *Intermills* v. *Commission*, n. 375 above, and in Cases 62/87 and 72/87 *Executif Régional Wallon & Glaverbel* v. *Commission* [1988] ECR 1573.

[398] Case 282/85, n. 248 above.

[399] Case 259/85 *France* v. *Commission* [1987] ECR 4393.

[400] In the general area of case law, the Court has always adopted a restrictive view on the *locus standi* of associations to bring annulment proceedings. See Joined Cases 16–17/62 *Confédération Nationale des producteurs de fruits et légumes & others* v. *Council*, n. 86 above, at 479, where the Court said: 'one cannot accept the principle that an association, in its capacity as the representative of a category of businessmen, could be individually concerned by a measure affecting the general interest of that category'; see also Case 60/79 *Fédération nationale des producteurs de vins de table et de vins de pays* v. *Commission* [1979] ECR 2429 at 2432; Case 117/86 *UFADE* v. *Council* [1986] ECR 3255, at point 12; Case 135/81 *Groupement des agences de voyages* v. *Commission* [1982] ECR 3799 and Case T–476/93 *FRSEA and FNSEA* v. *Council*, judgment of the CFI of 28 Oct. 1993. In the area of anti-dumping cases, however, the Court seems to have adopted a more lenient approach; see Case C–170/89 *Bureau Européen des Unions de Consommateurs (BEUC)* v. *Commission* [1991] ECR I–5709, see 170 below. Likewise, in a recent decision involving state aids (Joined Cases T–447/93, T–448/93, and T–449/93 *Associazione Italiana Tecnico Economica del Cemento* v. *Commission*, judgment of 6 July 1995, not yet reported), the CFI admitted that an Italian Association representing the interests of some Italian companies had *locus standi* to challenge a Commission decision authorizing an aid to be given to the competitors of the undertakings that the association represented. It was clear in those cases that the undertakings represented were directly and individually concerned and the Court allowed the association to bring the action on the ground that this fact would avoid a higher number of individual applications. The application for annulment was also successful on the merits and the Court annulled the decision.

the active role played by the applicants in the procedure leading to the adoption of the decision in question.[401]

In a later case, *Van der Kooy and others* v. *Commission*,[402] a different and more liberal view was taken by the Court. In this case, Van der Kooy, a limited liability company and the Landbouwschap[403] both brought proceedings against a Commission decision addressed to the Netherlands, whereby it was stated that the preferential tariff charged to glasshouse growers for natural gas in the Netherlands was an aid incompatible with the Common Market within the meaning of Article 92 EC Treaty. Finally the Dutch Government also brought proceedings under Article 173(1) EEC Treaty. The Court quickly dismissed the application presented by Van der Kooy, on the grounds that the decision affected a broad category of business and that the applicants were not affected differently from other traders.[404] After the ruling in *DEFI*, one would have thought that the application brought by Landbouwschap was also going to be rejected.[405] The Court, however,

[401] The Court seemed to regard as important the fact that the French Government had already begun proceedings for the annulment of the same measure. Thus it said (at consideration 19) that 'It should in any event be pointed out that the French Government has itself brought an action for a declaration that the contested decision is void and relies on exactly the same objections as those described by DEFI. That fact demonstrates that DEFI cannot claim that it is denied legal protection for the interests it is seeking to defend.' It could be thought that this circumstance had some influence on the final conclusion that the applicants were not directly and individually concerned. The strength of this argument diminishes in the light of later case law. Thus in Joined Cases 6765 and 70/85 *Van der Kooy* v. *Commission*, n. 391 above, the fact that the Member State addressee also brought annulment proceedings was seen as unimportant in terms of the determination of the *locus standi* of the applicants. In Case C–135/92 *Fiskarno* v. *Commission* [1994] ECR I–2885, the fact that the Member State addressee could challenge the contested measure by means of an arbitration procedure had no effect on the applicant's right to institute annulment proceedings (at point 28). Likewise in a case decided in the context of Art. 177 EC Treaty proceedings, Cases C–6 and C–9/90 *Francovich and Others* v. *Italy* [1991] ECR 1–5357, the Court admitted that a Member State is obliged to make good harm to individuals caused by the non-implementation of a dir., and did not make the protection of this right of individuals dependent on whether or not the Commission brought an enforcement action under Art. 169 EC Treaty. This line of case law indicates that the Court, apart from the isolated ruling in *DEFI* does not normally make the protection of individual rights contingent on whether somebody else has brought or intends to bring proceedings.

[402] Joined Cases 67–68 and 70/85, n. 391 above.

[403] See 93 above .

[404] Joined Cases 67–68 and 70/85, n. 391 above, at points 14–15. The Court did not follow the suggestions of its A.G., Sir Gordon Slynn (at 245), who believed that *Van der Kooy* ought to enjoy *locus standi*, due to its quality as a beneficiary of the preferential tariff on the basis of the Court's earlier judgments, like that in Case 730/79 *Philip Morris* v. *Commission*, n. 395 above. It would appear therefore that when an aid is a 'sectorial aid', i.e. one that benefits a broad category of business, individual undertakings do not enjoy *locus standi* to challenge the decision declaring the incompatibility of the aid with the Common Market. On the contrary, when an aid is intended to benefit a specific undertaking, this potential recipient is able to challenge the decision refusing to authorize the aid (see 95 above).

[405] The Commission objected to the admissibility of the action begun by this applicant (see n. 391 above, at 228) on the same grounds that had succeeded in the judgment of the Court in *DEFI* (Case 232/85, n. 248 above, and 95 above. The A.G. also believed that the application of the Dutch body was inadmissible for the identical reasons that the application of *DEFI* had been rejected (Case 232/85, n. 248 above, at 247). However, the ruling in *DEFI* was not mentioned anywhere, either by the defendant institution or by the A.G.

found this applicant directly and individually concerned, and abandoned its former approach of transposing its views on the *locus standi* of associations expressed in the general area of case law in this field. The involvement of the applicant in the procedure for the adoption of the decision at issue was regarded as a key element in the recognition that it was directly and individually concerned by the decision.[406]

The main difference between the rulings of the Court in *DEFI* and in *Van der Kooy* is again a matter of the adoption by the Court of a more flexible approach to the *locus standi* of private parties. In *Van der Kooy*, not only did the Court disregard the fact that the Dutch Government also initiated annulment proceedings[407] but it also regarded the involvement of the applicants in the procedure as a very important indication of their interest in the annulment of the contested decisions.

3.4.5 JUDICIAL REVIEW OF DECISIONS ADOPTED IN THE COURSE OF THE PRELIMINARY PROCEDURE FOR THE EXAMINATION OF NEW AIDS UNDER ARTICLE 93(3) EC TREATY

Recent case law of the Court has shown that interested private parties may also challenge decisions adopted by the Commission declaring the *prima facie* compatibility with the Common Market of new aids in the course of the preliminary examination in accordance with Article 93(3) EC Treaty.[408] These cases have consolidated and further developed the more open attitude of the Court to the *locus standi* of private parties than has been adopted generally in the area of state aids proceedings.

In *Comité international de la rayonne et des fibres synthétiques (CIFRS)* v. *Commission*,[409] the International Committee of Nylon and Synthetic Fabrics, together with a group of European associations and companies, brought annulment proceedings against a decision of the Commission which amounted in fact to a decision refusing to initiate proceedings under Article 93(2) EC Treaty. The Commission itself did not object to the admissibility of the action brought by CIFRS,[410] for, in its view, the status of CIFRS as a competitor of the recipients of the aid made its application admissible. The Court arrived at the conclusion that this applicant was directly and individually concerned by the Commission decision, given its role of negotiator with the Commission during the procedure prior to the enactment of the Commission decision, which had been shown in

[406] In the recent case, Case C–295/82 *Landbouwschap* v. *Commission*, n. 385 above, this body did not get involved in the procedure.

[407] For the standpoint taken by the Court in Case 232/85 *DEFI* v. *Commission*, see n. 248 above, and accompanying text.

[408] See 89 above.

[409] Case C–313/90, judgment of 24 Mar. 1993.

[410] On the importance of this factor, see n. 310 above.

particular by its frequent contacts with the Community authorities and by the submission of written observations.[411] The applicants succeeded on the merits and the decision was annulled. It is noteworthy that the Court thus based its reasoning on the fact that the applicant had been involved in the procedure that led to the adoption of the measure at issue and did not base it on its position as a competitor of the recipients of the aid, as the Commission had suggested.

It has been shown that the involvement of non-privileged applicants in the procedure leading to the adoption of a decision within the framework of state aids proceedings is a good guarantee that *locus standi* will subsequently be accorded to them. This is certainly true for decisions adopted within the context of Article 93(2) EC Treaty—although a recent decision of the Court of First Instance also suggests that factual circumstances may, in some cases, suffice to grant *locus standi* to private applicants.[412] However, the preliminary examination procedure under Article 93(3) EC Treaty is a *prima facie* examination carried out by the Commission that in some instances may be performed without the knowledge of potential interested parties, given that there are no publicity requirements akin to the one contained in Article 93(2) EC Treaty.[413] Consequently, if this preliminary procedure culminates in a Commission decision that establishes the compatibility of an aid with the Common Market, a third-party competitor of the potential recipient could find himself in a position where, whilst wanting to challenge the decision at issue, he did not have the opportunity of becoming involved in the procedure leading to the adoption of the decision in question. If *locus standi* depended exclusively on involvement in the procedure, such a third-party competitor might, perhaps unjustly, be excluded from access to the Article 173 review procedure.[414]

This point has recently been raised in *Cook* v. *Commission*.[415] In this case, the Spanish Government intended to grant an aid to a Spanish undertaking, PYRSA (Piezas y Rodajes SA) for the construction, in the province of Teruel, of a foundry to produce sprockets and GET parts.[416] Cook, a competitor undertaking, became aware of this and complained to

[411] Case C–313/90, n. 409 above, at point 29. The A.G., Mr Lenz, offered a similar view in his Opinion (see [1993] Rec. I–1167–1168).

[412] See Case T–435/93 *ASPEC* v. *Commission*, n. 393 above.

[413] In the framework of anti-dumping proceedings, the Commission has the duty to publish a notice in the Official Journal about the initiation of the proceedings—Art. 7(1)a of Reg. 2423/88 [1988] OJ L209/1. Likewise, in competition proceedings, the Commission normally publishes a notice in the Official Journal in relation to the initiation of proceedings so that interested parties may submit their views (see Art. 2(2) of Reg. 99/63, n. 300 above).

[414] In this respect see the Opinion of Tesauro A.G. in Case C–198/91 *Cook* v. *Commission*, n. 222 above, at paras 43–44, and the judgment of the CFI in Case T–435/93 *ASPEC* v. *Commission*, n. 393 above.

[415] Case C–198/91, n. 222 above.

[416] These items are used in the construction of earth-moving and excavation equipment.

the Commission seeking the initiation of Article 93(2) EC Treaty procedure. The project qualified as a 'new aid', and accordingly the Commission carried out the preliminary examination provided for in Article 93(3) EC Treaty. The Commission reached the conclusion that the aid was *prima facie* compatible with the Common Market. This decision was the subject of an application for annulment filed by Cook. The admissibility of this application was contested by the Commission.

The Opinion of the Advocate General, Mr Tesauro, was very enlightening. In his view, there were no doubts that the applicant was directly concerned by the decision, since the authorization granted to the Spanish Government to implement the aid would lead to an injury being sustained by Cook.[417] As for the question of individual concern, the Advocate General recalled the two conditions that the Court had indicated as important to satisfy this test in *COFAZ* v. *Commission*.[418] Those conditions were: (a) the fact that the applicants ought to be significantly affected by the aid, and (b) their procedural involvement in the adoption of the measure. Both elements were present in this case. In relation to the first condition, Mr Tesauro emphasized that Cook and PYRSA were competitors as regards a substantial proportion of their activities. In relation to the second condition, the Advocate General was satisfied by the fact that Cook had filed the complaint that drew the attention of the Commission to the projected aid.

Having said this, the Advocate General went a step further and made a very interesting observation as a matter of general interest. Mr Tesauro concluded: 'the participation of a third party in the preliminary procedure —a procedure of which that party is normally unaware—cannot constitute a *condition sine qua non* for bringing an action against a decision *to raise no objections* [emphasis added].'[419]

In Mr Tesauro's view, any undertaking competing with the one benefiting from an aid should be given standing to challenge the Commission decision not to raise objections under Article 93(3) EC Treaty, independently of whether or not it had played a part in the procedure leading to the adoption of the contested measure. In *Cook* it so happened that the applicant himself communicated to the Commission the plans of the Spanish Government, but this fact was purely coincidental and would not necessarily be so in other cases.

The Court reached the conclusion that Cook was directly and individually concerned by the decision. The Court first explained that the Commission was only obliged to notify 'concerned parties' so that they could submit their comments within the framework of proceedings under Article 93(2) EC Treaty. For the first time in the context of state aids proceedings,

[417] See Opinion of Mr Tesauro (Case C–198/91, n. 222 above, at para. 36).
[418] See 90 above.
[419] Case C–198/91, n. 222 above, at para. 43.

the Court recognized that this obligation to notify was a procedural guarantee for interested parties and that, in order to respect the principle underlying that guarantee, those applicants should be able to challenge Commission decisions taken under Article 93(3) EC Treaty. Thus, the Court said:

> Where without initiating the procedure under Article 93(2), the Commission finds, on the basis of Article 93(3), that an aid is compatible with the Common Market, the persons intended to benefit from those procedural advantages may secure compliance therewith only if they are able to challenge that decision by the Commission before the Court.[420]

The Court recalled that undertakings competing with the recipients of the aid were parties concerned for the purposes of Article 93(2) EC Treaty.[421] Therefore, Cook was found to be directly and individually concerned by the decision at issue, owing to his position as a competitor of the recipients of the aid and not by reason of his procedural involvement in the adoption of the contested decision.

The more liberal approach of the Court to the *locus standi* issue can be appreciated if this ruling is compared with the recent ones given in cases concerning competition and anti-dumping proceedings. In both those areas, a private applicant was normally granted standing when he became actively involved in the procedure that led to the adoption of the contested measure. Thus, in competition proceedings, in order for a natural or legal person to become entitled to the procedural advantages contained in the basic regulations, it was necessary that the applicant engage in conduct such as the lodging of a complaint or the submission of observations. The recent decisions of the Court of First Instance in the *Air France*[422] and *Mineral Waters*[423] cases could indicate that interested parties that have not participated in the administrative proceedings may also be entitled to bring annulment proceedings against the resulting decision. The same can be said about anti-dumping proceedings, where the judgment of the Court in *Extramet* granted *locus standi* to importers, in view of factual considerations and not due to the fact that the applicants had become procedurally involved in the adoption of the contested regulation. Likewise, in *Cook*, the Court reached the conclusion that the mere quality of the applicant as a competitor of the potential beneficiary of a state aid may suffice for him to be considered as directly and individually concerned by a decision declaring the *prima facie* compatibility of the aid with the Common Market, without any further consideration of its procedural involvement in the elaboration of the measure.[424] Future case law will show whether

[420] Case C–198/91, n. 222 above, at point 23.

[421] In this respect, see n. 375 above.

[422] See Case T–3/93, n. 351 above, and Case T–2/93, n. 351 above.

[423] See Case T–96/92, n. 364 above, and Case T–12/93, n. 364 above.

[424] The case law in state aids proceedings had also suggested hitherto that the procedural

this new approach can be extended to measures enacted within the framework of Article 93(2) EC Treaty.[425] It would seem, from the ruling of the Court of First Instance in *ASPEC* v. *Commission*,[426] that in that context, it would be necessary for the applicant not only to be in competition with the beneficiaries of an aid, but also to prove that the grant of aid would have very harmful effects on his position in the market. The reason for this could be, perhaps, that, in the context of Article 93(2) proceedings, private applicants always have the opportunity of securing compliance with the procedural advantages to which they are entitled.

involvement of the applicants in the elaboration of the contested decision was a crucial element in determining their *locus standi* to challenge it in annulment proceedings. Thus, see Case 169/84 *COFAZ* v. *Commission*, n. 136 above and Joined Cases 67–68 and 70/85 *Van der Kooy* v. *Commission*, n. 391 above

[425] Another case in the context of Art. 93(3) proceedings, Case C–225/91 *Matra* v. *Commission*, judgment of 15 June 1993, has confirmed the views in *Cook*. In that case, the applicant. a competitor company, complained to the Commission that the Portuguese Government intended to grant an aid to a joint venture between Ford of Europe and Volkswagen for setting up a manufacturing unit for multi-purpose vehicles in Sétubal. The Commission issued a decision under Art. 93(3) EC Treaty establishing the *prima facie* compatibility of the aid with the Common Market. The applicants brought annulment proceedings against the decision, and their *locus standi* was not contested by the defendant institution but by the intervener (Ford Werke). The Court concluded that the applicant had *locus standi* on the same basis as in *Cook* (*ibid.* , at points 10–19).

[426] Case T–435/93, n. 393 above.

4

The Locus Standi *of Non-Privileged Applicants to Challenge Measures in the Form of Regulations or of Directives*

This Chapter will be devoted mostly to the study of the case law of the European Court of Justice in connection with the attempts made by private parties to challenge Commission and Council regulations.[1] It has already been seen[2] that Article 173 EC Treaty excludes *a sensu contrario* any binding act other than decisions from the scope of challenge by natural and legal persons. Consequently, regulations and directives[3] are, in principle, excluded. However, and with the clear intention of preventing the European institutions from escaping the likelihood of review by choosing the form of a regulation for an act which is in substance a decision, the drafters of the EC Treaty established the principle that a private applicant could bring annulment proceedings against a decision which 'although in the form of a regulation is of direct and individual concern to the former'.[4] From the wording of Article 173(2) EEC Treaty, it would seem that three cumulative hurdles need to be overcome by natural or legal persons who wish to challenge a regulation. In the first place, it has to be proved that the measure, albeit in the form of a regulation, is in substance a decision; in the second place, that the decision is of individual concern to the applicant; in the third place, that it is of direct concern.[5] However, one feature of the case law in this area which could trouble any observer who wishes to find uniform criteria in the Court's approach to the question of *locus standi*. This is the fact that two divergent lines seem to emerge from the case law of the Court.

[1] After the Maastricht Treaty amendments, the Council and the Commission are no longer the only Community institutions that can enact regs. In those instances where the new conciliation and veto procedure is applicable, regs. may now be adopted jointly by the Council and the European Parliament (see 18 above). The European Central Bank may also enact regs. (Art. 108a (1) EC Treaty as amended by the Maastricht Treaty).

[2] See 26 above.

[3] For an analysis of the *locus standi* of non-privileged applicants to challenge dirs., see 170–3 below.

[4] Art. 173(2) EEC Treaty (now Art. 173(4) EC Treaty).

[5] In this respect see the Opinions of Lagrange A.G. in Joined Cases 16–17/62 *Confédération Nationale des Producteurs de Fruits et Légumes* v. *Council* [1962] ECR 471 at 484 and of Roemer A.G. in Cases 63/69 and 64/69 *La Compagnie Française Commerciale et Financière* v. *Commission* [1970] ECR 205 and [1970] ECR 221 at 215, and Case 65/69 *La Compagnie d'Approvisionnement, de Transport et de Crédit* v. *Commission* [1970] ECR 229.

On the one hand, in some of its decisions the Court highlighted the existence of three separate admissibility tests: legal nature, individual, and direct concern.[6] Therefore, throughout the case law in this area, private applicants, when bringing annulment proceedings against measures labelled as regulations, have needed to show that such measures were in reality 'disguised decisions' before going on to prove that they were of direct and individual concern to them. This matter would not have created further complications if the Treaties had offered clear guidance on the distinction between regulations and decisions. Unfortunately, this is not the case and the borderline between the two kinds of act is blurred in some instances.[7] The achievement of a clear criterion of distinction between the two kinds of act is a crucial point, for it will determine the extent of the right of private parties to obtain judicial review. Such a criterion has been elaborated by the European Court through its case law and has resulted in an almost insurmountable test, requiring proof of the existence of a causal link between the regulation at issue and the situation of the applicants, or, in other words, proof that the regulation was enacted not to deal with an objective situation in the market but in order to decide on the fate of a group of addressees. As a consequence, most of the actions were dismissed as inadmissible.

On the other hand, in some other instances, the Court ignored the first of those tests and resolved the admissibility issue on the basis of the tests of direct and individual concern.[8] In this group of cases, many more actions were declared admissible.

The existence of this conflicting judicial trend has been acknowledged by the majority of authors[9] and by the Advocates General of the Court,[10] but they have not adequately explained the reasons for such a division.[11] The present work has three main aims in this area.

In the first place, it is suggested that, with a few exceptions, there is a logic in the approach of the Court to these cases. In fact, the Court adopted the double admissibility test mostly in those instances where the contested

[6] See 112 below.

[7] In this respect, see the Opinion of Lagrange A.G. in Case 8/55 *Fédéchar* v. *High Authority* [1954–56] ECR 245 at 269, which, although delivered in the framework of an ECSC Treaty, case is very enlightening on this point.

[8] See 138 below.

[9] Thus, T. C. Hartley, *The Foundations of European Community Law* (3rd edn., Oxford, 1994), 368; H. G. Schermers and D. Waelbroeck, *Judicial Protection in the European Community* (5th edn., Deventer, 1992), 231–2; S. Weatherill and P. Beaumont, *EC Law* (London, 1993), 198–201, and R. Greaves, '*Locus Standi* under Article 173 EEC when Seeking Annulment of a Regulation' (1986) 11 *ELRev.* 119, 131.

[10] See the Opinion of Da Cruz Vilaça A.G. in Case 333/85 *Mannesmann-Röhrenwerke* v. *Council* [1987] ECR 1381 at 1390.

[11] One author felt that perhaps 'the Court decides first whether it wants the application to be admissible and then applies whichever test will produce the desired result': T. C. Hartley, n. 9 above, 368.

regulations affected *in their entirety* closed categories of people, and where it was not clear that a causal link existed between the aim of the regulations and the situation of the applicants. In these cases, had the European Court considered the test of legal nature, it would almost certainly have dismissed the actions. This group of cases amounts in itself to a liberalization of the *locus standi* conditions contained in Article 173(2) EEC Treaty.

In the second place, it is argued that the recent decision of the Court in *Sofrimport* v. *Commission*[12] has brought a further degree of liberalization by ignoring the test of legal nature in an application against three regulations affecting categories of people partially closed and partially open, a situation wherein the Court had normally dismissed actions for annulment brought by members of the closed category on the ground that such regulations were truly legislative acts.[13] The recent decision of the European Court of Justice in *Codorniu* v. *Council*[14] confirms this view.

Finally, it is argued that the judgment in *Sofrimport* has had a clear impact on the case law of the Court that followed where—with two exceptions[15]—the test of legal nature had not been taken into account and the cases were decided solely on the basis of the tests of direct and individual concern, even in cases where the regulations at issue affected open categories.

It seems therefore that the Court could be moving towards the elimination of this additional hurdle in the determination of the *locus standi* of private applicants in annulment proceedings—if not completely, at least in those cases where the applicants are individually and directly concerned. This tendency towards liberalization finds an echo in the case law involving anti-dumping proceedings,[16] where the Court has freed itself from the test of legal nature and has interpreted the question of standing of natural and legal persons in terms very similar to those that appeared in the case law of competition and state aids proceedings.[17] The result would be that non-privileged applicants could challenge true regulations, provided that such measures or some of their provisions concerned them directly and individually. This outcome would also represent a major step in the judicial protection of natural and legal persons, who hitherto have been barred from challenging acts of a general nature, or, in other words, a true

[12] Case C–152/88 [1990] ECR I–2477.
[13] See 132 below.
[14] Case C–308/89 [1994] ECR I–1853.
[15] Joined Cases C–15/91 and C–108/91 *Buckl* v. *Commission* [1992] ECR I–6061 and the *Gibraltar Airport cases* (Case C–336/90 *Gibraltar Development Corporation* v. *Council*, judgment of 12 July 1993; Case C–128/91 *Gibraltar and Gibraltar Development Corporation* v. *Council*, judgment of 12 July 1993; Case C–397/92 *Gibraltar and Gibraltar Development Corporation* v. *Council*, judgment of 12 July 1993; Case C–168/93 *Gibraltar and Gibraltar Development Corporation* v. *Council*, judgment of 12 July 1993).
[16] See 155 ff. below.
[17] See 75 ff. above.

re-drafting of the Treaty by the Court.[18] All these points will be dealt with in this Chapter. The starting point of this analysis is the achievement of a clear criterion of distinction between regulations and decisions. As a preliminary, however, it is important to recollect the limited but enlightening experience acquired by the Court in case law under Article 33 ECSC Treaty.

4.1 General and Individual Decisions Under the ECSC Treaty

It has already been seen how Article 33 ECSC Treaty imposed much more lenient *locus standi* conditions on private parties—undertakings and associations of undertakings—than Article 173(2) EEC Treaty.[19] One important difference between the two provisions is that under the ECSC Treaty, private parties are allowed to challenge general decisions[20] on the ground of the existence of a misuse of powers affecting them. Nevertheless, this is hardly an advantage given the enormous difficulty involved in successfully arguing this ground.[21] Thus, although Article 33 does not contain a proviso equivalent to the one in Article 173(2) which guards applicants against the possibility of a true individual decision appearing in the form of a general decision,[22] the truth is that, from early case law, private applicants tried to show, when challenging measures that were outwardly general decisions,

[18] It would not be the first time that the Court has altered the wording of a Treaty provision: see Ch. 3 above, n. 102.

[19] See 40 above.

[20] General decs. are the ECSC equivalent of regs. under the EC Treaty, and ECSC individual decs. are the equivalent of EC decs.

[21] In this respect, M. Waelbroeck, 'Examen de Jurisprudence 1955 à 1971, Communautés Européennes' [1971] *RCJB* 541, 546. Also T. C. Hartley, n. 9 above, 433–6.

[22] This was not always a non-contentious view. In an early case, Case 3/54 *Assider* v. *High Authority* [1954–56] ECR 63 at 66, the High Authority put forward the view that the expression in Art. 33 ECSC Treaty 'misuse of powers affecting them' reflected the intention of the authors of the Treaty to exclude actions against acts of a general nature and that Art. 33 ECSC Treaty only contained a proviso to prevent private parties from challenging individual decisions disguised as general ones. In the same case, Lagrange A.G. said (*ibid.*, at 87) that 'having just included misuse of powers amongst the grounds for annulment, the authors of the Treaty thought of the situation where a decision which, while in fact individually *affecting* an undertaking is "disguised" ("camouflaged", to use the word employed without hesitation in the written submissions) as, to all appearances, a general decision and is, in consequence, clearly invalidated as a misuse of powers'. See also A. de Labaudère, 'Traits Généraux du Contentieux Administratif des Communautés Européennes' (1964) 111 *Recueil des Cours, Académie de Droit International* 531, 567. This view, although consistent with the ensuing wording of Art. 173(2) EEC Treaty, would be tantamount to admitting that, in reality, what was to be avoided was not so much situations of misuse of powers but of misuse of procedure, and that natural and legal persons would be prevented from challenging 'true general acts'. The Court, however, dismissed these arguments in Case 8/55 *Fédéchar* v. *High Authority*, n. 7 above at 257, where it made clear that non-privileged applicants could indeed challenge true normative acts albeit only on the ground of misuse of powers.

that they were in reality individual decisions and presumably more easily reviewable in terms of *locus standi*.[23] The Court implicitly acknowledged the possibility that an apparent general decision could be, in reality, an individual decision by adopting a non-formalistic approach to the nature of measures subject to annulment proceedings.[24] Thus, in *Fédéchar* v. *High Authority*[25] the Court said that 'a disguised individual decision remains an individual decision, since its nature depends on its scope rather than on its form'.[26]

To elaborate a suitable criterion of distinction between general and individual decisions, the Court could not rely on the provisions of the ECSC Treaty. The only legal provision available was Article 14 ECSC Treaty, which merely distinguishes between decisions and recommendations[27] and does not provide any way of distinguishing general and individual decisions.

In *Wirtschaftsvereinigung Eisen- und Stahlindustrie* v. *High Authority*[28] the Court explained for the first time the essential features of a general decision by saying that 'it establishes a legislative principle, imposes abstract conditions for its implementation and sets out the legal consequences entailed thereby'.[29]

The central idea underlying this statement is that what characterizes general decisions is their legislative character. One of the features of normative measures is their abstract character or, in other words, that they affect *any* individual who finds himself fulfilling the conditions that determine their application. It is thus clear, that in the context of the ECSC Treaty, regulations are identified with legislative acts. This standpoint undoubtedly influenced the decisions rendered by the Court under the EC Treaty.

4.2 Regulations *versus* Decisions: Basic Criteria of Distinction: Article 189 EC Treaty

The different types of Community legislation are contemplated in Article 189 EC Treaty.[30] Article 189(2) EC Treaty provides that 'a regulation shall

[23] In Case 8/55 *Fédéchar* v. *High Authority*, n,. 7 above, the applicants believed that the decision, albeit in appearance a general one, was an individual one in substance.

[24] The point had been already raised by Roemer A.G. in his Opinion on Joined Cases 7 and 9/54 *Groupement des Industries Sidérurgiques Luxemburgoises* v. *High Authority* [1954–56] ECR 175 at 211.

[25] Case 8/55, n. 7 above.

[26] *Ibid.*, 257. See also Joined Cases 1/57 and 14/57 *Société des Usines à Tubes de la Sarre* v. *High Authority* [1957–58] ECR 105 at 114.

[27] Recommendations are the ECSC Treaty equivalent of EC Dirs.

[28] Case 13/57 [1957–58] ECR 265.

[29] *Ibid.* 276. In Joined Cases 36–38, 40 and 41/58 *Simet, Meroni & Others* v. *High Authority* [1959] ECR 157 at 166, the Court expressed the same view in very similar terms.

[30] These are regs., dirs., decs., recommendations, and opinions (see 5 above).

have general application. It shall be binding in its entirety and directly applicable in all member States'. Regulations appear thus defined in the first place in Article 189 EC Treaty, with the characteristics of true legislative acts.

Quite extraordinarily, only three provisions in the European Community Treaty expressly provide for the use of regulations in their implementation.[31] Conversely, in a great number of areas the Community institutions have been given the option of enacting either regulations, directives, or decisions.[32] In truth, a great number of areas regulations have been used to implement the Treaty. In this respect a very important distinction must be made between Council regulations and some Commission regulations. Council regulations are instruments of great generality, geared to the achievement of uniformity[33] in areas where this element is essential, like the uniform organization of the market in agricultural products,[34] anti-dumping,[35] or competition proceedings.[36] In the case of Commission regulations, a distinction must be made between certain regulations which are clearly of a legislative character[37]—which resemble Council regulations—and other Commission regulations, which clearly resemble general administrative acts.[38]

The three characteristics of regulations, according to Article 189, are

[31] Thus, Art. 48(3)(d) EC Treaty provides that the Commission shall enact regs. to regulate the right of workers 'to remain in the territory of a Member State after having been employed in that State'; Art. 94 EC Treaty (as amended by the Maastricht Treaty) provides that the Council shall enact regs. 'for the application of Articles 92 and 93'; finally, Art. 209(a) EC Treaty (as amended by the Maastricht Treaty) establishes that the Council shall 'make financial regulations specifying in particular the procedure to be adopted for establishing and implementing the budget and for presenting and auditing accounts'. This contrasts with the numerous areas where the Treaty expressly provides for the use of dirs. and decs. See S. Weatherill and P. Beaumont, n. 9 above, 791–5.

[32] S. Weatherill and P. Beaumont, n. 9 above.

[33] Dirs., on the other hand, are used in areas where it is sufficient to obtain a degree of harmonization: for instance, recognition of diplomas from other Member States. See Council Dir. (89/48) on a general system for the recognition of higher education diplomas awarded on completion of professional education and training of at least three years' duration: [1989] OJ L19/6.

[34] See Reg. 23 of the Council on the progressive establishment of a common organization of the market in fruit and vegetables: JO 965/62 of 20 Apr. 1962; [1959–62] OJ Spec. Ed. 97, or Reg. 19 of the Council on the gradual establishment of a common organization of the market in cereals: JO 933/62 of 20 Apr. 1962.

[35] See, for instance, Reg. 2423/88 of the Council on protection against dumped or subsidized imports from countries not members of the EEC: [1988] OJ L209/1.

[36] See for instance, Reg. 17 of the Council implementing Arts. 85 and 86 of the Treaty: JO 204/62 of 21 Feb. 1962; [1952–62] OJ Spec. Ed. 87.

[37] See Reg. 1251/70: [1970] JO L242/27; [1970] OJ Spec. Ed. 402, adopted in implementation of Art. 48(3)(d) EC Treaty or, in the area of competition law, Reg. 27 on the form and content of applications and notifications: JO 1118/62 of 10 May 1962; [1959–62] OJ Spec. Ed. 132.

[38] See, for instance, Commission Reg. 1182/78 [1978] OJ L145/46, and Commission Reg. 1392/78 [1978] OJ L167/53, on standing invitations to tender to determine export refunds on sugar.

that they are acts: (a) of general application; (b) binding in their entirety; and (c) directly applicable in all Member States. The first characteristic marks the fundamental point of distinction between regulations and decisions, and is the feature upon which the case law has elaborated most.[39] Decisions are individual acts, whereas regulations are essentially normative acts that bind not only Community institutions but also Member States and individuals. The second characteristic distinguishes regulations from directives—which, although they are measures of general application, are only binding in the results to be achieved and leave to the national authorities the choice of form and methods. The third feature reflects a double point: first, regulations become part of national law without any need of acts of ratification or reception in the national legal order;[40] secondly, their scope of application extends to the entire territory of the Community.

Article 189(4) EC Treaty reads: 'A decision shall be binding in its entirely upon those to whom it is addressed.' A glance at this legal provision reveals the different qualities of decisions as opposed to regulations. In the first place, it is clear that they are acts of individual application. Although they are binding in their entirety, such an effect is limited to the addressees of the measures. Such addressees are, by definition, individually and directly concerned.

These notions seem clear enough as outlined in the EC Treaty, but in practice they are difficult to apply. The criterion of generality emerges as the core of the distinction. It is clear in some cases that regulations affect very broadly determined categories of people.[41] In other cases, however, regulations contain provisions of such degree of specification that they greatly resemble decisions.[42] Conversely, some decisions addressed to Member States have such a very wide field of application that one could assume that they have legislative character.[43]

The Court therefore found itself in the difficult position of trying to elaborate a test to ascertain the legal nature of the measures under consideration, with the criterion of generality as its only guiding star.[44]

[39] See 112–23 below.

[40] Case 39/72 *Commission* v. *Italy* [1973] ECR 101, at point 17.

[41] e.g. see the reg. at issue in Case 40/84 *Casteels* v. *Commission* [1985] ECR 667, 125 below.

[42] e.g. see the reg. at issue in Case 232/81 *Agricola Commerciale Olio* v. *Commission* [1984] ECR 3881, 145 below.

[43] e.g. see the dec. at issue in Case 1/64 *Glucoseries Réunies* v. *Commission* [1964] ECR 413, 000 above. In a case under the ECSC Treaty, Case 8/55 Fédéchar v. *High Authority*, n. 7 above, at 269, Lagrange A.G. had warned of the potential difficulty in applying these criteria to what he termed 'intermediate cases'—i.e. 'where a decision regulates a specific situation directly but without naming the persons to whom it refers'.

[44] Academic writers in this field have repeatedly pointed out the difficulty involved in formulating in clear terms the test of legal nature. Thus, S. Weatherill and P. Beaumont, n. 9 above, 201.

4.3 The Reasons behind the Exclusion of Regulations from the Scope of Challenge of Private Parties

What is the origin of the limitation contained in Article 173(2) EEC Treaty?[45] Regulations are a very powerful instrument of implementation of the Common Market policies contained in the EC Treaty; they are measures of general application and have a direct impact on the sphere of interests of Community citizens. The fact that they fall outside the possibilities of review by private applicants amounts to a serious limitation in the system of judicial protection available to natural and legal persons,[46] especially if the lack of democracy still informing the Community legislative process is borne in mind. Some very powerful reasons must have guided the authors of the Treaty to adopt this restrictive approach. In the absence of *travaux préparatoires* it is difficult to ascertain the real intention of the drafters of the Treaty. For enlightenment on this matter, it is necessary to look at the opinions of academic writers, some of whom participated in the negotiation of the Treaty of Rome.

The two reasons commonly suggested are: (a) the extreme consequences that stem from the annulment of regulations, which, especially in the early years of Community life, were adopted after laborious negotiations conducted by a Council tied to the rule of unanimity in a great variety of fields,[47] and (b) the quasi-legislative character of regulations, which are normally identified with 'Community laws'.[48]

[45] This limitation has been repeatedly confirmed by the ECJ. The Court said in Joined Cases 16–17/62 *Confédération Nationale des Producteurs de Fruits et Légumes* v. *Council*, n. 5 above, at 478: 'It follows that such a person [natural or legal person] is not entitled to make an application for annulment of regulations adopted by the Council or the Commission.' The academic writers have also emphasized this view. See amongst others M. Waelbroeck, J. V. Louis, J. L. Dewost, and G. Vandersanden, *Le Droit de la CEE* (Brussels, 1983), x, 104; A. Barav, 'The Judicial Power of the EEC' (1979–80) 53 *South. Cal. LR* 461, 471; M. Angulo and F. G. Dawson, 'Access by Natural and Legal Persons to the European Court of Justice' (1967) 36 *Univ. Cinc. LR* 583, 606; A. R. Freedman, 'The Right of Private Parties to Appeal "Acts" of the EEC' (1963–64) 3 *Vir. Int. LJ* 199, 203; A. G. Toth, 'The Individual and European Law' (1975) 24 *ICLQ* 659, 677, and R. Joliet, *Le Droit Institutionnel des Communautés Européennes* (Liège, 1981), 71.

[46] In this respect see the text of the Exeter Lecture in European Community Law given by Sir Gordon Slynn at the University of Exeter, Centre for European Legal Studies, on Friday, 10 May 1985, where he expressed the wish that private parties had more direct access to challenging acts of a legislative nature.

[47] Opinion of Lagrange A.G. in Joined Cases 16–17/62 *Confédération Nationale des Producteurs de Fruits et Légumes* v. *Council*, n. 5 above, at 486.

[48] *Ibid.* 486. Also J. V. Louis, *Les Réglements de la CEE* (Brussels, 1969), 121 and C. F. Ophüls in 'Les Réglements et les Directives dans les Traités de Rome' [1966] 1 *CDE* 3, 16. The same line of reasoning had been followed within the framework of the ECSC Treaty. Under that Treaty, private parties are entitled to challenge general decisions on the ground of misuse of powers (see 105 above). When the applicants in one case, Case 8/55 *Fédéchar* v. *High Authority*, n. 7 above, at 258, tried to put forward the submission that private parties ought to

It is suggested that these arguments could be at least partly refuted. In relation to the first argument, it may be said that, whilst it could hold true for early Council regulations, it does not for Commission regulations, whose procedures of adoption are rather different.[49] Moreover, the Single European Act introduced the qualified majority vote[50] as the usual method for passing legislative measures, a circumstance that considerably eases the rigours of the negotiation process.[51]

In relation to the second argument, it must be stressed that regulations have been treated only as legislative acts, forgetting that some Commission regulations may be truly general administrative measures[52] and that the latter type of measure is challengeable in the majority of national legal systems by natural and legal persons.[53] As early as 1965, one author[54] was aware of this problem and, to mitigate it and its repercussions in the judicial protection available to private parties, suggested that the Court

be able to allege *any* ground for illegality in order to contest general decisions, the Court explained for the first time the reasons behind the limited access of private applicants to challenge normative acts. Thus, the Court said 'there is nothing in the Treaty from which it may be concluded that private undertakings have been granted such a right to review the "constitutionality" of general decisions, that is, their conformity with the Treaty, since they are quasi-legislative measures adopted by a public authority with legislative effect *erga omnes*'. It appears from this quotation that, in the context of the ECSC Treaty, the reason for excluding general decisions from the range of measures challengeable by individuals, is that they are generally identified with legislative measures.

[49] Most of the legislative powers of the Commission have been conferred by delegation of the Council and apply to a number of areas, amongst them competition, common agricultural policy, etc. The Council issued a dec. (Dec. 87/373 [1987] OJ L197/33) regulating the three procedures for the Commission's exercise of powers delegated by the Council (Art. 2 of the Dec.). In all three procedures, the intervention of a committee of representatives of the Member States is provided for in order to ensure that the Commission's action does not contradict the will of the Member States. The *first procedure* (Procedure I) leaves a great margin of discretion to the Commission, and the committee has mainly an advisory role. The *second procedure* (Procedure II) has two variants and provides for a greater degree of control by the committee of the Commission's action and can only curb the Commission's powers if both the Council and the committee adopt an unfavourable opinion on the Commission's proposal. The *third procedure* (Procedure III) also has two variants and may impose much greater restraint on the Commission's powers, because unless the committee delivers a favourable opinion, the Commission must submit the proposal to the Council and the same process as if delegation had not been effected would take place. In consequence, only if the Commission is acting under Procedure II or especially Procedure III will the process for enacting a reg. be exposed to the same tensions between Member States as described above.

[50] Art. 148(2) EC Treaty, and Art. 189(b) and (c) as amended by the Maastricht Treaty.

[51] Unanimity has been confined to some certain areas of the Treaty: thus, see S. Weatherill and P. Beaumont, n. 9 above, at 69, n. 45.

[52] In this respect, see the problem caused as a result of the absence of a clear distinction in the Community legal system between legislative measures and general administrative acts: 5 above.

[53] See 5 above.

[54] N. Catalano in his intervention in 'La Fusion des Communautés Européennes', in *Colloquium organised in Liège on the 28, 29 and 30 April 1965* (The Hague, 1965), 284–5. For a similar line of thought see S. Neri, 'Le Recours en Annulation dans les Communautés Européennes: role et limites' [1967] *RMC* 452, 455. See also A. W. Green, *Political Integration by Jurisprudence* (Leyden, 1969), 110 and 112.

ought to make a distinction in each case between laws and general administrative measures, with the result that, in the first case, the measure would not be challengeable by private parties, whereas in the second it would, provided of course the tests of direct and individual concern were also satisfied. Two other authors[55] however expressed strong objections to this view, for two main reasons: first the clear wording of Article 173, which leaves no room for interpretation, and secondly, the danger of allowing the Court to determine its own jurisdiction.

It is argued that this second view is more in accordance with the principles of division of powers and legal certainty that must rule a democratic society such as the Community aims to be. It was for the authors of the EC Treaty to establish a clear criterion of distinction between the two types of acts and then for the Court to apply them. In the absence of any acknowledgement of the existence of two types of regulations, let alone guidance on the criterion of distinction between them from the drafters of the EC Treaty, the Court could do nothing but apply the wording of Article 173 EC Treaty, which clearly excludes all regulations from judicial review.

It has been explained already that Council regulations have a clear legislative character. The Single European Act, and recently the Maastricht Treaty, have increased the European Parliament's powers of participation in the legislative process in a number of areas.[56] If this trend continues, it could well be that in the future Council regulations will resemble national laws and that the voice of the peoples of Europe will always be heard in the elaboration of Community laws. Under these conditions, the consequences of excluding private applicants from the challenge of Council regulations would be mitigated.[57] Currently, however, this exclusion is not fully justified.

In relation to Commission regulations, it has been stressed that they can neither be true laws nor general administrative acts. In the first case, those regulations are adopted by procedures in which the democratic deficit is obvious.[58] In such circumstances, the fact that they are excluded from judicial review by natural and legal parties seems rather unfair. However, and since they are 'true laws', the solution could be to modify the procedures of their elaboration so that the Parliament could intervene more effectively. In the second case, the fact that regulations resembling general administrative acts are excluded from judicial review amounts to a gap in

[55] G. Rasquin and R. M. Chevallier, 'L'Article 173, Alinéa 2 du Traité CEE' [1966] 2 *RTDE* 31, 42.

[56] Although there are a number of areas where the Council may still adopt legislation without consulting the European Parliament, i.e. common commercial policy, certain aspects of agricultural policy, etc. For a comprehensive list see S. Weatherill and P. Beaumont, n. 9 above, at 796–7.

[57] In this sense it must be remembered that in national legal systems private parties can only challenge legislative acts in exceptional cases: see 30 above.

[58] See n. 49 above.

the system of judicial remedies provided by the European Community Treaties, especially in view of the solutions adopted by national legal systems. It is in relation to this latter type of regulation that the second reason traditionally advanced for excluding them from review is not valid.

4.4 General Area of Case Law

In this section, the two lines[59] of case law followed by the European Court in approaching the *locus standi* of private parties to challenge regulations, i.e. cases decided on the basis of the triple admissibility test and cases decided on the basis of the double admissibility test, will be analysed. Within the framework of the first group of cases, the test of legal nature will receive ample consideration. The tests of direct and individual concern have in both groups been given the same construction as they have been given in the case law concerning decisions,[60] and therefore they will be considered only briefly here.

4.4.1 Cases decided on the basis of a triple admissibility test: the impact of the test of legal nature

The present section aims to shed some light on the approach adopted by the European Court in those cases where the problem of the *locus standi* of private parties has been decided by taking as a starting point the existence of three tests. The problem is why the Court adopted an irregular approach in applying the *locus standi* tests even in cases decided on the basis of three admissibility tests. Thus, in some instances the non-fulfilment of the test of legal nature has automatically determined the inadmissibility of actions without it being necessary also to decide on the basis of the other two tests. In some few instances the tests of individual concern *or* of direct concern have been given some consideration, along with the test of legal nature. Finally in some instances all three tests have been considered and found satisfied.

Whilst academic writers have agreed that the severity of the test of legal nature determined the inadmissibility of most of the actions,[61] the uneven approach of the Court to the different cases has never been explained. In the present work the solution proposed is that it is possible to divide the case law of the Court into four blocks of decisions where common features

[59] See 103 above.

[60] Thus, see for the notion of individual concern Case 40/64 *Sgarlata* v. *Commission* [1965] ECR 215 at 226 and for direct concern Joined Cases 41–44/70 *International Fruit Company* v. *Commission* [1971] ECR 411, at point 15.

[61] Thus see T. C. Hartley, n. 9 above, 368 and S. Weatherill and P. Beaumont, n. 9 above, 199.

have been found. However, before going into the detail of this division it is important to study the guidelines laid down by five early decisions of the Court[62] which provided models for each group.

4.4.1.1 Early Decisions of the Court: The Principles of Application of the Admissibility Tests

In the first group of cases that came before the Court in the area of challenge of regulations by private parties, the Court set out the guidelines for the application of the test of legal nature. These cases were *Confédération Nationale des Producteurs de Fruits et Légumes* v. *Council*.[63] A French trade association brought annulment proceedings against a provision in a regulation on the progressive establishment of a common organization of the market in fruit and vegetables that provided for the immediate abolition of quantitative restrictions on imports of agricultural products and ordered Member States to dispense with recourse to the transitional measures provided by Article 44 EC Treaty.

The following points may be extracted from the ruling of the Court:

1. It was firmly established that pure regulations are excluded from the scope of challenge of private parties.[64]
2. The Court acknowledged, however, that a measure labelled as a regulation could be a decision in substance and that '[i]n examining this question, the Court cannot restrict itself to considering the official title of the measure, but must first take into account its object and content'.[65] That confirms the non-formalistic approach that the Court has adopted in other instances.[66]
3. The Court sketched the main features of decisions and regulations as follows:

> Under the terms of Article 189 of the EEC Treaty, a regulation shall have general application and shall be directly applicable in all the Member

[62] Joined Cases 16–17/62 *Confédération Nationale des Producteurs de Fruits et Légumes* v. *Council* n. 5 above, and Case 30/67 *Industria Molitoria Imolese* v. *Council* [1968] ECR 115, exemplify the first group of cases (see 125 below); Case 6/68 *Zuckerfabrik Watenstedt* v. *Council* [1968] ECR 409 provided guidance for the second group (see 127 below); Case 64/69 *La Compagnie Française Commerciale et Financière SA* v. *Commission*, n. 5 above, exemplify the third group (see 131 below) and Joined Cases 41–44/70 *International Fruit Company* v. *Commission* n. 60 above, the fourth group (see 137 below).

[63] See n. 62 above. See also the judgment of the Court in Joined Cases 19–22/62 *Fédération Nationale de la Boucherie en Gros des Viandes* v. *Council* [1962] ECR 491 in almost identical terms.

[64] *Ibid.* at 478, The Court rejected the argument of the applicants that the satisfaction of the tests of direct and individual concern should suffice to render an action admissible even if directed against a reg. For the Court it was necessary that the act was shown to be a decision.

[65] *Ibid.*

[66] See 19 above. See also Joined Cases 789–790/79 *Calpak* v. *Commission* [1980] ECR 1949, at point 7, where the Court said that 'the choice of form cannot change the nature of the measure'.

> States, whereas a decision shall be binding upon those to whom it is addressed. The criterion for distinction must be sought in the 'general application' or otherwise of the measure in question.
>
> The essential characteristics of a decision arise from *the limitation of persons to whom it is addressed* whereas a regulation, being essentially of a legislative nature, is *applicable, not to a limited number of persons, defined or identifiable, but to categories of persons viewed abstractly and in their entirety.*[67]

The Court emphasized that the main character of regulations was the fact that they are measures of general application. The Court explained such generality in terms of the circle of people affected. Regulations were aimed at categories of people viewed in the *abstract*, whereas decisions were addressed to a limited number of people defined or identifiable. This approach is very clear in cases where the regulations affect very wide categories of people but it leads to confusion when the regulations apply to small groups. Perhaps that is why the Court, in a later judgment, *Zuckerfabrik* v. *Council*,[68] where the contested regulation affected a small and easily ascertainable category of producers, explained that in that case the *abstract* character of a regulation referred to its aim rather than to the circle of persons addressed.[69]

It is to be noted that with this statement the Court brought together the tests of legal nature and of individual concern. As already shown, an applicant was individually concerned by a measure when his individual rights under Community law had been affected. The notion of individual concern was normally related to the existence of a closed category, i.e. a category of people fixed and ascertained before the measure entered into force.[70] Therefore applicants individually concerned by a measure were elevated in many cases to a class of *de facto* addressees. This probably explains the statement of the Court that followed: 'in order to determine in doubtful cases whether one is concerned with a decision or a regulation, it is necessary to ascertain whether the measure is of individual concern to specific individuals'.[71]

Therefore it could have been concluded from this case that once the test of individual concern is fulfilled, the measure automatically becomes a decision.[72] This view introduced a degree of confusion between the two

[67] Joined Cases 16–17/62, n. 5 above, at 478, emphasis added. See also the statement of the Court in *Wirtschaftsvereinigung Eisen- und Stahlindustrie* v. *High Authority*, n. 28 above.

[68] Case 6/68, n. 62 above.

[69] See 117 below.

[70] See 51 ff. above.

[71] Joined Cases 16–17/62, n. 5 above, at 478.

[72] This was also the understanding that Roemer A.G. had of this case, as appears from his Opinion in Case 30/67 *Industria Molitoria Imolese* v. *Council*, n. 62 above, at 123–4). It is perhaps useful to recall in this context the case law under the ECSC Treaty. In Case 3/54 *Assider* v. *High Authority*, n. 22 above, at 256, the Court had explained that 'the question whether a decision is individual or general in nature must be decided on the basis of objective criteria'. In the cases that followed and in order to ascertain the nature of the measures at issue,

tests but was rectified by the Court in later cases, where the Court established a clear distinction between the two tests.[73]

4. Finally, the Court formulated the view that some provisions of a regulation could have the character of a decision without affecting the overall classification of the measure as a regulation. The Court said:

> [I]f a measure entitled by its author a regulation contains provisions which are capable of being not only of direct but also of individual concern to certain natural or legal persons, it must be admitted, without prejudice to the question whether that measure considered in its entirety can be correctly called a regulation, that in any case, those provisions *do not have the character of a regulation* and may be impugned by those persons under the terms of the second paragraph of Article 173.[74]

This statement does not settle the question of whether the same provision in a regulation could have the character of a decision in relation to a group of people and at the same time have the character of a regulation in relation to the rest of those affected. One author[75] believed that this was the case, and that the Court was really acknowledging that 'hybrid regulations'[76] do exist. This idea also appeared in the Opinions of the Advocates General.[77] However, the concept was conclusively dismissed by the Court in *Moksel* v. *Commission* where the Court said 'a single provision cannot at one and the same time have the character of a measure of general application and of an individual measure'.[78] From recent judgments, it

the Court looked at the terms in which the decision was drafted and, at the content and purpose of the measure. Thus, see Case 18/57 *Nold* v. *High Authority* [1959] ECR 51 at 50 and Joined Cases 36–38, 40 and 41/58 *Simet, Meroni & others* v. *High Authority*, n. 29 above, at 156. In a case decided after the ruling in Joined Cases 16–17/62 *Confédération Nationale des Producteurs de Fruits et Légumes* v. *Council*, n. 5 above, the Court, obviously influenced by this last decision, ruled that '[i]n order to ascertain whether a decision of the High Authority is general or individual, its content must in particular be examined to establish whether its provisions are likely to affect directly and individually the situations of the persons to whom they apply': Joined Cases 55–59/63 *Modena* v. *High Authority* [1964] ECR 211 at 228.

[73] See Case 6/68 *Zuckerfabrik Watenstedt* v. *Council*, see n. 62 above, and described at 117 below.

[74] Joined Cases 16–17/62, n. 5 above, at 479, emphasis added. Also see Case 30/67 *Industria Molitoria Imolese* v. *Council*, n. 62 above, at 121.

[75] See K. A. Parkinson, 'Admissibility of Direct Actions by Natural and Legal Persons in the European Court of Justice: Judicial Distinctions between Regulations and Decisions' (1989) 24 *Tex. Int. LJ* 433, 449.

[76] In the sense that the same provision could have a dual nature.

[77] See Opinion of Warner A.G. in the *Japanese Ball Bearing cases* (Cases 113 and 118–121/77 [1979] ECR 1185 at 1246) and of Da Cruz Vilaça in Case 333/85 *Mannesmann-Röhrenwerke* v. *Council*, n. 10 above, at 1391.

[78] Case 45/81 [1982] ECR 1129, at point 18. In the context of the ECSC Treaty, a similar result had been achieved. Thus Case 3/54 *Assider* v. *High Authority*, n. 22 above, at 269. Lagrange A.G. suggested that a general decision could be, in respect of certain people, an individual decision. The Court remained silent in that case, but in a later case, the Court affirmed that '[a]lthough the Treaty is silent in this matter, a decision which is individual in character in relation to the undertakings to which is directed cannot be at the same time

seems clear that the Court has no difficulty in concluding that a particular provision in a regulation may lose its regulatory character and become a (series) of decision(s) although the rest of the measure remains a regulation.[79]

The Court applied those principles to *Confédération Nationale des Producteurs de Fruits et Légumes*. First, the Court looked at the *content* of the provision and decided that it 'involved immediate legal consequences in all Member States for categories of persons viewed in a general and abstract manner',[80] in that it eliminated the restrictions on the freedom of traders to export or import within the Community, ordering the Member States to dispense with transitional measures. Secondly, the Court went on to consider whether the provision was of *individual concern* to the applicants. It must be stressed that when these cases were decided, the Court had not yet formulated the *Plaumann* test.[81] The Court decided that the measure was not of individual concern to the applicants in the short term.[82] The application was dismissed as inadmissible without the test of direct concern being considered.

In *Industria Molitoria Imolese* v. *Council*,[83] the applicants—milling undertakings in the provinces of Bologna and Ancona—instituted proceedings for the annulment of two provisions in a Council regulation that fixed the prices and principal marketing centres for cereals for the 1967–8 marketing year. In the applicants' view, the provisions fixed the intervention prices for common wheat for the regions of Bologna and Ancona at too high a level.

The Court followed the guidelines set by *Confédération Nationale des Producteurs de Fruits et Légumes*. It expressed the need to deal first with the test of legal nature.[84] Amongst the elements determining the true nature of the measure, the Court took into consideration the *purpose* of the regulation[85] and the *framework* within which the regulation had been enacted.[86] The contested regulation had been issued on the basis of a Council regulation on the creation of a single market in cereals which provided 'with a view in particular to stabilising markets and guaranteeing the free movement of cereals within the Community . . . for the fixing of derived intervention prices'.[87] The Court concluded that the system put in

regarded as a general decision in relation to third parties': Case 18/57 *Nold* v. *High Authority*, n. 72 above, at 50.

[79] See Case C–354/87 *Weddel* v. *Commission* [1990] ECR I–3847.

[80] Joined Cases 16–17/62, n. 5 above, at 478.

[81] See 46 above.

[82] The Court said that the applicants were concerned by the provision 'in the same way as all other agricultural producers of the Community': Joined Cases 16–17/62, n. 5 above, at 475, but did not elaborate *why* that was so.

[83] Case 30/67, n. 62 above.

[84] 'It is accordingly necessary to ascertain . . . the true legal nature of the measure entitled Regulation No 128/67 and more particularly of Articles 2 and 3 of that regulation: *ibid.* 120.

[85] *Ibid.*

[86] *Ibid.*

[87] *Ibid.*

place by the earlier Council regulation was necessary to ensure the establishment of a single market in cereals and that the contested regulation *was part* of that system by fixing the derived intervention prices for the marketing year 1967–8. The fact that the regulation was part of a group of measures which were undoubtedly of general application meant that it, too, was of a general character.[88] The Court considered briefly the test of individual concern but found that it was not fulfilled, on the ground that the applicants were not sufficiently individualized. The application was dismissed as inadmissible.

A landmark case was *Zuckerfabrik Watenstedt* v. *Council*,[89] In that case, a manufacturer of raw beet sugar felt aggrieved by a provision in a Council regulation that established discriminatory rules for raw beet sugar producers in relation to white and cane sugar producers, and brought annulment proceedings against the measure. *Zuckerfabric* claimed that it had *locus standi* as it was a member of a very small and ascertainable class of producers and that consequently, although the contested measure had been adopted in the form of a regulation, it nevertheless constituted a decision affecting a well-defined group of people, amongst them the applicant.[90]

The Court began by considering the legal nature of the measure and delivered the following statement:

> [A] measure does not lose its character as a regulation simply because it may be possible to ascertain *with greater or lesser degree of accuracy the number or even the identity of persons to which it applies at any given time as long as there is no doubt that the measure is applicable as the result of an objective situation of law or fact* which it specifies and which is in harmony with its ultimate objective. Furthermore, the fact that a legal provision may have *different practical effects on the different persons to whom it applies in no way contradicts its nature as a regulation* provided that the situation to which it refers is objectively determined.[91]

Two major points deserve careful consideration:

1. On the one hand the Court further clarified the *abstract* character of regulations. In *Confédération Nationale des Producteurs de Fruits et Légumes*[92] the main gist of the distinction between regulations and decisions was whether the measures referred to abstract or defined

[88] In later cases the Court followed a very similar trend. Thus, in Case 6/68 *Zuckerfabrik Watenstedt* v. *Council*, n. 62 above, at 415, the Court said that a provision that abrogates a provision of general application or places a time-limit on its application partakes of the general nature of the earlier provision: in Case 64/69 *La Compagnie Française Commerciale et Financière SA* v. *Commission*, n. 5 above, at point 12, the Court found that transitional measures assume the general character of the measure into which they are inserted. Likewise, in Joined Cases 103–109/78 *Société des Usines de Beauport* v. *Council* [1979] ECR 17, at point 19, the Court understood that a reg. introducing a clause derogating from the provisions of an earlier reg. participates in the general character of that regulation.

[89] Case 6/68, n. 62 above.

[90] *Ibid.* 413. As Roemer A.G. explained, the group of producers was not likely to increase in the near future (*ibid.* 420).

[91] *Ibid.* 415, emphasis added.

[92] See 114 above.

categories of people. That approach is clear when regulations are of a clear legislative nature and affect very large categories, i.e. all agricultural producers in the Community, but not when the regulations affect small groups. In a case like *Zuckerfabrik*, such a view would imply that, since the class of people affected is easily ascertainable, the measure is no longer a regulation but a decision. That is why the Court made clear that, in cases where the regulation affects a small group of people, it is irrelevant that the group of people potentially affected is practically defined before the measure enters into force, provided that the aim of the measure is to deal with an *objective situation of fact or law* that takes place, generally in the area of general management of the market.[93] In other words, it is the object of a regulation that determines its abstract character, not the circle of people affected by it. The new view of the Court was welcomed by academic writers[94] and remains firmly established in later case law.[95]

It is suggested that the argument of the Court is very sound. It would be quite unjust that in those cases—like the present one—where the measure affects a category with very few members, the applicant would be able to show straight away that the measure is a decision, by-passing all the difficulties of the test of legal nature which he would have had to confront if the measure affected a wide category of people. For instance, the facts in *Confédération Nationale des Producteurs de Fruits et Légumes* and in *Zuckerfabrik* were very similar. In both cases, the applicants were trying to challenge regulations (about the common organization of vegetables in the first case, and of sugar in the second case). In the first case, however, the applicants belonged to a very large class of people affected—all the agricultural producers in the Community. In the second, the applicants were part of a very small class not likely to increase. This purely accidental fact should not influence the views of the Court on *locus standi*.

2. On the other hand, the Court drew a clear distinction between the tests of legal nature and individual concern which the decision of the Court in *Confédération Nationale des Producteurs de Fruits et Légumes* had assimilated to the point of making them interchangeable.[96]

[93] In other areas, like cases concerning anti-dumping regs., the test of legal nature was ignored from early stages and therefore these problems never arose: see 155 ff. below.

[94] See R. Kovar, 'Chronique de la Jurisprudence de la Cour de Justice des Communautés Européennes. 11 juillet 1968. Affaire 6–68. *Zuckerfabrik* v. '*Conseil*' (1969) 96 *JDI* 455, 457.

[95] See Case 64/69 *La Compagnie Française Commerciale et Financière SA* v. *Commission*, see n. 5 above, at point 11; Case 101/76 *Koninklijke Scholten Honig* v. *Council* [1977] ECR 797, at point 23; Joined Cases 789–790/7 *Calpak* v. *Commission*, n. 66 above, at point 9, and Case 45/81 *Moksel* v. *Commission*, n. 78 above, at point 17.

[96] See n. 71 above, and accompanying text.

It has already been seen[97] that the case law showed that an applicant is individually concerned by a Community measure when, prior to the enactment of the measure, it took a course of action, i.e. an application for licences, to which certain individual rights had been attached.[98] In this sense, the applicants belonged to a closed category. The contested decision affected these rights,[99] and on this basis, the applicants were granted *locus standi*.

In *Zuckerfabrik* the Court said that even if a measure produces different practical effects on different parties, it may still be a regulation. To be individually concerned by a measure an applicant needs to prove that he is affected differently from the rest of the people generally affected. The Court's *dictum* in this case amounted to saying that, even in cases where the applicants belonged to a closed category and were individually concerned, the measure could still be a regulation.[100]

The difference between this approach and the one in *Confédération Nationale des Producteurs de Fruits et Légumes* is notable. In those cases, the Court had said that the fulfilment of the test of individual concern implied the fulfilment of the test of legal nature.[101] In *Zuckerfabrik*, it became clear that even when applicants are individually concerned by a regulation, the measure can still be a regulation in nature. A measure is a regulation when its aim is to deal with an objective situation in the market, quite independently of whether there is a group of people especially affected by it. The fulfilment of the test of legal nature is extremely difficult to obtain, as will be shown later on.[102] In *Zuckerfabrik* the question of individual concern was not considered,[103] but it is believed that the applicant was not individually concerned since he did not enjoy any individual rights under EC law that the regulation had affected. In the case law that followed, however, there were instances where the applicants

[97] See 51 ff. above.

[98] e.g. in Joined Cases 106–107/63 *Toepfer* v. *Commission* [1965] ECR 405, see 48 above, the applicants had applied for import licences and, on the basis of the measures in force, they had the right to import at a zero rate of levy. Likewise, in Case 11/82 *Piraiki-Patraiki* [1985] ECR 207, see 54 above, the applicants had entered into export agreements before the enactment of the contested decision, a circumstance that gave them the right to claim the protection afforded to traders in that situation by the Act of Accession before any protective measures were taken.

[99] In *Toepfer*, the applicants could not import at a zero rate of levy and in *Piraiki-Patraiki*, protective measures were adopted without taking into consideration the situation of traders who had entered into export agreements.

[100] In this sense, see the italicized words of the *Zuckerfabric dictum* (see n. 91 above).

[101] See n. 71 above. This view has not been repeated in cases since *Zuckerfabrik*.

[102] See Joined Cases 41–44/70 *International Fruit Company* v. *Commission*, n. 60 above and 121 below, for a résumé of the judgment.

[103] The Court considered only the test of legal nature, and took into account the *content* of the reg., and the *framework* in which it had been enacted.

were individually concerned, yet the Court dismissed their application on the ground that the measure was a true regulation.[104]

La Compagnie Française Commerciale et Financière v. *Commission*[105] involved a Commission regulation enacting measures of conjunctural policy as a result of the devaluation of the French franc. The Commission regulation was enacted in implementation of a Council regulation of 11 August 1969 which provided that France should, for a limited period, grant import subsidies and levy compensatory amounts on exports. The contested provision in the Commission regulation retroactively reduced the compensatory amounts charged on exports for export agreements concluded before 11 August 1969.[106] This possibility, however, could only avail the exporters if they had requested advance refunds. The applicants had concluded export agreements before 11 August but had not applied for advance refunds. The applicants brought annulment proceedings and argued that it was wrong to penalize them by excluding them from the application of transitional measures on the ground that they did not make use of a procedure that was purely optional, by applying for an advance refund.

The Court decided the case only on the basis of the non-fulfilment of the test of legal nature. Following its traditional line, it looked into the *framework* within which the regulation had been issued;[107] thus the measure was adopted to implement a Council regulation and was part of a group of provisions intended to adjust the functioning of the intervention mechanisms of the common organization of agricultural markets. It then looked at the *purpose* of the basic Council regulation[108] and of the contested provisions.[109] All these measures were of general application. The Court reached the conclusion that the provisions at issue, even though of a transitional nature, partook of the general nature of the measure that they sought to reconcile with earlier measures of equally general character.[110]

The Court decided the case on the basis that the provision at issue was of a regulatory nature. But were the applicants individually concerned? One author believed that they were,[111] since they belonged to a closed category. It is suggested, however, that this is not such a clear conclusion.

[104] See Joined Cases 103–109/78 *Société des Usines de Beauport* v. *Council*, n. 88 above.

[105] Case 64/69, n. 5 above.

[106] The measure was a wholly retroactive reg. that applied to a closed category of people, i.e. those exporters that concluded export agreements before 11 Aug. 1969.

[107] Case 64/69, n. 5 above, at point 4.

[108] *Ibid.*, at point 5.

[109] *Ibid.*, at point 6.

[110] The Court said, '[t]he fact that a transitional provision is applicable only to certain situations arising before a date fixed by it and therefore, often established before it comes into force, does not prevent that provision from being an integral part of the former and new provisions which it is designed to reconcile and, consequently, from partaking of their general nature' *ibid.*, at point 12.

[111] T. C. Hartley, n. 9 above, 370–1.

What is unusual in this case is the existence of two closed categories: first, the category of traders that had entered into export agreements before 11 August—to which the applicants belonged—and, secondly, within that category, the group of traders that had applied for advance fixed refunds, to which the applicants did not belong. The applicants did not contest the obligation imposed on them to pay compensatory amounts—which did not exist at the time they entered into agreements—but the fact that, *because* they had not applied for advance fixed refunds, they did not have the right to obtain a reduction in the amount to be paid. The applicants had not taken the course of action—i.e. application for advance fixed refunds—to become necessary holders of the right to obtain a reduction in the compensatory amounts they had to pay. Had they applied for advance fixed refunds, they would have been individually concerned by the aforesaid provisions.[112] Admittedly, this solution is not very fair, in so far as the Commission could have imposed such a condition—application for an advanced fixed refund—deliberately in order to avoid applications from a determined group of traders, but it is believed to be the one stemming from the application of the principles of *locus standi* set out by the Court.

International Fruit Company v. *Commission*[113] was one of the small group of cases where the test of legal nature was found to be fulfilled. These cases concerned the annulment of a provision in a regulation enacted within the framework of a series of regulations introducing protective measures taken with the object of limiting the import of dessert apples from non-member states. The aforementioned regulations provided that the importers should make applications for licences to the national authorities, which would inform the Commission, which in its turn would enact a regulation at the end of each week deciding the number of licences that would be granted. The applicants had been refused licences by the contested regulation and brought annulment proceedings against this measure.

The Court began by explaining the need to deal with the tests of direct and individual concern,[114] but in truth it also considered the nature of the measure. The Court said that at the time the Commission enacted the contested regulation the number of applications for licences was fixed,[115] or in other words that the regulation had retroactive character and affected a closed category of people. Then the Court stated that when the Commission enacted the regulation it 'decided, even though it took account *only of the quantities requested*, on the subsequent fate of each application which had been lodged'.[116] The Court concluded that:

Accordingly, Article 1 of Regulation N° 983/70 is not a provision of general application within the meaning of the second paragraph of Article 189 of the

[112] This explanation finds support in a later case: Case 100/74 *Cam* v. *Commission* [1975] ECR 1393, which involved very similar facts (see 143 below, for a résumé of the judgment).

[113] Joined Cases 41–44/70, n. 60 above.

[114] *Ibid.*, at point 15.

[115] *Ibid.*, at points 17–18.

[116] *Ibid.*, at point 20, emphasis added.

Treaty, but it must be regarded as *a conglomeration of individual decisions taken by the Commission under the guise of a regulation pursuant to Article 2(2) of Regulation N° 459/70, each of which decisions affects the legal position of each author of an application for a licence.*

Thus, the decisions are of individual concern to the applicants.[117]

The Court therefore found the test of legal nature fulfilled, in that the provision in the regulation was in truth a series of decisions and the test of individual concern was found to be satisfied automatically. The applicants were also found to be directly concerned according to the same criteria as those applied in the case law concerning decisions.[118]

Two points raise issues for discussion:

1. It appears from this case, that, in order to find the test of legal nature fulfilled, a causal link must exist between the measure at issue and the situation of the applicants.[119] In other words, it must be clear from the content of the regulation or of the provision in the regulation that it was enacted not to meet an objective situation in the market but to decide on the situation of a fixed group of people to which the applicants belong.[120] This is a circumstance extremely difficult to prove, and one that only appears in cases that involve extraordinary facts, like the present ones[121] or in cases where the applicants are named in the regulation.[122] In the present cases the Commission took into account the applications submitted and *then* decided, on the basis of an objective element—the quantities requested—which traders should be granted licences and which ones should not be granted them. Such a provision is clearly not one of

[117] Joined Cases 41–44/70, n. 60 above, at points 21–22, emphasis added.

[118] The Court said: 'Article 1(2) of Regulation N°459/70 . . . makes it clear that the national authorities do not enjoy any discretion in the matter of the issue of licences and the conditions on which applications for the parties concerned should be granted': *ibid.*, at point 25.

[119] Note the difference in the case of the notion of direct concern, which relates to the existence of a direct causal link between the measure and the *damage* caused to the interest of the applicants: see 63 ff. above.

[120] This view was recorded in very clear terms by Tesauro A.G. in his Opinion in Case C–244/88 *Usines Coopératives de déshydratation du Vexin* v. *Commission* [1989] ECR 3811 at 3824, where he said, referring to the present case, that '[i]n that case, not only . . . did the measure adopted by the Commission . . . relate to a specific and closed circle of traders but, what is more important, the import licences applications submitted by them . . . were the essential element taken into consideration by the Commission in defining the scope of the precautionary measures to be adopted. In those circumstances, therefore, there was a causal link between the applications for import licences submitted and the precautionary measure.' See also the Opinion of Da Cruz Vilaça A.G. in Case 333/85 *Mannesmann-Röhrenwerke* v. *Council* [1987] ECR 1381 at 1396. See also G. Vandersanden and A. Barav, *Contentieux Communautaire* (Brussels, 1977), 172.

[121] So far only one other case has presented a similar set of facts. See Case C–354/87 *Weddel* v. *Commission*, n. 79 above.

[122] See Case 138/79 *Roquette Frères* v. *Council* [1980] ECR 3333 and Case 139/79 *Maizena* v. *Council* [1980] ECR 3393.

general but of individual application. The test of legal nature would thus appear to be a detector of situations where the Community Institutions could be guilty of a misuse of powers, or rather a misuse of procedure.[123]

2. The test of individual concern was automatically fulfilled after the finding that the provision was a bundle of decisions. This is a logical outcome, for nobody can be more individually concerned by a measure than its addressee. The judgment of the Court in *Confédération Nationale des Producteurs de Fruits et Légumes*[124] had suggested that, in cases where the distinction between regulations and decisions was not clear, the fulfilment of the test of individual concern would mean that the measure would be a decision. The ruling in *Zuckerfabrik* made plain that this is not the case.[125] Finally, the decision of the Court in *International Fruit Company* shows that what is true is that the fulfilment of the test of legal nature will always mean the fulfilment of the tests of individual and direct concern.

The logical conclusion, therefore, is that the test of legal nature is much more stringent than the combined effect of the tests of direct and individual concern, in that it seeks to identify real addressees—who always have *locus standi*—and not parties particularly affected by a measure.

This distinction, at first sight complicated, is easily explained with an example. In *Cam* v. *Commission*,[126] a case decided on the basis of the double admissibility test, the applicants were declared directly and individually concerned by the regulation at issue, without any separate finding that the measure was a decision and not a regulation. Had the Court applied the test of legal nature, the action would most probably have been dismissed as inadmissible.

The case law that has followed these early decisions has conformed to the main lines of thought they represent. The Court's judgments on *locus standi* can be classified in four main categories. These four categories can be further grouped into two main divisions, according to whether the applicants belonged to open or closed categories. The division presented in this work depends on whether the regulations at issue affect wide, small, or closed categories of people.

[123] The existence of a misuse of procedure would be clear in those cases, since the Community institutions would be using the form of a regulation for an act that in reality should have adopted the form of a series of decisions. The presence of misuse of powers is more difficult to establish, since it requires the proof of a subjective element, i.e. that the measure at issue has been enacted for purposes other than those stated: see Joined Cases 18 and 35/65 *Gutmann* v. *Commission* [1966] ECR 103 at 117 and T. C. Hartley, n. 9 above, 433–6.

[124] See 113 ff. above.

[125] See 117 ff. above.

[126] Case 100/74, n. 112 above.

A. Applicants belonging to Open Categories

1. The first group of cases comprises those where the regulations at issue are clearly acts of a general nature and where the applicants normally belong to very large groups of people affected by the measures. These cases[127] partly followed the approach of the Court in the *Confédération Nationale des Producteurs de Fruits et Légumes* and *Industria Molitoria Imolese*[128] cases.

2. The second group of decisions refers to those cases where the regulations affect small categories easily ascertainable—i.e. by reason for the specific activity they carry out—to which the applicants belong but which were not fixed when the measures were enacted. These cases[129] were modelled on the *Zuckerfabrik* decision.[130]

B. Applicants belonging to Closed Categories

3. The third group encompasses those cases where the regulations at issue apply, either in their entirety[131] or partly[132] to closed categories of people and where the applicants belong to those closed categories. These cases followed the guidelines laid down by the Court in *La Compagnie Française Commerciale et Financière.*[133]

4. The fourth group of cases comprises those where the regulations at issue apply exclusively to those closed categories and there is a clear causal link between the measures and the situation of the applicants (who are members of that closed category). These cases[134] followed in the footsteps of the Court's ruling in *International Fruit Company.*[135]

These categories of cases will be considered in turn in the following pages.

[127] Case 40/84 *Casteels* v. *Commission*, n. 41 above; Case 117/86 *Union de Federaciones Agrarias de España (UFADE)* v. *Council and Commission* [1986] ECR 3255; Case 191/87 *Cooperativa Veneta Allevatori Equini (COVALE)* v. *Commission* [1988] ECR 515; and *Gibraltar Airport cases* (n. 15 above).

[128] See 113–17 above.

[129] Case 101/76 *Koninklijke Scholten Honig* v *Council and Commission*, n. 95 above; Case 147/83 *Binderer* v. *Commission* [1985] ECR 257; Case 26/86 *Deutz und Geldermann* v. *Council* [1987] ECR 941; Joined Cases 97, 193, 99 and 215/86 *Asteris* v. *Commission* [1988] ECR 2181; Joined Cases C–15/91 and C–108/91 *Bulck* v. *Commission*, n. 15 above.

[130] See 117 above.

[131] Joined Cases 103 to 109/78 *Société des Usines de Beauport* v. *Council*, n. 88 above.

[132] Case 162/78 *Wagner* v. *Commission* [1979] ECR 3467; Case 45/81 *Moksel* v. *Commission*, n. 78 above; Case C–244/88 *Usines Coopérative de Déshydratation du Vexin* v. *Commission*, n. 120 above; Case C–229/88 *Cargill* v. *Commission* [1990] ECR I–1303.

[133] See 120 above.

[134] Case C–354/87 *Weddel* v. *Commission,* n. 79 above; Case 138/79 *Roquette Frères* v. *Council*, n. 122 above; and Case 139/79 *Maizena* v. *Council*, n. 122 above.

[135] See 121 above.

4.4.1.2 Cases Involving Regulations Affecting Open Categories (Large Groups)

In these cases, the regulations at issue are at first sight measures of general application. They set out legislative principles which apply to any private party falling within their scope of application in any Member State. As a rule, they apply to wide categories of people. The approach of the Court in these cases has been to state briefly that the act is a general legislative measure—and therefore non-challengeable by private parties—without analysing further the content of the measure, given that it is apparent that it affects categories of people viewed generally and in the abstract. In this respect these decisions resemble the Court's approach in *Confédération Nationale*. The difference between those and this earlier ruling is that the Court has not discussed whether the applicants have been individually concerned but, from the fact that the measure is a true regulation, it has followed automatically that the applicants are not individually concerned. The Court was most probably acting in accordance with the principle of economy in the judicial reasoning given that in all these cases it is suggested that the applicants were not individually concerned.

Several decisions of the Court illustrate this line of thought. Thus, in *Casteels* v. *Commission*,[136] a French importer of windscreen wipers and parts of windscreen wipers into the Community challenged a Commission regulation intended to determine the tariff classification of those products. In *Unión de Federaciones Agrarias de España (UFADE)* v. *Council and Commission*,[137] a Spanish association of agricultural producers brought an action directed against a Council regulation laying down general rules for the application of the supplement mechanism applicable to trade and an implementing Commission regulation. In both cases, the Court did not examine in detail the content of the regulations, but only emphasized that they were clearly acts of a general nature, and therefore, the applicants could not be individually concerned.[138]

Finally, *Cooperativa Veneta Allevatori Equini (COVALE)* v. *Commission*,[139] is another example. In this case, three co-operative societies brought annulment proceedings against a provision in a Commission regulation that laid down rules for the importation of male bovine animals for fattening. According to former regulations in this area, in order to be able to import such animals without paying a levy, security had to be lodged and the competent authorities had to be informed at which production unit the animals were to be fattened. The contested regulation provided

[136] Case 40/84, n. 4 above.
[137] Case 117/86, n. 127 above.
[138] Case 40/84, n. 4 above, at point 10, and Case 117/86, n. 127 above, at points 9–11.
[139] Case 191/87, n. 127 above.

that any delay in performing these obligations would lead to the forfeiture of 15 per cent of the security and for a further reduction of 20 per cent of the remaining amount for each day by which the time-limit was exceeded. The applicants, who had been late in fulfilling the second obligation, alleged that the regulation infringed the principle of proportionality,[140] in that the latter was just a secondary obligation to the principal one—i.e. the lodging of a security. The Court simply dismissed the action on the ground that the regulation was a truly normative measure.[141]

In this case, it was clear that the measure was a general one. Furthermore, and although the Court did not tackle this issue, it was clear the applicants were not individually concerned. There was nothing in their position that could make them different from the rest of the traders affected by the regulation. However, the result of applying strict *locus standi* conditions was that the Court did not investigate a possible serious infringement of a general principle of law.[142]

In a group of very recent judgments, the *Gibraltar Airport* cases,[143] the Court decided the *locus standi* of the applicants according to the guidelines set out in this section. In these cases, the Government of Gibraltar and the Gibraltar Development Corporation (owner of the civil terminal of Gibraltar airport) brought annulment proceedings against a common provision in four Council regulations. Two of these regulations concerned access by air-carriers to scheduled intra-Community air services;[144] one regulation concerned the operation of air cargo services between the Member States;[145] and one regulation concerned the allocation of slots at Community airports.[146] All four regulations contained a provision that suspended the application of the regulation in relation to Gibraltar airport until the arrangements of the Joint Declaration made between Spain and the United Kingdom on 2 December 1987 came into operation.[147] The Council objected to the admissibility of the action on the ground that the applicants were not directly and individually concerned. The Court dismissed the actions as inadmissible on the grounds that the regulations at issue were of a general character, and therefore the provisions that introduced a suspen-

[140] The principle of proportionality is one of the general principles of law in the European Community. See Case 9/73 *Schülter* v. *Hauptzollamt-Lörrach* [1977] ECR 1135, at point 22.

[141] *Ibid.*, at point 10.

[142] See also Case 55/86 *ARPOSOL* v. *Council* [1988] ECR 13. See 146 below.

[143] N. 15 above.

[144] Thus Reg. 2423/90 [1990] OJ L217/8 was at issue in Case C–336/90 *Gibraltar Development* v. *Council*, n. 15 above, and Reg. 2408/90 [1992] OJ L240/80 was at issue in Case C–397/92 *Gibraltar and Gibraltar Development* v. *Council*, n. 15 above.

[145] Reg. 294/91 [1991] OJ L36/1 was at issue in Case C–128/91 *Gibraltar and Gibraltar Development* v. *Council*, n. 15 above.

[146] Thus Reg. 95/93 [1993] OJ L14/1 was at issue in Case C–168/93 *Gibraltar and Gibraltar Development* v. *Council*, n. 15 above.

[147] Art. 1(3) of Reg. 2423/90, n. 144 above; Art. 1(3) of Reg. 2408/90, n. 144 above; Art. 1(3) of Reg. 294/91, n. 145 above; and Art. 1(3) of Reg. 95/93, n. 146 above.

sion in the application of such regulation partook of that general character. In consequence, the applicants were denied *locus standi*, without any consideration being given to the tests of direct and individual concern.[148] The regulation applied to a very wide category, i.e. all air traders that might wish to operate a service between a Community airport and Gibraltar airport. This is one of the few cases decided after 1990 where the Court applied the triple admissibility test to decide the *locus standi* issue. It must not be forgotten, however, that political issues (i.e. the long-standing dispute between Spain and the United Kingdom over the sovereignty of Gibraltar) underlined the facts of these cases and that the challenge of the regulations at issue was something politically undesirable.

4.4.1.3 Cases Involving Regulations Affecting Open Categories (Small Groups)

The regulations at issue in these cases have in common that they affect small categories of people—easily ascertainable and not likely to increase after the regulations enter into force—to which the applicants belonged but which were not fixed when the regulation was issued. In such cases, it is much more difficult to ascertain the real nature of that measure given that the Community institution concerned might be using the form of a regulation to cover real decisions addressed to the members of that group. That may be why the Court in these cases discussed at length the nature of the regulations under consideration—unlike in the cases belonging to the first category—mainly looking at the *content* of the regulations and at the *framework* in which they were enacted. In recent cases belonging to this group it seems that the Court has also analysed the test of individual concern.

In *Koninklijke Scholten Honig* v. *Council and Commission*[149] a producer of glucose with a high fructose content brought annulment proceedings against a Council regulation and an implementing Commission regulation that had reduced the amount of production refund for starch used in the manufacture of glucose. The applicants believed that the measures were in truth a series of decisions, in that the producers of glucose with high fructose content were in reality a very small group not likely to increase.[150] The Court dismissed the action as inadmissible on the grounds that the measures were true regulations. However, to reach this conclusion it analysed at length the *framework* within which the regulations were

[148] Thus see Case C–336/90, n. 15 above, at points 16–19; Case C–397/92, n. 15 above, at points 14–17; Case C–128/91, n. 15 above, at points 15–18; and Case C–168/93, n. 15 above, at points 12–15.

[149] Case 101/76, n. 95 above.

[150] In this respect see the Opinion of Roemer A.G. in Case 6/68 *Zuckerfabrik Watenstedt* v. *Council*, n. 62 above, at 420.

issued,[151] and then looked at the *preambles* of the contested regulations in order to ascertain the reasons for the reduction and subsequent abolition of refunds.[152] On basis of all these elements, the Court concluded that the measures were indeed regulations rather than a series of decisions. Finally the Court repeated its *dictum* in *Zuckerfabrik*[153] stating that the fact that the applicants belonged to a small category did not alter the general nature of the measure.[154]

Binderer v. *Commission*[155] involved a Commission regulation that prohibited the use of certain adjectival forms to describe wines[156] imported into Germany and originating in Hungary and the former Yugoslavia in order to prevent consumers from being misled into believing those wines were of the same quality as German wines similarly described. *Binderer* claimed to be directly and individually concerned by the provisions of that regulation, since only he and two other undertakings imported and distributed such wines in Germany. The Court analysed first the nature of the measure and concluded that it was a legislative measure and not a disguised decision. This conclusion was not altered by the fact that the applicant belonged to such a small category.[157] The issue of individual concern was not discussed, but it followed automatically from the fact that the measure was clearly one of general application, and that the applicants were not individually concerned.[158]

In *Deutz und Geldermann* v. *Council*[159] the Court adopted a slightly different approach. In that case, a German sparkling-wine producer brought annulment proceedings against a Council regulation laying down general rules for the description and presentation of sparkling wines and aerated sparkling wines in so far as that regulation provided that reference could only be made to the production method called *méthode champenoise* if usage was traditional, for eight wine growing years. The applicant argued that the category of producers using that method was small and not susceptible of increase and that therefore they were directly and individually concerned by the regulation.[160]

The Court first held that the measure was a regulation and that the fact that the applicants belonged to a small group of producers did not change the nature of the measure.[161] The Court then analysed whether the applic-

[151] Case 101/76, n. 95 above, at point 11. The Court explained that production refunds had been granted by a former Council reg. on the common organization of the market in cereals, given the special situation of the market at the time.

[152] *Ibid.*, at points 12–16.

[153] N. 91 above.

[154] Case 101/76, n. 95 above, at point 23.

[155] Case 147/83, n. 129 above.

[156] e.g. *Spätlese* (late harvest) and *Aüslese* (selected grapes).

[157] Case 147/83, n. 129 above, at point 13, where the *Zuckerfabrik* statement was repeated (n. 91 above).

[158] *Ibid.*, at point 15. The same principle of economy in judicial reasoning referred to above (see 125 above) appears here.

[159] Case 26/86, n. 129 above.

[160] *Ibid.*, at 944.

[161] *Ibid.*, at point 8.

ants were individually concerned, concluding that there was nothing in their position that could distinguish them from the rest of the traders affected. The Court concluded—with an argument that is very familiar in relation to individual concern in cases decided in the area of decision[162]—by saying '[i]n fact the contested measure concerns the applicant only in its objective capacity as a sparkling wine producer which has traditionally used a particular method of production in just the same way as any other producer or trader in the same position'.[163]

In other words, the applicants had not taken a course of action before the enactment of the contested regulation that entitled them to some individual rights that the contested regulation had affected to a certain extent. They were affected merely in their capacity as wine producers. They were not therefore, individually concerned.[164]

The *Asteris* v. *Commission*[165] cases illustrate how stringent *locus standi* conditions can hinder the proper administration of justice. The Court had annulled in an earlier judgment[166] a Commission regulation that had fixed the coefficient to be applied to the production aid for tomato concentrates for the 1983–4 marketing year. In that decision the Court had also ruled that the Commission had the duty to fix a new coefficient for Greece or to devise other systems of compensation. The Commission enacted the contested regulation, whereby it only granted additional aid for the 1983–4 marketing year, without making provision for subsequent years. The Commission was called upon to act by the applicants—a group of Greek producers of tomato concentrates—in compliance with the judgment of the Court. The Commission, refusing to take action, addressed a decision to the applicants.

Asteris challenged both the regulation itself and the Commission's decision of refusal to comply with the judgment. As far as the annulment of the regulation was concerned, the Court reiterated the principles of distinction between regulations and decisions[167] and the *Zuckerfabrik* statement in

[162] See *Plaumann* v. *Commission*, 45–7 above, n. 115.

[163] Case 26/86, n. 129 above, at point 12. Even national laws bring about changes that unavoidably upset some private parties which operate in the sector affected. Their mere capacity as traders does not suffice to give them standing to challenge such laws. For instance, if a national law imposes on all producers of sparkling wine the obligation to label their bottles, including a certain requirement—e.g. that all bottles should be recycled—all producers, even if they had a large stock of bottles with labels not complying with this requirement, would have to abide by such a law, without being entitled to challenge it. It must be recalled that in the national legal systems laws are only susceptible of challenge by private parties in very exceptional cases. On the other hand, general administrative measures may be challenged by natural and legal persons upon proof of a direct and individual interest (see 39 above). The measure at issue in *Deutz und Geldermann* v. *Council* was clearly of a legislative nature.

[164] In the case law concerning decisions see Case 231/82 *Spijker* v. *Commission* [1983] ECR 2559, at points 9–10.

[165] Joined Cases 97, 193, 99 and 215/86, n. 129 above.

[166] Case 192/83 *Hellenic Republic* v. *Commission* [1985] ECR 2791.

[167] Joined Cases 97, 193, 99 and 215/86, n. 129 above, at points 12–13.

relation to small classes.[168] It did not, however, apply them to the present case, preferring to focus on individual concern. The applicants were clearly not individually concerned, in that there was nothing in their situation that could distinguish them from the rest of the producers of tomato concentrates.[169] The action against the decision of refusal was equally dismissed as inadmissible.[170]

Greece also challenged the regulation and the Commission decision of refusal. The action against the regulation was dismissed as inadmissible because there was no flaw *per se* in the limited measures that it put in place. However, the action against the decision of refusal succeeded on the merits. The Commission was therefore obliged to enact further regulations, fixing additional coefficients for production aid to tomato concentrates for the years following the 1983–4 marketing year—which was, of course, the result sought by Asteris.

The extreme stringency of the *locus standi* tests is clear from this case. If Greece had not brought an action, the substantive issues would never have been considered, yet the Commission's conduct was illegal.

Recently, in *Bulck* v. *Commission*[171] the applicants were enterprises which ran the majority of slaughter-houses for ducks and geese in Germany. They had asked the Commission to re-establish the levy on the importation of these birds from non-member countries, which a former Council regulation had reduced by 50 per cent. The Commission, however, took a decision addressed to the applicants refusing to take such action. *Bulck* brought an action for the annulment of that decision and, since the measure that the Commission would have adopted would have been a regulation, the issue of *locus standi* had to be assessed in relation to this latter measure.[172] The Court dismissed the application. The regulation itself was a legislative measure and the applicants were not individually concerned, even though they belonged to a small category. There was nothing in their position that could distinguish them from the rest of the traders affected.[173]

[168] Joined Cases 97, 193, 99 and 215/86, n. 129 above.

[169] *Ibid.*, at point 15.

[170] *Ibid.*, at point 17. The reason for declaring the inadmissibility of the action against the dec. of refusal was that the applicants, when calling upon the Commission to act, sought the adoption of a measure that would have taken the form of a reg. The Court has made clear on numerous occasions that applicants may not use a dec. addressed to them to circumvent the *locus standi* requirements of Art. 173(2) EEC Treaty: see Case 42/71 *Nordgetreide* v. *Commission* [1972] ECR 105.

[171] Joined Cases C–15/91 and C–108/91, n. 129 above.

[172] The same situation had arisen in Joined Cases 97, 193, 99 and 215/86 *Asteris* v. *Commission*, n. 129 above.

[173] Joined Cases C–15/91 and C–108/91, n. 129 above, at points 22–27.

4.4.1.4 Cases Involving Regulations Affecting Closed Categories

In these cases, the regulations at issue have affected either wholly—in one case[174]—or partly closed categories of people. It is in these cases that the severity of the test of legal nature is most noticeable and has prevented access to the Court by private applicants whose actions would have been admissible if they had been directed against decisions. In the two previous categories of cases, it is clear that applicants were *never* individually concerned by the regulations at issue. In the cases belonging to the present group it is argued that applicants *were* individually concerned, either by the regulations at issue or by some of their provisions. The Court, however, took into account only the test of legal nature to decide the admissibility of the actions. As a result, all the actions were dismissed as inadmissible. This group of cases reaffirms the existence of a marked difference between the tests of legal nature and individual concern.[175]

A. Regulations Affecting Exclusively Closed Categories

A particularly striking example is the decision of the Court in *Société des Usines de Beauport* v. *Council.*[176] These cases arose in the context of the common organization of the market in sugar. A 1974 Council regulation had provided for the allocation by the Member States of basic quotas to undertakings. The quota rules were valid from 1 August 1975 to 31 July 1980. A subsequent Council regulation—the one at issue in this case—contained a provision that derogated from the provisions of the earlier regulation and that authorized the French Republic to reduce the basic quota for each undertaking established in the French overseas departments for the entire period of the marketing years 1977 to 1980. The regulation was therefore *wholly retroactive*. The applicants were sugar undertakings which had been granted a quota under the earlier regulation and which saw it reduced as a consequence of the contested regulation. The Advocate General, Mr Warner, did not consider the issue of the real nature of the regulation. He had no hesitation in saying that the applicants were individually concerned, in so far as they belonged to the closed category of traders that had been allocated quotas for five years.[177] The applicants had an individual right under Community law—in particular the right to maintain their quotas—which was affected by a later measure. The regulation affected in its entirety a closed category of traders. However, he

[174] Joined Cases 103 to 109/78 *Société des Usines de Beauport* v. *Council*, n. 88 above.

[175] In this respect see the early standpoint of the Court in Joined Cases 16–17/62 *Confédération National des Producteurs de Fruits et Légumes* v. *Council*, n. 5 above, where the Court suggested that the satisfaction of the test of individual concern would imply that the measure was not a reg.

[176] Joined Cases 103–109/78, n. 88 above.

[177] *Ibid.* 30.

considered that the traders were not directly concerned, in that only if the French Republic decided to reduce the quota would the regulation affect the undertakings. Consequently, he explained that the action should be declared inadmissible.[178]

The Court focused first on the nature of the measure, stressing that it aimed to derogate from the provisions of an earlier legislative measure. It concluded that the contested regulation was also a general legislative measure[179] and therefore not challengeable by private parties. In a quite unusual move for the Court in this area of case law, it also considered the issue of direct concern and concluded, following the Opinion of the Advocate General, that the applicants were not directly concerned.[180] The Court did not consider whether the applicants were individually concerned. It is suggested that they were, but this fact did not seem to be important provided it was shown that the measure was a true regulation.

It is difficult not to be critical of this decision by the Court, in that it does not appear at all clear that the regulation was a genuine legislative measure. The *only* people affected were the closed category of traders that had been allocated a quota. This situation is very far from the definition of a regulation as a measure that affects 'abstract categories of people'. Fortunately, in all other cases where a regulation has affected only closed categories, the Court has decided the *locus standi* issue solely on the basis of the tests of direct and individual concern,[181] ignoring the intricacies of the test of legal nature. It is argued, though, that in this case, given that it was clear the applicants were not directly concerned, the action would have been inadmissible anyway.

B. Regulations Affecting Mixed Categories

The gap between the tests of legal nature and individual concern becomes more evident in cases where the regulations at issue affected partly closed and partly open categories. In them, applicants belonging to the closed categories who, it is suggested, were individually and directly concerned by provisions in regulations, were denied *locus standi* on the ground that the measures were of a general nature.[182]

[178] Joined Cases 103–109/78, n. 88 above, 31.

[179] The Court said: 'It is necessary to conclude from this that the amendment made by the contested regulation shares, in the same way as Article 2 of Regulation No 3331/74, in the nature of a regulation'; *ibid.*, at point 19.

[180] *Ibid.*, at points 21–22. It may be that the Court was deliberately avoiding the test of individual concern, in that, given that direct concern was not present, the practical outcome of the case—inadmissibility—would have been the same.

[181] See 143 below.

[182] See Case 162/78 *Wagner* v. *Commission*, n. 132 above; Case 45/81 *Moksel* v. *Commission*, n. 7 above; Case C–244/8 *Usines Coopératives de Vexin*, n. 120 above; and Case C–229/88 *Cargill* v. *Commission*, n. 132 above. The only exception in this consistent line of case law is Case 333/85 *Mannesmann-Röhrenwerke* v. *Council*, n. 10 above, where the reg. at issue affected mixed categories. In this instance the Court decided the *locus standi* of an applicant belonging

Thus, in *Wagner* v. *Commission*,[183] the applicants were sugar exporters who had been granted licences before 1 June 1978 to export sugar for which refunds had been fixed in national currencies. At the time the licences were awarded, the amount of the export refunds only had to be multiplied by a coefficient if they had been fixed in units of account. Three subsequent Commission regulations then provided that the coefficient should also be applied to refunds fixed in national currencies. All the regulations contained a provision that applied this measure retroactively to transactions where customs formalities had been completed before 1 June 1978, provided that exportation took place after that date. The applicants argued that the regulations, whilst being measures of general application in relation to transactions entered into *after* their entry into force, nevertheless constituted decisions in relation to exporters whose refunds had already been fixed and who suffered a retroactive application of the coefficient which resulted in the reduction of the refunds.[184]

The Court in this case clearly marked the distinction between the tests of legal nature and individual concern and laid down the guidelines for a series of cases that followed and that involved regulations affecting partially closed and partially open categories of people. At this point, it is important to recall that, in the case law concerning measures in the form of decisions, there is abundant evidence that applicants who belong to a closed category (by reason of their particular conduct prior to the enactment of the measure) to which certain rights were attached—and who are retroactively affected by a provision in a decision may challenge such a provision even though the rest of the measure applies to open categories of people.[185] The applicant in the present case, *Wagner*, was in an identical position. At the time when he had been granted the licence, he was entitled to obtain a refund not multiplied by the coefficient. His situation was, therefore, adversely affected by the later Commission regulations.

to the closed category on the basis of the double admissibility test. In fact the Court only decided on the question of direct concern (at points 15–16) and having found that the applicants were not directly concerned (see also the Opinion of Da Cruz Vilaça A.G. at 1398–4400), did not consider it necessary to decide on individual concern and dismissed the action. It is suggested that the difference between this case and all the others involving mixed categories lies in that the applicants in the latter cases were directly and individually concerned and therefore, had the Court applied to double admissibility test, the actions would have been admissible. In *Mannesmann-Röhrenwerke*, however, the outcome of the case would have been the same whichever approach the Court had taken.

[183] Case 162/78, n. 132 above.

[184] *Ibid.* 3473. Likewise, Warner A.G. did not discuss the real nature of the measure but had little difficulty in concluding that *Wagner* was individually concerned since he belonged to a category fixed and ascertained before the measure entered into force: *ibid.* 3494.

[185] In Joined Cases 106–107/63 *Toepfer*, n. 98 above and 48 above, Case 62/70 *Bock* [1971] ECR 897 and 50 above, and Case 11/82 *Piraiki-Patraiki*, n. 98 above and 54 above, successful applicants had pending licences or transactions which were affected by the decs. at issue and they were declared to be individually concerned by decs. that affected the conditions in which the licences were going to be granted or the transactions performed.

The Court, however, took a very grim stand and dismissed the actions as inadmissible on the basis that the test of legal nature had not been fulfilled and that the measures were real regulations. The Court explained that the *purpose*[186] of the introduction of the coefficient was mainly to avoid deflections on trade and it was aimed not at reducing the refunds to which the applicants were entitled but was 'only a technical way of adjusting, in trade with non-member countries, the basic monetary compensatory amount which is fixed at a uniform level calculated on the basis of the Community prices'.[187] In other words, the Court was saying that the regulations were intended to deal with a particular situation in the market and did not have the specific aim of deciding on the situation of the applicants. The Court completed its judgment on the admissibility of the application by saying that the system introduced by the regulation 'applies to all successful traders, whatever the date of the award, provided that exportation took place after the 1st June 1978'.[188] The tests of direct and individual concern were not considered.[189]

Two points may be made. First, it is clear that the traders that had pending transactions were particularly affected, as the application of the coefficient would mean that their refunds would be lower than they had expected, whereas all future exporters would enter into agreements already expecting a refund multiplied by a coefficient and consequently could still decide whether or not to enter into transactions. In other words, although future exporters would be able to strike bargains on the basis of new arrangements, Wagner and the traders belonging to the closed category were bound by existing contracts. The Court based the test of legal nature on a purely objective analysis of the market, regardless of the actual effects that a measure had on different private parties.

It is suggested that this stand is unnecessarily restrictive. It is clear that, in the area of general management of the market, private interests will have sometimes to give way to the requirements of public interest. However, it seems unfair that private applicants individually and directly concerned by provisions in a regulation—and the test of individual concern is restrictive enough—do not have the opportunity of making their submissions on the substance and of challenging the Community institution's action only because the act in question is a regulation.[190] Of course, the fundamental issue underlying the *locus standi* problem arises here: if the

[186] Case 162/78, n. 132 above, at point 19.

[187] *Ibid.*, at point 20.

[188] *Ibid.*, at point 22.

[189] The fact that the applicants belonged to a closed category was not contemplated at all.

[190] Fortunately, in a recent case where the issue of *locus standi* was decided solely on the basis of the tests of direct and individual concern, this situation changed. Thus, in Case C–152/88 *Sofrimport* v. *Commission*, n. 12 above, the Court did not consider the legal nature of the reg. and the applicants had *locus standi* on the ground that they were directly and individually concerned by the contested provision. The same can be said of the decision of the Court in Case C–308/89 *Codorniu* v. *Council*, n. 14 above.

Court shows more leniency in the interpretation of *locus standi* conditions, a flood of applications for annulment against Community regulations would most probably arrive at the Court Registry; if on the other hand, the Court adopts a more restrained approach, in some situations (like the present one) applicants would be treated unjustly.[191] A fairer view would perhaps be to grant standing to those applicants and to decide on the merits whether the institution's action was lawful or not.[192]

Secondly, it would also seem that, when a regulation affects a category of natural and legal persons that is partially closed and partially open, the test of legal nature could only be fulfilled if the regulation discriminated openly against the applicants and treated them differently from the rest of the traders affected.[193] In all other cases, the use of a sufficiently broad formula by the institution concerned would guarantee immunity against annulment proceedings brought by private parties.

A similar approach was followed in *Moksel* v. *Commission*.[194] In that case a German exporter of meat had submitted several applications to the competent national authority for export licences with advanced fixing of export refunds. While his application was being considered, the contested regulation was issued, suspending the advance fixing of refunds. Moksel's application was therefore rejected. Moksel brought annulment proceedings against the regulation in so far as it applied to pending licences. The situation was very similar to the one in *Wagner*.[195] The Court indeed, took the same view as it had taken in the *Wagner* case and rejected the action as inadmissible on the ground that an examination of the nature of the measure showed that it was a genuine regulation which applied equally to both pending and future applications for licences.[196]

The new element in *Moksel* was that the Court clearly identified the elements to be taken into account when applying the test of legal nature: '[c]onsequently, it must be deduced from the *purpose* of the contested measure, from the *framework* of the regulations of which it forms part and

[191] This is so especially if it is borne in mind that the reg. at issue in Wagner presented all the characteristics of what would have been a general administrative act in the national legal systems. In those systems—e.g. the Spanish administrative legal system—general administrative acts are challengeable by private parties showing a legitimate interest, like the one that Wagner had in this case (see Dec. of the Constitutional Tribunal 160/1985 of 28 Nov.).

[192] In this respect see the Opinion of Warner A.G. in this case where, after declaring the action admissible, he dismissed it as unfounded: Case 162/78, n. 132 above, at 3495.

[193] As the court itself said in Joined Cases 789 and 790/79 *Calpak* v. *Commission* [1980] ECR 1949, at point 10, it would be necessary that the reg. was 'a decision adopted specifically in relation to them [the applicants] and as such, entitling them to institute proceedings under the second paragraph of Article 173'.

[194] Case 45/81, n. 78 above.

[195] VerLoren Van Themaat A.G. believed, as Warner A.G. had concluded in *Wagner*, that the applicant was individual concerned: *ibid.* 1152.

[196] *Ibid.*, at point 16. The ruling was severely criticized by T. C. Hartley ('Article 173. The Right of Private Parties to bring Proceedings. *Moksel* v. *Commission*' (1983) 8 *ELRev.* 41, 42.

from *its very nature* that it is indeed a regulation which is of general application'.[197]

All of these elements had been present in earlier rulings[198] but in this case the Court expressly enumerated them and considered them systematically.

To ascertain the *purpose* of the regulation and the *framework* of which it formed part, the Court looked at three points: (a) the references in the preamble of the regulation, (b) the statement of reasons, and (c) the wording of its provisions.[199]

In relation to the *purpose* of the regulation, it was clear that it was aimed at dealing with an objective situation in the market where difficulties had arisen. In relation to the *framework*, the Court explained that, since the regulations conferring the right of advance fixing refunds were of general application, any measure modifying this right was likewise of general application.[200]

Finally, in relation to the *nature* of the provision at issue the Court only emphasized that the same provision could not be at the same time a measure of general and of individual application.[201]

Likewise, in *Usines Coopératives de Déshydratation du Vexin* v. *Commission*,[202] the applicants had requested the French intervention agency to issue them with certificates fixing in advance the aid applicable to various quantities of dried fodder. While their applications were pending, the Commission enacted a regulation suspending the advance fixing of the aid. The applicants challenged the regulation in so far as it affected pending applications, and suggested that the Commission had used a very broad formula, encompassing past and future applications whereas it intended to block the pending applications, which it regarded as speculative.[203] The Court remained unimpressed and applied the same principles as in earlier decisions. The application was dismissed as inadmissible in so far as the measure was found to be a real regulation.

[197] Case 45/81, n. 78 above, at point 19, emphasis added.

[198] See Case 30/67 *Industria Molitoria Imolese* v. *Council*, n. 62 above, at 121; Case 64/69 *La Compagnie Française Commerciale* v. *Commission*, n. 5 above, at points 4–5; Joined Cases 41–44/70 *International Fruit Company* v. *Commission*, n. 60 above, at points 16–22; Case 101/76 *Koninklijke Scholten Honig* v. *Council and Commission*, n. 95 above, at points 11–16; and Case 162/78 *Wagner* v. *Commission*, n. 132 above, at points 19–22.

[199] Case 45/81, n. 78 above, at point 16.

[200] *Ibid.*, at point 17.

[201] *Ibid.*, at point 18.

[202] Case C–244/88, n. 120 above. See also Case C–229/88 *Cargill* v. *Commission*, n. 132 above.

[203] Case C–244/88, n. 202 above, at 3818.

4.4.1.5 Cases Involving Regulations Affecting Exclusively Closed Categories and where a Clear Causal Link Existed Between the Measure and the Situation of the Applicants

Throughout the case law that has been studied in the earlier sections the main problem posed to applicants was to prove that the act or provision was in reality of an individual nature. The cases in this section, which have been modelled on the decision in *International Fruit Company*,[204] showed that the fulfilment of the test of legal nature would occur in very rare circumstances. In fact, there are only three cases in which the Court has acknowledged that the regulations at issue or one of their provisions were, in reality decisions. In two of them, *Roquette Frères* v. *Council* and *Maizena* v. *Council*[205] it did not even need to apply the test of legal nature, in that the applicants were expressly named in the contested provision. The third case, *Weddel* v. *Commission*,[206] involved very similar facts to those in *International Fruit Company*.

Roquette Frères v. *Council* and *Maizena* v. *Council* were cases of great importance for the constitutional issues they raised. In those cases, the applicants, manufacturers of isoglucose, brought annulment proceedings against a provision of a Council regulation and the Annex thereto fixing the production quota to be allocated to them. Roquette and Maizena alleged that the fixing of the quota was void, in that the Council had failed to obtain the opinion of the European Parliament before enacting the regulation. Since the measure was in the form of a regulation, the applicants needed to overcome the *locus standi* barrier. Advocate General Reischl concluded that the provision in the regulation was in truth a series of individual decisions, each one addressed to a particular undertaking,[207] on the basis that the six undertakings were mentioned by name in the Annex to which the contested provision referred. The Court reached an identical conclusion.[208]

[204] Joined Cases 41–44/70, n. 60 above.

[205] Case 138/79 (*Roquette*) and Case 139/79 (*Maizena*), n. 122 above.

[206] Case C–354/87, n. 79 above.

[207] Case 138/79, n. 122 above, at 3369.

[208] See Case 138/79 *Roquette* v. *Council*, n. 122 above, at point 16 and Case 139/79 *Maizena* v. *Council*, n. 122 above, at point 16. F. G. Jacobs ('Isoglucose Resurgent: Two Powers of the European Parliament Upheld by the Court' (1981) 18 *CMLRev.* 219, 225–6, made an interesting observation in relation to this case. He pointed out that, although the applicants were the addressees of the particular provision in the reg., it was clear that the rest of the reg. was an act of a general nature. In spite of this, the Court annulled the whole reg. and not just the particular provision. The approach of the Court in these cases contrasts with its traditional approach, which is to annull only the provision that concerns the applicants directly and individually: see Case C–152/88 *Sofrimport* v. *Commission*, n. 12 above and 147 below, and Case 11/82 *Piraiki-Patraiki*, n. 164 above, 55 above). Another author (T. C. Hartley, 'Consulting the European Parliament: *Roquette* v. *Council* and *Maizena* v. *Council*' (1981) 6 *ELRev.* 181, 185) believed that the unusual step taken by the Court in these cases reflected the fact that the lack of consultation with the European Parliament vitiated the whole reg.

In *Weddel* v. *Commission*,[209] the applicant, a trading company whose business was the importation and exportation of meat, had submitted to the Dutch Cattle and Meat Board an application for import licences for a quantity of beef and veal. The relevant regulations provided that the Commission could, if the quantities for which licences had been requested exceeded the quantities available, reduce the amounts requested by a fixed percentage. Accordingly, the Commission enacted the contested regulation which retroactively reduced the amounts requested by a fixed percentage. The applicants suffered considerable losses as a result of this measure and brought an action for the regulation's annulment.

The Court followed a very similar approach to that adopted in *International Fruit Company*, although in this case it considered first the tests of direct and individual concern. The applicants were directly concerned since no discretion had been left to the national authorities and therefore the regulation was the direct cause of the losses they had suffered.[210] They were also individually concerned in that they belonged to a closed category of traders[211]—i.e. the ones that had submitted applications for licences before the regulation was issued. Finally, the existence of a causal link between the quantities of beef and veal for which applications were submitted and the percentage fixed by the regulation was the element that determined that the regulation was in reality a bundle of decisions. In other words the percentage had been fixed exclusively on the basis of quantities already submitted.[212]

On this basis, the Court concluded that the provision was in reality a bundle of individual decisions, each one affecting the legal position of each applicant.

4.4.2 CASES DECIDED ON THE BASIS OF A DOUBLE ADMISSIBILITY TEST

In this group of cases the Court appears to have ignored completely the test of legal nature and decided *locus standi* exclusively on the basis of the tests of direct and individual concern. There are three main blocks of decisions, which in turn form two main groups.

A. *Applicants belonging to open categories*

1. Cases where the regulations at issue affected very wide categories of people.[213]

[209] Case C–354/87, n. 79 above.
[210] *Ibid.* at point 19.
[211] *Ibid.*, at points 20–21.
[212] *Ibid.*, at points 21–22.
[213] Case 30/64 *Sgarlata* v. *Commission*, n. 60 above; Case C–257/93 *Van Parijs* v. *Council and Commission*, judgment of 21 June 1993; Case C–276/93 *Chiquita Banana* v. *Council*, judgment of 21 June 1993; Case C–107/93 *Asociación Española de Fabricantes de Margarina (AEFMA)* v. *Commission*, judgment of 12 July 1993; and Case T–476/93, *FRSEA and FNSEA* v. *Council*, Order of the CFI of 28 Oct. 1993.

2. Cases where the regulations affected very small groups easily ascertainable but nevertheless not fixed, to which the applicants belonged.[214]

B. *Applicants belonging to closed categories*

1. Cases where the regulations at issue affected exclusively closed categories.[215]

2, Cases where the regulations at issue affected partly closed categories and partly open categories.[216]

It is believed that the ruling of the Court in *Sofrimport*[217] in 1990 could be considered as a turning point in the case law. Prior to this decision, most of the cases where the regulations at issue affected either open categories or partially closed and partially open categories had been decided on the basis of the triple admissibility test. Only in three cases did the Court apply the double admissibility test.[218] After *Sofrimport*, most of the cases decided by the Court—whether involving regulations affecting solely open categories or mixed categories—have been decided on the basis of the double admissibility test. That is why a distinction between the case law *before* and *after Sofrimport* is made in the following sections.

4.4.2.1 Cases Involving Regulations Affecting Open Categories (Large Groups)

Prior to 1990, only in one case where the regulation at issue affected large categories did the Court, when deciding the *locus standi* of the applicants, apply the double admissibility test. As has already been seen, in those cases the Court normally applied the triple admissibility test.[219] This case was *Sgarlata* v. *Commission*.[220] The applicant and nine other Italian producers

[214] Case 123/77 *Unione Nazionale Importatori e Commercianti Motoveicoli Esteri (UNICME)* v. *Council* [1978] ECR 845; Joined Cases C–232/91 and C–233/91 *Petridi* v. *Commission* [1991] ECR I–5351; Case C–131/92 *Arnaud* v. *Council*, judgment of 24 May 1993; Case C–213/91 *Abertal* v. *Commission*, judgment of 15 June 1993; and Case T–472/93 *Campo Ebro* v. *Council*, judgment of the CFI of 21 February 1995, not yet reported.

[215] Case 100/74 *Cam* v. *Commission*, n. 112 above; Case 88/76 *Société pour l'Exportation des Sucres* v. *Commission* [1977] ECR 709; Case 232/81 *Agricola Commerciale Olio* v. *Commission*, n. 42 above); Case 264/81 *Savma* v. *Commission* [1984] ECR 3915; Case 55/86 *Asociación Provincial de Armadores de Pesca de Gran Sol de Pontevedra (ARPOSOL)* v. *Council*, n. 142 above.

[216] Case 333/85 *Mannesmann-Röhrenwerke* v. *Council*, n. 10 above; Case C–152/88 *Sofrimport* v. *Commission*, n. 12 above; Case C–309/89 *Codorniu* v. *Council*, n. 14 above; and Case T–489/93 *Unifruit Hellas* v. *Commission* [1994] ECR II–1201.

[217] See n. 12 above.

[218] See (a) open categories: Case 40/64 *Sgarlata* v. *Commission*, n. 60 above; Case 123/77 *Unione Nazionale importatori e Commercianti Motoveicoli Esteri (UNICME)* v. *Council*, n. 214 above, and (b) mixed categories: Case 333/85 *Mannesmann-Röhrenwerke* v. *Council*, see n. 10 above.

[219] See 125 above.

[220] Case 40/64, n. 60 above.

of citrus fruits brought annulment proceedings against a Commission regulation fixing the reference price for lemons, mandarins, clementines, and sweet oranges. Two important points need to be emphasized: first, the Court expressly said that it was not necessary to take into account the test of legal nature,[221] it being sufficient to decide upon the question whether the applicants were directly and individually concerned; secondly, the Court transposed the definition of individual concern made in the case law concerning decisions in this area.[222] The Court concluded that the applicants were not individually concerned and dismissed the action as inadmissible. The interpretation followed by the Court in this case was very restrictive.[223]

Since the judgment of the Court in *Sofrimport*, the same technique has been applied in a number of very recent cases. Thus, in *Van Parijs* v. *Council and Commission*[224] and in *Chiquita Banana* v. *Council*,[225] the applicants, a group of undertakings in the sector of banana supply, brought annulment proceedings against a Council regulation on the common organization of the market in bananas. Similarly, in *Asociación Española de Fabricantes de Margarina (AEFMA)* v. *Commission*,[226] the applicants, a group of Spanish associations of manufacturers of margarine, brought proceedings against a Commission regulation relating to the suspension of customs duties and fixed components for trade between the Community of Ten and Spain. The regulations at issue in those cases were ones of very wide application and affected very large categories of people. In all these cases the Court concluded that the applicants were not individually concerned, given that there was nothing in their position that could distinguish them from the rest of the undertakings affected.[227] The Court of First Instance adopted the same approach in *Fédération Nationale des Syndicats d'Exploitants Agricoles (FNSEA)* v. *Council*.[228]

4.4.2.2 Cases Involving Regulations Affecting Open Categories (Small Groups)

Similarly, prior to 1990 only one case where the contested regulation affected small categories was decided by the Court on the basis of the tests of direct and individual concern. This was *Unione Nazionale Importatori e*

[221] Case 40/64, n. 60 above, 226. Roemer A.G. had considered first the legal nature of the measure and had reached the conclusion that it was of a true normative character: *ibid.* 233.

[222] *Ibid.* at 226, where the *Plaumann* definition of individual concern was repeated (see Ch. 3, n. 114).

[223] See 43 above, n. 94.

[224] Case C–257/93, n. 213 above.

[225] Case C–276/93, n. 213 above.

[226] Case C–107/93, n. 213 above.

[227] See Case C–257/93 *Van Parijs*, n. 213 above, at points 7–10; Case C–276/95 *Chiquita Banana*, n. 213 above, at points 7–10; and Case C–107/93 *AEFMA*, n. 213 above, at points 14–18.

[228] Reg. 1697/77 [1977] OJ L188/1.

Commercianti Motoveicoli Esteri (UNICME) v. *Council*.[229] In this case, an association of Italian importers of Japanese motorcycles brought annulment proceedings against a Council regulation[230] that imposed protective measures on imports of certain motorcycles originating in Japan for the year 1977. There was some evidence that the measure had been enacted in response to a request from the Italian Government, after the Japanese authorities had imposed a ban on the import into Japan of ski-boots originating in the Community, which in fact applied mainly to the Italian industry.[231] The regulation established that the imports would be dependent on the production of an import authorization by the Italian authorities and that only 18,000 items should be imported during 1977. The importers of Japanese motorcycles into Italy were a small and easily ascertainable group of traders. The Court dismissed the annulment proceedings as inadmissible due to lack of direct and individual concern of the applicants.[232]

On the one hand the Court decided first that *UNICME* was not directly concerned in so far as only when the Italian authorities refused to them an import permit would the applicants be directly concerned.[233] Two criticisms of this view suggest themselves. First, the ruling in *Bock*[234] had established that, even in cases where the Member State addressee enjoyed a theoretical degree of discretion in the implementation of a Community measure, private applicants could be directly concerned by such a measure if the Member State had made clear beforehand how its discretion would be used. In this case, the Italian Government *had requested* the protective measure, therefore it was quite clear how the discretion was to be exercised. The only discretion that the Italian Government really retained was the choice of the particular importers that would be awarded import licences. Secondly, the prohibition imposed, i.e. not to import more than 18,000 items, was clearly direct and did not need any implementation.

On the other hand, it was clear, in view of the existing case law, that the applicants were not individually concerned. Although they belonged to a small group, they did not constitute a closed category, and because they had not engaged in a conduct prior to the enactment of the regulation, to which certain rights had been attached. The Court said:

> The possibility of determining more or less precisely the number of even the identity of persons to whom measure applies, by no means implies that it must be regarded as being of individual concern to them.[235]

[229] Case 123/77, n. 214 above.
[230] Reg. 1697/77 [1977] OJ L188/1.
[231] This fact was acknowledged in the 3rd recital to the Reg. Furthermore, the 4th recital to the Reg. provided that the protective measures should be limited to imports into Italy.
[232] Hartley criticized the severe approach of the Court to the *locus standi* of the applicants in this case: see T. C. Hartley, '*Locus Standi* to Challenge Regulations. *UNICME* v. *Council*' (1978) 3 *ELRev*. 387.
[233] Case 123/77, n. 214 above, at point 11.
[234] Case 62/70 [1971] ECR 897. See 67 above. Even more liberal was the dec. of the Court in Case 11/82 *Piraiki-Patriaki*, n. 98 above and 69 above.
[235] Case 123/77, n. 214 above, at point 16.

In other words, the Court explained that the fact that the applicants belonged to a small group did not imply that they were individually concerned.[236] It will be recalled that, in *Zuckerfabrik*, the Court also made clear that the fact that applicants belong to small categories easily ascertainable does not mean that the measure ceases to be a regulation.[237]

Since the judgment in *Sofrimport*, the Court has applied the same technique in a number of cases in order to dismiss actions for annulment brought by members of small groups challenging regulations affecting them. In all the cases that followed, the Court explained that neither the fact that the applicants belonged to a very small category, nor their sole capacity as economic operators would suffice to make them individually concerned. Thus, in *Petridi* v. *Commission*,[238] two Greek undertakings brought annulment proceedings against a Commission regulation opening an invitation to tender for the sale of tobacco held by the German, Greek, and Italian intervention agencies. The applicants belonged to the small group most likely to be affected by the measure. The Court refused to grant them *locus standi* on the basis they were not individually concerned.[239] Likewise, in *Arnaud* v. *Council*,[240] the action for annulment brought by a group of operators of French fishing vessels against a provision in a regulation relating to certain measures of conservation of fishing resources was dismissed on the ground that the applicants were not individually concerned.[241] Finally, in *Abertal* v. *Commission*,[242] Abertal and eighteen other organizations of Spanish nut and locus bean producers brought annulment proceedings against a Commission regulation laying down detailed rules for the application of the specific measures for nuts and locust beans provided by a former Council regulation. The applicants were not given standing to challenge the regulation on the ground that they were not individually concerned.[243]

The Court of First Instance has adopted the same approach as the European Court in *Campo Ebro* v. *Council*,[244] where the only Spanish producer of isoglucose tried to challenge a Council regulation on the

[236] This idea has been repeated in later case law. Thus see Joined Cases C–232/91 and C–233/91 *Petridi* v. *Commission*, n. 214 above, at point 10; Case C–131/92 *Arnaud* v. *Council*, n. 214 above, at point 13; and Case C–213/91 *Abertal* v. *Commission*, n. 214 above, at point 17. In the case law concerning the challenge of decisions, see Case 231/82 *Spijker* v. *Commission*, n. 164 above.

[237] For a fuller discussion of this issue see Case 6/68 *Zuckerfabrik* v. *Council*, n. 62 above; Case 101/76 *Koninklijke Scholten Honig* v. *Council and Commission*, n. 95 above; Case 26/86 *Deutz und Geldermann* v. *Council*, n. 129 above; Joined Cases 97, 193, 99 and 215/86 *Asteris* v. *Commission*, n. 129 above; and Joined Cases C–15/91 and C–108/91, *Bulck* v. *Commission*, n. 129 above.

[238] Joined Cases 232/91 and 233/91, n. 214 above.

[239] *Ibid.*, at point 11.

[240] Case C–131/92, n. 214 above.

[241] *Ibid.*, at points 13–15.

[242] Case C–213/91, n. 214 above.

[243] *Ibid.*, at points 17–24.

[244] Case T–472/93, judgment of 21 Feb. 1995, not yet reported.

common organization of the market in sugar which granted aid to beet and sugar cane growers.

4.4.2.3 Cases Involving Regulations Affecting Closed Categories

A. Regulations Affecting Exclusively Closed Categories

Most of the cases decided by the Court on the basis of a double admissibility test involved regulations affecting in their entirety closed categories.

Cam v. *Commission*[245] involved a set of facts quite similar to those in *La Compagnie Française Commerciale*.[246] In pursuance of a Council regulation on the common organization of the market in cereals, exporters could ask for advance fixing of export refunds. Those refunds were the subject of monthly adjustments in accordance with the threshold price in force during the month of exportation. The Council, in order to take account of the effects of general inflation on agriculture, enacted a regulation that established a single and exceptional increase in the target prices as from 7 October 1974. This increase affected the threshold prices and, consequently, the amount of the refunds. On 4 October 1974, the Commission enacted the contested regulation—which was to enter into force on 7 October—which provided that the increase in the threshold prices should not be followed by an increase in the refunds that had been subject to advanced fixing, where the applications had been lodged before 7 October. It was not possible to ask for advance fixed refunds after 26 July 1974. The applicants had applied and obtained export licences with advance fixed refunds before 26 July. They had exported part of their consignments, but the remainder had not been exported by 7 October. Had it not been for the contested regulation, the applicants would have obtained a substantial refund.[247]

In the first case, the Court considered whether the applicants were directly concerned. The Court explained:

The contested measure, by denying to a class of traders the benefit of an increase in the amount of refunds for specific exporters, which was on the contrary

[245] Case 100/74, n. 112 above.

[246] Case 64/69, n. 5 above.

[247] Warner A.G. believed that the facts were indistinguishable from those at issue in Case 64/69*La Compagnie Française* v. *Commission*, n. 5 above, at 1414 (see also T. C. Hartley, n. 9 above, at 371). In fact, the similarity between the two cases is quite striking, as both involved retroactive regs. that denied to a group of traders a benefit generally given to others. Thus, in *La Compagnie Française*, traders who entered into export agreements before a determined date but did not apply for advance fixed refunds were denied the right to pay reduced compensatory amounts whereas, in the *Cam* case, traders who applied for licences and advanced fixed refunds before a determined date were denied the right of increased export refunds. In the first of these cases, however, the Court dismissed the action as inadmissible on the grounds that it was a true reg.

granted to those whose applications for advanced fixing were made at a later date, directly concerns the said traders.[248]

The Court's statement clearly reflects the conclusions reached earlier[249] about the notion of direct concern. For an applicant to be directly concerned, the important point is the existence of a causal link between the measure in question and the damage created to the applicant's rights. In this case, the discriminatory treatment suffered by Cam, clearly resulted in damage to the applicant, i.e. loss of substantial refunds.

In the second place, the Court analysed the question of individual concern. The Court acknowledged that the applicants belonged to a closed category,[250] i.e. those exporters who applied for advance fixed refunds before 26 July 1974 and who still had current licences on 7 October 1974, and who therefore were 'distinguished by reason of the individual course of action which they had pursued or are regarded as having pursued during a particular period'.[251] The Court concluded:

> Such a measure, even if it is one of a number of provision having a legislative function, individually concerns the persons to whom it applies in that it affects their legal position because of a factual situation which differentiates them from all other persons and distinguishes them individually, just as in the case of the persons addressed.[252]

The application was declared admissible but it was dismissed on the merits.

Three points stand out from this decision:

1. The Court ignored the test of legal nature. It is suggested that, had the Court considered the true nature of the measure at issue, most probably the action would have been dismissed as inadmissible on the ground that the measure was a true regulation.[253] Instead, the Court considered whether the applicants were directly and individually concerned. It is noticeable that the Court did not conclude that the regulation was in truth a series of decisions but simply that the provision, 'even if it is one of a number of provisions having a legislative function', was of direct and individual concern to the applicants. Despite this fact, one author concluded that it followed from the fulfilment of the tests of direct and individual concern that

[248] Case 100/74, n. 112 above, at point 14.
[249] See 73 above.
[250] Case 100/74, n. 112 above, at point 15.
[251] *Ibid.*, at point 18.
[252] *Ibid.*, at point 19.
[253] The reg. was part of a series of regs.—definitely of a legislative nature—aimed at counteracting the effects of inflation on agriculture, and the Commission had acted in pursuance of the derogatory powers that the Council reg. establishing the threshold prices had conferred upon it. In this context it must be recalled that the Court had consistently held that a provision derogating from the provisions of an act of a general nature partakes of the general character of the latter: see n. 88 above.

the measure was a decision.[254] In this work, it is argued that the measure was a true regulation and that the Court deliberately avoided the test of legal nature in order to declare the action admissible. Support for this argument is found in that the word 'decision' does not appear anywhere in the judgment.

2. It is submitted that this case is the first indication that the Court could have been ready to ignore the test of legal nature in situations where the measure applied exclusively to closed categories. In those situations the *only* people affected by the measure are the members of the closed category and it would have been very unfair to deprive them of the opportunity of bringing annulment proceedings.[255]

3. The tests of direct and individual concern were given a very similar construction to that in the area of case law concerning decisions.[256]

A very similar approach was adopted by the Court in *Société pour l'Exportation des Sucres* v. *Commission*.[257] In that case, a Commission regulation retroactively abolished the right of cancellation for export licences with advance fixed refunds issued before 15 March 1976 and still valid on 1 July 1976. The regulation applied in its entirety to a closed category of traders, namely those holders of export licences issued before 15 March who had not used them by 1 July. The applicants belonged to that category, and the Court had no difficulty in concluding that they were directly and individually concerned by the regulation.

Two other cases are *Agricola Commerciale Olio* v. *Commission*[258] and *Savma* v. *Commission*.[259] A Commission regulation had required the Italian intervention agency (AIMA) to sell a quantity of olive oil. Lots were drawn and six undertakings were declared successful tenderers. Subsequently, the Commission enacted another regulation cancelling the sale. The applicants (the undertakings that had been allocated lots) brought annulment proceedings against the latter regulation. The Commission objected to the admissibility of the action on the ground that the regulation was a true one aimed at the management of the olive oil market.[260] Advocate General

[254] T. C. Hartley believed that in the judgment 'there was no specific finding that the measure was a decision; the Court must have considered that this followed automatically from the finding that it applied individually to those affected', '*Locus Standi* to Challenge Regulations' (1978) 3 *ELRev.* 385, 386, in other words that the fulfilment of the test of individual concern implies that the measure is, by nature a decision.

[255] In those situations where the regs. affected categories partly closed and partly open, however, the Court normally decided the issue of the *locus standi* of the members of the closed category on the basis of the triple admissibility test (see 132 above) until its decision in *Sofrimport* where the Court ignored the test of legal nature and considered only direct and individual concern (see 147 below).

[256] In this context see R. Kovar and A. Barav, 'Variations Nouvelles sur un Thème Ancien; les Conditions de Recevabilité du Recours Individuel en Annulation' [1976] *CDE* 73, 94.

[257] Case 88/76, n. 215 above.

[258] Case 232/81, n. 42 above.

[259] Case 264/81, n. 215 above.

[260] Case 232/81, n. 42 above, at 3885.

Lenz ignored the test of legal nature and concluded that the applicants were directly and individually concerned, given that the purpose of the contested regulation was to cancel the effect of the sale and, therefore, it only affected the traders individualized by the drawing of lots.[261] The Court basically agreed with the Advocate General and declared the action admissible without taking into account the test of legal nature. The Court said:

> [F]rom the time when lots were drawn, at the very latest, the situation as between the parties to the sale was determined. Regardless of when ownership was transferred, it follows that any intervention on the part of the Community Institutions preventing AIMA from carrying out its obligations to the traders designated by the drawing of lots, necessarily constitutes a measure of direct and individual concern to them.[262]

In *Asociación Provincial de Armadores de Pesca de Gran Sol de Pontevedra (ARPOSOL)* v. *Council*,[263] a Spanish association formed to represent and defend the interests of forty-six Spanish fishing businesses brought annulment proceedings against a Council regulation laying down the measures to be taken in respect of certain operators who do not comply with the provisions relating to fishing contained in the Act of Accession of Spain and Portugal. All the members of ARPOSOL appeared in Annex IX to the Act of Accession and, consequently, they were authorized to fish in Community waters.[264] Article 2 of the contested regulation[265] provides that the Member States must notify the Commission of any infringement of the provisions of the Act without delay. After such notification, the vessel concerned is automatically excluded from the periodical lists which the Member States submit to the Commission. The applicants believed that the provision violated the principles of *audi alteram parte*[266] and *non bis in idem*.[267]

The Court dismissed the action exclusively on the grounds that the applicants were not directly concerned, given that they could only be

[261] Case 232/81, n. 42 above, at 3903.

[262] See *Agricola Commerciale*, at point 11, and *Savma*, at point 11.

[263] Case 55/86, n. 142 above.

[264] For a brief description of the system provided by the Act of Accession, see 58 above.

[265] Reg. 3781/85 [1985] OJ L363/26.

[266] In relation to this point two authors pointed out that, in cases where the alleged infringement was decided in the course of administrative proceedings, as opposed to judicial proceedings (i.e. before a French administrative authority), the penalty of exclusion from the periodical list would be applied without giving the master of the vessel the chance to be heard; in other words, it would constitute a breach of the principle of the right to a fair hearing. See R. R. Churchill and N. G. Foster, 'Double Standards in Human Rights? The Treatment of Spanish Fishermen by the EEC' (1987) 12 *ELRev*. 430, 440.

[267] These principles are general principles of European Community law and as such have been acknowledged by the Court on numerous occasions: see Case 85/76 *Hoffmann-La Roche* v. *Commission* [1979] ECR 461, at point 9, for the principal of *audi alteram parte* and Joined Cases 18 and 35/65 *Gutmann* v. *Commission* [1966] ECR 103 for the principle of *non bis in idem*.

affected 'if the State in which they are registered, refused under Article 2 of the contested regulation, to enter their names on the drafts of periodical lists and if these draft lists are approved by the Commission'.[268]

It is suggested that the applicants were not directly concerned because no direct damage had been caused to them as a result of the regulation; it would be necessary first to commit an infringement of the provisions of the Act of Accession and to be excluded from the list. It is believed that they were individually concerned in that they formed part of the closed category of fishing vessels named in Annex IV of the Act of Accession as authorized to fish in Community waters.[269]

Although it is clear, in view of the principles underlying the existing case law governing the *locus standi* of private parties, that ARPOSOL's action could not be declared admissible, this case raises an important issue. The regulation at stake in the present case could have been infringing two general principles of Community law: *non bis in idem* and *audi alteram parte*. The restrictive *locus standi* conditions of Article 173(2) EEC Treaty prevented the applicants from putting forward their submissions on the substance of the case. It must be recalled that in some national legal systems, although natural and legal persons do not have a wide right of action against legislative measures, in some cases they may challenge even a statute when it allegedly violates certain fundamental rights.[270] It is thought that, in cases like the present one, private applicants should be given *locus standi* to challenge regulations that could be infringing general principles of law.[271]

B. Regulations Affecting Mixed Categories

In *Sofrimport* v. *Commission*[272] the Court moved a step towards a more liberal construction of the *locus standi* of private parties to challenge

[268] Case 55/86, n. 142 above, at point 12. Mischo A.G. had arrived at an identical conclusion: *ibid.* 20.

[269] This view finds support in the decision of the Court in Case 207/86 *APESCO* v. *Commission* [1988] ECR 2151; see 000 above.

[270] For instance, the Spanish Constitution protects as one of these rights the principle of *audi alteram parte*: see art. 24(4), Art. 161(b), and Art. 53(2). See also Arts. 103(1) and (3) of the German Constitution, which refers to the principles of *audi alteram parte* and *non bis in idem*, and Art. 93(4), which allows the review of the constitutionality of laws that could be violating those principles.

[271] In this respect see the similarities between the present case and Case 191/87 *COVALE* v. *Commission* (n. 127 above, and accompanying text). For a discussion as to why alternative means of review would be unsatisfactory in this case, see 192 ff. below. It is important to note in this respect that the ECJ in its recent report on certain aspects of the application of the TEU (source: 'Les Activités de la Cour et du Tribunal de Première Instance des Communauts Européennes', Week 22 to 26 May 1995, at 14), has encouraged the idea that the 1996 Intergovernmental Conference should examine the problems that could arise from the introduction of a catalogue of fundamental rights in the Treaty. In particular, the Court indicated that, in the event of such a catalogue being introduced, it would be necessary to consider whether the burdensome *locus standi* conditions of Art. 173 EC Treaty would allow effective judicial protection of the rights of natural and legal persons.

[272] Case C–152/88, n. 12 above.

normative acts. In this case, a French importer of fresh fruit sought the annulment of three Commission regulations that suspended the issue of import licences, including pending licences, for dessert apples originating in Chile. Sofrimport had lodged applications for import licences and had a shipment of applies on the way to the Community when the regulations were enacted. The French intervention agency refused to issue the licences on the basis of those measures. The regulations at issue therefore applied to categories of traders partially closed (the ones with pending licences and goods in transit, i.e. Sofrimport) and partially open (other traders).

It has been shown in a series of cases where the regulations at issue affected partly closed categories, and where the applicants belonging to those categories were directly and individually concerned, how the Court had decided that the actions were inadmissible because the measures were true legislative acts.[273] The Court, however, took a different stand in *Sofrimport*. First of all, it ignored the test of legal nature and decided the issue of admissibility on the basis of the tests of direct and individual concern.

The Court concluded that the applicants were directly concerned, given that the national authorities were left with no choice except to reject the pending applications for licences.[274]

In discussing the issue of individual concern, the Court first emphasized that the applicant belonged to a category fixed and ascertained, that of traders with products in transit when the regulations were issued.[275] Secondly, the Court explained that a provision in the basic Council regulation in the sector[276] gave traders with products in transit specific protection. The Court believed, therefore, that those applicants 'ought to be able to enforce observance of that protection by bringing legal proceedings for that purpose'.[277] The finding that the applicants were individually concerned was therefore derived from the fact that they belonged to a closed category, in that they had pursued a distinctive conduct in the past—they

[273] In this respect, see 57 above. For the exceptional circumstances that arose in Case 333/85 *Mannesmann-Röhrenwerke* v. *Council*, see n. 10 above. It was on the basis of the existing case law that Tesauro A.G. concluded that the application for annulment brought by *Sofrimport* should be declared inadmissible on the ground that the measure was a true reg. He concluded that 'the suspension at issue here derives from the exercise of a legislative power intended to regulate and maintain the equilibrium of the market . . . whilst it is true that, the measure in question applies to a number of persons it is also true that, to use an expression from a previous decision, that comes about, by virtue of an objective legal or factual situation defined by the measure in relation to its purpose': Case C–152/88, n. 12 above, at I–2494.

[274] *Ibid.*, at point 9. Compare this case with Case 55/86 *ARPOSOL*, n. 142 above, where it was clear that the Member State did have a separate role to play.

[275] Case C–152/88, n. 12 above, at point 10.

[276] Art. 3(3) of Council Reg. 2707/72, on the conditions for applying protective measures for fruit and vegetables ([1972] JO L291/3; [1972] OJ Spec. Ed. 3) provides that the Commission, when adopting protective measures, should take into account the special position of products in transit to the Community.

[277] Case C–152/88, n. 12 above, at point 12.

had applied for licences and their goods were in transit to the Community —to which an individual right was attached—the right to come within the safeguarding clause of the earlier Council regulation for importers with goods in transit. The Commission violated that right by enacting the protective measures without taking into account the situation of traders with goods in transit.[278] On this basis the applicants were individually concerned. The ruling in *Sofrimport*, therefore accords with the conclusions reached earlier[279] about the notion of individual concern.[280] The Court went on to annul the regulations in so far as they applied to traders with pending licences and goods in transit; further, it awarded them damages. This is a very rare case, in that the applicants obtained everything they asked for, the annulment of the regulations in so far as they affected them, and moreover, financial compensation.

The recent decision of the Court in *Codorniu* v. *Council*[281] has confirmed this liberal trend of the Court. *Codorniu* is a Spanish company that manufactures and markets quality sparkling wines. It owns the graphic trademark 'Gran Crémant de Cordorniu' and has been using it since 1924 to designate one of its wines. Other Spanish producers also use the term 'Gran Crémant'. A provision of a Council regulation reserved the use of the term 'Crémant' to certain quality sparkling wines manufactured in France and Luxembourg. *Codorniu* brought annulment proceedings against this provision, arguing that its inability to use the term at issue would involve a loss of 38 per cent of its total turnover.[282] The Court decided that the applicant was individually concerned in that the effect of the contested provision was to deprive the applicant of the use of its own trade mark.[283] The tests of direct concern and of legal nature were neither mentioned nor applied,[284] and the action

[277] Case C–152/88, n. 12 above, at point 12.

[278] The CFI has emphasized, in its recent decision in Case T–489/93 *Unifruit Hellas* v. *Commission* [1994] ECR II–1201, the importance of the existence of an individual right of the applicants that was disregarded by the Community institution concerned when it enacted the contested reg. In that case (which involved facts remarkably similar to those in *Sofrimport*), the applicant was a company that imported and exported fruit and vegetables to and from non-Member States and which brought annulment proceedings against three Commission regs. that established a countervailing charge on the importation of apples from Chile. The applicants belonged to the closed category of traders with goods in transit when the contested measures were enacted, but, unlike the situation in *Sofrimport*, they did not hold an individual right that the Commission had disregarded when enacting the contested measures. The CFI refused to grant them *locus standi* on the basis that they were not individually concerned: *ibid.*, at point 25.

[279] See 52 ff. above.

[280] See in particular the similarities between the ruling of the Court in this case and in Case 11/82 *Piraiki-Patraiki*, n. 98 above. For a discussion of this latter case, see 54 above.

[281] Case C–308/89, n. 14 above.

[282] See also the Opinion of Lenz A.G.: *ibid.*, at 1869–71, who concluded that the applicant was individually concerned on the basis of the damaging effect that the provision at issue could have on the applicant's position in the market.

[283] *Ibid.*, at point 21.

[284] Furthermore, the Court readily admitted that the provision was of a legislative nature. The Court said: '[a]lthough it is true that according to the criteria in the second paragraph of Article 173 of the Treaty, the contested provision is by nature and by virtue of its sphere of

was declared admissible. On the merits, the contested provision was annulled on the grounds that it discriminated between producers in the Community.

The contested provision affected a category of traders partially closed (the users of the term 'crémant') and partially open (all future users of the term). *Codorniu* was a member of the closed category but furthermore was distinguished by the fact that it had a specific right (the right to use its trade mark) that was affected by the contested provision.[285] As a consequence, the applicant was individually concerned by the provision. The *Codorniu* case therefore, confirms the interpretation in this work of the notion of individual concern.[286]

4.5 Some Tentative Conclusions

So far, the following conclusions seem to emerge from the case law of the Court on the *locus standi* of non-privileged applicants to bring annulment proceedings against regulations.

1. *Regulations affecting exclusively closed categories.* The existence of two divergent lines of case law, i.e. whether to apply the double or triple admissibility test, is not merely capriciousness on the part of the Court; it represents a deliberate effort to avoid the rigours of the test of legal nature in cases where the whole regulation at issue affected a closed category and where it was not clear whether or not there was a causal link between the regulation and the situation of the applicants.[287] If the test of legal nature had been applied in those cases, the actions for annulment would probably have been dismissed as inadmissible. It is noteworthy that, prior to *Sofrimport*, most of the cases[288] decided on the basis of the double admissibility test referred to regulations affecting exclusively closed categories.[289]

application, of a legislative nature, in that it applies to the traders concerned in general, that does not prevent it from being of individual concern to some of them': Case C–309/89, n. 14 above, at point 19.

[285] The CFI, in a recent case involving the annulment of a dir., referred back to the *Codorniu* case, explicitly saying that *Codorniu* was individually concerned because the contested provision had affected the specific rights of the applicant: Case T–99/94 *Asocarne* v. *Council* [1994] ECR II–873, at point 20.

[286] See 53 above.

[287] Those cases where the existence of such causal link has been clear: see Joined Cases 41–44/70 *International Fruit Company* v. *Commission*, n. 60 above; and Case C–354/87 *Weddel* v. *Commission*, n. 79 above; or where the applicants named in the reg.: see Case 148/79 *Roquette* v. *Council*, n. 122 above, and Case 139/79, *Maizena* v. *Council*, n. 122 above, were decided in accordance with the triple admissibility test.

[288] The only exceptions being Case 40/64 *Sgarlata* v. *Commission*, n. 60 above; Case 123/77 *Unicme* v. *Council*, n. 214 above; and Case 333/84 *Mannesmann-Röhrenwerke* v. *Council*, n. 10 above.

[289] Thus see Case 100/74 *Cam* v. *Commission*, n. 112 above; Case 88/76 *Société pour l'Exportation des Sucres* v. *Commission*, n. 215 above; Case 232/81 *Agricola Commerciale Olio*

2. *Regulations affecting open categories.* In contrast, most of the actions for annulment brought before 1990 involving regulations affecting open categories—either large or small groups—have been decided according to the triple admissibility test.[290] In many of those cases, the non-fulfilment of the test of legal nature has automatically determined the inadmissibility of the actions. A growing trend has been observed, however, in cases concerning small groups, where the Court has also ruled on whether the applicants were individually concerned.[291] In none of those cases concerning open categories were the applicants deemed to be individually concerned, and therefore the practical outcome of these cases would have been the same if the double admissibility test had been applied.

3. *Regulations affecting mixed categories.* Cases involving regulations affecting partially closed and partially open categories were traditionally dealt with by the Court on the basis of the triple admissibility test.[292] In consequence, applicants belonging to the closed category and individually and directly concerned by provisions in those regulations were nevertheless refused *locus standi* to challenge such measures, on the ground that the measures were true regulations. It is in such cases that the application of the test of legal nature has caused damage to the rights of action of private parties. Fortunately, the recent decisions of the Court in *Sofrimport*[293] and in *Codorniu*[294] have modified this line of case law and have allowed the applicants belonging to closed categories and holding specific rights to bring annulment proceedings against the provisions of a regulation retroactively affecting them.

4. It follows that the Court has progressively moved towards a more liberal construction of the *locus standi* conditions of private parties to challenge regulations. The first step has been to free itself from the application of the test of legal nature, at least in those cases where applicants have been individually and directly concerned.[295] The case law after the decision in *Sofrimport* has mostly reflected the Court's intention to extent this trend

v. *Commission*, n. 42 above; Case 264/81 *Savma* v. *Commission*, n. 215 above; and Case 55/86 *ARPOSOL* v. *Council*, n. 142 above.

[290] See Joined Cases 16–17/62 *Confédération Nationale de Producteurs de Fruits et Légumes* v. *Council*, n. 5 above; Case 30/67 *Industria Molitoria Imolese*, n. 62 above; Case 40/84 *Casteels* v. *Commission*, n. 41 above; Case 117/86 *UFADE* v. *Council*, n. 127 above; Case 191/87 *COVALE* v. *Commission*, n. 127 above; Case 6/68 *Zuckerfabrik* v. *Council*, n. 62 above; Case 101/76 *Koninklijke Scholten Honig* v. *Commission*, n. 95 above; Case 147/83 *Binderer* v. *Commission*, n. 95 above; Case 26/86 *Deutz und Geldermann* v. *Council*, n. 129 above; and Joined Cases 97, 193, 99 and 215/86 *Asteris* v. *Commission*, n. 129 above.

[291] See Case 26/86 *Deutz und Geldermann* v. *Council*, n. 129 above; and Joined Cases 97, 193, 99 and 215/86 *Asteris* v. *Commission*, n. 129 above.

[292] See Case 162/78 *Wagner* v. *Commission*, n. 132 above; Case 45/81 *Moksel* v. *Commission*, n. 78 above; Case C–244/88 *Usines Coopérative de Déshydratation du Vexin* v. *Commission*, n. 120 above; and Case C–228/88 *Cargill v. Commission*, n. 132 above.

[293] Case C–152/88, n. 12 above.

[294] Case C–309/89, n. 14 above.

[295] See 143 above.

even to cases where the regulations at issue have affected open categories and the applicants have not been individual concerned.[296] If this trend continues in the future, it means that the Court may be ready to dispense with the hurdle of having to prove that the measure is not a true regulation but a decision. The Court's approach finds support in its case law in cases concerning anti-dumping regulations, where very soon the Court began to ignore the test of legal nature and decided the issue of the *locus standi* of natural and legal persons on the basis of the tests of direct and individual concern,[297] and in more general terms with the overall tendency of the Court in recent years towards greater leniency in affording *locus standi* to private parties in annulment proceedings.[298]

4.6 The *Locus Standi* of Private Parties to Challenge Measures Adopted in the Course of Anti-Dumping Proceedings

4.6.1 Background to Anti-Dumping Proceedings

Dumping is a form of price discrimination that consists of selling products at higher prices in the home market than abroad. From the beginning of this century steps have been taken first by national legislation (Canada in 1904, the United States in 1906) and subsequently at an international level (General Agreement on Tariffs and Trade[299]) to curb the practice of dumping.[300] The EEC Treaty provided for the adoption of measures to protect trade, such as anti-dumping and anti-subsidy measures, as part of the objectives of the establishment of a common commercial policy.[301] Council Regulation 2423/88 on protection against dumped or subsidized imports

[296] See Joined Cases C–232/91 and C–233/91 *Petridi* v. *Commission*, n. 214 above; Case C–131/92 *Arnaud* v. *Commission*, n. 214 above; Case C–213/9 *Abertal* v. *Commission*, n. 214 above; Case C–257/93 *Van Parijs* v. *Council and Commission*, n. 213 above; Case C–276/93 *Chiquita Banana* v. *Council*, n. 213 above; Case 10793 *AEFMA* v. *Commission*, n. 213 above; Case T–476/93 *FRSEA and FNSEA* v. *Council*, n. 213 above; and Case T–472/93 *Campo Ebro* v. *Council*, n. 213 above. All these cases were decided on the basis of the tests of direct and individual concern. The only exceptions to this line of case law are Joined Cases C–15/91 and C–108/91 *Bulck* v. *Commission*, n. 15 above, and the *Gibraltar Airport* cases, n. 15 above, where the admissibility issue was decided on the basis of the triple test.

[297] See 155 below.

[298] In the case law concerning decisions, see 60 above; in the case law concerning competition proceedings, see 86 above, and in the context of state aids cases, see 98 above.

[299] See Art. VI of the GATT and also Art. 14 of the Anti-Dumping Code.

[300] For a survey of the classical objections to the practice of dumping, see 1. Van Bael and J. F. Bellis, *Anti-dumping and other Trade Protection Laws in the European Economic Community* (2nd edn., Bicester, 1990), 30 ff. For a historical introduction on anti-dumping laws, see J. Buhart, 'Le Régime Communautaire de l'Anti-dumping; Vingt Ans d'Experiénce' (1988) 24 *RTDE* 253, 254–7.

[301] Art. 113(1) Ec Treaty. Art. 91 EC Treaty provided for the adoption of such measures during the transitional period, in order to curb dumping practised within the Common Market.

from non-Member countries of the EC is now the basic regulation in force in this area.[302]

Anti-dumping proceedings are normally initiated following a complaint submitted by natural or legal persons, or by an association acting on behalf of the Community industry.[303] The Commission, after consultations with the Advisory Committee,[304] may decide that there is sufficient evidence to initiate proceedings. In that case, the investigation phase is open[305] and the Commission needs to determine the existence of dumping,[306] the existence of injury,[307] the existence of a causal link between the existence of dumping and the injury caused,[308] and that the interests of the EC call for intervention.[309]

During the investigation phase, interested parties enjoy several rights and procedural guarantees.[310] Thus, the Commission has to advise 'exporters, importers and complainants known to be concerned' of the initiation of the proceedings.[311] Complainants, importers, and exporters may inspect all the information made available to the Commission provided it is relevant and not confidential.[312] Exporters and importers have the right to be informed of the essential facts and considerations on the basis of which it is intended to recommend the imposition of definitive duties or the definitive collection of the amounts secured by way of provisional duties.[313] Complainants, exporters, and importers have the right to be heard.[314] Interested parties may, upon request, meet the Commission 'so that opposing views may be presented and any rebuttal arguments put forward'.[315]

Once the investigation phase is over, proceedings may end in various ways. It may be that no anti-dumping duties are imposed, either because the exporters concerned give undertakings, because it is disclosed that no dumping had taken place, or because it becomes evident that protective measures are no longer necessary. Otherwise, the Commission may impose provisional anti-dumping duties and in due course definitive anti-dumping duties may be imposed by the Council.

[302] The first basic reg. was Council Reg. 459/68 [1968] JO L93/1, amended by Council Reg. 2011/73 [1973] OJ L206/3; Council Reg. 1411/77 [1977[OJ L160/4; consolidated by Council Reg. 3017/79 [1979] OJ L339/1; replaced by Council Reg. 2176/84 [1984] OJ L201/1; amended by Council Reg. 176/87 [1987] OJ L167/91; replaced by Council Reg. 2423/88 [1988] OJ L209/1.

[303] See Art. 5 of Reg. 2423/88, n. 302 above.

[304] *Ibid.*, Art. 6.

[305] *Ibid.*, Art. 7.

[306] *Ibid.*, Art. 2.

[307] *Ibid.*, Art. 4.

[308] *Ibid.*

[309] *Ibid.*, Arts. 11(1) and 12.

[310] In this respect, see the similarities with competition regs.: see 79 above.

[311] Art. 7(1)b of Reg. 2423/88, n. 302 above.

[312] *Ibid.*, Art. 7(4)(a). It must be pointed out that most of the price information is confidential and therefore this right is less extensive than it appears to be.

[313] *Ibid.*, Art. 7(4)(b).

[314] *Ibid.*, Art. 7(5).

[315] *Ibid.*, Art. 7(6).

4.6.2 REVIEWABLE ACTS IN ANTI-DUMPING PROCEEDINGS

Annulment proceedings may be brought only against acts producing legal effects.[316] In the course of anti-dumping proceedings, several measures can be susceptible of review.

First, after receiving a complaint, the Commission may either decide *not to initiate proceedings*, in which case the decision is reviewable,[317] or *to initiate proceedings*,[318] in which case it is suggested that the decision would not be open to judicial review in so far as it would be a decision that simply paves the way for later steps in the proceedings.

Secondly, after the Commission investigation takes place, the Commission may decide to terminate the procedure or to impose duties.

On the one hand, the Commission may decide to *terminate the proceedings* either because *protective measures are not necessary*,[319] *or because protective measures are no longer necessary*,[320] or because the Commission *accepts the undertakings of the exporters*,[321] in which cases the measures would be reviewable in so far as they would be final decisions having legal effects upon interested parties.[322] Conversely, the Commission decision *not accepting the undertakings of exporters* is not susceptible of review since it would be an intermediary measure preparatory to the final one imposing the duties.[323]

On the other hand, the Commission may decide to *impose provisional duties* which may be made definitive by the Council. According to Article 13(1) of Regulation 2423/88 both provisional and definitive duties shall be imposed by regulation. A Commission regulation *imposing provisional duties* is a reviewable act,[324] but recent cases have made clear that, when the amounts secured as provisional duties are collected at the rate of the duties definitively imposed, the regulation imposing the provisional duties

[316] See 19 above.

[317] Case 191/82 *FEDIOL* v. *Commission* [1983] ECR 2913.

[318] There is no anti-dumping case to support this argument, but it seems that the decision of the Court in Case 60/81 *IBM* v. *Commission* [1981] ECR 2639 in the area of competition proceedings provides support for this view.

[319] For instance when dumping is non-existent; or when the existence of injury is not proved: e.g. *Wheeled loaders* (Japan), Commission Dec. of 9 Feb. 1989 [1989] OJ L39/35, or when the interests of the Community do not call for intervention: e.g., *Electric Typewriters* (Taiwan), Commission Dec. of 23 May 1986 [1986] OJ L140/52.

[320] e.g. *Shovels* (Brazil), Commission Dec. of 12 Dec. 1984 [1984] OJ L330/28.

[321] See Case 295/86 *Garelly* v. *Commission* [1987] ECR 3117.

[322] See in the area of competition law the judgment of the Court in Joined Cases 8–11/66 *Société Anonyme Cimentières CBR* v. *Commission* [1967] ECR 75.

[323] See Joined Cases C–133/87 and C–150/87 *Nashua Corporation* v. *Commission and Council* [1990] ECR I–719 and Case C–156/87 *Gestetner Holdings* v. *Council and Commission* [1990] ECR I–781.

[324] See Joined Cases 239 and 275/82 *Allied Corporation* v. *Commission* [1984] ECR 1005.

doe not produce separate legal effects.[325] A regulation *imposing definitive duties* is reviewable in that it is a final measure having legal effects on interested parties.[326]

4.6.3 CASE LAW OF THE EUROPEAN COURT OF JUSTICE ON THE *LOCUS STANDI* OF PRIVATE PARTIES TO CHALLENGE ANTI-DUMPING MEASURES

Most of the annulment actions concerning measures adopted in the course of anti-dumping proceedings brought by natural and legal persons have been lodged against the regulations imposing either provisional or definitive duties.[327] In this area of case law, the Court has followed a noticeably more liberal approach to the *locus standi* issue and that is the reason why these cases are considered in a separate section.

The case law of the Court in this area on the *locus standi* conditions imposed on private parties is highly relevant, given the more lenient approach adopted by the Court in contrast to the generally restrictive attitude taken in the area of case law concerning the challenge to regulations adopted in the general management of the market.[328]

Two features characterize the case law of the Court on the issue of *locus standi* of private parties to challenge anti-dumping measures: (a) the early elimination of the test of legal nature, and (b) the different treatment accorded to the various categories of parties normally involved in the anti-dumping proceedings.

4.6.3.1 The Elimination of the Test of Legal Nature

As explained earlier, the basic anti-dumping regulation provides that anti-dumping duties should be imposed by regulation.[329] This implies that the

[325] See Joined Cases 294/86 and 77/87 *Technointorg* v. *Commission and Council* [1988] ECR 6077, at point 12; Case 56/85 *Brother Industries* v. *Commission* [1988] ECR 5655, at point 12; and Joined Cases C–305/86 and C–160/87 *Neotype Techmashexport* v. *Commission and Council* [1990] ECR I–2945.

[326] See the *Japanese Ballbearing cases*: *NTN Toyo Bearing* v. *Council* (Case 113/77 [1979] ECR 1185); *Import Standard Office* v. *Council* (Case 118/77 [1979] ECR 1277); *Nippon Seiko* v. *Council* (Case 119/77 [1979] ECR 1303); *Koyo Seiko* v. *Council* (Case 120/77 [1979] ECR 1337); and *Nachi Fujikoshi* v. *Council* (Case 121/77 [1979] ECR 1363).

[327] There are only a few cases concerning decisions, like Case 191/82 *FEDIOL* v. *Commission*, n. 317 above, or the *Plain paper photocopiers cases*, which partly involved a Commission dec. refusing to accept undertakings from exporters: see *Nashua Corporation* v. *Commission and Council* and *Gestetner Holdings* v. *Council and Commission*, n. 323 above and 167 below.

[328] In this sense, it is interesting also to recall the contrast in the approach of the Court to the *locus standi* of private parties in the case law concerning decisions in the area of general management of the market on the one hand (see 45 above) and in the areas of competition (see 81 above), and state aids (see 90 above) on the other. There is a close kinship between these latter two areas and anti-dumping cases.

[329] See 154 above.

institution concerned cannot validly impose such duties except by regulation. In accordance with the wording of Article 173 EC Treaty, three obstacles need to be overcome by private parties before an action for annulment against a measure in the form of a regulation is declared admissible: these are the fulfilment of the tests of legal nature, and of direct and individual concern.[330] Strictly speaking, therefore, an applicant wishing to challenge a regulation imposing provisional or definitive duties would be confronted with these three hurdles. Nevertheless, if the Court had followed *ad litteram* the wording of Article 173(2) EEC Treaty in the case of anti-dumping regulations, it would have found itself in a difficult situation.

First, the difficulty in fulfilling the test of legal nature is well-known.[331] Application of that test would have rendered inadmissible most of the actions brought by natural or legal persons. This seems a rather unfair result, bearing in mind that there is a series of interested parties—exporters, complainants, importers—which actively participated in the procedure of elaboration of the contested regulations and whose rights and procedural guarantees are described in Regulation 2423/88.[332]

Secondly, if the Court reached the conclusion that an action for annulment brought by a private party was admissible, the Court would automatically have to annul the regulation for having been adopted in the wrong form.[333]

The Court solved this delicate problem by simply ignoring the test of legal nature. Only in one case, *Alussuise* v. *Council and Commission*[334] did the Court decide the *locus standi* of the applicant on the basis of the triple admissibility test. In that case, an independent importer brought annulment proceedings against a Commission regulation and a Council regulation imposing provisional and definitive anti-dumping duties on the imports of orthoxylene originating in Puerto Rico and the United States respectively. The Court decided that the measure was a general act and therefore not

[330] See 102 above.

[331] See 122 above.

[332] See n. 302 above. See also the position of interested parties in cases involving competition decisions, 79 ff. above, and state aids decisions, 98 ff. above.

[333] This point was made by T. C. Hartley, n. 9 above, 379, and by J. A. Usher ('Regulations, General and Individual at the Same Time?' (1984) 9 *ELRev.* 263 at 264). This stems from the fact that the imposition of anti-dumping duties has to be effected by means of a reg. (see Art. 13(1) of Reg. 2423/88). In order to overcome this difficulty, Warner A.G. in his Opinion in the *Japanese Ballbearing cases*, n. 326 above, 1246, explained that anti-dumping regs. were 'hybrid regulations' (for definition of this concept, see 115 above) or, in other words, that their provisions could be at the same time decs. in relation to a group of traders and regs. in relation to the rest of traders. In this respect see also the Opinion of VerLoren Van Themaat A.G. in Joined Cases 239 and 275/82 *Allied Corporation* v. *Commission*, n. 324 above. As seen above, in the area of general management of the market, the Court dismissed that view in Case 45/81 *Moksel* v. *Commission*, n. 78 above. In the area of anti-dumping proceedings the Court has never endorsed the views of these Advocates General.

[334] Case 307/81 [1982] ECR 3463.

challengeable by private parties.[335] It is unclear why the Court took this approach in the *Alussuise* case.

The approach adopted in *Alussuise* has not been repeated in later cases. Starting with the judgment of the Court in *Allied Corporation* v. *Commission*[336] and continuing in later cases, the Court disregarded the test of legal nature and only considered whether the applicants were directly and individually concerned by the regulations at stake. In *Allied*, the Court said:

> Although it is true that, in the light of the criteria set out in the second paragraph of Article 173, such measures are in fact, as regards their nature and scope, *of a legislative character* inasmuch as they apply to all the traders concerned, taken as a whole, their provisions may none the less be of direct and individual concern to those producers and exporters charged with practising dumping.[337]

It is noticeable that the word 'decision' does not appear in the judgment. This is a powerful indication that the measure remains a regulation but may nevertheless contain provisions of direct and individual concern of certain traders.

It is argued that the approach of the Court, although at variance with the precise wording of Article 173(2) EEC Treaty, is justified[338] on grounds of facilitating the access of private parties to judicial review in the European Community, in a fashion similar to the case law concerning regulations in those cases where the measures or some of their provisions affected closed categories of people.[339]

This view has remained constant in later case law[340] and has been endorsed by the Court in very clear terms in its recent judgment in *Extramet* v. *Council*.[341]

[335] *Ibid.*, at points 8–13.

[336] Joined Cases 239 and 275/82, n. 324 above.

[337] *Ibid.*, at point 11, emphasis added.

[338] Unlike other areas, like the case law concerning the *locus standi* of the European Parliament (see 25 above), where the Court gave reasons for adopting a more liberal approach in recent cases, the Court has seldom explained the reasons behind its moves toward a more lenient construction of the *locus standi* of private parties. Exceptions to this are, in competition cases the *First Metro* case (Case 26/76 [1977] ECR 1875), in anti-dumping cases *FEDIOL* v. *Commission* (Case 191/82, n. 317 above), and in the general area of case law *Parti Ecologiste 'Les Verts'* v. *European Parliament* (Case 394/83 [1986] ECR 1339). A survey of these exceptional cases reveals that it was necessary for the Court to explain why such a new approach had been adopted, given the revolutionary line of thought the cases introduced in their respective areas.

[339] See 143 above.

[340] See, for instance, Case 279/86 *Sermes* v. *Commission* [1987] ECR 3109, at point 15; Case 301/86 *Pedersen* v. *Commission* [1987] ECR 3123, at point 14; Joined Cases C–133/87 and C–150/87 *Nashua Corporation* v. *Commission and Council*, n. 523 above, at point 14; and Case C–156/87 *Gestetner Holdings* v. *Council and Commission*, n. 323 above, at point 14.

[341] The Court said: '[i]t follows that measures imposing anti-dumping duties may, *without losing their character as regulations*, be of individual concern in certain circumstances to certain traders who therefore have standing to bring an action for their annulment': Case C–358/89 [1991] ECR I–2501 at point 14, emphasis added. In this respect see also D. Wyatt and A. Dashwood, *European Community Law* (3rd edn., London, 1993), 130.

4.6.3.2 Locus Standi *Conditions Imposed on Parties Concerned by Anti-dumping Proceedings*

As already seen,[342] Regulation 2423/88 was drafted bearing in mind the rights of parties interested in the proceedings. Some of these parties are expressly enumerated in the regulation[343]—exporters, importers, and complainants. Others have appeared as such from the case law of the Court,[344] i.e. associations of consumers and users. The Court has adopted an uneven approach regarding their *locus standi* to challenge anti-dumping regulations. In the following pages, the basis on which the Court granted *locus standi* to these parties will be analysed. There are great similarities in the trend followed by the Court in these cases and those decided in the area of competition and state aids proceedings. These similarities will be stressed in individual instance.

4.6.3.2.1 Exporters

The first cases where the issue of the *locus standi* of exporters arose were the *Japanese Ballbearing* cases.[345] Following a complaint by the Federation of European Bearing Manufacturers that Japanese ballbearings were being dumped in the Community, the Commission adopted a regulation imposing provisional anti-dumping duties on the importation of such products. The Council then adopted the contested regulation[346] on the same day that the Commission had accepted the undertakings of the producers. Four Japanese producers (*Toyo*, *Nippon Seiko*, *Koyo Seiki* and *Nachi*), hereafter referred to as the 'Big Four', were the main target of the regulation. The Council regulation imposed a definitive anti-dumping duty on all Japanese ballbearings, but suspended its application[347] so long as those specific undertakings were observed; imposed on the Commission the duty to be vigilant that the undertakings given by the producers were not violated;[348] and finally ordered the definitive collection[349] of the provisional anti-dumping duties imposed on the products manufactured by the 'Big Four', who were expressly named in the regulation.

The 'Big Four' and their subsidiaries brought annulment proceedings against the Council regulation. The Court had to decide first on the admissibility of their actions. As a preliminary point, it made clear that the 'Big Four' and their subsidiaries were sufficiently closely associated and, therefore, regarding the question of whether they were individually and

[342] See 153 above.
[343] *Ibid.*
[344] See 169 below.
[345] N. 326 above.
[346] Reg. 1778/77 [1977] OJ L196/1.
[347] *Ibid.*, Art. 1.
[348] *Ibid.*, Art. 2.
[349] *Ibid.*, Art. 3.

directly concerned by the regulation, there was no need to distinguish between producers and subsidiaries.[350]

The Court held that the actions brought by the exporters and their subsidiaries were admissible, in that the provision they were contesting[351] was in truth a collective decision relating to named addressees.[352] The Court ruled that the provision only concerned importers who had imported products manufactured by the 'Big Four' and consequently it was of direct and individual concern to the latter.[353]

From the decisions of the Court in those cases it appears that when exporters are named in the regulation at issue they are granted standing to challenge the measure,[354] which logically ceased to be a regulation and became a series of decisions addressed to them.[355] The Court's standpoint prompted fears that exporters would only be given *locus standi* in those cases where they were named in the operative part of a regulation.[356] As

[350] See Case 113/77 *NTN Toyo Bearing* v. *Council*, n. 326 above, at point 9; Case 119/77 *Nippon Seiko* v. *Council*, n. 326 above, at point 11; Case 120/77 *Koyo Seiko* v. *Council*, n. 326 above, at point 14; and Case 121/77 *Nachi Fujikoshi* v. *Council*, n. 326 above, at point 6.

[351] Art. 3 of the Reg: see n. 346 above.

[352] See Case 113/77 *NTN Toyo Bearing* v. *Council*, n. 326 above, at point 11; Case 119/77 *Nippon Seiko* v. *Council*, n. 326 above, at point 14; Case 120/77 *Koyo Seiko* v. *Council*, n. 326 above, at point 23; and Case 121/77 *Nachi Fujikoshi* v. *Council*, n. 326 above, at point 11.

[353] It is noticeable that the Court has always decided with more leniency on the *locus standi* of subsidiaries or co-subsidiaries, both in anti-dumping and in competition cases: see Joined Cases 228–229/82 *Ford of Europe and Ford Werke* v. *Commission* [1984] ECR 1129, 000 above, and accompanying text).

[354] In later cases, whenever exporters have been named in the reg. at issue, the admissibility of their applications has never been contested by the defendant institutions. Thus see Case 250/85 *Brother Industries* v. *Council* [1988] ECR 5683; Case 301/85 *Sharp* v. *Council* [1988] ECR 5813; Joined Cases 260/85 and 106/86 *TEC* v. *Council* [1988] ECR 5855; Joined Cases 273/85 and 207/86 *Silver Seiko* v. *Council* [1988] ECR 5927; Case C–69/89 *Nakajima* v. *Council* [1991] ECR I–2069; and the recent decision of the CFI in Joined Cases T–163/94 and T–165/94 *NTN Corporation* v. *Council*, judgment of 2 May 1995, not yet reported.

[355] It is useful to recall here that this view also appeared in the area of general case law. See Case 138/79 *Roquette* v. *Council*, n. 122 above, and Case 139/79 *Maizena* v. *Council*, n. 122 above. This idea, however, conflicts with the point made earlier that anti-dumping duties should be imposed by reg., see 272 above. The Court itself declared that the contested provision was a 'bundle of decisions' in these judgments but it did not comment on this underlying conflict. Warner A.G. did, and that is why he put forward the theory that anti-dumping regulations could be *hybrid regulations* (see n. 77 above). The Court however did not seem to adopt his view (see n. 78 above). In later cases involving named exporters this conflict did not arise, given that the admissibility of their applications was never contested by the defendant institutions (see n. 354 above).

[356] See C. Norall, 'Judicial Review of Anti-dumping Measures: Further Developments' (1984) 9 *ELRev.* 46, 49 and J. F. Bellis, 'Judicial Review of EEC Anti-dumping and Anti-subsidy Determinations after *Fediol*: The Emergence of a New Admissibility Test' (1984) 21 *CMLRev.* 539, 545. In fact, in Case 307/81 *Alussuise* v. *Council and Commission* (see n. 334 above, and accompanying text), this view was repeated. In that case, the Court said (referring to the admissibility of an action brought by an independent importer): '[c]onsequently, such measures constitute, as regards independent importers who, *in contrast to exporters, are not expressly named in the regulation*, measures of general application': *ibid.*, at point 9, emphasis added.

one author pointed out,[357] this view had many drawbacks, especially in relation to undertakings which, although not named in the regulation at issue, actively participated in the proceedings leading to its adoption and which were the subject of the Commission's investigations.[358]

In *Allied Corporation* v. *Commission*,[359] three American exporters and one independent importer brought annulment proceedings against a Commission regulation imposing provisional anti-dumping duties on imports of chemical fertiliser originating in the United States.[360] The Court, when dealing with the *locus standi* issue of the exporters, introduced a new element. First, it explained that it was clear from the basic anti-dumping regulation[361] that anti-dumpling duties may 'only be imposed on the basis of findings resulting from investigations concerning the production prices of undertakings individually identified'.[362] Then the Court concluded that:

It is thus clear, that measures imposing anti-dumping duties are liable to be of direct and individual concern to those producers and exporters who are liable to establish that they were identified in the measures adopted or *concerned* by the preliminary investigations.[363]

The decision of the Court in *Allied* widened the *locus standi* of exporters and producers in relation to earlier case law, allowing them to bring annulment proceedings against regulations imposing anti-dumping duties, not only in cases where they were named in the contested measures, but also when they had participated in the investigations led by the Commission.[364] Thus, procedural involvement of exporters in the adoption of the contested measures appeared as a key element in determining their standing in annulment proceedings.[365] This approach has appeared not only in the case law that followed in cases involving regulations imposing anti-

[357] C. Norall, n. 356 above, 51.

[358] The European Parliament also at this time expressed its concern that 'there should be adequate opportunities for appeal from Commission decisions and judicial review of the procedures and the international legal concepts of dumping and subsidization' (Report of 1 Sept. 1981, drafted by the Committee on External Economic Relations on the EEC Anti-dumping activities: Doc. 1–422/81. 'The Welsh Report', 14).

[359] Joined Cases 239 and 275/82, n. 324 above.

[360] In a later case, Case 53/83 *Allied Corporation* v. *Council* [1985] ECR 1621, the applicants challenged the Council reg. that imposed definitive anti-dumping duties.

[361] At the time it was Reg. 3017/79: see n. 302 above.

[362] Joined Cases 239 and 275/82, n. 324 above, at point 11.

[363] *Ibid.*, at point 12, emphasis added.

[364] The Court has also explained that '[a] regulation imposing different anti-dumping duties on a series of traders is of direct concern to any one of them only in respect of those provisions which impose on that trader a specific anti-dumping duty and determine the amount thereof and not in respect of those provisions which impose anti-dumping duties on other undertakings': Case 258/84 *Nippon Seiko* v. *Council* [1987] ECR 1923, at point 7, and Case C–174/87 *Ricoh* v. *Council* [1992] ECR I–1335, at point 7.

[365] When this case was decided, the procedural involvement of private parties in the course of anti-dumping proceedings had already appeared as an important element in the *locus standi* issue in a case involving complainants: see Case 191/82 *FEDIOL* v. *Commission*, n. 317 above.

dumping duties[366] but also in cases involving decisions adopted in the course of competition[367] and state aids decisions.[368]

The Court did not tackle the issues of direct and individual concern on the same basis as in its general area of case law. First, as in cases involving competition and state aids decisions, the two issues have never been dealt with separately. Secondly, in relation to individual concern, the concept has not been construed on the basis of the existence of a closed category[369] but on the basis of the role played by applicants in the anti-dumping proceedings. The reason for this more liberal approach by the Court was well-expressed by one author:

> Regardless of the form of the instrument by which the proceeding is concluded, determinations made by the institutions at the end of the proceedings are bound to be of 'individual' concern to all those who have participated in it: for them, the outcome of the proceedings reflects *per force* the institution's judgement on the input which they have brought into the proceedings.[370]

The test of direct concern has never been discussed in these cases but it is argued that it is connected with the existence of a causal link between the anti-dumping regulation and the damage caused in the interests to the applicants.

4.6.3.2.2 Complainants

It has already been seen that anti-dumping proceedings are normally initiated following a complaint submitted by a natural or legal person, or association, acting on behalf of the Community industry.[371]

The first case where the situation of complainants was debated was *Fédération de l'Industrie de l'Huillerie de la CEE (FEDIOL)* v. *Commission*,[372] a case decided in the closely related field of anti-subsidy

[366] Thus, statements similar to the one in *Allied* appeared in Case 279/86 *Sermes* v. *Commission*, n. 340 above, at point 15; Case 301/86 *Pedersen* v. *Commission*, n. 340 above, at point 14; Joined Cases C–133/87 and C–150/87 *Nashua Corporation* v. *Commission and Council*, n. 340 above, at point 14; Case C–156/87 *Gestetner Holdings* v. *Council and Commission*, n. 323 above, at point 14; Case 205/87 *Nuovo Ceam* v. *Commission* [1987] ECR 4427, at point 11; and Case C–358/89 *Extramet* v. *Council*, n. 323 above, at point 15. The intervention of a company (on which the Commission did not impose anti-dumping duties) as a mere transmitter of documents between the Commission and the company found to be practising dumping does not suffice, however, to make that company directly and individually concerned: Case C–75/92 *Gao Yao* v. *Council* [1994] ECR I–3141.

[367] See *Second Metro Case* (Case 75/84 [1986] ECR 3021), see 84 above.

[368] See Joined Cases 67–68 and 70/85 *Van der Kooy* v. *Commission* [1988] ECR 219; see 96–7 above.

[369] Although, as happened in cases involving competition proceedings, the fact that the applicants participated in the proceedings put them in a closed category, since no one could participate after the contested decision was enacted. The difference between this area and the area of general case law is that, in the case of anti-dumping proceedings, the fact that the applicants had participated in the procedure only gave them certain procedural rights and not individual substantive rights under Community law: see 82 above.

[370] J. F. Bellis, n. 300 above, 549.

[371] See 153 above.

[372] Case 191/82, n. 317 above.

proceedings[373] and one which involved a Commission decision instead of a regulation. The Commission, following a complaint from *FEDIOL*—the European Seed Crushers and Oil Processors Federation—addressed a decision to the latter, refusing to initiate anti-subsidy proceedings relating to the import of soya bean oil cakes from Brazil into the Community. In this case, it was not the *locus standi* of *FEDIOL* to challenge the decision of refusal which was contested (addressees always have *locus standi*) but its right to obtain a Commission decision commencing anti-dumping proceedings.

The Court analysed the case in a fashion very similar to the approach adopted in the *First Metro Case*[374] in the area of competition proceedings. The Court initially stated that the basic anti-dumping regulation[375] recognized the existence of a legitimate interest on the part of complainants, manifested by the fact that a series of procedural rights are granted to them.[376] On this basis the Court explained that complainants had to be accorded the right to bring annulment proceedings not only when the EC institutions disregarded those rights,[377] *but also*:

> [I]n the spirit of the principles which lie behind Articles 164 and 173 of the Treaty, complainants have the right to avail themselves, with regard both to the assessment of the facts and to the adoption of the protective measures provided for by the regulation, of a review by the Court appropriate to the nature of powers reserved to the Community Institutions on the subject.[378]

The point made by the Court in this judgment is that, from the moment a complainant files a complaint and the Commission considers it,[379] the institution acknowledges that the latter has a legitimate interest in the outcome of the proceedings. As a consequence, a series of procedural rights are granted to complainants, i.e. they may submit observations, they may examine the file and non-confidential information, they may request to be heard, etc. As a result of their procedural involvement, they hold a *legally protected interest*. These parties must therefore be given the right to review not only any violation of those rights but also, in the spirit of the principle of attainment of an overall system of judicial protection,[380] the

[373] Anti-subsidy proceedings (also called countervailing measures) are another type of measure for trade protection against subsidized imports whose release and free circulation in the Common Market cause damage to the Community industry. They are governed by the same legislative instrument as anti-dumping proceedings, i.e. Reg. 2423/88 (see n. 302 above), and share many provisions in common with anti-dumping proceedings.

[374] Case 26/76 [1977] ECR 1875; see 81 above.

[375] At the time, Reg. 3017/79, n. 302 above.

[376] Case 191/82, n. 317 above, at point 25. (These rights are described at 153 above.)

[377] *Ibid.*, at point 28.

[378] *Ibid.*, at point 29.

[379] As for the difficulties that arise from an approach based on procedural involvement, see 169.

[380] See also, in the area of competition proceedings, the judgment of the Court in the *First Metro Case* (Case 26/76, n. 374 above, at point 14).

resulting measures adopted by the Community institution.[381] In summary, the procedural involvement of private parties again plays a key role in the ultimate recognition of the admissibility of their actions.[382]

The position of complainants was discussed again in *Timex* v. *Council and Commission*.[383] In this case, Timex, the leading manufacturer of mechanical watches in the EC, brought annulment proceedings against a Council regulation imposing definitive duties on the importation of mechanical watches originating in the former Soviet Union, on the grounds that the duty imposed was too low. Three elements determined the *locus standi* of the applicants.

First, the complaint lodged by Timex, triggered the investigation of the Commission, and Timex's views were heard during the proceedings.[384] In other words, the Court took into account Timex's procedural involvement.

Secondly, the Court pointed out that Timex was the leading manufacturer of mechanical watches in the Community.[385] This is a factual circumstance which points towards the degree of damage that the applicants may suffer as a consequence of the contested measure.[386]

Thirdly, the Court explained that the regulation was based on the applicant's own situation because 'the conduct of the investigation procedure was largely determined by Timex's observations and the anti-dumping duty was fixed in the light of the effect of the dumping on Timex .[387]

The Court therefore concluded that the applicants had *locus standi* to challenge the contested regulation.

Complainants are therefore granted standing on the basis of their procedural involvement in the elaboration of the measure at issue. The fact that they are involved in the procedure means that the Commission has acknowledged that they are interested parties, and as a consequence they

[381] See J. P. Kuyper, 'Some Reflections on the Legal Position of Private Complainants in Various Procedures Relating to Commercial Policy' [1983–85] *LIEI* 115, 128.

[382] See J. F. Bellis, who explained that the Court in this case 'shifted the admissibility enquiry from the nature of the measures to that of the proceedings leading to the adoption of the measures' (n. 300 above, 549).

[383] Case 264/82 [1985] ECR 849.

[384] *Ibid.*, at points 13–14.

[385] *Ibid.*, at point 15, emphasis added.

[386] It must be recalled here that in the area of case law on general management of the market, the Court did not normally take these circumstances into account. Thus, see Case 1/64 *Glucoséries Réunies* v. *Commission* [1964] ECR 413, where the applicant was a leading manufacturer of glucose, and Joined Cases C–15/91 and C–108/91 *Bulck* v. *Commission*, n. 15 above In one judgment, however, a factual element appeared in the determination of *locus standi*: see Case 294/81 *Control Data* v. *Commission* [1983] ECR 911. In competition cases these elements appeared in the *Second Metro Case* (Case 75/84 [1986] ECR 3021). In anti-dumping proceedings, see Case C–358/89 *Extramet* v. *Council*, n. 341 above.

[387] Case 264/82, n. 383 above, at point 15. In this respect, see the Court's ruling in *Allied Corporation* v. *Commission* (see 160 above) where it also made clear that anti-dumping duties are imposed on the basis of findings resulting from investigations concerning undertakings individually identified.

have a series of procedural rights that have to be respected.[388] Their right to judicial review, though, is not limited to obtaining the protection of those rights but also extends to an examination of the substantive measures subsequently adopted by the Commission or the Council.[389]

4.6.3.2.3 Importers

In the case of importers, there has been an evolution from very restrictive *locus standi* conditions to more lenient ones, but the process has taken longer than for complainants or exporters. Until the recent judgment of the Court in *Extramet* v. *Council*,[390] importers were not granted *locus standi* to challenge regulations imposing anti-dumping duties, even if they had participated in the proceedings leading to the adoption of the measure in question. That seems a little unfair if their situation is compared with the situation of exporters and complainants. This section has been subdivided into two. The first sub-section deals with the case law before *Extramet*; the second with the *Extramet* judgment.

A. The Case Law before *Extramet*: Principles and Foundations of the *Locus Standi* of Importers in Annulment Proceedings: Special Consideration of the Position of Original Equipment Manufacturers (OEMs)

In one of the *Japanese Ballbearing* cases,[391] the *locus standi* of importers was first considered. In that case, an exclusive importer (ISO) associated with one of the 'Big Four' (Nachi) brought annulment proceedings against the regulation at issue in those cases.[392] The Court declared ISO's action admissible on the ground that ISO and Nachi were so closely associated that, in order to determine the existence of dumping, the export price had to be 'constructed' on the basis of the resale price at the first independent buyer.[393] It would seem therefore that importers would only be granted

[388] In a case decided in the area of general management, Joined Cases C–15/91 and C–108/91 *Bulck* v. *Commission*, n. 15 above, the applicants maintained that they had become involved in the elaboration of the reg. at issue in that they had let the Commission know that they would suffer great damage as a result of the reg. and that the Commission had taken into account their prices in the course of its investigations. The Court refused their contentions and explained that, although in the area of anti-dumping cases complainants have a series of procedural rights recognized in the basic anti-dumping reg., the basis market regs. do not make provision for similar rights of interested third parties: *ibid.*, at points 29–30.

[389] This point was also made by the Court in Case 264/82 *Timex*, n. 383 above, at point 16.

[390] Case C–358/89, n. 341 above.

[391] Case 118/77 *Import Standard Office (ISO)* v. *Council*]1979] ECR 1277.

[392] See n. 326 above.

[393] Case 118/77, n. 391 above, at point 15. In order to establish the existence of dumping, the basic anti-dumping reg. provides for comparison between the *normal value* and the *export price* (Art. 2(9) of Reg. 2423/88, n. 301 above). The *normal value* is 'the price actually paid or payable in the ordinary course of trade for the like product intended for consumption in the exporting country or country of origin' (*ibid.* , Art. 3(a)). The *export price* can be either (a) the price actually paid or payable for the product sold for export to the Community (*ibid.*, Art. 8(a)), or (b) the constructed export price, i.e. the price of first resale to an independent buyer

locus standi in very specific circumstances, i.e. when during the anti-dumping investigations, the Commission had to use the constructed export price to determine the existence of dumping.

In *Allied Corporation* v. *Commission*,[394] the Court decided that, although an exporter who had participated in the preliminary investigations was granted *locus standi*,[395] an independent importer was refused *locus standi*—even though it too had participated in the procedure—on the ground that the export price was not calculated by taking into account the resale prices charged by the importer.[396]

This narrow conception has been the subject of severe criticism.[397] Notwithstanding this fact, the Court reiterated its view in later cases.[398]

The criteria used by the Court to ascertain the *locus standi* of importers in annulment proceedings seem very restrictive.[399] One may wonder *why*

(*ibid.*, Art. 8(b)). The Commission normally uses the constructed export price to determine the existence of dumping in those cases where there is an association or compensatory arrangement between the exporter and the EC importer. The provisions referring to the method of determination of the export price have appeared in very similar or identical terms in all the basic anti-dumping regulations prior to Reg. 2423/88, the one currently in force. At the time the *Japanese Ballbearing* cases were decided the basic reg. in force was Reg. 459/68 (see n. 302 above), and the provision dealing with the method of determination of the export price was Art. 3(3) of that Reg.

[394] Joined Cases 239 and 275/82, n. 324 above. [395] See 000 above.

[396] Joined Cases 239 and 275/82, n. 324 above, at point 15.

[397] See J. F. Bellis, n. 300 above, 550; A. M. Matarasó, 'The Independent Importer's Right of Review of Anti-dumping Regulations before the European Court of Justice' (1988) 12 *Fordham Int.LJ* 682; J. A. García López, 'Derecho Económico Internacional y Relaciones Privadas: La Interdependencia Funcional del Régimen GATT y el Ordenamiento Jurídico Comunitario en la Aplicación de Normas de Intervención Comercial, con Particular Referencia al Derecho Anti-dumping' (1992) 54 *R Esp.D Int* 443, 460. E. van Ginderachter, 'Problématique de la Recevabilité au regard de la Réglementation CEE en Matière de Dumping et de Subventions: Etat de la Question et Perspectives d'Avenir' [1987] *CDE* 635, 649.

[398] In two cases concerning the imposition of provisional anti-dumping duties on the importation of multi-phase electric motors, the Court applied the same criteria: see Case 279/86 *Sermes* v. *Commission*, n. 340 above, and Case 301/86 *Pedersen* v. *Commission*, n. 340 above. In those cases, the applicants were the sole importers into France and into Denmark respectively of the aforesaid products. The Court explained that they were not directly and individually concerned by the reg. at issue, in so far as the Commission had not determined the export prices by reference to the importers' resale prices (see *Sermes* v. *Commission*, at points 14–17 of the judgment, and *Pedersen* v. *Commission*, at points 14–17 of the judgment). Likewise, in Joined Cases 277 and 300/85 *Canon* v. *Council* [1988] ECR 5731, where a group of Community importers brought annulment proceedings against a Council reg. imposing definitive duties on the importation of electronic typewriters originating in Japan. The Court declared the actions inadmissible, given that the export price had not been calculated by taking into account the importer's resale prices in the Community.

[399] In this respect see E. Van Ginderachter, n. 397 above, 650, where he explains that there are two main objections to this approach. In the first place, an importer may have a greater degree of dependence on the exporter than if it were associated with him in the form of a compensatory agreement, e.g. when it uses the dumped product as raw material to manufacture a product essential to its economic activities. In the second place, the parameter used by the Court cannot be applied to anti-subsidy proceedings where the concept of export price has no place at all, given that the proceedings have their origin in the acts of public authorities of non-member Countries.

the Court has never explained its reasons for choosing an element such as the method of determination of the export price by the Commission, when so many other factors intervene in the determination of the existence of dumping. In the cases of both exporters[400] and complainants,[401] the *locus standi* conditions imposed on them referred to their procedural involvement in the process of elaboration of the measure at issue and, as a consequence of the latter, to the procedural rights granted to them in the basic anti-dumping regulation. Both elements appear equally in the case of importers. Thus, in many of the cases where actions were dismissed as inadmissible, the importers had actively participated in the Commission investigations.[402] Likewise, Regulation 2423/88[403] acknowledges importers as 'concerned parties'[404] and grants them the same procedural rights as exporters and complainants.[405] Therefore it could be said that from the time importers become involved in the Commission investigations, the Commission has *de facto* recognized that those importers have a legitimate interest in the outcome of the proceedings. Consequently, those importers should be given *locus standi*, if they wish to challenge the legality of the resulting measures. On this basis, the approach taken by the Court seems rather unfair, especially if it is borne in mind that importers are the ones paying the duties.[406] One might also add that granting *locus standi* to importers where the Commission has used constructed export prices but refusing *locus standi* where other methods of calculation are used is rather arbitrary, as it makes the outcome of *locus standi* depend on which method of calculation the Commission chooses to use.

Fortunately the Court began to adopt a more liberal approach to the *locus standi* of importers in two groups of cases.

The first group of cases involved regulations imposing duties on the importation into the EC of multi-phase electric motors. The Court declared admissible the actions for annulment brought by Community im-

[400] See 158–61 above.
[401] See 161–4 above.
[402] Thus see Case 307/81 *Alussuise* v. *Council and Commission*, n. 334 above at 3469; Joined Cases 239 and 275/82 *Allied Corporation* v. *Commission*, n. 324 above; Case 279/86 *Sermes* v. *Commission*, n. 340 above, at point 10; Case 301/86 *Pedersen* v. *Commission*, n. 340 above, at point 10.
[403] See n. 302 above.
[404] *Ibid.*, Art. 7(1)b.
[405] See 153 ff., above.
[406] T. C. Hartley thought that the approach of the Court was partly due to the fact that importers could have recourse to national courts: n. 9 above, 381. The Court has repeatedly made reference to this possibility open to importers. Thus see Case 307/81 *Alussuise* v. *Council and Commission*, n. 334 above, at point 13; Joined Cases 239 and 275/82 *Allied Corporation* v. *Commission*, n. 324 above, at point 15; Case 279/86 *Sermes* v. *Commission*, n. 340 above, at point 19.; Case 301/86 *Pedersen* v. *Commission*, n. 340 above, at point 19; Case C–205/87 *Nuova Ceam* v. *Commission*, n. 366 above, at point 17. However, as Jacobs A.G. explained in his Opinion in Case C–358/89 *Extramet* v. *Council*, n. 341 above, at I–2523–2525, recourse to national courts is not always a satisfactory alternative to annulment proceedings. In this respect see 188 below.

porters whose resale prices had not been used to determine the existence of dumping but to calculate the anti-dumping duty itself.[407]

The second group of cases involved a Council regulation imposing definitive anti-dumping duties on imports of plain paper photocopiers.[408] These cases concerned the particular situation of OEMs (Original Equipment Manufacturers), i.e. companies that supply under their own brand name products manufactured by other undertakings. Two OEMs (Nashua and Gestetner) were independent importers whose resale prices had not been taken into consideration by the Commission in order to determine the export price in its findings in relation to the existence of dumping. The Court, however, granted Nashua and Gestetner *locus standi* in annulment proceedings against the Council regulation, on the grounds that, given the particular features adopted in the business dealings between OEMs and exporters, the OEMs' sales were taken into account by the Commission in the calculation of the normal value and the weighted dumping margin on the basis of which the anti-dumping duty was fixed. The OEMs were granted *locus standi* because they 'were concerned by the findings relating to the existence of dumping'.[409] The Court, therefore, seemed to be beginning to transpose the reasoning followed in cases concerning the *locus standi* of exporters and complainants and to be attaching importance to the procedural involvement of the applicants. Nevertheless, in view of the features of these cases, and in particular of the special relationship between OEMs and exporters, it would have been premature to reach the conclusion that the Court had definitely changed its view on the *locus standi* of independent importers. Fortunately, the Court reviewed its standpoint in *Extramet* v. *Council*,[410] a landmark case on the *locus standi* of importers to challenge anti-dumping measures.

B. The *Extramet* Judgment

The Council, following an increase in the imports of calcium metal from China and the former Soviet Union, imposed a definitive anti-dumping duty on such imports,[411] given that the EC industry was experiencing difficulties. *Extramet* was an undertaking in the Common Market producing pure calcium from calcium metal. Pechiney was a major producer of Calcium metal and also transformed it. In the recital to the regulation imposing the duties,[412] the Council stated that the 'Community producer'

[407] Joined Cases C-305/86 and C-160/87 *Neotype Techmashexport* v. *Commission and Council*, n. 325 above, at point 20; Joined Cases C-320/86 *Stanko France* v. *Commission and Council* [1990] ECR 3013, summary publication § 2, and Case C-157/87 *Electroimpex* v. *Council* [1990] ECR 3021, summary publication § 2.

[408] Joined Cases C133/87 and C-150/87 *Nashua Corporation* v. *Commission and Council*, n. 323 above, and Case C-156/87 *Gestetner Holdings*, n. 323 above.

[409] *Ibid.* at points 15-20 and 17-23 respectively.

[410] Case C-358/89, n. 341 above.

[411] Reg. 2808/89 [1989] OJ L271/1.

[412] See recitals 2 and 3 of the Reg., n. 302 above.

. Pechiney) and 'an independent importer' (i.e. *Extramet*) had their ,ws heard during the proceedings. Extramet and Pechiney were in direct ›mpetition with each other, and in its submissions, Extramet pointed out that Pechiney had refused to supply it with calcium metal, obviously to prevent competition from Extramet.

Extramet brought annulment proceedings against the regulation. The Council objected that the action was inadmissible, on the well-known ground that, in the findings relating to the existence of dumping, the applicant's resale prices had not been taken into account to determine the export price.[413] Extramet in its turn, stressed that it was the principal importer into the Community of calcium metal from China and the former Soviet Union and that it had actively participated in the anti-dumping proceedings.[414] Advocate General Jacobs reviewed the case law of the Court on *locus standi* of importers and concluded that, in his view, there should be two cases where importers ought to be granted standing to challenge anti-dumping regulations: (a) in those cases where importers are identified, even implicitly in the anti-dumping regulation, and (b) in those cases where importers have actively participated in the anti-dumping proceedings, at least when their position in the market has been significantly affected.[415] In the present case, the applicant satisfied both conditions.

The Court declared the action admissible but it did not do so on the basis that Advocate General Jacobs had suggested. For the Court, Extramet was individually and directly concerned on two counts:

1. It was the largest importer of calcium metal and, at the same time, end-user of the product.[416]
2. Its business activities depended to a large extent on those imports and were seriously affected by the regulation, given: (a) the limited number of manufacturers of the product, and (b) the difficulties in obtaining supplies from Pechiney, which was its main competitor.[417]

Hence the Court reached the conclusion that the applicant had *locus standi* without taking into account that it had been identified in the anti-

[413] Case C–358/89, n. 341 above, at I–2505.

[414] *Ibid.*

[415] *Ibid.* I–2523. The second situation suggested by Jacobs A.G. recalls significantly the judgment of the Court in Case 169/84 *COFAZ* v. *Commission* [1986] ECR 391, see 90 above.

[416] *Ibid.*, at point 17. It must be recalled here that in Case 264/82 *Timex* v. *Council and Commission*, n. 383 above, the fact that the applicant in that case was a leading manufacturer of the products at issue influenced in the issue of its *locus standi*. In the area of general case law, see Case 294/81 *Control Data* v. *Commission* [1983] ECR 911, see 60 above.

[417] *Ibid.*, at point 17. The consideration of the economic damage that the contested measure may cause to the applicants had appeared in very few occasions in the case law of the Court. Thus, see in the area of state aids Case 169/84 *COFAZ* v. *Commission*, n. 415 above, and Case C–198/91 *Cook* v. *Commission*, judgment of 19 May 1993; in the arena of competition proceedings see the judgment of the CFI in the *Air France* cases (see 86 above) and in the area of general management of the market, Case C–354/89 *Schiocchet* v. *Commission*, n. 104 above.

dumping regulation or that it had participated in the proceedings. Instead, the Court chose to take into account only factual circumstances, like the importance of the applicant in the market in question and the extent to which its economic activities would be disrupted as a consequence of the measure.[418] If the Court had regarded as conclusive the method of determination of the export price—as it had done consistently in earlier case law[419]—a very unfair situation would have arisen.[420]

The *Extramet* judgment is a clear example of a situation where the Court has been more concerned with upholding the rule of law and protecting interested parties than with following the literal wording of Article 173(2) EEC Treaty. Thus, the test of legal nature was ignored, and even the tests of direct and individual concern received a construction very different from that in earlier cases. The Court did not even look at the procedural involvement of the applicants in the proceedings, a key element for the determination of the *locus standi* of exporters and complainants, but decided on the basis of the devastating economic consequences that the regulation would bring upon the applicant.[421] With this interpretation, moreover, the Court has overcome some difficulties engendered by equating *locus standi* with procedural involvement in the anti-dumping proceedings. This would arise, for instance, in the case of an importer who did not intervene in the Commission investigations, i.e. either because the Commission failed to notify it of the initiation of the proceedings, or because the Commission did not take into account the importer's data, but who suffers great economic damage as a consequence of the regulation adopted. On the basis of *Extramet*, such an importer would be granted standing. The questions left open by *Extramet* are, of course, (a) the degree of importance that an importer must hold in the market, i.e. principal importer, one of the main importers, etc.; (b) the degree of damage that he must sustain as a consequence of the contested measure.

4.6.3.2.4 Other Parties

In this section the most important point is the study of the situation of associations of users and consumers. In *Bureau Européen des Unions de*

[418] In the view of two authors, the Court should have chosen, as a criterion for assessing the *locus standi* of importers, whether they had participated in the proceedings or not: E. A. Vermulst and J. J. Hooijer, 'Note on *Extramet* v. *Council*' (1992) 29 *CMLRev*. 385, 387.

[419] See 164–7 above.

[420] The most conclusive proof in this respect is that the Court has subsequently annulled the reg. at issue in its judgment on the substance of this case: Case C–358/89 *Extramet* v. *Council* [1992] ECR I–3813.

[421] This is an element consistently argued by private applicants in the case law of the Court on admissibility of annulment actions, e.g. Case 40/64 *Sgarlata* v. *Commission*, n. 60 above, Case 1/64 *Glucoseries Réunies* v. *Commission* [1964] ECR 413, Case 123/77 *UNICME* v. *Council*, n. 214 above, but it has rarely been accepted by the Court.

Consommateurs (BEUC) v. *Commission*[422] the European Office of Consumer Unions brought a plea of illegality in order to obtain a declaration of inapplicability to it of Article 7(4)(a) of Regulation 2423/88,[423] on the ground that this provision did not regulate the right of associations of users and consumers to inspect the Commission's non-confidential file. The Court concluded that it was for the Community legislature to consider whether such parties ought to be granted that right.[424] The Court, however, also said that 'there is nothing in the wording of Article 7(4)(a) of the Basic Anti-dumping regulation to prevent the Commission from allowing persons who have a legitimate interest to inspect the non-confidential file'.[425] In other words, the Court admitted that the Commission could acknowledge that such parties are interested parties. In the light of the case law so far studied it may be concluded that, if these parties are allowed to participate in the proceedings leading to the adoption of an anti-dumping measure, most probably they will be granted *locus standi* in subsequent annulment proceedings. Further case law will no doubt provide some enlightenment on this point.

4.7 The *Locus Standi* of Private Parties to Challenge Measures in Form of Directives

As has already been seen, it is clear from the wording of Article 173 EC Treaty that decisions are the only acts challengeable by private parties by means of annulment proceedings.[426] However, in view of the case law of the Court on the *locus standi* of private parties to challenge regulations,[427] academic writers began to put forward their views on whether directives could also be susceptible of review.[428]

It was not until recently that the European Court faced a case where private parties challenged a directive. Thus, in *Fédération Européenne de la*

[422] Case C–170/89 [1991] ECR 5709.
[423] See n. 302 above.
[424] Case C–170/89, n. 4523 above, at point 30.
[425] *Ibid.*, at point 29.
[426] But see the case law concerning regs., see 150–2 above.
[427] *Ibid.*
[428] The authors are divided on this point. Thus, R. Joliet, *Le Droit Institutionnel des Communautées Européennes* (Liège, 1981), 72–3 and P. J. Kapteyn and T. P. VerLoren Van Themaat, *Introduction to the Law of the European Communities* (2nd edn., Deventer, 1989), 291 believed that dirs. ought to be excluded from the scope of challenge by natural and legal persons due to: (a) the clear wording of Art. 173(2) EEC Treaty and (b) the fact that the original and most essential function of dirs. is to harmonize legislation, which necessarily implies that they are general in nature. Other authors, like M. Waelbroeck ('Le Recours en Annulation' [1971] *RCJB* 513, 536) believe that the possibility of challenging dirs. could be open to private parties, especially bearing in mind the innovative case law of the Court on the effects of these measures and the non-formalistic approach of the Court in the *ERTA* case (see 19 above). Similarly, D. Wyatt and A. Dashwood, n. 341 above, 124, explain that if individuals are able to challenge decisions addressed to Member States (provided they are of direct and individual concern to them), it is not impossible that they may be allowed to challenge dirs. if they fulfil the tests of direct and individual concern.

Santé Animale v. *Council*,[429] a European association for the protection of animal health brought annulment proceedings against a directive prohibiting the use in livestock farming of certain substances having a hormonal action. The applicants had first requested the adoption of interim measures,[430] which were dismissed as inadmissible on the ground that directives are measures of general application and therefore fall outside the scope of review of private parties.[431] When the Court delivered its judgment on the annulment proceedings, the action was dismissed as inadmissible, but on different grounds. This time, the Court put aside the general nature of the measures and stated only that the directive was not of individual concern to the applicants.[432] From this case, it would seem *a sensu contrario* that, had the applicant been individually and directly concerned by the directive, its action would have been declared admissible.

In a recent case, however, the Court decided the admissibility of an action brought by a private party against a provision in a directive on the basis of the triple admissibility test. In this case, *Government of Gibraltar* v. *Council*,[433] a Full Court dismissed the application for annulment brought by the applicant against a provision in a directive. The directive at issue concerned the authorization of scheduled inter-regional services for the transport of passengers, mail, and cargo between the Member States. The contested provision suspended the application of the directive to Gibraltar airport until the Joint Declaration made by Spain and the United Kingdom on 2 December 1987 came into operation.

The Court analysed the legal nature of the directive. It pointed out: first that it affected *very wide categories of people* (i.e. all carriers wishing to operate a direct inter-regional air service between another Community airport and Gibraltar airport); secondly, that other airports had likewise been excluded (i.e. those of the Greek and Atlantic islands); finally, that the *reason* for the exclusion was the existence of an obstacle of an objective nature (i.e. the differences between the United Kingdom and Spain on the sovereignty of Gibraltar).

The case law of the Court of First Instance appears not to be completely uniform in this area either. Thus, in *Guna* v. *Council*,[434] two provisions in a Council directive on homoeopathic products were challenged by a manufacturer and importer of those products. The Court decided the case only on the basis of the tests of direct and individual concern, and explained that the applicant was not individually concerned, in that the contested provisions affected him as a member of an open category, all manufacturers of homoeopathic products.[435] The Court did not hint at all that

[429] Case 160/88 [1988] ECR 6399.
[430] Case 160/88R [1988] ECR 4121.
[431] *Ibid.*, at point 27.
[432] Case 160/88, n. 430 above, at point 13.
[433] Case C–298/89, judgment of 29 June 1993.
[434] Case T–463/93, Order of the CFI of 29 Oct. 1993.
[435] *Ibid.*, at point 17.

directives are *a priori* excluded from applications for judicial review brought by private parties.[436]

In its recent decision in *Asocarne* v. *Council*,[437] however, the Court adopted a different approach, and took as a starting point the strict wording of Article 173 EC Treaty, which does not mention the right of private parties to challenge directives. The Court explained that those applicants would have means of redress before the national courts, once the directives have been implemented by national authorities.[438] The Court applied the test of legal nature[439] and concluded that the measure was a true directive, and not a 'disguised decision', and therefore excluded from challenge by private parties. Only incidentally did the Court examine the question of individual concern. The application for annulment was dismissed as inadmissible.

The decisions of the European Court in the *Gibraltar* case and of the Court of First Instance in *Asocarne* seem to recall the early decisions of the European Court in actions against regulations.[440] Those decisions could be read in two ways: (a) that the Court of First Instance will, in future cases, analyse first the test of legal nature before going into individual and direct concern, in which case it could be that even natural and legal persons directly and individually concerned by a provision in a directive could be barred from challenging it on the basis of its general nature;[441] (b) that the European Court and the Court of First Instance respectively chose in those cases to deal with legal nature, given that, in any event, the applicants were not individually concerned and the practical result—inadmissibility—would have been the same even if only the latter of the two tests had been applied. Only future case law will clarify the Court of First Instance's approach to the problem of the *locus standi* of private applicants to challenge directives.

It is thought that, although it is difficult to imagine a situation where a natural or legal person is directly and individually concerned by a directive, the test of legal nature should not be added to the already exacting tests of direct and individual concern, particularly in view of the recent case law of the European Court of Justice on regulations. Several arguments support this conclusion. First the case law on regulations proves that, in some cases, private applications have *locus standi* to challenge provisions in a regulation, despite its general nature.[442] Secondly, the case law on the

[436] That was so even though the main argument of the Council was that the terms of Art. 173 EC Treaty do not allow natural and legal persons to challenge dirs.: *ibid.*, at point 9.

[437] Case T–99/94, Order of the CFI [1994] ECR II–873.

[438] *Ibid.*, at point 17. This argument does not appear to be completely valid if other decs. of the Court are considered. See 96, n. 401 above.

[439] *Ibid.*, at point 18.

[440] See 113 ff. above.

[441] In this sense, see the case law concerning regs. affecting mixed categories (see 132 above).

[442] See 149 above.

effects of directives has been very liberal and there is no reason why such a trend could not be transposed to the area of judicial review of those measures. Finally, in *Alcan* v. *Commission* the Court said, referring to Article 173(2) EEC Treaty:

> The aim of this provision is to ensure legal protection of individuals in all cases in which they are individually concerned by an EEC measure—*in whatever form it appears*—which is not addressed to them.[443]

This statement would mean, therefore, that directives can also be reviewable by natural or legal persons directly and individually concerned by those acts.

[443] Case 69/69 [1970] ECR 385, at point 4, emphasis added.

PART II

Alternative Means of Review

5

Preliminary Rulings on Validity

5.1 General Features

As well as fulfilling the purpose of preserving the uniformity of Community law throughout the Community and of ensuring co-operation between the national courts and the European Court of Justice, the system of preliminary rulings offers an alternative route for the challenge of illegal action by the Community institutions.[1]

All three Community Treaties contemplate the possibility of obtaining a review of the validity of Community acts by means of preliminary rulings delivered by the European Court.[2] Thus, once a Community measure (e.g. an agricultural regulation) has been implemented by the national authorities, a private party may challenge the national measure before the national court, which may, in turn, refer a question about the validity of the Community measure to the European Court.

Under Article 177(1)(b) of the EC Treaty,[3] the European Court of Justice of the European Communities has jurisdiction to give preliminary rulings relating to 'the validity and interpretation of acts of the Institutions of the Community *and of the European Central Bank*'.[4] Article 41 ECSC Treaty gives jurisdiction to the European Court to deliver preliminary rulings on the validity of acts of the Commission and the Council 'where such validity is in issue in proceedings brought before a national court or tribunal'.

Preliminary rulings on the validity of Community measures constitute an indirect method of judicial review of the legality of Community action. Given that the greatest number of actions brought before the national courts are lodged by private parties, the system of preliminary rulings opens up a useful additional channel that allows private parties to obtain the review of potentially illegal Community acts.[5] Furthermore, given the

[1] Thus see Case 294/83 *Parti Ecologiste 'Les Verts'* v. *European Parliament* [1986] ECR 1339, at point 23, and Case 314/85 *Foto-Frost* v. *Haulptzollamt Lübeck-Ost* [1987] ECR 4199, at points 18–19.

[2] Art. 177(1)(b) EC Treaty, Art. 41 ECSC Treaty, and Art. 150(1)(b) Euratom Treaty.

[3] Art. 150(1)(b) Euratom Treaty reads in very similar terms.

[4] The italicized words represent the Maastricht Treaty amendments.

[5] Thus see T. L. Early, 'The Scope of Preliminary Rulings on the Validity of Community Law' (1980) 15 *The Irish Jurist* 237 at 239; G. Bebr, *Development of Judicial Control in the European Communities* (The Hague, 1981), 494; C. Harding, 'The Impact of Article 177 on the Review of Community Action' (1981) 1 *YEL* 93 at 112–13; H. G. Schermers and D. Waelbroeck, *Judicial Protection in the European Communities* (5th edn., Deventer, 1992),

restrictions placed by Article 173(2) EEC Treaty on the direct challenge of Community acts, Article 177 has become a widely used route for private applicants.[6]

Several aspects of the system of preliminary references need to be considered here.

> 1. In relation to the *kinds of acts* that may be challenged, Article 41 ECSC Treaty refers to acts enacted by the Council and the Commission, whereas Article 177 uses the broader formula of 'acts of the institutions of the Community and *of the European Central Bank*'. This formula—considerably broader than that of Article 173—would certainly cover regulations, directives, and decisions enacted jointly by the Council and the Parliament, and the Commission, and the regulations and decisions enacted by the European Central Bank,[7] i.e. acts producing legal effects in accordance with the list in Article 189 EC Treaty. This statement, however, needs to be tempered in accordance with the case law of the Court.

In the first place, the European Court of Justice has consistently held that the concept of a reviewable act must encompass all measures adopted by the institutions that are intended to produce legal effects, regardless of their denomination.[8]

Secondly, the Court—which had already given interpretative rulings on recommendations[9]—has ruled that, unlike Article 173 (which excludes the review of non-binding acts[10]), 'Article 177 confers on the Court jurisdiction to give a preliminary ruling on the validity and interpretation of all acts of the institutions of the Community without exception'.[11] It would follow, therefore, that opinions and recommendations are included in the scope of Article 177.[12]

Finally, the question arises whether international agreements entered into by the Community under powers given in the Treaties are reviewable.

271; see also the Opinion of Roemer A.G. in Joined Cases 73–74/63 *Internationale Crediet* v. *Minister van Landbouw en Visserij* [1964] ECR 1 at 22.

[6] Thus see C. Vadja, 'Some Aspects of Judicial Review within the Common Agricultural Policy' (1979) 4 *ELRev.* 244 at 244–5, and H. Rasmussen, 'The Court of Justice of the European Communities', in *Thirty Years of Community Law* (European Communities, Brussels, 1981), 187.

[7] See Art. 108(a) EC Treaty.

[8] Thus see Case 22/70 *Commission* v. *Council* [1971] ECR 263, see 19 above.

[9] Case 113/75 *Frecatessi* v. *Amministrazione delle Finanze dello Stato* [1976] ECR 983. See also Case 90/76 *Van Ameyde* v. *Uci* [1977] ECR 1091.

[10] But see the observations offered at 00 above.

[11] Case C–322/88 *Grimaldi* v. *Fonds des Maladies Professionelles* [1989] ECR 4407, at point 8.

[12] Some authors doubt whether such review would be of any practical value: see G. Bebr, n. 5 above, 465 and the Opinion of Roemer A.G. in Joined Cases 73–74/63 *Internationale Crediet* v. *Minister van Landbmouw en Visseri*, n. 5 above, at 22.

The Court had already given rulings on the interpretation of international agreements.[13] Now, after the decision of the Court in *France* v. *Commission*,[14] where the reviewability of international agreements was confirmed in the context of annulment proceedings,[15] there is little doubt that these acts may also be reviewed by means of a preliminary ruling on their validity.

In conclusion it may be said that the wording of Article 177(1)(b) is so wide that it allows private parties to obtain the review of practically any kind of Community act, unlike annulment proceedings, which, in practice, seek to limit the kinds of challengeable acts to decisions[16] and the plea of illegality, which only allows the indirect challenge of regulations.[17]

2. The procedure under Article 177 is unique from the point of view of the rights of private parties. Unlike the other avenues of judicial review—action for annulment, plea of illegality, and action for a failure to act—where a private party challenges directly or indirectly before the European Court of Justice the illegality of the action or omission of the Community institutions, here the national court is the only one entitled to request the review of the validity of a Community act. This derives from the fact that the system of preliminary rulings was conceived more as a kind of constitutional control than as a direct method of protection of the rights of private parties. The system of preliminary rulings is, therefore, distinguished from other methods of challenge of the legality of Community measures, which adopt the structure of a contentious procedure between the private party and the Community Institution. As the Court explained in *Hessische Knappschaft* v. *Maison Singer*:

> The Court has jurisdiction to give preliminary rulings concerning the interpretation of the Treaty provisions pursuant to article 177 of the Treaty, which establishes direct co-operation between the Court and the courts and tribunals of the Member States by way of a non-contentious procedure, excluding any initiative of the parties who are merely invited to be heard in the course of that procedure.[18]

3. As far as the grounds of review are concerned, it must be noted that the wording of Articles 177 EC Treaty and 41 ECSC Treaty refer to the examination of the *validity* of a Community measure without specifying the grounds, whereas Articles 173 and 33 ECSC Treaty

[13] Case 181/73 *Haegeman* v. *Belgium* [1974] ECR 449, at points 4–6; Case 87/75 *Bresciani* v. *Amministrazione Italiana delle Finanze* [1976] ECR 129; Case 720/80 *Polydor* v. *Harlequin* [1982] ECR 329; Case 12/86 *Demirel* v. *Stadt Scwäbisch Gmünd* [1987] ECR 3719.

[14] Case C–327/91 [1994] ECR I–3641, at points 13–17.

[15] See 20 above.

[16] See 26 above.

[17] See 197 below.

[18] Case 44/65 [1965] ECR 965 at 970. See also Case C–364/92 *SAT Fluggesellschaft* v. *Eurocontrol* [1994] ECR I–43, at point 9.

refer to the review of the *legality* of Community acts and expressly enumerate the grounds that may be invoked.[19] This different wording was used by the German Government in *Internationale Crediet* v. *Minister van Landbouw en Visserij*[20] to put forward the view that perhaps the concept of validity is more restrictive than that of legality, and that the European Court could only, by means of a preliminary ruling on validity, rule on the formal aspects of an act (i.e. whether it is a legal act or a non-existent act) but not on its intrinsic legality. However, this view was rejected by the Advocate General[21] and implicitly by the Court when it went on to examine whether the Commission was entitled, under the relevant provision of the Treaty, to enact the contested decision.[22] In a later case, the Court gave a very wide formulation and accepted that a Community act may be subject to review on any grounds of invalidity.[23] Usually, the national courts, in their requests for a preliminary ruling, will invoke the same grounds of illegality that appear in Article 173.

4. The European Court has exclusive competence to declare an act invalid by means of a preliminary ruling. In the framework of the ECSC Treaty, Article 41 expressly declares that the European Court has exclusive jurisdiction to decide on the validity of a Community act. In the framework of the EC Treaty, the decision of the Court in *Firma Foto-Frost* v. *Hauptzollamt Lübeck-Ost*[24] makes it clear that national courts did not have the power to decide the invalidity of Community acts for two reasons: (a) the threat that this would pose to the uniformity of Community law,[25] and (b) in order to maintain the coherence of the system of judicial review.[26]

5. As to the *effects* of a preliminary ruling on validity, it must be recalled that, in the case of a successful action for annulment, the contested decision is declared null and void and it is treated as if it had never existed. In the case of a preliminary ruling on validity, strictly speaking the declaration of invalidity is only addressed to the referring national court, by virtue of the special nature of the system of preliminary references.[27] Thus, it would appear that the effect of

[19] The plea of illegality may also be invoked on the same grounds as those of Art. 173. See 200 below.

[20] Joined Cases 73–74, n. 5 above, at 9–10.

[21] *Ibid.* 19–20.

[22] *Ibid.* 12–13.

[23] Thus see Joined Cases 21–24/72 *International Fruit Company* v. *Produktschap voor Groenten en Fruit* [1972] ECR 1219, at point 5.

[24] Case 324/85 [1987] ECR 4199.

[25] *Ibid.*, at point 15.

[26] The Court said 'since Article 173 gives the Court exclusive jurisdiction to declare void an act of a Community Institution, the coherence of the system requires that where the validity of a Community act is challenged before a national court, the power to declare the act invalid must also be reserved to the Court of Justice': *ibid.*, at point 17.

[27] See Case 29/68 *Milch-, Fett- und Eierkontor* v. *Hauptzollamt Saarbrücken* [1969] ECR 165, where the Court said: 'A judgment by the Court under Article 177 is binding on the national courts hearing the case in which the decision is given' (at 180).

the ruling ought to be limited to the litigants in the national court's proceedings.[28] The Court has ruled, however, that national courts may rely on a previous preliminary ruling declaring the invalidity of a Community act addressed to another national court in order to regard that Community act as invalid for the purposes of the judgment that it has to give.[29] This is a logical conclusion, given that, otherwise, a great deal of unnecessary litigation could take place before the Court. From the point of view of the rights of private parties, the Court has accepted that the effect of both remedies is, in practice, almost the same.[30] After a preliminary ruling declaring the invalidity of a Community measure, the Community institution concerned will most probably replace the act found to be invalid.[31]

6. A final point that needs to be made in this area is that most of the key doctrines and principles of European Community law are the result of Article 177 rulings, a fact that gives a very strong indication

[28] In fact, this was the Opinion of Gand A.G. in Case 16/65 *Schwarze* v. *Einfuhr- und Vorratsstelle für Getreide und Futtermittel* [1965] ECR 877, at 886.

[29] See Case 66/80 *International Chemical Corporation* v. *Amministrazione delle Finanze dello Stato* [1981] ECR 1191, at point 13, where the Court said: 'It follows therefrom that although a judgment of the Court given under Article 177 of the Treaty declaring an act of an institution, in particular a Council or Commission regulation, to be *void* is directly addressed only to the national court, which brought the matter before the Court, it is sufficient reason for any other court to regard that act as *void* for the purposes of a judgment which it has to give'. It must be noted that the French version of the judgment (Aff. 66/80 [1981] Rec. 1191, at point 13) speaks of the *invalidité* or a Community measure, whereas the English version, in what appears to be an error of translation, speaks of the Community measure as being *void*. (This point was raised by Dr. R. Lane, private communication, Sept. 1994.) Likewise, in the skimmed-milk cases, the English translation of the judgments uses the expression that the regulation in question was *null and void* (Case 114/76 *Bela-Mühle* v. *Grows-Farm* [1977] ECR 1211, at point 8; Case 116/77 *Granaria* v. *Hoofdproduktschap voor Akkerbouwprodukten* [1977] ECR 1247, at point 26, and Joined Cases 119–120/76 *Ölmühle Hamburg* v. *Hauptzollamt Hamburg Waltershof* [1977] ECR 1269), at point 8, whereas the French version of those judgments uses the expression *'le réglement . . . n'est pas valide'* (Aff. 114/76 [1977] Rec. 1211, at point 8; Aff. 116/77 [1977] Rec. 1247 at point 26, and Aff. Jointes 119–120/76 [1977] Rec. 1269 at point 8). It would appear that the French version is the more appropriate, given that nullity is the result of a successful action for annulment and not of a preliminary ruling, where the Court may declare the act in question to be invalid and not void. Accordingly, in later cases the English version of the judgments has used the term *invalidity* (Case 4/79 *Providence Agricole de la Champagne* v. *ONIC* [1980] ECR 2823, at points 42–46; Case 107/79 *Maiseries de Beauce* v. *ONIC* [1980] ECR 2883, at points 42–46; Case 145/79 *Roquette* v. *French Customs* [1980] ECR 2917, at points 50–55. See also Case 120/86 *Mulder* v. *Minister van Landbouw en Visserij* [1988] ECR 2321, at point 8.

[30] For a comprehensive discussion of the retroactive effects of preliminary rulings on validity, see C. Harding, n. 5 above, at 102–6. See the judgments of the Court in Case 4/84 *Pinna* v. *Caisse d'Allocations Familiales de la Savoie* [1986] ECR 1, at 26; Case 112/83 *Société des Produits de Maïs* v. *Administration des Douanes*[1985] ECR 719, at point 17; and Case C–228/92 *Roquette Frères* v. *Hauptzollamt Gelden* [1994] ECR I–1465, at point 20.

[31] Thus see Joined Cases 117/76 and 16/77 *Ruckdeschel* v. *Hauptzollamt Hamburg-St Annen* [1977] ECR 1753, at point 28. See also the example of Dir. 90/366 [1990] OJ L180/30 (dir. on the right of residence for students) which was declared void in Case C–295/90 *Parliament* v. *Council*, judgment of 7 July 1992.

of the creative role played by the Court in the context of these proceedings.

The principles of supremacy,[32] direct effect,[33] and need for effective legal protection of rights claimed under EC law,[34] for instance, are not to be found in the EC Treaty, and the Court has developed them in its case law through preliminary references. Similarly, general principles of law, such as proportionality,[35] equality,[36] legal certainty,[37] and respect for fundamental human rights[38] were progressively ingrained in the EC legal system mostly by way of preliminary references.

The Court has also proved willing, in the field of preliminary references, to uphold a comprehensive system of judicial protection even against the wording of the Treaty. Thus, in *ECSC* v. *Acciaierie e Ferriere Busseni*[39] the Court held that, despite the wording of Article 41 ECSC Treaty,[40] that indicates that the Court is only competent to give preliminary rulings on the *validity* of acts of the High Authority and of the Council, it would have been inconsistent with the system of remedies of the Treaty not to recognize the ability of the Court to give rulings on the *interpretation* of ECSC Treaty provisions and acts of the institutions. In *Amministrazione delle Finanze dello Stato* v. *SPI*,[41] the Court ruled on its competence to interpret provisions of the GATT even though the wording of Article 177 does not provide for such a possibility. In both *Busseni* and *SPI* the Court departed from the traditional formula that describes the jurisdiction of the Court as a *compétence d'attribution*. The Court has, in fact, enlarged the limits of its jurisdiction beyond those established by the provisions of the Treaty, in order to attain a system of judicial protection without any gaps. The Court's approach to preliminary references contrasts markedly with the restraint shown by the Court in the area of actions brought by private parties under Article 173(2) EEC Treaty, where the Court has sometimes preferred to abide by the restrictive wording of that legal provision.[42]

[32] e.g. Case 6/64 *Costa* v. *ENEL* [1964] ECR 585 at 594.

[33] e.g. Case 26/62 *Van Gend en Loos* v. *Nederlandse Administratie der Berlastingen* [1963] ECR 1 at 13.

[34] Case 106/77 *Amministrazione delle Finanze dello Stato* v. *Simmenthal SpA* [1978] ECR 629, at points 13–24 and Case C–213/89 *R.* v. *Secretary of State for Transport, ex parte Factortame* [1990] ECR 2433, at points 18–23.

[35] e.g. Case 9/73 *Schlüter* v. *Hauptzollamt Lörrach* [1973] ECR 1135, at point 22.

[36] e.g. Joined Cases 117/76 and 16/77 *Ruckdeschel* v. *Hauptzollamt Hamburg St-Annen* [1977] ECR 1753, at point 7.

[37] e.g. Case 13/61 *Bosch* v. *Van Rijn* [1962] ECR 45 at 52.

[38] e.g., Case 29/69 *Stauder* v. *City of Ulm* [1969] ECR 419, at point 7.

[39] Case C–221/88 [1990] ECR I–495.

[40] Art. 41 ECSC Treaty is the equivalent of Art. 177 EC Treaty.

[41] Joined Cases 267–9/81 [1983] ECR 801.

[42] For instance, in Case 66/76 *CFDT* v. *Commission* [1977] ECR 305, in an action for annulment brought in the context of the ECSC Treaty, the applicant, a trade union, warned the Court that if the action was declared inadmissible they would be left without a remedy. The Court replied: '[w]hilst the principles upon which the applicant relies call for a wide interpreta-

5.2 The Relationship between Article 177(1)(b) and Article 173 EC Treaty

The pages that follow comprise a study of the advantages and disadvantages of preliminary rulings as an alternative to annulment proceedings. It would appear that a natural or legal person who wishes to contest the legality of a reviewable Community measure has two immediate routes open to him: either to bring a direct action before the European Court under Article 173 EC Treaty, or to challenge before a national court the measure implementing the Community act in the hope that the national court will refer to the Court of Justice a question on the validity of the Community measure under Article 177(1)(b).[43] This could, however, be a very superficial approach to the problem: can private parties really choose between either route, or can they only bring proceedings before the national courts (with the possibility that the national court may raise a question about the validity of a Community act) in situations where Article 173 is not available to them?

On the one hand, an affirmative answer to the second question would mean a serious impediment to the judicial protection of natural and legal persons, as it may be doubtful—particularly bearing in mind the intricate case law of the Court in this area—whether they enjoy *locus standi*. On the other hand, in those situations where it was beyond doubt that the applicants had *locus standi* under Article 173 and nevertheless they did not bring annulment proceedings, the possibility of bringing an action before the national courts would have meant the use of Article 177 as a parallel method of judicial review in direct evasion of the time-limits imposed by Article 173.[44]

tion of the provisions concerning the institution of proceedings before the Court with a view of ensuring the individual's legal protection, they do not permit the Court on its own authority to amend the actual terms of its jurisdiction': *ibid.*, at point 8. See also Case 30/64 *Sgarlata* v. *Commission* [1965] ECR 215, see 43 above, n. 94. In the framework of the ECSC Treaty, see Case 12/63 *Schilieker* v. *High Authority* [1963] ECR 85 at 89.

[43] As the Court explained in Case 314/85, *Firma Foto-Frost* v. *Hauptzollamt Lübeck-Ost*, n. 24 above, at point 16: 'requests for preliminary rulings, like actions for annulment constitute means for reviewing the legality of acts of the Community Institutions'. See also Case 294/83 *Parti Ecologiste 'Les Verts'* v. *European Parliament*, n. 1 above, at point 23.

[44] It must be recalled here that the Court has consistently held in its case law that alternative methods of review may not be used when the Community act in question could have been challenged by means of an action for annulment, and the purpose of using an alternative route is a direct evasion of the time-limits of Art. 173. Thus, see for the plea of illegality, Joined Cases 31 and 33/62 *Wöhrmann* v. *Commission* [1962] ECR 501 at 507 in the framework of the EC Treaty; in the framework of the ECSC Treaty, there is a consistent line of case law to the effect that an applicant may not, in the context of annulment proceedings against an individual decision, invoke the illegality of another individual decision addressed to him that has become definitive due to the expiry of the time-limit provided for annulment proceedings: see Case 41/85 *Sideradria* v. *Commission* [1986] ECR 3917, at point 5 and also the decision of the CFI in

In *Universität Hamburg* v. *Hauptzollampt Hamburg-Kehrwieder*,[45] the Court mentioned the *locus standi* difficulties of Article 173, stressed the role of Article 184 (plea of illegality) in conjunction with Article 177, and on that basis deliberately refused to consider the wider issue of the general relationship between Articles 173 and 177.[46] In *Walter Rau Lebensmittelwerke* v. *Bundesanstalt für Landwirtshaftliche Marktordnung*,[47] the Court admitted that the possibility of bringing an action under Article 173(2) EEC Treaty did not exclude the possibility of another action before a national court against the national measure of implementation. In that case, however, the applicants had simultaneously brought annulment proceedings and an action before the national courts, therefore there was no question of their trying to avoid the time-limits of Article 173.

In a recent case before the Court, *TWD Textilwerke Deggendorf* v. *Germany*,[48] the plaintiff in the national proceedings was an undertaking manufacturing polyamide and polyester yarn that had received aid from the German Government. The Commission, after initiating the procedure under Article 93(2) EC Treaty,[49] reached the conclusion that the aid was unlawful and addressed a decision to Germany ordering its recovery. The competent German authorities forwarded to the German undertaking a copy of the Commission decision, pointing out the fact that it could bring annulment proceedings against the decision. TWD did not initiate proceedings under Article 173(2) EC Treaty but did bring an action before the national courts when the German authorities, in implementation of the Commission decision, addressed a decision to the undertaking, ordering the recovery of the aid.

The national court referred two questions to the European Court, the first of them being whether it was bound by the Commission decision. The Court replied that, it was beyond doubt that TWD could have brought an action for annulment against the Commission decision (a) because there was a consistent line of case law accepting that an undertaking in receipt of individual aid may directly challenge a Commission decision declaring an aid incompatible with the Common Market;[50] and (b) furthermore, the German Government had informed the undertaking of the possibility of

Case T–26/90 *Finsider SpA* v. *Commission* [1992] ECR II–1789, at point 61. A similar doctrine appears in the case law on the action for a failure to act: thus see Joined Cases 10 and 18/68 *Eridania* v. *Commission* [1969] ECR 459 at 483 in the framework of the EC Treaty and Joined Cases 21 to 26/61 *Meroni* v. *High Authority* [1962] ECR 73 at 78 in the framework of the ECSC Treaty.

[45] Case 216/82 [1983] ECR 2771.

[46] *Ibid.*, at points 5–12. In this respect see the very enlightening Opinion of Sir Gordon Slynn A.G. at 2795–7.

[47] Joined Cases 133–136/85 [1987] ECR 2289, at point 12.

[48] Case C–188/92 [1994] ECR I–833.

[49] See 90–7 above.

[50] Case C–188/92, n. 48 above, at point 14. See also 90 ff. above for examples of this line of case law.

bringing annulment proceedings.[51] The Court concluded that the Commission decision had therefore become definitive and could no longer be challenged in Article 177 proceedings.

Since the Court's decision in *TWD Textilwerke*, the role of the system of preliminary rulings on validity appears more than ever to be an alternative to annulment proceedings rather than a parallel method of review. The situation can be summarized as follows: (1) if it is clear beyond doubt that the private party could have brought annulment proceedings (i.e. because it was the addressee of the Community decision, or, if it was not the addressee, because there is a consistent line of case law that points in that direction and the applicant had been informed in good time of the possibility of directly challenging the decision) but it did not do so during the time-limit set in Article 173, the Community decision becomes definitive and can no longer be challenged before the national courts; (2) if it appears doubtful whether the private party had *locus standi* or if the applicant had no means of learning of the Community act and the only act addressed to it was one of the national authority, it would appear that the private party can bring proceedings before the national court, hoping that a reference concerning the validity of the Community act would be made by the national court;[52] (3) finally, in the case of a challenge to regulations, the wording of Article 173(4) EC Treaty and the restrictive interpretation followed by the Court would suggest that private parties may always bring proceedings before the national courts against the measures of implementation, given that it is quite difficult to imagine a situation where it is clear beyond doubt that they enjoy *locus standi*.[53]

The decision in *TWD* seems clear enough, but it is suggested that it has to be treated with caution; a prudent lawyer would probably advise his client always to bring proceedings both under Article 173 EC Treaty and before a national court in any circumstance where there is the slightest doubt whether they have *locus standi* in annulment proceedings.

5.2.1 ADVANTAGES OF PRELIMINARY RULINGS ON VALIDITY

The most obvious advantage that the procedure set out in Article 177 EC Treaty presents is that applicants in proceedings before the national court do not have to fulfil strict *locus standi* conditions (contrary to what happens in annulment proceedings in the European Court) before a national court raises a reference.[54] Therefore both individual and general

[51] Case C–188/92, n. 48 above, at point 26.

[52] The dec. of the Court in Case 216/82 *Universität Hamburg* v. *Hauptzollamt Hamburg-Kehrweder* [1983] ECR 2771 lends support to this view.

[53] See Case 294/83 *Parti Ecologiste 'Les Verts'* v. *European Parliament*, n. 1 above, at point 23.

[54] On the *locus standi* conditions imposed by the national legal systems on private parties to obtain review of administrative action, see 31 ff. above.

Community acts may be challenged without meeting the stringent conditions of direct and individual concern. For this reason, Article 177 EC Treaty has always been seen as the logical alternative to an action under Article 173(2) EEC Treaty by the European Court,[55] by the Advocates General,[56] and by the national courts.[57]

The case law of the European Court provides plentiful examples of cases where preliminary references from national courts have allowed individuals and undertakings to obtain a ruling on the validity of EC regulations and decisions that they could not possibly have challenged by means of a direct action before the European Court, owing to their lack of *locus standi*.[58] Thus it was through preliminary rulings that the regulations or provisions of the regulations at issue in the skimmed milk,[59] maize,[60]

[55] See Case 123/77 *UNICME* v. *Council* [1978] ECR 845, at point 12. The case law involving *locus standi* of importers in anti-dumping proceedings provides ample evidence of the constant reference made by the Court to Art. 177: see 166 above, n. 406.

[56] See Opinion of Gand A.G. in Case 38/64 *Getreide-Import* v. *Commission* [1965] ECR 203 at 213 and of Sir Gordon Slynn in Case 216/82 *Universität Hamburg* v. *Hauptzollamt-Kehrwieder*, n. 52 above.

[57] Thus, the Finanzgericht, Munich, said in *Re Bulgarian Dessert Grapes* [1967] CMLR 156 at 159 that '[a] reference under Article 177 to the Court of Justice for a preliminary ruling will give the appellants an opportunity not afforded to them by the narrow wording of the right of petition under Article 173(2) to test the validity of the regulation'.

[58] For instance it may be recalled that in Case 101/76 *Koninklijke Scholten Honig* v. *Council and Commission* [1977] ECR 797, 127–8 above, the action for annulment brought by the applicants was dismissed as inadmissible in so far as it was directed against a Council and a Commission reg. The applicants then brought proceedings before a national court against the national measure implementing the regs. and that court raised a reference with the ECJ on the validity of the latter (Case 125/77 *Koninklijke Scholten Honig* v. *Hoofdproduktschap voor Akkerbouwprodukten* [1978] ECR 1991). Likewise in the *Berlin Butter* cases, the applicants, German producers of margarine, brought annulment proceedings against a dec. addressed to Germany which were dismissed as inadmissible (Case 97/85 *Deutsche Lebensmittelwerke GmbH* v. *Commission* [1987] ECR 2265). The applicants had, at the same time, initiated proceedings before the national courts, and the national court raised a reference with the ECJ on the validity of the Commission dec. (Joined Cases 133–136/85 *Walter Rau Lebensmittelwerke GmbH* v. *Bundesanstalt für Landwirtschaftliche Marktordnung*, n. 47 above). See also Joined Cases C–133/93, C–300/93, and C–362/93 *Crispoltoni* v. *Fattoria Autonama Tabacchi* [1994] ECR I–486, where the national court requested a ruling on the validity of a Council reg. on the common organization of the market in raw tobacco and where the plaintiff in national proceedings was a tobacco planter who would have not enjoyed *locus standi* in a direct action for annulment.

[59] In the skimmed-milk cases (Case 114/76 *Bela-Mühle* v. *Grows-Farm* [1977] ECR 1211; Case 116/76 *Granaria* v. *Hoofdproduktschap voor Akkerbouwprodukten* [1977] ECR 1247, and Joined Cases 119/76 and 120/76, *Ölmühle Hamburg* v. *Hauptzollamt Hamburg Waltershof* [1977] ECR 1269) the Court declared invalid a Council reg. which, in order to reduce the stocks of skimmed-milk powder in the Community, imposed the compulsory purchase of skimmed-milk powder (instead of soya protein which is much cheaper) on animal feed producers. The reg. was found to infringe the principle of proportionality.

[60] In the maize cases (Case 4/79 *Providence Agricole* v. *ONIC* [1980] ECR 2823; Case 109/79 *Maïseries de Beauce* v. *ONIC* [1980] ECR 2883, and Case 145/79 *Roquette* v. *French Customs* [1980] ECR 2917) the Court declared invalid three Commission regs. that established the system of fixing monetary compensatory amounts for products processed from maize, on the ground that they contravened the basic Council reg. and Art. 43(3) EEC Treaty.

isoglucose,[61] and milk-quota cases,[62] and more recently in *Lomas and others*[63] were declared invalid. All these regulations were general market regulations, and actions by non-privileged applicants under Article 173 EC Treaty would most probably have been declared inadmissible. However, these regulations infringed general principles of law,[64] or Treaty provisions,[65] or reflected situations where the Community institutions had exceeded their powers,[66] and ought, in a Community subject to the rule of law, to have been reviewed by the European Court. In other cases, like the quellmehl[67] and gritz[68] cases, the Court did not declare the regulations at issue invalid but, after declaring their incompatibility with a general principle of law of the Community (in those cases, the principle of equality),[69] established that 'it was for the competent institution to adopt the measures necessary to correct this incompatibility'.[70]

Article 177(1)(b) EC Treaty has a further advantage, in that the European Court has recently declared in *Zuckerfabrik Süderdithmarschen* v. *Hauptzollamt Itzehoe*[71] that a national court may grant interim relief in certain circumstances.[72]

Thus far, both the advantages outlined above and the creative role played by the Court in the context of preliminary references would seem to indicate that the option offered by Article 177 EC Treaty is the perfect

[61] In the isoglucose cases (Joined Cases 103 and 145/77 *Royal Scholten Honing* v. *Intervention Board for Agricultural Produce* [1978] ECR 2037) the Court declared invalid two provisions in a Council reg. that imposed a levy on isoglucose, in order to mitigate the competitive effect of this new produce on sugar, on the ground that they infringed the principle of equality by discriminating between isoglucose producers and sugar producers.

[62] In the milk-quota cases (Case 120/86 *Mulder* v. *Minister van Landbouw en Visserij* [1988] ECR 2321 and Case 170/86 *Von Deetzen* v. *Hauptzollamt Hamburg-Jonas* [1988] ECR 2355) the Court declared invalid a Council reg. that imposed a system of milk quotas to control the supplies of milk in the Community on the grounds that was adopted in breach of the principle of legitimate expectations.

[63] Joined Cases C–38/90 and C–151/90 [1992] ECR I–1781. In these cases, where the defendants in the main proceedings were exporters of sheep and sheepmeat, the Court declared invalid a provision in a reg. on the common organization of the market in sheepmeat and goatmeat on the ground that the Commission had exceeded its powers.

[64] See the skimmed-milk cases, n. 59 above; isoglucose cases, n. 61 above; and milk-quota cases, n. 62 above.

[65] See the maize cases, n. 60 above.

[66] See Joined Cases C–38/90 and C–151/90 *Lomas and others*, n. 63 above.

[67] Joined Cases 117/76 and 16/77 *Ruckdeschel* v. *Hauptzollamt Hamburg-St Annen*, n. 36 above.

[68] Joined Cases 124/76 and 20/77 *Moulins et Huileries de Pont-à-Mousson* v. *Office National Interprofessionnel des Céréales* [1977] ECR 1795.

[69] In the quellmehl and gritz cases, nn. 67 and 68 above, a Council reg. had granted a production subsidy to producers of quellmehl, starch, and gritz. The reg. at issue in the proceedings withdrew the subsidy for quellmehl and gritz but not for starch. The ECJ found that the reg. was incompatible with the principle of equality, given that it discriminated against quellmehl and gritz producers in relation to starch producers.

[70] Joined Cases 117/76 and 16/77, n. 36 above, at point 13 and Case 124/76, n. 68 above, at point 28.

[71] Joined Cases C–143/88 and C–92/89 [1991] ECR I–415.

[72] *Ibid.*, at point 33.

remedy for the deficiencies of Article 173 EC Treaty. In this sense, one author[73] believes that proceedings under Article 177 EC Treaty not only provide for a suitable alternative to Article 173 but are the main remedy available to private parties to protect themselves against the action of the EC institutions. In his view, the restrictive approach of the Court to the interpretation of Article 173(2) EEC Treaty has been a deliberate move to divert all applications to Article 177 EC Treaty.[74]

However, despite the benefits that the system of preliminary references could offer to natural and legal persons it is also necessary to identify those situations where proceedings under Article 177 EC Treaty are not a suitable alternative to a direct action, either because they offer a less satisfactory remedy or because they are not available at all. In such situations private parties may be left without a remedy and gaps in the system of legal protection appear.

5.2.2 DISADVANTAGES OF PRELIMINARY RULINGS

The first set of problems arises in connection with the special nature of the system of preliminary references. This system is aimed at ensuring co-operation between the national courts and the European Court.[75] According to the terms of Article 177(2) EC Treaty, the proceedings commence before a national court, and the court 'may, *if it considers* that a decision on the question is necessary to enable it to give judgment' [emphasis added], refer a question on the interpretation or validity of a point of EC law. *The decision therefore lies with the national court whether to make a reference to the European Court.* The European Court of Justice has repeatedly said that it has no power to judge the appropriateness of the reference raised by the national court.[76] The parties thus have no guarantee that the national court will judge it opportune to ask the European Court for a preliminary ruling and cannot compel the national court to make a reference.[77] If the national court decides not to make a reference, the parties will have to appeal against that decision, several times if necessary,

[73] See H. Rasmussen, 'Why is Article 173 Interpreted Against Private Plaintiffs? (1980) 5 *ELRev.* 112, at 114 and 122–7.

[74] *Ibid.* 123 and 129. But see C. Harding, 'The Private Interest in Challenging Community Action' (1980) 5 *ELRev.* 354.

[75] See 177 above.

[76] Thus see Case 155/73 *Sacchi* [1974] ECR 409, at point 3; Case 83/78 *Pigs Marketing Board* v. *Raymond Redmond* [1978] ECR 2347, at point 25; Case C–368/89 *Crispoltoni* v. *Fattoria Autonoma Tabacchi di Cità di Castello* [1991] ECR I–36905, at point 10; and Case C–186/90 *Durighello* v. *INPS* [1991] ECR I–5773, at points 8–9. However, the judgments in Case 104/79 *Foglia* v. *Novello* [1980] ECR 745 and in Case C–83/91 *Meilicke* v. *ADV/ORGA* [1992] ECR I–4871, at points 24–34 seem to offer a different conclusion.

[77] Case 93/78 *Mattheus* v. *Doego* [1978] ECR 2203, at point 6.

until they reach the highest court that can judge the case.[78] That involves extra delay and extra cost.

In theory, Article 177(3) EC Treaty should ensure that a reference will always eventually be made. The so-called *acte clair* doctrine means that this is not exactly true. This doctrine implies that a court will not ask for a reference when it is thought that the answer is sufficiently clear.[79] Although the conditions under which the *acte clair* doctrine can be applied are—if applied correctly—very difficult to fulfil,[80] the truth is that, as Hartley[81] points out, it can imperil the uniformity of EC law throughout the Community and therefore it has to be used with the utmost caution. The doctrine of *acte clair* usually appears in connection with interpretative rulings but it is thought that it may also apply to preliminary rulings on validity. Thus a court of final appeal may decide that the Community act in question is clearly valid[82] and refrain from asking a preliminary reference.[83] While this approach is desirable from the point of view that it preserves the principle of legal certainty by assuming that a Community act is valid, it may nevertheless be prejudicial to private parties who believe that the measure in question is invalid. The relevance of the *acte clair* doctrine to the present work is that, even before courts of final appeal, private parties cannot be certain that a reference on the validity of the Community measure they are trying to challenge will be made.

Once a reference is made, two further limitations arise from the nature of preliminary rulings. First, *private parties may not contest the description of the facts submitted by the national court* on the basis of which the European Court will deliver a ruling.[84] Secondly, it is also *the discretion of*

[78] This can also create problems in countries like England, where (for instance) leave from the CA is needed to go to the HL. The situation could arise where the CA could refuse to make a reference to the ECJ and also refuse to grant leave to appeal. Fortunately the situation was solved after *Hagen* v. *Fratelli Moretti* ([1980] 3 CMLR 253 at 255 (CA)) where it was decided that the CA would make a reference, if leave to appeal was refused.

[79] See Case 283/81 *CILFIT* v. *Ministry of Health* [1982] ECR 3415, where the Court said that a national court of final appeal would be obliged to make a reference 'unless it has established that the question raised is irrelevant or that the Community provision in question has already been interpreted by the Court or that the correct application of Community law is so obvious as to leave no scope for any reasonable doubt': *ibid.*, at point 21.

[80] *Ibid.*, at points 18–20.

[81] T. C. Hartley, *The Foundations of European Community Law* (3rd edn., Oxford, 1994), 292.

[82] As explained above, a national court may never declare a Community act invalid: see 180 above.

[83] In this respect see *R.* v. *Secretary of State for the Home Office, ex parte Flynn*, judgment of 7 July 1995 [1995] TLR 425.

[84] See Case 104/77 *Oehschläger* v. *Hauptzollamt Emmerich* [1978] ECR 791, at point 4, and Case C-364/92 *SAT Fluggesellschaft* v. *Eurocontrol*, n. 18 above, at points 12–14.

the national court to decide the scope of the questions referred. Thus, in *Hessiche Knappschaft* v. *Singer*[85] the Court said that:

Under Article 177, it is for the court or tribunal of a Member State and not the parties in the main action, to bring a matter before the Court of Justice. Since the right to determine the questions to be brought before the Court thus devolves upon the Court or Tribunal of the Member State alone, the parties may not change their tenor or have them declared to be without purpose.[86]

Admittedly, this statement of the Court has been tempered, at least in part, by subsequent decisions, where the Court has decided on questions submitted by the litigant parties in certain specific circumstances.[87] The general rule remains, however, that it is for the national court to determine the scope of the questions submitted and that, when those questions are sufficiently precise, private parties will not be allowed to submit additional questions.[88]

It would appear that it is not by any means clear that, once the national court decides to make a reference, the questions referred by the national court will exactly reflect what the parties wanted or that the grounds upon which the illegality of the Community measure is sought will be the same as the ones intended by the parties. In the *Berlin butter* cases[89] this circumstance put the applicants at a disadvantage. One of the arguments that the margarine producers put forward in order to obtain the admissibility of their action of annulment[90] was that, in the preliminary reference, the national court referred to only some of the allegations which they had set out in support of their application, and that therefore their rights could receive adequate protection only if the direct action was declared admissible. The Court vigorously rejected their argument.[91]

[85] Case 44/65 [1965] ECR 965.

[86] *Ibid.*, at 970.

[87] Thus H. G. Schermers and D. Waelbroeck, *Judicial Protection in the European Communities* (5th edn., Deventer, 1992) 443–5, point out that the Court has decided on questions submitted by the litigant parties when they constitute, either a qualification to general questions on validity submitted by the national courts (Joined Cases 103 and 145/77 *Koninklijke Scholten Honig* v. *Intervention Board for Agricultural Produce* [1978] ECR 2037, at points 16–17) or when they have been incorporated by the national courts in their own references (Case 17/72 *Getreidehandel* v. *Einfur- und Vorratsstelle für Getreide* [1972] ECR 1071, at point 2). In this respect, see also the interesting observations put by G. Bebr ('Examen en Validité de l'Article 177 du Traité CEE et Cohesion Juridique de la Communauté' [1975] *CDE* 379 at 388), where he explains that if the national courts adopted a policy of referring very general questions on validity, leaving it to the litigants in national proceedings to invoke the grounds of illegality that they think fit, the procedure under Art. 177(1)(b) could end up being a means of redress very similar to the direct actions.

[88] Thus, in Case 270/81 *Felicitas* v. *Finanzamt Hamburg* [1982] ECR 2771, where the *Finanzgericht Hamburg* asked two questions on the interpretation of the provisions of a Council dir. concerning indirect taxes on the raising of capital. The plaintiff in the national proceedings in its observations submitted an additional question to the ECJ on the interpretation of two provisions of the dir., different from the one on which the national court requested an interpretative ruling . The Court refused to reply to the question posed by the plaintiffs in national proceedings, given that it had not been submitted by the national court.

[89] See n. 58 above.

[90] Case 97/85, n. 58 above, at 2269.

[91] Thus, the Court said: '[t]he fact that the national court is empowered to determine which

Another disadvantage of proceedings under Article 177 EC Treaty is that for the applicants to be able to bring proceedings before a national court, with the intention of obtaining a ruling on the validity of a Community measure, there must be a *national measure implementing the Community measure.*[92] In many cases EC measures will require measures of implementation, with or without the exercise of further discretion by the Member State in question. In other cases, however, the EC measures are directly applied to Community individuals and undertakings without any intervention by the Member States. In the first case it is clear that private parties can bring proceedings before the national court. In the second situation, however, the applicants cannot bring proceedings before the national courts and the possibility of a reference to the European Court is ruled out.[93]

The applicants could effectively be left without any means of redress,[94] which contradicts the repeated statements of the Court on the need for an effective judicial protection.[95]

Intimately connected with that problem is the situation where a measure of implementation does exist but there are no national procedures available to the potential applicant to challenge it. This is what happened in *CFDT* v. *Commission*,[96] a case in the context of the ECSC Treaty. In that case, a trade union sought the annulment of a Council decision that had failed to appoint it to a seat on the ECSC Consultative Committee. The action for annulment was declared inadmissible and the Court of Justice pointed out that the applicants could bring proceedings before the national court.[97] The applicants brought proceedings before the French *Conseil d'Etat* which held that it had no jurisdiction to hear the matter. Ultimately, CFDT brought a complaint before the European Commission of Human Rights

questions it intends to submit to the Court is an inherent feature of the system of means of redress established by the Treaty and is not therefore an argument which is capable of justifying a broad interpretation of the conditions of admissibility laid down in the second paragraph of Article 173': Case 97/85 *Union Deutsche Lebensmittelwerke* v. *Commission*, n. 58 above, at point 12.

92 See A. G. Toth, 'The Individual and European Law' (1975) 24 *ICLQ* 659, 701.

93 This is the problem that seems to have arisen in Case 30/64 *Sgarlata* v. *Commission* (see n. 42 above and 139 above, for a summary of the facts). The applicants alleged in their submissions that proceedings before national courts could not be brought and that, if the direct action was declared inadmissible, they would have no means of redress. The Court, however, declared the action inadmissible: *ibid.* 227.

94 See R. Kovar's criticism of the ruling of the Court in *Sgarlata* in 'Chronique de la Jurisprudence de la CJCEE' (1966) 93 *JDI* 707, 710.

95 e.g., /case 222/84 *Johnston* v. *Chief Constable of the Royal Ulster Constabulary* [1986] ECR 1651, at point 18. See also Case 294/83 *Parti Ecologiste 'Les Verts'* v. *European Parliament*, n. 1 above, at point 23, and Case C–2/88 Imm. *Zwartveld* [1990] ECR I–3365, at point 16.

96 Case 66/76, n. 42 above.

97 *Ibid.*, at point 12. The Court was aware that the applicants could be left without a remedy before the national court. See n. 42 above.

that was also declared inadmissible.[98] Sometimes it may also happen that the procedure provided by national law is recourse to an administrative authority and not to a court.[99] Undoubtedly, it is for the national system to provide a suitable means of redress,[100] but the fact is that in the situations described above, Article 177 does not provide an effective means of alternative redress.

Another inconvenience arises in those situations where *in order to bring national proceedings with the intention of challenging the validity of a Community measure, the applicants would have first to break EC law*. The clearest example to illustrate this proposition is provided by *ARPOSOL* v. *Council*.[101] In that case the action of the applicants against a Council regulation was dismissed as inadmissible owing to lack of *locus standi*. Previously, the applicants had made an application for interim measures[102] which was dismissed by the President of the Court, who pointed out that a fishing vessel caught committing an infringement would have the opportunity of recourse to the courts of the Member State in whose territorial waters the infringement was committed, and that, once excluded from the periodical lists, it could then have recourse to its national courts and to the European Court.[103] In the main action, the Court suggested that ARPOSOL could have a means of redress, once excluded from the periodical lists at national and Community level.[104] In other words, the Court was saying that, until the applicants had been caught illegally fishing in the waters of another Member State and until this State had informed the Commission and the Spanish Government had excluded them from the periodical lists, they could not have the opportunity to challenge a regulation that could be infringing the general principles of Community law. It is suggested that this is a clearly undesirable outcome and that the system of preliminary references is not an ideal alternative to a direct action in these cases.

[98] Case 8030/77 *CFDT* v. *The European Communities, the Member States of the European Community collectively and the Member States of the European Communities individually* [1979] 2 CMLR 229.

[99] In this respect see *Jensen and others* v. *The Corporation of the Trinity House of Deptford* [1982] 2 Lloyd's Rep. 14 (CA) *per* Kerr LJ at 27: '[t]here is no warrant whatever, as far as I can see, for the assertion, in relation to all disputes in which issues of EEC law arise, that there is an automatic right of resort to the courts, coupled with a right to disregard whatever other judicial or administrative machinery may have been set up for their resolution'.

[100] See the Opinion of Reischl A.G. in Case 138/79 *Roquette Frères* v. *Council* [1980] ECR 3333 at 3367, where he said that 'the admissibility of actions under Article 173 naturally does not depend on whether, after contested Community arrangements are applied by the national authorities, they may be challenged before a national court which may, if necessary, make a reference for a preliminary ruling under Article 177 EEC Treaty. The Treaty obviously does not recognise such ancillary relationship between the various possibilities of legal recourse.'

[101] Case 55/86 [1988] ECR 13. For a description of the facts, see 146 above.

[102] Case 55/86R [1987] 1 CMLR 113.

[103] See Case 207/86 *APESCO* v. *Commission* [1988] ECR 2151, at point 19.

[104] Case 55/86 note 101 above, at point 12.

Another problem could arise if *the European Court refuses to give a preliminary ruling*[105] when asked to do so by the national court or if it declares a reference made by a national court inadmissible, which amounts to the same thing . This is a very rare situation but it has occurred in the case law of the European Court. In some cases, the Court has refused to give a ruling: for example, when the question asked by the national court was one of national law,[106] or where no question of EC law arose,[107] or when at the time the preliminary reference was made the national proceedings had been terminated.[108] The Court's decision is fully justified in these cases, for the questions fall outside the scope of the system of preliminary references. However, in *Foglia* v. *Novello*[109] the Court refused to give a ruling on the ground that no genuine dispute was involved in the case.[110] In so doing, the Court passed judgment on the appropriateness of the reference, which contradicts the principle of co-operation with national courts that the European Court has defended in so many instances.[111] The ruling of the Court in *Foglia* v. *Novello* was severely criticized by academic writers.[112] In *Vinal* v. *Orbat*,[113] the Italian Government argued that no genuine dispute was involved and that the reference should be declared inadmissible.[114] However, after analysis,[115] the Court concluded that the reference was admissible. It is argued that the fact that the Court sometimes investigates the appropriateness of an Article 177 reference introduces a further element of uncertainty, and means that in some cases the system provided by Article 177(1)(b) EC Treaty is not a complete alternative to a direct action. Fortunately, there are not many instances in the case law where the European Court has done this,[116] but it is enough that the

[105] See E. V. E. Sharpston and C. Barnard, 'The Jurisdiction of the Court of Justice to hear Article 177 References: Which Way are We headed, Please?' (forthcoming) for *CMLRev.*

[106] Case 93/75 *Adlerblum* v. *Caisse Nationale d'Assurance Vieillesse des Travailleurs Salariés de Paris* [1975] ECR 2147.

[107] Case 132/81 *Rijksdienst voor Werknemerspensioenen* v. *Wlaeminck* [1982] ECR 2953, at point 4.

[108] Case 338/85 *Pardini* v. *Ministero del Commercio con l'Estero* [1988] ECR 2041, at point 11.

[109] Case 104/79, n. 76 above.

[110] See also Case C–83/91 *Meilicke* v. *ADV/ORGA*, n. 76 above, where the Court declined to answer a lengthy and complex series of questions on the Second Company Law Dir. referred to it by the *Landgericht* Hannover.

[111] See 179 above.

[112] A. Barav ('Preliminary Censorship? The Judgment of the European Court in *Foglia* v. *Novello*' (1980) 5 *ELRev.* 443, 467) said: '[o]nce the courts or tribunals of the member States have determined that a reference is necessary and that a decision on a position of EEC law was required, the ECJ may not censor such decision'. Barav recognized the necessity of protecting the ECJ against abuses of procedure but he also thought that more rulings like the one in *Foglia* v. *Novello* would diminish the confidence of the national courts in the ECJ: *ibid.* 468.

[113] Case 46/80 [1981] 77 at 82.

[114] For another case where, on the facts, it is doubtful whether a real dispute was involved see Case C–47/90 *Delhaize* v. *Promalvin* [1992] ECR I–3669. The Court, however, did not scrutinize the appropriateness of the reference.

[115] *Ibid.*, a points 5–7.

[116] The ECJ has acknowledged its duty to reply to the questions submitted by the national courts, unless it appears that the questions submitted have 'no bearing on the real situation or

possibility exists. Furthermore, three recent judgments suggest that there could be further restrictions in the admissibility of preliminary references. Two of those cases[117] concerned interpretative rulings in the area of competition law. In both cases the Court refused to give a ruling on the ground that the national court failed to define the factual and legislative background to the questions which it submitted and, as a result, the Court claimed that it had insufficient knowledge of the facts upon which the national proceedings were based and therefore it could not interpret Community law.[118] Similarly in *La Pyramide Sàrl*,[119] the Court refused to reply to a question formulated without any explanation of the legislative and factual background.[120]

There too, proceedings under Article 177 EC Treaty have failed to produce a suitable alternative to a direct action.

From a *procedural point of view* there are two important points that deserve attention. First, it has been said that proceedings under Article 177 EC Treaty involve an extra delay in relation to proceedings in direct actions,[121] in the sense that the applicants have to wait until the measure is implemented by the national authorities, then bring their case before the national court, and then wait for the reference of the European Court. Although it is true that in some instances obtaining a preliminary ruling on validity could take a long time, this is not always the case.[122] Proceedings

on the subject-matter of the case in the main proceedings' (Case C–186/90 *Durighello* v. *INPS* [1991] ECR I–5773, at point 9; Case C–343/90 *Lorenço Dias* v. *Director da Alfândega do Porto* [1992] ECR I–4673, at point 18; Case 67/91 *Dirección General de Defensa de la Competencia* v. *Asociación de la Banca Privada* [1992] ECR I–4785, at points 25–26; Joined Cases C–332/92, C–333/92, and C–335/92 *Eurico Italia* v. *Ente Nazionale Risi* [1994] ECR I–711, at point 17; Case C–18/93 *Corsica Ferries* v. *Corpo dei Piloto del Porto di Genova* [1994] ECR I–1783, at point 14; and Case C–306/93 *SMW Winzersekt* v. *Land Rheinland-Pfalz* [1994] ECR I–5579, at point 15.

[117] Joined Cases C–320–322/89 *Telemarsicabruzzo SpA and others* v. *Circostel*, judgment of 26 Jan. 1993, at points 6–9; Case C–157/92 *Pretore di Genova* v. *Banchero*, judgment of 19 Mar. 1993, at points 4–7.

[118] It must be recalled here that the Court has consistently held that the fact-finding task is to be performed by the national court. See the recently decided case, Case C–127/92 *Enderby* v. *Frenchay Health Authority and Secretary of State for Health*, judgment of 27 Oct. 1993, at point 25.

[119] Case C–378/93 [1994] ECR I–3999.

[120] The Court however, has given a reference in a case where, although the national court failed to define the legislation and factual background, the Court was familiar with it by reason of a previous reference: see Joined Cases C–133/93, C–300/93, and C–362/83 *Crispoltoni* v. *Fattoria Autonoma di Tabacchi di Citá di Castello*, n. 58 above.

[121] Thus C. Harding, n. 4 above, at 357. Also A. M. Mataraśó, 'The Independent Importer's Right of Review in Anti-dumping Regulations before the ECJ' (1988) 12 *Fordham International Law Journal* 682.

[122] At 31 Dec. 1989, the time taken to obtain a preliminary ruling was on average 16.6 months, whereas for a direct action it was 22.9 months: source: 'Synopsis of the work of the Court of Justice and Court of First Instance of the European Communities in 1988 and 1989', 50. At 31 Dec. 1993, the time taken to obtain a preliminary ruling was 20.4 months, whereas for a direct action it was 22.9 months before the ECJ and 23.3 months before the CFI: source:

before the Court may be shorter in the case of preliminary rulings, and even when the extra time for the implementation of the measure and to initiate proceedings before the national court are taken into consideration, in some cases the route of Article 177 EC Treaty may not be much slower than that of Article 173(2) EEC Treaty.[123]

Secondly, the way the parties submit their written observations is different in the case of preliminary references and direct actions. In the case of direct actions the applicants have the chance to expose their views in their application and then they can give a reply to the points made by the defence.[124] In the case of preliminary rulings, the parties to the main action before the national court are entitled to submit written observations[125] but they can only submit one written plea.[126] It is thought that the parties would benefit more from a procedure where there is a full exchange of pleadings; that is to say, in this respect, proceedings under Article 177 are more disadvantageous to private parties than direct actions.

'Les Activités de la Cour de Justice et du Tribunal de Première Instance des Communautés Européennes en 1993', 29. At 31 Dec. 1994, the time taken to obtain a preliminary ruling was 18 months and for a direct action 20.8 months before the ECJ, and 23 months before the CFI: source: statistics that appeared in the 'Proceedings before the Court of Justice and the Court of First Instance of the European Communities' No 34/94 at 34.

[123] Some direct actions take a very long time to process, as (for instance) Case C–156/87 *Gestetner Holdings* v. *Council* [1990] ECR I–781 where the written procedure alone took over a year (Ms E. V. E. Sharpston, private communication, May 1993).

[124] Art. 19 Statute of the ECJ and Art. 41 Rules of Procedure.

[125] Case 62/72 *Bollman* v. *HZA Hamburg-Waltershof* [1973] ECR 269.

[126] Art. 20, Statute of the ECJ.

6
The Plea of Illegality

6.1 General Features

The plea of illegality, unlike annulment proceedings, is an indirect method of challenging Community acts. It allows a party to plead the illegality of a normative act which serves as the legal basis of a measure at issue in the main action. This judicial remedy, which is familiar to the legal system of the Member States,[1] appears regulated in all three Community Treaties.[2]

Thus, Article 184 EC Treaty reads:

> Notwithstanding the expiry of the period laid down in the *fifth* paragraph of Article 173, any party may, in proceedings in which a *regulation adopted jointly by the European Parliament and the Council or a regulation* of the Council, of the Commission *or of the ECB is at issue*, plead the grounds specified in the *second* paragraph of Article 173 in order to invoke before the Court of Justice the inapplicability of that regulation.[3]

Within the framework of the ECSC Treaty, Article 36(3) allows private parties to invoke the plea of illegality only in the course of an appeal against pecuniary sanctions or periodic penalty payments. This provision reads 'In support of its application, a party may under the same conditions as in the first paragraph of Article 33 of this Treaty, contest the legality of the decisions or recommendations which that party is alleged not to have observed.'

In other words, a party on whom a penalty has been imposed may, in the course of annulment proceedings against the decision imposing the penalty, contest the legality of the measure that it infringed and for the violation of which the fine was imposed.

Several aspects of these legal provisions will be considered here:

1. It appears clear from a comparison of the two legal provisions that Article 36(3) ECSC Treaty gave the plea of illegality a more restrictive scope, in so far as it could only be invoked in the course of an appeal against fines. The European Court, however, soon

[1] In this respect, see the Opinion of Lagrange A.G. in Case 15/57 *Compagnie des Hauts Forneaux de la Chasse* v. *High Authority* [1957–58] ECR 211, 235–6.

[2] Art. 36(3) ECSC Treaty, Art. 184 EC Treaty, and Art. 156 Euratom Treaty.

[3] The italicized words represent the Maastricht amendments. Art. 156 Euratom is almost identical.

extended the scope of this provision; in *Meroni* v. *High Authority*,[4] the Court said that Article 36(3) 'should not be regarded as a special rule . . . but as the application of a general principle'. The plea of illegality can therefore be invoked in the context of disputes other than those concerning fines.[5]

2. Article 184 EC Treaty limits the *kind of acts* that may be challenged by means of the plea of illegality to regulations.[6] The European Court of Justice has nevertheless followed a liberal interpretation, extending the possibility of challenge to acts producing similar effects, although not presented in the form of a regulation.[7] Article 36(3) ECSC Treaty seems to open the possibility of challenging both individual and general acts. The European Court[8] and the Court of First Instance,[9] however, have restricted the use of the plea of illegality to the challenge of general acts.

The question arises why the authors of the Treaty limited the kinds of acts that could be challenged to general acts. The answer commonly accepted by the academic writers[10] is that this judicial remedy reflects the specific wish of the drafters of the Treaties to mitigate the restricted right of private parties to challenge directly acts of a normative nature.[11]

[4] Case 10/56 [1957–58] ECR 157, 162.

[5] Another example of the liberal interpretation of the plea of illegality by the ECJ appears in the context of staff cases, where the Court has allowed the plea to be invoked, even though there is no provision to that effect in the Staff Regulations: see Case 20/71 *Sabbatini* v. *European Parliament* [1972] ECR 345 and the Opinion of Roemer A.G. at 354.

[6] See the Opinion of Roemer A.G. in Joined Cases 6 and 11/69 *Commission* v. *France* [1969] ECR 523 at 550, when, in an action brought against France for failure to fulfil its obligations under the EC Treaty, France maintained that the dec. which it was accused of disregarding was illegal, Mr Roemer said: 'it is only in respect of regulations that Article 184 EC Treaty does not exclude the objection of illegality after the expiration of the limit period, whereas no such provision is made for decisions (with which we are concerned in the present case)'.

[7] See Case 92/78 *Simmenthal* v. *Commission* [1979] ECR 777, at point 40, where the Court said that the field of application of Art. 184 must include 'acts of the institutions, which although they are not in the form of a regulation, nevertheless they produce similar effects and on those grounds may not be challenged under Article 173 by natural or legal persons other than Community institutions and Member States'; see also Case 294/83 *Parti Ecologiste 'Les Verts'* v. *European Parliament* [1986] ECR 1339, at point 23. The CFI has also adopted this view; see Joined Cases T–6/92 and T–32/92 *Reinarz* v. *Commission*, judgment of 26 Oct. 1993 at point 56.

[8] See Case 21/64 *Dalmas* v. *High Authority* [1963] ECR 175 at 187; Case 76/83 *Böel* v. *Commission* [1984] ECR 859, at point 4; Case 270/82 *Esteel* v. *Commission* [1984] ECR 1195, at point 5.

[9] Case T–26/90 *Finsider* v. *Commission* [1992] ECR II–1789, at point 61.

[10] G. Bebr, *Development of Judicial Control in the European Communities* (The Hague, 1981), 193, n. 3; A. Barav, 'The Exception of Illegality in Community Law: A Critical Analysis' (1974) 11 *CMLRev.* 366, 367; H. G. Schermers and D. Waelbroeck, *Judicial Protection in the European Communities* (5th edn., Deventer, 1992), 261; M. Waelbroeck, J. V. Louis, D. Vignes, J. L. Dewost, and G. Vandersanden, *Le Droit de la Comunauté Economique Européenne* (Brussels, 1983), x, 356.

[11] Thus the statement of the Court in Case 294/83 *Parti Ecologiste 'Les Verts'* v. *European Parliament*, n. 7 above, at point 23, seems to confirm this view: '[i]n particular, in Articles 173

3. It would seem that, if the plea of illegality was engineered to compensate for the restricted right of challenge of private parties, the category of *potential applicants* should be restricted to natural and legal persons, given that Member States and Community institutions can always bring a direct action. The wording of Article 184 EC Treaty, however, gave the right to *any party* to invoke the plea. Some authors[12] expressed their opposition to the recognition of such a right, mainly on the ground of the privileged position that Member States and Community institutions hold in the context of annulment proceedings. For the majority of academic writers, however, such a right could not be excluded,[13] given the wording of the Treaty and, in the case of Member States, the implicit recognition of this possibility by the Court in two cases.[14] In the context of the ECSC Treaty, it would appear that Article 36(3) opens this judicial remedy only to private parties—undertakings and associations of undertakings—in so far as only those applicants may be the subject of fines under the ECSC Treaty. After the decision of the Court in *Meroni* v. *High Authority*,[15] where the Court extended the scope of the plea of illegality to other types of proceedings, it follows that Member States and Community institutions cannot be excluded.

4. The Plea of illegality appears as an *incidental and subsidiary* method of judicial review, in so far as it cannot be used independently, but only when there are other proceedings pending before the

and 184 on the one hand, and Article 177, on the other, the Treaty established a complete system of judicial remedies and procedures designed to permit the Court of Justice to review the legality of measures adopted by the Institutions. Natural and legal persons are, thus, protected against the application of general measures which they cannot contest before the Court by reason of the special conditions of admissibility laid down in the second paragraph of Article 173 of the Treaty. Where the Community institutions are responsible for the administrative implementation of such measures, natural and legal persons may bring a direct action before the Court against the implementation of such measures, which are addressed to them or which are of direct and individual concern to them, and, in support of that action, plead the illegality of the general measure on which they are based.' See also Case 92/78 *Simmenthal* v. *Commission*, n. 7 above, at points 39–41.

[12] G. Bebr, 'Judicial Remedy of Private Parties against Normative Acts of the European Communities: The Role of the Exception of Illegality' (1966–7) 4 *CMLRev.* 7, 12–13.

[13] A. Barav n. 10 above, at 371–2; D. Wyatt and A. Dashwood, *European Community Law* (3rd edn., London, 1993), 155; P. Dubois, 'L'Exception d'Illégalité devant la Cour de Justice des Communautés Européennes' [1978] *CDE* 407, 411–13; H. G. Schermers and D. Waelbroeck, n. 10 above, 265. Other authors remain doubtful whether this possibility exists; thus see T. C. Hartley, *The Foundations of European Community Law* (3rd edn., Oxford, 1994), 423.

[14] In Case 32/65 *Italy* v. *Council and Commission* [1966] ECR 389, the Italian Government invoked the illegality of one Council reg. and of one Commission reg . in support of its action for annulment directed against a Council reg. In Case 116/82 *Commission* v. *Germany* [1986] ECR 2519, the German Government was allowed, in the context of proceedings under Art. 169 EC Treaty, to invoke the illegality of a Commission reg.

[15] Case 10/56, n. 4 above.

European Court of Justice,[16] and now, in the case of private parties, before the Court of First Instance.[17] The issue arose in *Wöhrmann* v. *Commission*.[18] In that case, the Commission had addressed two decisions fixing the countervailing charge on imports of whole powdered milk into Germany, which had been implemented by the appropriate German authorities. The applicants brought proceedings before the national courts against the implementing measures, and at the same time they raised directly a plea of illegality before the European Court against the Commission decisions. The Court made clear that proceedings needed to be pending before the European Court under some other provision of the Treaty and that, consequently, applicants could not plead directly the illegality of a regulation or of a measure of similar effect under Article 184 EC Treaty.[19]

The nature of the proceedings in the course of which the plea of illegality may be invoked by private parties is varied, although most frequently it appears in the course of annulment proceedings against a decision implementing the normative act whose legality is being questioned.[20]

In the framework of the ECSC Treaty, the European Court has expressly ruled that the plea of illegality may arise in the course of an action for a failure to act.[21] In this respect, it must not be forgotten that Article 35(3) ECSC Treaty[22] creates the fiction that, if the Commission does not act

[16] In the framework of the ECSC Treaty, it appeared clear that the court before which proceedings had to be pending was the ECJ, given that an action against pecuniary sanctions or periodic penalty payments is the exclusive competence of the ECJ. Under the wording of Art. 184 EC Treaty, however, it is not clear before which court proceedings must be pending. In Joined Cases 31 and 33/62 *Wöhrmann* v. *Commission* [1962] ECR 501 at 505–7, the Court explained that proceedings need to be pending before the ECJ.

[17] See Art. 4 of Dec. 88/591 [1988] OJ L319/1; corrected version [1989] OJ C215/1, and Art. 1(3) of Dec. 93/350 [1993] OJ L144/21. See 9 above.

[18] Joined Cases 31 and 33/62, n. 16 above.

[19] In this respect, see also Joined Cases 87 and 130/77, 22/83, 9 and 10/84 *Salerno* v. *Commission and Council*, at point 36, where the Court said: 'in allowing a party to plead the inapplicability of a regulation, Article 184 does not create an independent right of action, such a plea may only be raised indirectly in proceedings against an implementing measure, the validity of the regulation being challenged, in so far as it constitutes the legal basis of that measure'. See Case 33/80 *Albini* v. *Council and Commission* [1981] ECR 2141, at point 17.

[20] See, in the framework of the ECSC Treaty, Case 10/56 *Meroni* v. *High Authority*, n. 4 above; Case 15/57 *Compagnie des Hauts Forneaux de la Chasse* v. *High Authority*, n. 1 above; Case 18/62 *Barge* v. *High Authority* [1963] ECR 259; Case 21/64 *Dalmas* v. *High Authority*, n. 8 above; Joined Cases 154, 205, 206, 226 to 228, 263, 264/78, 39, 31, 83 and 85/79 *Valsabbia* v. *Commission* [1980] ECR 907; Case 15/83 *Alpha* v. *Commission* [1984] ECR 3519; and Joined Cases 140, 146, 221 and 226/82 *Walzstahl* v. *Commission* [1984] ECR 951. In the context of the EC Treaty, see Case 92/78 *Simmenthal* v. *Commission* [1979] ECR 777 and Joined Cases T–6/92 and T–52/92 *Reinarz* v. *Commission*, n . 7 above . See also Case 20/71 *Sabbatini* v. *European Parliament*, n. 5 above and Case 262/80 *Andersen* v. *European Parliament* [1984] ECR 185 (staff cases).

[21] Joined Cases 32 and 33/58 *Société Nouvelle des Usines de Pontlieu Aciéries du Temple (SNUPAT)* v. *High Authority* [1959] ECR 127 at 139; Case 42/58 *Société des Aciers Fins de l'Est (SAFE)* v. *High Authority* [1959] ECR 183 at 191.

[22] See 210 below.

within a month after being called upon to act, it is deemed to have adopted an implied decision of refusal.[23] In other words, the action for a failure to act is turned under the ECSC Treaty into a special action for annulment. In the framework of the EC Treaty, the silence of the Community institution concerned is interpreted not as a negative decision but as an omission against which the action for a failure to act may be brought.[24] Academic writers appear divided as to whether the plea of illegality may arise in the context of an action for a failure to act. For some,[25] the fact that the Court has repeatedly emphasized that the action for annulment and the action for a failure to act are two aspects of the same remedy,[26] justifies the fact that the plea may be invoked in the course of an action for a failure to act. Other authors express their doubts whether this possibility exists.[27] It is thought that, although it is difficult to imagine a situation where the plea of illegality could be invoked in the course of an action for a failure to act,[28] the possibility should not be excluded.

Finally, the plea of illegality could also, at least theoretically, arise in the context of an action for damages (i.e. where the applicant claims damage has resulted from a decision taken in implementation of an earlier, allegedly unlawful, regulation). The possibility, however, is quite remote, because in the framework of the action for damages there is no limit as to the type of act that may be challenged and, in consequence, the applicant could directly challenge a regulation.

It is clear that the plea of illegality could not arise in the context of Article 177 proceedings.[29]

> 5. Both Article 36(3) ECSC Treaty and Article 184 EC Treaty refer to the same *grounds of illegality* that appear in the context of annulment proceedings,[30] a further indication of the role of the plea of illegality as a complement to annulment proceedings.

[23] Joined Cases 7/54 and 9/54 *Groupement des Industries Sidérurgiques Luxembourgeoises* v. *High Authority* [1954–56] ECR 175.

[24] Joined Cases 10 and 18/68 *Eridania* v. *Commission* [1969] ECR 459 at 483.

[25] Thus H. G. Schermers and D. Waelbroeck, n. 10 above, 262; M. Waelbroeck, J. V. Louis, D. Vignes, J. L. Dewost, and G. Vandersanden, n. 10 above, x, 360, and T. C. Hartley, n. 13 above, 417.

[26] See 209 below.

[27] Thus see P. Dubois, n. 13 above, 425; G. Bebr, n. 10 above, 201.

[28] The following situation, for instance, could be imagined: a Council reg. empowers the Commission to take implementing measures; the Commission fails to do so, on the ground that the Council reg. is partly unlawful; an action for a failure to act is brought against the Commission by the Council; in the course of those proceedings, the Commission, as defendant, invokes the plea of illegality against the Council reg.

[29] There is nothing in the wording of Art. 184 EC Treaty that prevents the plea of illegality from arising in the context of preliminary rulings. It is nevertheless clear, in view of the way the Court describes the system of judicial protection, that it is very unlikely that Art. 184 could be used in conjunction with Art. 177. (See Case 294/83 *Parti Ecologiste 'Les Verts'* v. *European Parliament*, n. 7 above, at point 23.

[30] See Art. 33(1) ECSC Treaty and Art. 173(2) EC Treaty.

6. A further element that the European Court has made clear through its case law is that an applicant may not plead the illegality of any regulation to in support of its application. The Court has explained that a certain connection must exist between the contested measures in the main proceedings and the general act whose legality is being questioned. In earlier judgments, the Court expressed this degree of connection in various wordings.[31] In later judgments, the Court has adopted a uniform wording and has determined that the general act must form 'the legal basis of the decision which is being attacked'.[32]

7. As to the *effects* of the plea of illegality, the wording of Article 184 EC Treaty clearly reveals that a successful plea would culminate in the inapplicability of the general act in issue to the particular case. This would mean that the regulation would continue to be in force but would not be applied to the particular case.[33] If the plea has arisen in the context of annulment proceedings—as it very often does—it operates as a ground of illegality and, if successful, determines the annulment of the implementing decision while the general act would continue to be in force. In practice, however, if a plea is successful the Community institution will normally replace the challenged measure in order to avoid similar challenges by other parties.[34] In this respect there are great similarities between the effect of a successful plea of illegality and the effect of a preliminary ruling declaring the invalidity of a regulation.[35]

[31] Thus in Case 18/62 *Barge* v. *High Authority*, n. 20 above, 279, the Court said that the measure at issue in the main proceedings should constitute a 'direct and immediate application' of the general act; in Case 21/64 *Dalmas* v. *High Authority*, n. 8 above, 187, the Court explained that 'a direct legal connexion should exist between the two measures'; in Case 32/65 *Italy* v. *Council and Commission*, n. 14 above, 409, the Court said that the general act must 'be applicable directly or indirectly to the issue with which the application is concerned'.

[32] See Case 92/78 *Simmenthal* v. *Commission*, n. 7 above, at point 39; Joined Cases 275/80 and 24/81 *Krupp* v. *Commission* [1981] ECR 2489, at point 32; Joined Cases 87 and 130/77, 22/83, 9 and 10/84 *Salerno* v. *Commission and Council*, n. 19 above, at point 36; Joined Cases 140, 146, 221, and 226/82 *Walzstahl* v. *Commission*, n. 20 above, at point 20; and Joined Cases T-6/92 and T-5/92 *Reinarz* v. *Commission*, n. 7 above, at point 56. It seems that the term 'legal basis' is more restrictive than the terms used in the earlier cases (see n. 31 above).

[33] In other words, a successful plea would have an *inter partes* effect, in contrast to annulment proceedings, which have an *erga omnes* effect, where the act is declared null and void and treated as it if had never existed.

[34] In this respect, see the amendment of Art. 4(3) of Annex VII to the Staff Regulations of Officials of the European Communities following the judgment of the Court in Case 20/7 *Sabbatini* v. *European Parliament*, n. 5 above, in [1973] JO L55/1.

[35] See 180 above. See T. C. Hartley, n. 13 above, at 416–17 and 425.

6.2 The Efficacy of the Plea of Illegality as an Alternative to Annulment Proceedings

The main and obvious advantage of the plea of illegality is that it allows natural or legal persons to challenge regulations[36] that have been applied to them outside the strict time-limits of Article 173 EC Treaty. The Court of Justice has accepted this view.[37] As one author points out,[38] the plea of illegality is a particularly useful means of challenging 'chains of regulations'. In relation to the *locus standi* requirements, it could be said that Article 184 EC Treaty could allow non-privileged applicants to contest the legality of a regulation (or an act producing similar effects), which they did not have the *locus standi* to challenge under Article 173 EC Treaty.[39]

Having said this, there are two main features of this remedy which limit its effectiveness as an alternative procedural route for private parties.

1. In the first place, it seems that *natural and legal persons may only challenge regulations or acts producing similar effects*[40] by this means. Private parties, therefore, may not use the plea of illegality to challenge decisions.[41] In those cases where the decision was addressed to the applicant or was clearly of direct and individual concern to it—and therefore challengeable by means of annulment proceedings —the impossibility of challenging the decision by means of a plea of illegality is another reflection of the principle that alternative methods of judicial review may not be used when they would result in a direct evasion of the time-limits of the action for annulment.[42]

[36] A successful action under Art. 184 EC Treaty does not render a reg. void but it only declares it inapplicable to the applicant. In practice, however, the effects would be very similar to a declaration of nullity.

[37] Thus the Court said, in Joined Cases 31 and 33/62 *Wöhrmann* v. *Commission*, n. 16 above, at 507, that '[t]he sole object of Article 184 is thus to protect an interested party against the application of an illegal regulation, without thereby in any way calling in issue the regulation itself, which can no longer be challenged because of the expiry of the time-limit laid down in Article 173'. See also Joined Cases 87 and 130/77, 22/83, 9 and 10/84 *Salerno* v. *Commission and Council*, n. 19 above, at point 36, and G. Bebr, n. 10 above, 8.

[38] See E. V. E. Sharpston, *Interim and Substantive Relief in Claims under Community Law* (London, 1993), 130.

[39] In this sense see S. Weatherill and P. Beaumont, *EC Law*, 241 and D. Wyatt and A. Dashwood, *European Community Law* (London, 1993), 153.

[40] See 197 above.

[41] In Case 92/78 *Simmenthal* v. *Commission*, n. 7 above, the Court admitted that a private party could invoke the illegality of a general notice of periodic invitations to tender, given its general character, although it did not appear in the form of a reg. It is perhaps conceivable that e.g. a decision addressed to all Member States might be so general in character as to be assimilable to a reg.

[42] See Joined Cases 31 and 33/62 *Wöhrmann* v. *Commission*, n. 16 above, 507, in the sense that Art. 184 cannot be used as a direct evasion of the time-limits of Art. 173 EC Treaty. In the context of the ESCS Treaty, there is an abundant body of relevant case law. Very frequently, undertakings fined by the Commission tried to challenge, in an action for annulment against

2. The real limitation arises in so far as Article 184 can only be used where there is *a further Community measure implementing the contested regulation or general act*, i.e. a decision addressed to or of direct and individual concern to the applicant and which is the subject of the main action, e.g. annulment proceedings.[43] It is quite unusual for the Community to address further measures of implementation individually to private parties since this task is normally delegated to the competent organs of the Member States.[44] This gives an idea of the limited efficacy of this remedy to challenge Community regulations.[45]

the decisions that imposed the fine, former Commission decs. (e.g. fixing their production quotas) that had been addressed to them and which they had disregarded. The Court explained that '[i]t is well established case-law that an applicant may not, in an application for a declaration that an individual decision is void, raise an objection of illegality relating to another individual decision addressed to him which has become final': Case 76/83 *Böel* v. *Commission*, n. 8 above, at point 4. See also Case 21/64 *Dalmas* v. *High Authority*, n. 8 above, at 187; Case 270/82 *Estel* v. *Commission*, n. 8 above, at point 11; Case 41/85 *Sideradria* v. *Commission* [1986] ECR 3917, at point 5.

[43] See Case 92/78 *Simmenthal* v. *Commission*, n. 7 above, at point 39; Case 294/83 *Parti Ecologiste 'Les Verts'* v. *European Parliament*, n. 7 above, at point 23.

[44] In this case proceedings could be brought before the national courts which could raise a preliminary reference under Art. 177.

[45] In fact the plea of illegality is seldom invoked before the Court, and since 1973, the number of actions brought under Art. 184 has not appeared in the statistics of the Court.

7
The Action for Damages

7.1 General Features

The system of judicial protection provided for by the Community Treaties would not be complete if there was no action aimed at obtaining compensation for loss caused by acts of the Community institutions. The determination of the non-contractual liability of the European Community is one of the competences attributed to the European Court of Justice, in addition to its other heads of jurisdiction. This remedy is regulated by Articles 178, 215(2), and 215(3) EC Treaty which read:

> The Court of Justice shall have jurisdiction in disputes relating to compensation for damage provided for in the second paragraph of Article 215 [Article 178].
>
> In case of non-contractual liability, the Community shall, in accordance with the general principles common to the laws of the Member States, make good any damage caused by its Institutions or by its servants in the performance of their duties [Article 215(2)].
>
> *The preceding paragraph shall apply under the same conditions to damage caused by the ECB or by its servants in the performance of their duties* [Article 215(3)].[1]

The case law of the European Court has developed the conditions that are the basis of non-contractual liability. Relevant to this work are those situations where non-contractual liability arises from acts intended to produce legal effects. The Court made clear that in order to obtain damages from acts of the Community institutions, there must be (a) the existence of a wrongful act or omission, (b) damage, and (c) the existence of a causal relationship between the wrongful act and the damage caused.[2]

As far as the first requirement is concerned, whether liability arises from a decision,[3] or from a regulation[4] it is necessary that the act be declared unlawful. Initially, the Court required the act to be annulled first and only *then* could an action for damages be brought.[5] This would clearly have been

[1] The italicized words represent the Maastricht amendments to Art. 215. See also Arts. 151 and 188 Euratom Treaty. In the framework of the ECSC Treaty, see Art. 40.

[2] Case 4/69 *Lütticke* v. *Commission* [1971] ECR 325, at point 10;. Case 153/73 *Holtz & Willemsem* v. *Council and Commission* [1974] ECR 675 at point 7; Joined Cases 197 to 200, 243, 245 and 247/80 *Ludwigshafener Walzmülhle* v. *Council and Commission* [1981] ECR 3211, at point 18.

[3] Case C–200/89 *Funoc* v. *Commission* [1990] ECR I–3669, at point 30; Case 59/84 *Tezi Textiel* v. *Commission* [1986] ECR 887, at point 70.

[4] Case 5/71 *Aktien-Zuckerfabrik Schöppenstedt* v. *Council* [1971] ECR 975, at point 11.

[5] Case 25/62 *Plaumann* v. *Commission* [1965] ECR 95 at 108.

an undesirable solution, for it would have meant that the same conditions of admissibility applying to the action of annulment would have applied to the action for damages, thus restricting its utility. Fortunately, this stand by the Court was soon changed and in *Lütticke* v. *Commission*[6] the Court acknowledged the autonomy of the action for damages.[7] In *Aktien-Zuckerfabrik Schöppenstedt* v. *Council* the Court said even more clearly that the action for damages 'differs from an application for annulment in that its end is not the abolition of a particular measure, but compensation for damage caused by an institution in the performance of its duties'.[8]

In the event of liability arising from decisions, the Court has to find that the measure is illegal, but does not need to make a specific finding as to the gravity of the illegality, and then examines damage and the causal relationship between the damage and the measure in question.[9]

In the case of liability arising from a regulation, however, the illegality needs to be of a special gravity. Thus, in *Aktien-Zuckerfabrik Schöppenstedt*[10] the Court promulgated the '*Schöppenstedt* formula', ruling that:

> Where legislative action involving measures of economic policy is concerned, the Community does not incur non contractual liability for damage suffered by individuals as a consequence of that action, by virtue of the provisions contained in Article 215, second paragraph of the Treaty, *unless a sufficiently flagrant violation of a superior rule of law for the protection of the individual has occured.*[11]

This formula has been repeated by the Court in numerous cases[12] but its conditions have been so very difficult to satisfy that only in very few cases has the action been successful. Thus, in *HNL* v. *Council and Commission*[13] the Court said that it was necessary for the institution concerned to have 'manifestly and gravely disregarded the limits of the exercise of its powers'.[14] In the isoglucose cases,[15] where a Community regulation imposed a disproportionate levy on isoglucose, the Court did not award damages and went

[6] Case 4/69, n. 2 above, at point 6.

[7] Thus, the Court implicitly overruled its decision in Case 25/62 *Plaumann* v. *Commission*, n. 5 above.

[8] Case 5/71, n. 4 above, at point 3. See also Case 43/72 *Merkur* v. *Commission* [1953] ECR 1055, at point 5.

[9] Although in some cases in this area the Court changes the order of consideration of the requirements Case 253/84 *GAEC* v. *Council and Commission* [1987] ECR 123, where the existence of damage and the causal relationship were considered first.

[10] Case 5/71, n. 4 above.

[11] *Ibid.*, at point 11, emphasis added.

[12] See among others Joined Cases 9–11/71 *Compagnie d'Approvisionnement de Transport et de Crédit SA* v. *Commission* [1972] ECR 391, at point 13; Case 43/72 *Merkur* v. *Commission*, n. 8 above, at point 8; and Case 153/73 *Holtz & Willemsem* v. *Council and Commission*, n. 2 above, at point 7.

[13] Joined Cases 83 and 94/76, 4, 15, and 40/77 [1978] ECR 1209.

[14] *Ibid.*, at point 6.

[15] Case 143/77 *Koninklijke Scholten Honig* v. *Council and Commission* [1979] ECR 3583; Joined Cases 116 and 124/77 *Amylum and Tunnel Refineries* v. *Council and Commission* [1979 ECR 3497.

as far as to say that the conduct of the defendant institutions 'was not verging on the arbitrary'.[16] It seems that the Court has followed a very restrictive approach in the access of non-privileged applicants to the action for annulment and to the action for damages.[17] In the first case, the restrictions are imposed by the standing requirements of Article 173 EC Treaty which stop the actions in the admissibility stage. In the second case, the actions are admitted and consideration is given to the merits of the action, but they are dismissed as unfounded because the kind of illegality that the Court is seeking amounts to situations of clear misuse of powers, which are extremely difficult to prove.[18]

It is noticeable that even though the unlawfulness of a regulation may be established in the course of proceedings in an action for damages, in most cases the applicants first brought proceedings before the national courts (against the measures of implementation of those regulations), in the course of which references on the validity of the Community measures were made to the European Court.[19] Once a declaration of invalidity had been

[16] Case 143/77, n. 15 above, at point 16, and Joined Cases 116 and 124/77, n. 15 above, at point 19. For examples of a successful action for damages see 207 below.

[17] Recent case law in actions for damages brought by private parties suggest, however, that the Court may be beginning to adopt a more lenient approach to the interpretation of the *Schöppenstedt* formula: see Case C–220/91 P *Stahlwerke Peine Salzgitter AG* v. *Commission*, Judgment of 18 May 1993.

[18] Thus, at 31 Dec. 1990, only 13 out of 177 actions for damages brought before the Court were successful: source: offprint from the *XXIVth General Report on the Activities of the European Communities* (Brussels, 1990), at 449. Many of these actions for damages are brought by Community producers that have been affected by the interventionism practised by the EC institutions within the framework of the common agricultural policy. The Commission and the Council have a duty of general management of the market that unavoidably upsets some economic operators. It seems that the Court has decided to refrain voluntarily from giving judgment on such action of the Community executive unless a sufficiently clear violation or a misuse of powers has occurred. Thus, in Case 55/75 *Balkan-Import Export* v. *Hauptzollamt Berlin-Packhof* [1976] ECR 19, the Court said: '[a]s the evaluation of a complex economic situation is involved, the Commission and the Management Committee enjoy, in this respect, a wide measure of discretion. In reviewing the legality of the exercise of such discretion, the court must confine itself to examining whether it contains a manifest error or constitutes a misuse of power or whether the authority did not clearly exceed the bounds of its discretion': *ibid.*, at point 8. In other words, it is believed that the Court acknowledges that the action of the Community executive in the framework of the common agricultural policy may upset the interests of some private parties within the EC but that they have to suffer this inconvenience for the benefit of the 'public interest' unless a very grave and manifest violation of the law has occurred. This could be a reason why the Court is so reluctant to admit the challenge of normative acts by natural or legal persons. Thus reluctance is shown in the context of annulment proceedings by rarely granting standing to private parties, and in the case of actions for damages by very seldom awarding damages, unless a breach so serious as to amount to a misuse of powers has taken place.

[19] Thus preliminary rulings were given in the following set of cases:

Skimmed milk cases: Case 114/76 *Bela-Mühle* v. *Grows-farm* [1977] ECR 1211; Case 116/76 *Granaria* v. *Hoofdproduktschap voor Akkerbouwprodukten* [1977] ECR 1247; and Joined Cases 119 and 120/76 *Ölmühle Hamburg* v. *Hauptzollamt Hamburg Waltershof* [1977] ECR 1269.

obtained, the applicants brought actions for damages before the European Court which in some cases were successful.[20] This would seem the logical route, in that it makes sense to get the measure declared invalid through the route of Article 177 (where no strict *locus standi* conditions apply) in order to avoid further damages and, if this result is achieved, to try to obtain compensation for damage already suffered.[21] Out of all the cases where private applicants brought just actions for damages,[22] in very few[23] did the Court award damages.

Gritz cases: Joined Cases 124/76 and 20/77 *Moulins et Huileries de Pont-à-Mousson* v. *Office National Interprofessionnel des Céréales* [1977] ECR 1795.

Quellmehl cases: Joined Cases 117/76 and 16/77 *Ruckdeschel* v. *Hauptzollamt Hamburg-St Annen* [1977] ECR 1753.

Isoglucose cases: Joined Cases 103 and 145/77 *Royal Scholten Honing* v. *Intervention Board for Agricultural Produce* [1978] ECR 2037.

Milk cases: Case 120/86 *Mülder* v. *Minister van Landbouw en Visserij* [1988] ECR 2321.

[20] The actions for damages brought subsequently were:

Skimmed-milk cases: Joined Cases 83 and 94/76, 4, 15 and 40/77 *HNL* v. *Council and Commission*, n. 13 above: dismissed as unfounded.

Gritz cases: Joined Cases 64 and 113/76, 167, 239/78, 27, 28 and 45/79 *Dumortier Frères* v. *Council* [1979] ECR 3091; and Joined Cases 241, 242, and 245 to 250/78 *DGV* v. *Council and Commission* [1979] ECR 3017: successful claims.

Quellmehl cases: Case 238/78 *Ireks-Arkady* v. *Council and Commission* [1979] ECR 2955 and Joined Cases 261 and 262/78 *Interquell Stärke-Chemie* v. *Council and Commission* [1979] ECR 3045: dismissed as unfounded.

Isoglucose cases: Case 143/77 *Koninklijke Scholten Honig* v. *Council and Commission*, n. 15 above, and Joined Cases 116 and 124/77 *Amylum and Tunnel Refineries* v. *Council and Commission*, n. 15 above: dismissed as unfounded.

Milk cases: Joined Cases C–104/89 and C–37/90 *Mülder* v. *Council and Commission* [1992] ECR I–3061: successful claims.

[21] The Court itself acknowledged this fact. Thus, in Case 143/77 *Koninklijke Scholten Honig* v. *Council and Commission* the Court said: 'even though an action for damages under Articles 178 and 215 of the Treaty constitutes an independent action, it must nevertheless be assessed having regard to the whole of the system of legal protection of individuals set up by the Treaty. If an individual takes the view that he is injured by a Community legislative measure which he regards as illegal, he has the opportunity, when the implementation of the measure is entrusted to the national authorities, to contest the validity of the measure, at the time of its implementation, before a national court in an action against the national authority. Such a court may, or even must, in pursuance of Article 177, refer to the Court of Justice, a question on the validity of the Community measure in question. The existence of such an action is by itself of such a nature as to ensure the efficient protection of the individuals concerned': n. 15, at point 11.

[22] See for instance Joined Cases 197 to 200, *Ludwigshafener Walmühle* v. *Council and Commission*, n. 2 above; Case 5/71 *Aktien Zuckerfabrik Schöppemstedt* v. *Council*, n. 4 above; Joined Cases 9–11/71 *Compagnie d'Approvisionnement, de Transport et de Crédit* v. *Commission*, n. 12 above; Case 153/73 *Holtz & Willemsem* v. *Commission and Council*, n. 2 above; Case 74/74 *CNTA* v. *Commission* [1975] ECR 533; and Case 27/85 *Vandermoortele* v. *Commission* [1987] ECR 1129.

[23] e.g. Case 74/74 *CNTA* v. *Commission*, n. 22 above.

7.2 The Suitability of the Action for Damages as an Alternative to Annulment Proceedings

The action for damages is a remedy with an essentially different purpose from Article 173 EC Treaty.[24] When a non-privileged applicant brings an action for annulment, and provided it is declared admissible, it will obtain a *declaration* from the European Court that the contested measure is either legal or illegal. If the measure is declared illegal it will be treated as null and void, in other words, as if it had never existed. If a private party brings an action for damages, what it seeks is to obtain financial compensation in relation to an economic loss it has suffered as a consequence of a Community measure. Although the finding of the illegality of the measure at issue is one of the conditions for a successful action for damages, a private applicant obtains an award of damages and not a formal ruling on the validity or legality of the Community act. It would seem, therefore, that an action for damages may only be an alternative for a natural or legal person who does not satisfy the *locus standi* conditions of Article 173 EC Treaty and who wishes to challenge a Community act when he has suffered an economic loss of sufficient gravity and when there are no measures of implementation of the Community act, in which case an action before the national courts is not feasible. In those limited circumstances an action for damages may be a suitable alternative in that (a) there are no limitations as to the kinds of acts likely to give rise to Community liability, or in other words, acts producing legal effects, whether general or individual, are included; (b) there are no *locus standi* conditions to be satisfied by a prospective applicant other than having suffered prejudice caused by a Community institution, and (c) there is a five-year time-limit for bringing an action for damages against the strict time-limits of Article 173 EC Treaty.[25]

[24] See 205 above. See also Joined Cases 9 and 12/60 *Vloeberghs* v. *High Authority* [1961] ECR 197 at 213, where the Court, in an action in the context of the ECSC Treaty, said: '[t]he action for reparation referred to in Article 40 differs from an application for annulment both in its subject matter and in the nature of the grounds which may be pleaded. As regards its subject matter, an action for reparation is directed, not to the abolition of a particular measure but only to reparation of damage caused by an act or failure to act amounting to a wrongful act or omission.'

[25] Art. 43 of the Statute of the ECJ. The Court has interpreted this requirement with great leniency: see Case 145/83 *Stanley Adams* v. *Commission* [1985] ECR 3539, at points 26–27 and 48–52.

8

The Action for a Failure to Act

8.1 General Features

The action for a failure to act is a remedy closely related to the action of annulment in so far as, whilst annulment proceedings aim at the removal of illegal acts, the action for a failure to act seeks to challenge the unlawful inaction of Community Institutions. Therefore, it represents the logical complement[1] in judicial review in relation to the action of annulment. If only the action of annulment were available to ensure that the EC institutions acted within the limits of the law, there would be situations where the Community executive could abstain with impunity from adopting legislation or from taking decisions in situations where it ought to act. The closeness between the two recourses is evident and, as the Court has repeated consistently 'both prescribe one and the same method of recourse'.[2]

This remedy appears regulated in all three Community Treaties. Thus, Article 175 EC Treaty reads:

> Should *the European Parliament*, the Council or the Commission, in infringement of this Treaty, fail to act, the Member States and the other institutions of the Community, may bring an action before the Court of Justice to have the infringement established.
>
> The action shall be admissible only if the institution concerned has first been called upon to act. If, within two months of being called upon, the institution concerned has not defined its position, the action may be brought within a further period of two months.
>
> Any natural or legal person may, under the conditions laid down in the proceedings paragraphs, complain to the Court of Justice that an institution of the Community has failed to address to that person any act other than a recommendation or an opinion.
>
> *The Court of Justice shall have jurisdiction, under the same conditions, in actions or proceedings brought by the European Central Bank in the areas falling within the latter's field of competence and in actions or proceedings brought against the latter.*[3]

[1] A. G. Toth (*Legal Protection of Individuals in the European Communities* (Amsterdam, 1978), ii, 97 and 'The Law as it Stands on the Appeal for a Failure to Act' [1975/2] *LIEI* 65 refers very appropriately to this remedy as 'the other side of the coin' in judicial review in respect of the action for annulment.

[2] Case 15/70 *Chevalley* v. *Commission* [1970] ECR 975, at point 6. T. C. Hartley (*The Foundations of European Community Law* (3rd edn., Oxford, 1994), 395) refers to the closeness of these two methods of recourse as the 'unity principle'.

[3] The words in italics represent the Maastricht amendments. See Art. 148 Euratom Treaty, which has retained its original version—identical with the original version of Art. 175 EC Treaty—and has not been affected by the Maastricht Treaty.

Several conditions have to be met in order to use Article 175. In the first place, the institution concerned must have an obligation to act. Secondly, the institution must have been called upon to act. Finally, only if within the period of two months the institution does not define its position can an action for failure to act be brought before the European Court.[4]

Article 35 ECSC Treaty considers the action for a failure to act as a variation of annulment proceedings. Thus, once the Commission has been called upon to act, if after two months the Commission remains silent, the silence is to be interpreted as an implied decision of refusal, against which annulment proceedings may be brought under Article 33 ECSC Treaty.

Several features of the action for a failure to act will be considered here.

> 1. As far as the *kinds of applicants* that may bring an action for a failure to act are concerned, Article 175 EC Treaty makes a distinction between (a) privileged applicants, that is Member States, and 'other institutions of the Community'[5] and the European Central Bank,[6] and (b) non-privileged applicants, i.e. natural and legal persons.[7]

There are several differences in the wording of Article 173: (1) in the first place, the expression 'other institutions of the Community' would, strictly speaking, include the European Court of Justice[8] and the Court of Auditors,[9] although it appears unlikely, given that those institutions do not have a right to bring any other of the actions in the Community system of judicial review; (2) in the second place, the European Parliament has, under Article 175, the status of a privileged applicant; under Article 173 it only has the status of a semi-privileged applicant and it can only act in defence of its prerogatives;[10] (3) in the third place, the European Central Bank can always bring an action for a failure to act (and not only for the defence of its prerogatives) in matters falling within its area of competence; (4) finally, non-privileged applicants (natural and legal persons) need to satisfy some *locus standi* conditions in order to bring an action for a failure to act, in other words they can only bring an action when 'a Community institution has failed to address to that person an act other than a recommendation or

[4] Such definition of position does not need to adopt a particular form, it being sufficient that the institution make clear that it has no intention of acting.

[5] Art. 175(1) EC Treaty.

[6] Art. 175(4) Ec Treaty.

[7] Art. 175(3) EC Treaty.

[8] This is not a unanimous view amongst academic writers. For some, the ECJ could be included, although that is unlikely (T. C. Hartley, n. 2 above, 399): others believe that the safeguard of the 'unity principle' between the action for annulment and the action for a failure to act determines that the ECJ does not have a right of action under this provision (A. G. Toth, n. 1 above, 77–8).

[9] The Maastricht Treaty has given the Court of Auditors the status of a Community institution (Art. 4(1) EC Treaty).

[10] See 16 above. The question arises why the Parliament should have different status under these two provisions, especially in view of the fact that the Maastricht Treaty has given the Parliament plenty of opportunities as a semi-privileged applicant.

an opinion'. Such wording appears more restrictive than that of Article 173(4) EC Treaty, which admits the challenge by a private applicant of a decision addressed to a third party, provided that it was of direct and individual concern to the applicant.[11]

The potential defendants in those proceedings are the European Parliament,[12] the Council, the Commission, and the European Central Bank.

Article 35 ECSC Treaty does not make a distinction between privileged and non-privileged applicants bringing an action for a failure to act. Thus Article 35 ECSC Treaty enables the Member States, the Council, undertakings, and associations of undertakings to call upon the Commission to act. There are two comments to be made on this statement: (1) first, and given that the authors of the Treaty created the fiction of an implied decision of refusal following the silence of the Commission, private parties would anyway need to satisfy the *locus standi* requirements of Article 33(2) ECSC Treaty in order to bring annulment proceedings against that decision of refusal; (2) secondly, the European Parliament does not have a right of action under Article 35 ECSC Treaty, unlike the case in annulment proceedings.[13]

The only potential defendant under the ECSC Treaty is the Commission, unlike the case in annulment proceedings, where the Commission may also bring proceedings against the European Parliament and the Council.[14]

Finally, as a general observation to this section, it is submitted that, given the increasing complexity of the Community system, sooner or later the question of the rights of other potential applicants (e.g. the Committee of the Regions) will have to be addressed by the Court.

2. In relation to the *kinds of omissions* that are reviewable, there is a distinction under Article 175 EC Treaty between the omissions reviewable by privileged and by non-privileged applicants.

Privileged applicants may bring an action when the Community institution 'has failed to act'. The wording of Article 175 EC Treaty is yet again more general than that of Article 173 EC Treaty. It is clear that it includes the omission to enact a legally binding act, but the question arises whether applicants may institute an action for the failure of a Community institution to adopt a recommendation or an opinion.[15] Academic writers appear

[11] See 27 above. See 213 below, on the *locus standi* of non-privileged applicants.

[12] The European Parliament has been added to the list by the Maastricht amendments. See 209 above.

[13] Art. 33(4) ECSC Treaty, see 15 above, n. 1.

[14] Art. 38 ECSC Treaty. The exclusion of the Council and of the European Parliament is probably logical, given that in annulment proceedings the Commission may only challenge acts of the European Parliament and of the Council on the grounds of lack of competence and infringement of an essential procedural requirement, which is a quite impossible situation if the institution has failed to act. Moreover, in the case of the Parliament, it would be quite unfair that, whilst being excluded from the list of potential applicants, it could nevertheless have *légitimation passive*.

[15] It must be recalled here that only legally binding acts are reviewable by means of an

divided on this matter.[16] It was explained[17] how the decisions of the Court in *Grimaldi*[18] and *Saarland*[19] recognized the possibility that recommendations and opinions respectively may produce legal effects. It was said then that the next step could be the recognition of its reviewability. In that case, it is thought that the wide interpretation of Article 175 EC Treaty will prevail.

Non-privileged applicants may only review decisions, because decisions are the only acts that may be addressed to a private party. Regulations are excluded from the scope of application of Article 175, given that they do not have an identified addressee but are of general application.[20] A similar reasoning would apply to directives, given that these are always addressed to the Member States.

In the framework of the ECSC Treaty, it appears clear that only the failure of the Commission to adopt a legally binding act is reviewable.[21]

3. In relation to the *grounds of illegality*, Article 175 EC Treaty speaks of those situations where the institution concerned fails to act 'in infringement of this Treaty'. Academic writers have agreed that, although there is no case law on this matter, such expression would be interpreted widely and that it would include, for instance, the failure to act in violation of a general principle of law[22] and in misuse of powers. [23] Other examples would be the failure of a Community Institution to carry out a duty imposed by the Treaty (whether general[24] or specific[25]).

action for annulment according to the wording of Art. 173 EC Treaty. But see the observations submitted on Case 322/88 *Grimaldi* [1989] ECR 4407 and Case 187/88 *Saarland* [1989] ECR 4407: see 20 above.

[16] Thus H. G. Schermers and D. Waelbroeck (*Judicial Control in the European Communities* (5th edn., Deventer, 1992), 249) and A. G. Toth (n. 1 above, 80) take the view that recommendations and opinions ought to be included in the scope of the action for a failure to act; other authors, like S. Weatherill and P. Beaumont (*EC Law* (London, 1993), 401–2) reject this view. In this respect see the observations of T. C. Hartley (n. 2 above, 401–2) on the possible conflict with the 'unity principle' that would arise if recommendations and opinions were to be included in the scope of Art. 175 EC Treaty.

[17] See 20 above.

[18] Case 322/88, n. 15 above.

[19] Case 187/88, n. 15 above.

[20] See D. Wyatt and A. Dashwood, *European Community Law* (3rd edn., London, 1993), 138; T. C. Hartley, n. 2 above, 411, and H. Schermers and D. Waelbroeck, n. 16 above, 257.

[21] Art. 35(1) and (2) ECSC Treaty. According to this legal provision, there are two cases when applicants may bring an action for a failure to act: (a) where the Commission was obliged to take a decision or to make a recommendation, and (b) where the Commission was empowered to take a decision or to make a recommendation and abstained from doing so and such abstention constituted a misuse of powers.

[22] See H. G. Schermers and D. Waelbroeck, n. 16 above, 252–3.

[23] A. Barav, 'Considérations sur la Spécificité du Recours en Carence en Droit Communautaire' (1975) 11 (2) *RTDE* 53, 70.

[24] e.g. the general duty imposed on the Commission by Art. 155 EC Treaty.

[25] e.g. the duty of the Commission to investigate suspected infringements of the principles of competition law imposed by Art. 89 EC Treaty.

4. Although Articles 35 ECSC Treaty and 175 EC Treaty do not establish a time-limit for calling upon the institution to act, the European Court of Justice made clear that 'the exercise of the right to raise the matter with the Commission may not be delayed indefinitely.[26] Once the institution concerned has been called upon to act, it has two further months in which to define its position (Article 175(2) EC Treaty and Article 35(3) ECSC Treaty); failure to do so, in the case of ECSC Treaty, results in an implied decision of refusal, subject to annulment proceedings and, in the case of the EC Treaty, renders possible action for a failure to act.

5. The *effect* of a successful action for a failure to act is a declaration that the omission of the Community institution was illegal. The European Court cannot enact the desired measure; it is for the institution concerned to take steps to comply with the judgment.[27]

8.2 *Locus Standi* of Non-Privileged Applicants

It has already been stated[28] that non-privileged applicants need to satisfy certain *locus standi* conditions in order to bring an action for a failure to act. In the framework of the EC Treaty, those conditions appear at first sight to be more restrictive than those applying to the action for annulment.[29] If the principle of unity between both methods of review is to be respected, disparities between them, such as the *locus standi* of private parties, should not be encouraged. The main reason for this is that a Community institution could choose not to adopt a measure (and avoid an application for judicial review from a private applicant) instead of adopting it and being subject to an action for annulment brought by a private party. A typical situation of 'denial of justice' would then arise.

The wording of Article 175(3) EC Treaty suggests that only in those cases where a Community institution failed formally to address a decision to an applicant would the action be declared admissible.[30] By contrast, a natural or legal person may seek the annulment under Article 173 EC Treaty of a decision addressed to a third party which is of direct and individual concern to the applicant. What would happen if an applicant tried to use Article 175 EC Treaty to challenge the failure of a Community institution to address a decision to a third party that would have been of direct and individual concern to the applicant? In other words, where a non-privileged applicant

[26] Case 59/70 *Netherlands* v. *Commission* [1979] ECR 639, at points 15–19.

[27] Art. 176 EC Treaty and Art. 34 ECSC Treaty.

[28] See 210 above.

[29] As already explained in the framework of the ECSC Treaty it appears clear that, by creating the fiction of an implied decision of refusal, private parties must satisfy the same *locus standi* conditions as in annulment proceedings under Art. 33; see 211 above.

[30] See 212 above.

would have had *locus standi* under Article 173 if only the Community institution had acted, would it have *locus standi* to challenge a failure to act?

In *Mackprang* v. *Commission*,[31] the Advocate General, Mr Dutheillet de Lamothe, made clear that, to safeguard the unity of annulment proceedings and the action for a failure to act, the kind of acts susceptible to review and the *locus standi* conditions ought to be the same for both remedies. In consequence, he advocated the view that private parties should be able to challenge the failure of the EC institution to adopt a decision, which, although addressed to a third party, would have been of direct and individual concern to them.[32] The Court did not rule on this matter in that case, but in later decisions gave some indication that it considered that the *locus standi* conditions ought to be the same for both methods of review.[33]

The decision of the Court in *Empresa Nacional de Urânio SA* v. *Commission*[34] finally gave a clear answer to this question. In that case, a company producing uranium complained that the Commission had failed to take a decision under Article 53 Euratom Treaty. One of the objections of the Commission to the admissibility of the action was that the decision that the applicants were requesting the Commission to adopt would have been addressed to the Supply Agency and not to the applicants. According to the strict wording of Article 148 Euratom Treaty,[35] therefore, the applicants did not have *locus standi* to challenge the Commission's default. The Court did not accept the Commission's contention and very briefly stated that, had the decision been enacted, it would have been challengeable by the applicants (since it was clear that it would have been of direct and individual concern to them). Consequently, the failure of the Commission to enact such a decision was equally challengeable.[36] Without saying so in so many words, the Court seems here to have accepted another manifestation of the principle of unity, namely the fact that *locus standi* conditions are the same for annulment proceedings as for the action for a failure to act. A private party may challenge the failure of a Community institution not only to address a decision to it but to address a decision to a third party which would have been of direct and individual concern to that private party.[37]

[31] Case 15/71 [1971] ECR 797.

[32] *Ibid.*, at 807–8.

[33] Thus see Case 42/71 *Nordgetreide* v. *Commission* [1972] ECR 105, where the Court declared inadmissible an action for a failure to act because the applicants wanted the Commission to amend a former reg. The Court said: '[s]uch a provision would have affected the applicant only in so far as it belongs to a category viewed in the abstract and in its entirety and not as the person to whom *an act of direct and individual concern to him* was addressed [emphasis added]': *ibid.*, at consideration 5. See also Case 246/81 *Lord Bethell* v. *Commission* [1982] ECR 2277, at points 11–17.

[34] Case C–107/91, judgment of 16 Feb. 1993, not yet reported.

[35] Art. 175 EC Treaty and Art. 148 Euratom Treaty are substantially identical.

[36] Case C–107/91, n. 34 above, at point 17.

[37] By contrast, private parties may not bring an action for the failure of a Community institution to adopt a dec. that would not have concerned them directly and individually. In

In the case of regulations, the inability of private parties to challenge the failure of the EC institutions to adopt a general act would be the logical consequence of the restrictive wording of Article 173 EC Treaty, which does not allow non-privileged applicants to challenge regulations. For instance, in *Holtz & Willemsen GmbH* v. *Council*[38] the applicants tried to challenge the failure of the Council to enact a regulation, and the Court rejected the application as inadmissible in so far as the failure to act referred to an act of a regulatory nature. Nevertheless, it has been seen that, in some instances, private parties may challenge true regulations[39] when one or more of their provisions concern those private parties directly and individually. The logical corollary of this view is that theoretically it should be possible for natural and legal persons to challenge a failure to enact a regulation that would have contained provisions of direct and individual concern to the applicants. This possibility seems however, rather vague in that it is very difficult to foresee what the regulation would have said had it been enacted.[40]

8.3 The Relationship between the Action for a Failure to Act and the Action for Annulment

Private parties will use the action for a failure to act in order to challenge the illegal inaction of a Community institution. This method of review appears as a useful complement to a system of judicial review where the action for annulment and other alternative means (preliminary rulings on validity, plea of illegality, and action for damages) aim to challenge potentially illegal Community acts. In particular, the close association between

particular, there is a consistent line of case law to the effect that private parties may not bring an action against a failure of the Commission to initiate proceedings under Art. 169 EC Treaty, namely to take action against a Member State for a failure to fulfil its obligations under the Treaty. The Court explained that, in the context of those proceedings, the only measures that the Commission may be induced to take are addressed to Member States: see Case C-37/89 *Emerich* v. *Commission* [1990] ECR I-1555 at points 5–6; Case C-72/90 *Asia Motor* v. *Commission* [1990] ECR I-21821, at points 10–11.; Cast T-5/94 *J* v. *Commission* [1994] ECR II-391, at point 11; Case T-13/94 *Century Oil Hellas* v. *Commission* [1994] ECR II-431, at point 13; Joined Cases T-479/93 and T-559/93 *Bernardi* v. *Commission*, Order of the CFI of 29 Nov. 1994.

[38] Case 134/73 [1974] ECR 1. See also Joined Cases 97, 193, 99 and 215/86 *Asteris* v. *Commission* [1988] ECR 2181; Case 90/78 *Granaria* v. *Council and Commission* [1979] ECR 1081;. Joined Cases C-15/91 and C-108/91 *Bulck* v. *Commission* [1992] ECR I-6061. Also see the Opinion of Roemer A.G. in Case 42/71 *Nordgetreide* v. *Commission*, n. 33 above, 116.

[39] See 150–2 above.

[40] The possibility must not, however, be ruled out: e.g. a complainant who, having participated in the administrative proceedings conducted by the Commission, challenges the failure of the Commission to enact a final anti-dumping reg. The case law of the Court in the area (see 161 ff. above) makes it quite certain that the complainant would have had *locus standi* to challenge the reg., had it been adopted by the Commission.

the action for annulment and the action for a failure to act has been emphasized. The relationship between both actions is complementary rather than one of substitution. The *locus standi* conditions are the same under both remedies and the same time-limits apply to both actions.[41] Therefore the action for a failure to act can hardly be seen as an alternative to the deficiencies of annulment proceedings before the European Court.

[41] Joined Cases 10–18/68 *Eridania* v. *Commission* [1969] ECR 459, at 483. In this case the Court made clear (*ibid.*, at 483) that Art. 175 cannot be used to get round the conditions of Art. 173 EC Treaty. In the framework of the ECSC Treaty see Joined Cases 21–26/61 *Meroni* v. *High Authority* [1962] ECR 73 at 78.

9

Conclusions and Recommendations

This work set out to study the rights of private parties seeking to obtain a review of the legality of Community acts. Given that the Community law-making process is not yet entirely driven by democratic principles, it appeared to be of the utmost importance to ensure that private parties could obtain a review of the legality of Community acts that are harmful to their interests. Accordingly, the European Community Treaties provided for a system of judicial review open to private parties. In this system, the action for annulment occupies a central position, although there are other means by which a consideration of the legality of a Community act may be undertaken.

Action for Annulment

In the context of annulment proceedings, strict limitations were imposed on private parties wishing to contest the legality of a Community act. These limitations resulted from the adoption of draconian *locus standi* requirements attached to actions under Article 173(2) EEC Treaty (now Article 173(4) EC Treaty). The reason for them is thought to be the long-standing desire to prevent Community measures from being continuously challenged. The result is that, in many cases, actions brought by private parties are dismissed as inadmissible. Article 173 EC Treaty imposes on *non-privileged applicants* (natural and legal persons) two types of limitation: (a) only measures which are substantially decisions may be challenged by those applicants, and (b) if the applicant is not the addressee of the decision, he will have to satisfy cumulatively the tests of direct and individual concern. In consequence, a private party wishing to challenge a measure in the form of a decision addressed to a third party will have to show that the decision directly and individually concerns the private party. If he wishes to challenge a measure in the form of a regulation, he will have to overcome the additional hurdle of showing that the measure is a decision in substance (in other words, he will have to fulfil the test of legal nature).

The severity of these conditions is particularly marked when they are compared with those imposed by the drafters of the EC Treaty on *privileged applicants* (Commission, Council, and Member States) and *semi-privileged applicants* (the European Parliament and the European Central Bank) under

Article 173 EC Treaty. The first group of applicants does not have to fulfil any condition in respect of standing, whereas the second group can act only in defence of their prerogatives. The European Parliament and the European Central Bank did not enjoy the right to bring annulment proceedings under the original version of the Treaties. The European Court granted the Parliament the right to bring those proceedings on the condition described above only after difficult juridical evolution. The Maastricht amendments to the EC Treaty have confirmed this point and, moreover, the European Central Bank has been given the status of a *semi-privileged* applicant. The Parliament's experience shows how the Court has finally chosen to uphold the rule of law and the existence of a comprehensive system of judicial review even at the expense of re-drafting the wording of the EC Treaty.

The conditions imposed by Article 173(2) EEC Treaty on private parties as interpreted by the Court also contrast with the more lenient standards of the national legal systems. In the legal systems of the Member States, there is a clear distinction between legislative and general administrative acts. Legislative acts are challengeable by individuals in very limited circumstances, if at all. In earlier stages, in most legal systems the applicants had to show an infringement of one of their rights before they could bring an action to review the legality of administrative action. Nowadays, in all Member States (with the exception of Germany and Luxembourg) it is possible to challenge general administrative acts upon proof of direct and individual interest. With small variations, in all Member States, individual acts are always reviewable by the addressees (who always enjoy *locus standi*) and by non-addressees upon proof of a direct and individual interest. National courts have been fairly lenient in the interpretation of the notions of direct and individual interest. In the Community legal system the clear distinction between legislative and administrative acts does not exist. Although it is clear that Council regulations adopt the form of true 'Community laws' it is also undisputed that some Commission regulations greatly resemble general administrative acts. The wording of Article 173 excludes *all* regulations from judicial review by private parties.

The wording of Article 173(2) EEC Treaty is also more strict than its immediate precedent, Article 33 ECSC Treaty. This latter provision specifies that *non-privileged* applicants (undertakings and associations of undertakings) may challenge both general decisions on the ground of a misuse of powers affecting them and individual acts that *concern* them. Moreover, the European Court of Justice followed a very liberal trend in the interpretation of the notion of 'concern', and finally a notion very close to that of interest in the national legal systems has arisen. Thus, for instance, competitors of the addressees of a decision have been granted standing to challenge it.

Analysis of the case law of the Court on the issue of the *locus standi* of private parties to challenge measures in the form of decisions within the framework of the EC Treaty produces the following results.

A uniform trend and some exceptional instances appear in the interpretation by the Court of the tests of direct and individual concern in cases involving decisions adopted by the area of general management of the market.

INDIVIDUAL CONCERN

The fact that an applicant belongs to a closed category—that is, one the membership of which was fixed when the decision entered into force—is normally the external indicator that the applicant may be individually concerned by that measure. This is the view defended by the majority of academic writers. In this work it is argued that a further question always has to be asked, namely, whether the individual rights of the applicants have been affected by the contested decision. It is clear from the case law that the mere capacity of the applicant as a trader or as a member of a well-defined group but not one fixed before the decision was issued does not suffice to render him individually concerned. Likewise, even in cases where the applicant had a clear interest in the annulment of the decision (e.g. because he was a competitor of the undertakings favoured by the decision), he has not been declared individually concerned. It is submitted that only in those cases where the applicant's individual rights have been affected by the decisions at issue has the Court acknowledged that he was individually concerned. Very frequently, the fact that prospective applicants belong to closed categories will mean that they will be individually concerned by a decision, but that is not *always* the case. The recent decision of the Court of First Instance in *Unifruit Hellas* v. *Commission* (in a case involving the challenge of a regulation) explains very clearly that applicants belonging to closed categories could not be individually concerned, given that they did not have any individual rights that had been affected by the measure at issue. Furthermore, the decision of the European Court in *Codorniu*, a case concerning a case concerning a regulation, emphasizes the importance of the existence of an individual right for the applicant.

DIRECT CONCERN

The test of direct concern has traditionally been interpreted according to the premise of whether or not the implementation of the contested decision requires the exercise of discretion by the addressee. It appears that, when the addressee is left with no measure of discretion, the applicant would be directly concerned by the decision. This seems to be an idea flowing especially from early case law. The Court introduced a degree of flexibility by declaring applicants directly concerned by decisions which left a certain degree of discretion to the addressees in their implementation, provided that the latter had made clear, either by express declaration or implicitly, how the discretion was to be used. It is suggested that, although this criterion may be quite useful in interpreting direct concern in the case of decisions addressed to Member States, there are three fundamental weaknesses: (a) in some cases, it is difficult to determine the real meaning of discretion; (b) it does not explain those cases where Member State addressees did not have any discretion in the implementation of a decision and prospective applicants were not directly concerned; (c) it does not explain the notion of direct concern in cases where the decisions were addressed to other private parties. It is argued that what is really central to the notion of direct concern in all cases is the existence of a relationship of causality between the decision and the damage inflicted on the applicant.

In summary, the Court seems to require in general that direct damage shall have been caused to the individual rights of the prospective applicant. In this respect there is a certain parallel with the early requirements of standing imposed in similar proceedings by the Member States, and particularly in the German legal system. The criteria are quite restrictive, especially if it is borne in mind that some natural and legal persons (e.g. competitors) might well suffer damage to their *interests* as a result of a Community decision, without actually suffering damage to their *rights*.

In a few instances, however, the Court has adopted a more liberal interpretation of the test of individual concern. Thus, in *Control Data*, *Schiocchet* and *'Les Verts'*, the applicants did not suffer damage to their rights from the decisions at issue and yet they were granted standing. These instances amount to a liberalization of the interpretation by the Court of the conditions of Article 173(2) EEC Treaty and more particularly of the test of individual concern. In *Control Data* and in *Schiocchet*, the applicants were highly individualized by certain factual circumstances, whereas in *'Les Verts'* considerations arising from the merits of the case determined the admissibility of the action.

It is the unanimous view of academic writers that the Court has followed a more lenient approach in the interpretation of the *locus standi* conditions contained in Article 173(2) EEC Treaty in cases involving decisions adopted in the area of competition and state aids. This has generally been related to the fact that particular features govern the procedures of adoption of this type of decision.

DECISIONS ADOPTED IN THE COURSE OF COMPETITION PROCEEDINGS

Whereas decisions adopted in the area of general management of the market are largely discretionary, and the intervention of private parties in the elaboration of those decisions is not provided for, the basic procedural regulations in competition law grant to individual parties a series of procedural rights which create a legitimate interest in the outcome of those proceedings. This circumstance has exerted great influence on the subsequent determination of those parties' *locus standi* in annulment proceedings. The Court's interpretation has been as follows.

Initially, the tests of direct and individual concern were not considered separately. The test of direct concern was rarely considered but it is clear that it was not related to the absence of discretion bestowed on the addressee, given that all the decisions at issue were addressed to third parties. The recent decision of the Court of First Instance in the *First Air France Case* has confirmed that an applicant is directly concerned when there is a direct relationship of causality between the decision and the damage caused to the applicant.

The test of individual concern was given a different construction from that adopted by the Court in decisions in the area of general management of the market. Thus, applicants were declared to be *individually concerned* when they had become procedurally involved in the adoption of the contested decision. The reason for this approach seems to be that the Commission implicitly recognized during the course of the competition proceedings that such parties had a legitimate interest in the outcome of the proceedings, and that is why they were allowed to participate. The corollary of the existence of that interest is the ability of these parties of bringing annulment proceedings. The decisions of the Court in the *First* and *Second Metro Cases* and in *Ancides* support this view, as does the decision of the Court of First Instance in *Nederlandse Bankiersvereniging en Nederlandse Vereniging van Banken*. This line of thought demonstrates the weakness of continuing to exclude from the opportunity of access to judicial review those parties who, whilst having a clear interest in the annulment of the decision, did not participate in the administrative proceedings for a variety of reasons (e.g. they missed the notice in the Official Journal announcing the initiation of proceedings).

A degree of leniency has been introduced by the recent decisions of the Court of First Instance, both in the field of merger control. In its decisions in the *Air France* and *Mineral Waters* cases, the Court granted *locus standi* to applicants, not on the basis of their participation in the administrative proceedings, but because they had a clear interest (whether factual or legally protected) in the annulment of the measure in question.

DECISIONS ADOPTED IN THE COURSE OF STATE AIDS PROCEEDINGS

In this area of case law there are no basic procedural regulations specifying the position of interested third parties. The Court has nevertheless applied the tests of direct and individual concern in the same way as in competition decisions. The test of direct concern has not been related to the absence of discretion bestowed on the addressee (even though all the decisions at issue have been addressed to Member States and therefore the concept could have been workable) but to the existence of a direct link between the decision and the damage inflicted on the applicant's interest. Applicants have been declared individually concerned as a result of becoming involved in the proceedings that led to the adoption of the decision. This has been the criterion applied in challenging decisions adopted under Article 93(2) EC Treaty (in both cases, i.e. decisions declaring the compatibility of an aid and decisions declaring the incompatibility of an aid with the Common Market). The Court adopted the same approach in one case involving a decision under Article 93(3) EC Treaty (*CIFRS*) where the Commission reached the conclusion that the aid in question was, *prima facie*, compatible with the Common Market.

As with competition cases, recent decisions have brought about a further degree of liberalization in the interpretation of the *locus standi* issue. Thus, the decision of the European Court in *Landbouwschap* v. *Commission*, concerning the challenge of a decision under Article 93(2) EC Treaty, seems to suggest that the sole capacity of the applicant as a competitor of the beneficiary of the aid could suffice to grant the former *locus standi* in annulment proceedings. In much clearer terms, the decision of the Court of First Instance in *ASPEC* v. *Commission* has emphasized that *locus standi* could be granted on the basis of the devastating economic consequences that a decision may cause to applicants, regardless of whether or not they participated in the administrative proceedings. In *Cook* v. *Commission*, the European Court granted standing to a private applicant in annulment proceedings against a decision under Article 93(3) EC Treaty, *exclusively* on the basis of his position as a competitor of the beneficiary of the aid (even though the applicant in this case had, in fact, participated in the administrative proceedings).

The analysis of the case law of the European Court of Justice and of the Court of First Instance on the *locus standi* of private parties to challenge Community regulations offers the following results.

As already explained, the wording of Article 173(2) EEC Treaty suggests that private applicants, in addition to fulfilling the tests of direct and individual concern, have to show that the regulation is in truth a decision. In other words, potential applicants need to satisfy three cumulative tests: legal nature, individual concern, and direct concern. The case law of the European Court of Justice has reflected the existence of two divergent lines of case law in the consideration of the *locus standi* issue. Although in some instances, the Court has decided the admissibility of actions brought by private parties on the basis of this triple admissibility test, in others it has ignored the first of these tests and has decided the *locus standi* issue solely on the basis of the tests of direct and individual concern. Academic writers have expressed their bewilderment when faced with these apparently conflicting lines of thought.

This work suggests, however, that the changing approach of the European Court of Justice is not arbitrary. A survey of the case law has shown that there are common threads in the Court's approach. It is believed that what appears as a disconcerting line of case law is responding in fact to the continuing effort of the Court to soften the severity of the *locus standi* conditions imposed by Article 173(2) EEC Treaty. This has become even more apparent, since the decision of the Court in *Sofrimport* in 1990, a landmark case in this area, and, more recently, with the decision of the European Court in *Codorniu*.

In the first place, the test of legal nature is very difficult to fulfil. Authors in the field have expressed their concern about the limited guidance that the Court has given so far in the interpretation of this test. Those rare decisions of the Court where the tests of legal nature has been found to be fulfilled make it appear that proof will be needed that the defendant institution enacted the regulation, not to deal with an objective situation in the market, but exclusively to deal with the situation of a group of people to which the applicants belong. If it is borne in mind that regulations are, by definition, measures of general application intended to deal with an objective situation in the market (and as such they are drafted in very general germs), it can easily be seen how difficult it is to obtain proof of existence of a causal link between the measure and the situation of the applicants. In truth, only in cases where the regulations at issue display very particular features (i.e. the defendant institution enacted the measure establishing the situation of the applicants *after* taking into consideration solely the material submitted by the applicants), or where the applicants are named in the measure itself, will it be possible for private applicants to surmount this admissibility condition successfully. The tests of direct and individual concern were interpreted by the Court on the same terms as the case law concerning decisions.

It is submitted that, prior to the decision of the Court in *Sofrimport* in 1990, the Court applied the double admissibility test mostly in those cases where the regulations at issue affected exclusively closed categories but where the existence of the causal link explained above was not clear. In all these cases the applicants (belonging to those closed categories) were directly and individually concerned. All these cases can already be seen as a reflection of the willingness of the Court to relax the *locus standi* conditions contained in Article 173(2) EEC Treaty given that, had the test of legal nature been applied, the actions would probably have been dismissed as inadmissible. This would have been a very unfair result, in that in all these cases the applicants belonged to a clearly identifiable group of persons who had suffered direct damage to their rights as a consequence of the contested regulations.

In contrast, most of the actions decided prior to 1990 involving regulations affecting open categories (whether large or small) were decided on the basis of the triple admissibility test. It is suggested that in none of these cases were the applicants in fact directly and individually concerned. In consequence, the outcome of the proceedings would have been exactly the same if the Court had simply applied those two tests to determine the admissibility of the actions.

In those cases where the regulations affected categories that were partially open and partially closed, the *locus standi* of the applicants belonging to closed categories had traditionally been decided on the basis of the triple admissibility test. As a consequence, actions brought by applicants who were in fact directly and individually concerned by provisions in the regulations at issue were dismissed as inadmissible as a result of applying the test of legal nature. This approach was rather unfair if one considers the damage inflicted on the applicants. Fortunately, the decisions of the Court in *Sofrimport* and *Codorniu* have given *locus standi* (in a case involving a regulation possessing precisely those characteristics) to applicants belonging to the closed category.

It follows that the existence of a divergent line of case law reflects the willingness of the Court to move towards a more liberal construction of the *locus standi* of private parties to challenge regulations. The first step for the Court was to free itself from the application of the test of legal nature, at least in those cases where the applicants were directly and individually concerned, i.e. when their rights suffered direct damage as a consequence of the contested regulation. The implication of this is that, despite the wording of Article 173(2) EEC Treaty, regulations may be challengeable by private parties when the tests of direct and individual concern are satisfied. The decision of the Court of First Instance in *Unifruit Hellas* lends support to the view that the Court of First Instance will also be ready to grant *locus standi* to private parties who have individual rights that have been affected by a regulation.

The case law of the Court after *Sofrimport* has shown further signs of the Court's intention of eradicating the test of legal nature in deciding the *locus standi* of non-privileged applicants. In fact, in all but two of the subsequent cases, the European Court and the Court of First Instance have decided the *locus standi* of natural and legal persons solely on the basis of the tests of direct and individual concern.

Anti-dumping proceedings share many features with competition and state aids proceedings. Most of the actions for annulment brought in the context of anti-dumping measures involve regulations imposing provisional or definitive anti-dumping duties. Accordingly, the *locus standi* of private parties should have been decided, in accordance with the letter of Article 173(2) EEC Treaty, on the basis of the triple admissibility test. The Court, however, from an early stage and with only one exception (*Alussuise*), ignored the test of legal nature and decided this issue on the basis of the tests of direct and individual concern. *Alussuise* is a puzzling case which the Court appears to have decided implicitly to disregard in its subsequent decisions.

The parties normally involved in anti-dumping proceedings are exporters, importers, and complainants, although other parties (i.e. associations of users and consumers) may also be interested in the outcome. Direct concern has never been examined separately in these cases. Individual concern has been applied in the same way as in cases involving competition and state aids decisions. For exporters and complainants, procedural involvement in the elaboration of the regulations has been the key factor affording them *locus standi*. Importers, however, were treated differently for many years and, even though in many cases they had become procedurally involved, they were only given standing when, in the determination of the existence of dumping, the export price had been constructed on the basis of the resale price to the first independent buyer. Fortunately, the recent judgment of the Court in *Extramet* has granted *locus standi* to an importer (who had, moreover, participated in the administrative proceedings) solely on the basis of factual circumstances: the importance of the applicant in the market in question and the devastating economic consequences that the regulation would impose on him.

Although directives are not mentioned in Article 173 EC Treaty, academic writers soon began to debate whether private parties might challenge these acts. The case law of the European Court and of the Court of First Instance in this area is still scarce and not consistent. Only future case law of the Court of First Instance will shed some light on this matter.

Recommendations and opinions are, in principle excluded from the circle of reviewable acts by Article 173 EC Treaty, given their non-binding character. However, the decisions of the Court in *Saarland* and *Grimaldi* suggest that opinions and recommendations respectively may produce legal effects. The next step, therefore, *could* be to permit their review under Article 173.

Alternative Means of Review

Preliminary rulings on the validity of Community measures constitute an indirect method of judicial review of the legality of Community action. Once a Community measure has been implemented by the national authorities, a private party may challenge the national measure before the national court, which in turn may refer a question about the validity of the

Community measure to the European Court. It would seem that proceedings under Article 177 EC Treaty are the perfect alternative to the deficiencies of annulment proceedings, because they have the obvious advantage that applicants do not have to fulfil strict *locus standi* conditions (in fact, the case law of the European Court provides a host of examples of cases where preliminary references submitted by national courts have allowed individuals and undertakings to obtain a ruling on the validity of Community measures—especially regulations—that they could not possibly have challenged by means of a direct action, due to their lack of *locus standi*). The recent decision of the Court in *TWD Textilwerke*, however, has limited the availability of Article 177 proceedings to those cases where it is not clear that applicants would have had *locus standi* under Article 173 EC Treaty; in other words, in all those cases where applicants would, without a shadow of doubt, have had *locus standi* under Article 173 EC Treaty, and nevertheless did not bring annulment proceedings, the route of Article 177 EC Treaty would be no longer available to them.

The system of preliminary rulings also has several disadvantages in relation to the route offered by annulment proceedings (once the *locus standi* barrier has been dealt with). In particular: (a) the decision to make a reference lies with the national court, which introduces a degree of uncertainty, in that private parties have no guarantee that a reference will ultimately be made; (b) the national court has discretion to decide the scope of the questions referred, which may result in prejudice against the applicants, who may wish to put forward different allegations; (c) exceptionally it may happen that there are no national measures of implementation of the Community measure, or, even if measures of implementation do exist, that there are no national procedures available to the applicant for challenging those measures—in those cases, the possibility of a preliminary reference is ruled out; (d) in some cases, in order to bring national proceedings with the intention of challenging the validity of a Community measure, applicants would have first to break Community law; (e) another problem arises in those cases where the European Court refuses to give a reference, which again means, from the point of view of private parties, further uncertainty; (f) finally, from a procedural point of view, it is thought that private parties benefit more from a procedure where there is a full exchange of pleadings, as in annulment proceedings, rather than from the system of submission of one written plea in the context of preliminary rulings.

The plea of illegality is another indirect method of challenging Community acts. It allows a party to plead the illegality of a normative act which is the legal basis of a measure at issue in the main action. The plea of illegality serves the purpose of allowing private parties to challenge regulations, or acts producing similar effects, once they are implemented, by means of a decision addressed to or of direct and individual concern to them. This remedy is an incidental and subsidiary method of judicial review, as it cannot be used independently but only when there are other proceedings pending before the European Court (and now, in the case of private parties, before the Court of First Instance). The nature of the proceedings in the course of which the plea of illegality may be invoked by natural and legal persons is varied, although most frequently it appears in the course of annulment proceedings.

The efficacy of the plea of illegality as an alternative to annulment proceedings is limited by the fact that only general acts may be challenged and, especially, by the fact that an implementing decision addressed to, or of direct and individual concern to, the applicant must exist.

The action for damages is aimed at obtaining compensation for loss caused by the acts of the Community institutions. Relevant to this work are those situations where non-contractual liability arises from acts intended to produce legal effects. Before any damages award is made, the European Court (and now, in the case of natural and legal persons, the Court of First Instance) has to reach the conclusion that the contested act is illegal. The action for damages thus provides an additional vehicle for obtaining a review of the legality of a Community act. However, the principles governing the action for annulment and the action for damages are essentially different and both actions have a very different purpose; through the action for annulment the Court will make a declaration that the contested measure is either legal or illegal, whereas through the action for damages the applicant will obtain an award for damages. The case law has imposed very strict conditions on which fulfilment damages may be granted and, in view of this, private parties will very frequently try first to obtain a ruling on the legality of the contested act, by bringing proceedings before the national courts, in the hope that a preliminary reference on the validity of the Community measure will be made by the national court, and only then will they bring an action for damages. It is suggested that the action for damages can only be a true alternative to annulment proceedings in those cases where an applicant has suffered a loss of sufficient gravity and there are no measures of implementation (which renders non-feasible access to the national court).

The action for a failure to act is a remedy closely related to the action for annulment in so far as, whereas annulment proceedings aim at the removal of illegal acts, the action for a failure to act seeks to challenge the unlawful inaction of the Community institutions. The relationship between both remedies is complementary rather than a matter of substitution. Given that the remedies are two aspects of the same method of recourse, disparities between them should not be encouraged, since this would translate into gaps in the system of judicial protection. The *locus standi* conditions imposed on private parties in the context of the action for a failure to act appear at first sight to be more restrictive than those applying to the action for annulment. Fortunately, the case law on this remedy, especially the recent decision of the Court of Justice in *Empresa Nacional de Urânio*, has gradually worked in the direction of ensuring that the *locus standi* conditions are the same in both remedies. The efficacy of the action for a failure to act as an alternative to annulment proceedings is therefore very limited, especially since the same *locus standi* conditions apply.

CONCLUSION

Although the *locus standi* conditions attached to annulment proceedings under Article 173(2) EEC Treaty (now Article 173(4) EC Treaty) are very strict, and despite the fact that the Court interpreted them rather narrowly in its early case law, there are indications that the Court is progressively adopting a more liberal approach in all areas of case law. From 1 August 1993 (from 15 March 1994 in anti-dumping cases), jurisdiction to deal with all actions brought by private parties has been transferred to the Court of First Instance. In the context of annulment proceedings, the decisions of the Court of First Instance in the *Air France* and *Mineral Water* cases in the field of competition and in *ASPEC* in the field of state aids suggest that the Court of First Instance is willing to follow the liberal trend inaugurated by the European Court of Justice.

This trend is a very welcome step towards the enhancement of the protection of natural and legal persons within the Community legal system. The consequences of systematically denying *locus standi* to private applicants in annulment proceedings have been serious. Academic writers, and indeed the European Court, have repeatedly suggested that alternative means of review are open to those applicants who wish to obtain a review of Community acts. The survey by this work of these alternative remedies suggests however, that they do not always fill the gap. It is quite possible (and some examples have been given) that private parties may thus be deprived of all judicial protection against potentially illegal Community acts. If the trend of the European Court continues, these gaps in judicial protection will be reduced. It is submitted that private applicants showing a clear individualized interest should be allowed to challenge decisions in the area of general management of the market (e.g. competitors). In the case of regulations, too liberal an interpretation of the *locus standi* conditions could, of course, imperil the stability of the Community's secondary legislation, especially in the case of regulations with a clear legislative character. If the Parliament had even greater powers of intervention in the legislative process (i.e. more extensive than results from the Maastricht amendments), it would play a role more closely resembling that of a national parliament. The availability of judicial review and the democratic control of legislative acts, as distinct from administrative acts, would thus more closely mirror what is considered acceptable within the tradition of the Member States. In any case it is thought that, in those rare cases where there is a reasonably arguable case that a regulation violates a general principle of Community law, private applicants should always be able to challenge them, so that situations like those giving rise to *COVALE* and *ARPOSOL* are not repeated.

Bibliography

GENERAL WORKS

AUBY, J. M., and DRAGÓ, R., *Traité des Recours en Matière Administrative* (Paris, 1992).

BAEL, I. VAN, and BELLIS, J. F., *Anti-dumping and other Trade Protection Laws of the EEC* (2nd edn., Bicester, 1990).

BEBR, G., *Development of Judicial Control in the European Communities* (The Hague, Boston, London, 1981.

BLAUSTEIN, A. P., and FLANZ, G. H., *Constitutions of the Countries of the World* (20 Vols., New York, London, Rome, 1971).

BOULOUIS, J., and CHEVALLIER, R. M., *Grands Arrêts de la Cour de Justice des Communautés Européennes* (Paris, 1974).

BRAIBANT, G., *Le Droit Administratif Français* (2nd edn., Paris, 1988).

BÜHLER, O., *Die Subjektiven Öffentlichen Rechte und ihr Schutz in der Verwaltungsrechtsprechung* (Berlin, 1914).

CANE, P. P., *An Introduction to Administrative Law* (2nd edn., Oxford, 1992).

CHAPUS, R., *Droit du Contentieux Administratif* (3rd edn., Paris, 1991).

DEBBASCH, C., *Administration et Administrés en Europe* (Paris, 1984).

DIJK, P. VAN, *Judicial Review of Governmental Action and the Requirement of an Interest to Sue* (The Netherlands, 1980).

FAVOREU, L., and JOLOWICZ, J. A., *Le Contrôle Juridictionnel des Lois* (Paris, 1985).

FOULKES, D., *Administrative Law* (7th edn., London, 1990).

GARNER, B. A., *A Dictionary of Modern Legal Usage* (Oxford, 1987).

GREEN, A. W., *Political Integration by Jurisprudence. The Work of the Court of Justice of the European Communities in European Political Integration* (Leyden, 1969).

HARTLEY, T. C., *The Foundations of European Community Law* (3rd edn., Oxford, 1994).

HOGAN, G., and MORGAN, D., *Administrative Law in Ireland* (2nd edn., London, 1991).

JACOB, SIR JACK I. H. (gen. ed.), *The Supreme Court Practice (1993)* (2 Vols., London, 1992).

JACOBS, F. G. (gen. ed.), *European Law and the Individual* (Amsterdam, New York, Oxford, 1976).

JOLIET, R., *Le Droit Institutionnel des Communautés Européennes* (Liège, 1981).

KAPTEYN, P. J. G., and VERLOREN VAN THEMAAT, P., *Introduction to the Law of the European Communities* (2nd edn., Deventer, Boston, 1989).

LEWIS, C. B., *Judicial Remedies in Public Law* (London, 1992).

LOUIS, J. V., *Les Réglements de la Communauté Economique Européenne* (Brussels, 1969).

MILLETT, T., *The Court of First Instance of the European Communities* (London, 1990).

MOSLER, H. (ed.), *Gerichtsschutz gegen die Exekutive* (Köln, 1969).

NEVILLE BROWN, L., and JACOBS, F. G., *The Court of Justice of the European Communities* (2nd edn., London, 1983).

PACTEAU, B., *Contentieux Administratif* (Paris, 1985).
RITTER, L., BRAUN, D., and RAWLINSON, F., *EEC Competition Law* (Deventer, 1991).
SCHERMERS, H. G., and WAELBROECK, D., *Judicial Protection in the European Communities* (5th edn., Deventer, 1992).
SCHINA, D., *State Aids under the EEC Treaty. Articles 92 to 94* (Oxford, 1987).
SHARPSTON, E. V. E., *Interim and Substantive Relief in Claims under Community Law* (London, 1993).
SHERIDAN, M., CAMERON, J., and TOULMIN, J., *EC Legal Systems: An Introductory Guide* (London, 1992).
SMITH, SIR THOMAS, and BLACK, R. (gen. eds.), *The Laws of Scotland*, Stair Memorial Encyclopaedia (25 Vols., Edinburgh, 1989).
STEINER, J., *Textbook on EEC Law* (2nd edn., London, 1990).
TOTH, A. G., *Legal Protection of Individuals in the European Community* (2 Vols., Amsterdam, New York, Oxford, 1978).
—— *The Oxford Encyclopædia of European Community Law* (Oxford, 1991).
VANDERSANDEN, G., and BARAV, A., *Contentieux Communautaire* (Brussels, 1977).
WADE, H. W. R., *Administrative Law* (6th edn., Oxford, 1988).
WAELBROECK, M., LOUIS, J. V., VIGNES, D., DEWOST, J. L., and VANDERSANDEN, G., *Le Droit de la Communauté Economique Européenne* (15 Vols., Brussels, 1983).
WEATHERILL, S., and BEAUMONT, P., *EC Law* (London, 1993).
WEINHARDT, D., *Die Klagebefugnis des Konkurrenten* (Göttingen, 1973).
WHISH, R., *Competition Law* (3rd edn., London, 1993).
WYATT, D., and DASHWOOD, A., *European Community Law* (3rd edn., London, 1993).
ZANOBINI, G., *Corso di Diritto Amministrativo* (4 Vols., 6th edn., Milan, 1950).

ARTICLES

ANDERSEN, P., [1925] 'Ugeskrift for Retsvaesen (a weekly law journal) B 244.
ANGULO, M. R., and DAWSON, F. G., 'Access by Natural and Legal Persons to the Court of Justice of the European Communities' (1967) 36 *Univ. of Cinc. LR* 583.
BARAV, A., 'Direct and Individual Concern: An Almost Insurmountable Barrier to the Admissibility of Individual Appeals to the European Court' (1974) 11 *CMLRev.* 191.
—— 'The Exception of Illegality in Community Law' (1974) 11 *CMLRev.* 366.
—— 'The Judicial Power of the European Economic Community' (1979–80), 53 *South Cal. LR* 461.
—— 'Preliminary Censorship? The Judgment of the European Court in *Foglia* v. *Novello*' (1980) 5 *ELRev.* 443.
BELLIS, J. F., 'Judicial Review of EEC Anti-dumping and Anti-subsidy Determinations after *Fediol*: The Emergence of a New Admissibility Test' (1984) 21 *CMLRev* 539.
BEBR, G., 'Judicial Remedies of Private Parties Against Normative Acts of the European Communities: The Role of the Exception of Illegality' (1966–7) 4 *CMLRev.* 7.
—— 'Examen en Validté de l'Article 177 du Traité CEE et Cohésion Juridique de la Communauté' [1975] *CDE* 379.
—— 'The Standing of the European Parliament in the Community System of Legal Remedies: A Thorny Jurisprudential Development' (1990) 10 *YEL* 171.

BUHART, J., 'Le Régime Communautaire de l'Antidumping: Vingt Ans d'Expérience' (1988) 24 *RTDE* 253.

CAETANO, M., 'La Protection Juridictionelle du Particulier contre le Pouvoir Exécutif au Portugal' in H. Mosler (ed.), *Gerichtsschutz gegen die Exekutive* (2 vols., Köln and Dobbs Ferry, 1970), 887.

CATALANO, N., 'Ancora sulla Tutela Giurisdizionale degli Exportatori di Prodotti Agricoli' [1965] IV *Foro It.* 124.

—— Text of Intervention in 'La Fusion des Communautés Européennes', colloquium organized in Liège on 28, 29, and 30 April 1965 (Martinus Nyhoff, The Hague, 1965), 284.

CHURCHILL, R. R., and FOSTER, N. G., 'Double Standards in Human Rights? The Treatment of Spanish Fishermen by the European Community' (1987) 12 *ELRev.* 430.

CONSTANTINESCO, V., and DENYS, S., 'Note sur *Parti Ecologiste "Les Verts"* c./ *P.E.*' [1987] *Recueil Dalloz (Jur.)* 79.

DINNAGE, J., '*Locus Standi* and Article 173 EEC Treaty; the Effect of the *Metro SB-Großmärkte* v. *Commission* judgement' (1979) 4 *ELRev.* 15.

DUBOIS, P., 'L'Exception d'Illegalité devant la Cour de Justice des Communautés Européennes' (1978) *CDE* 407.

EARLY, T. L., 'The Scope of Preliminary Rulings on the Validity of Community Law' (1980) 15 *The Irish Jurist* 237.

FREEDMAN, A. R., 'The Rights of Private Parties to Appeal Acts of the EEC' (1993–4) 3 *Vir. Int. LJ* 199.

FRIGNANI, A., 'Observations sur la Cour de Justice, 25 Octobre 1977, Aff. 26/76, *Metro*' [1978] *CDE* 440.

FROMONT, M., 'L'Influence du Droit Français et du Droit Allemand sur les Conditions de Recevabilité du Recours en Annulation devant la Cour de Justice des Communautés Européennes' (1966) 2 *RTDE* 47.

GARCÍA LÓPEZ, J. A., 'Derecho Económico Internacional y Relaciones Privadas: La Interdependencia Funcional del Régimen GATT y el Ordenamiento Jurídico Comunitario en la Applicación de Normas de Intervención Comercial, con particular Referencia al Derecho Anti-dumping' (1992) 54 *Rev. Esp. D Int.* 443.

GINDERACHTER, E. VAN, 'Problématique de la Recevabilité au Regard de la Réglementation CEE en Matière de Dumping et de Subventions' [1987] *CDE* 635.

GOFFIN, L., 'Jurisprudence. Affaires Jointes 106 et 107/63' [1966] *CDE* 72.

GORMLEY, P. W., 'The Procedural Status of the Individual before Supranational Tribunals' (1963–5) 41–42 *Univ. of Det. LJ* 405.

GREAVES, R., '*Locus Standi* under Article 173 EEC Treaty when Seeking Annulment of a Regulation' (1986) 11 *ELRev.* 131.

HARDING, C., 'The Private Interest in Challenging Community Action' (1980) 5 *ELRev.* 354.

HARTLEY, T. C., '*Locus Standi* in Actions under Article 173 EEC Treaty. *Metro Großmärkte* v. *Commission* (1978) 3 *ELRev.* 209.

—— 'Article 173: *Locus Standi* to Challenge Regulations. *Unicme* v. *Council*' (1978) 3 *ELRev.* 385.

—— 'Consulting the European Parliament. *Roquette* v. *Council* and *Maizena* v. *Council*' (1981) 6 *ELRev.* 181.

HARTLEY, T. C., 'Article 173. The Right of Private Parties to bring Proceedings. *Moksel* v. *Commission*' (1983) 8 *ELRev.* 41.

HENDRY, K., '*Ford* Sheds Further Light on the Commission's Power to Grant Interim Measures' (1984) 9 *ELRev.* 344.

JACOBS, F. G., 'Isoglucose Resurgent: Two Powers of the European Parliament Upheld by the Court' (1981) 18 *CMLRev.* 219.

JACQUÉ, J. P., 'Notes sur CJCE, 23 Avril 1986, *Parti Ecologiste "Les Verts"* c./ *P.E.*' (1986) 22 *RTDE* 491.

JOLIET, R., and VOGEL, W., 'Le Tribunal de Première Instance des Communautés Européennes' [1989] *RMC* 423.

KENNEDY, T., 'The Essential Minimum: The Establishment of the Court of First Instance' (1989) 14 *ELRev.* 7.

KOVAR, R., 'Chronique de la Jurisprudence de la Cour de Justice des Communautés Européennes. Aff. Jointes 106 et 107/63 *Alfred Toepfer* c./ *Commission*' (1966) 93 *JDI* 707.

—— 'Chronique de la Jurisprudence de la Cour de Justice des Communautés Européennes, 11 juillet 1968, Aff. 6–68 *Zuckerfabrick* c./ *Conseil*' (1969) 96 *JDI* 455.

—— 'Les Accords liant les Communautés Européennes et l'Ordre Juridique Communautaire: A Propos d'une Jurisprudence Récente de la Cour de Justice' [1974] *RMC* 345.

—— 'Observations sur la Cour de Justice CEE, 23 avril 1986, Aff. 294/83 "*Les Verts* c./ *PE*" [1987] *CDE* 300.

KOVAR, R., and BARAV, A., 'Variations Nouvelles sur un Thème Ancien: Les Conditions du Recours Individuel en Annulation dans la CEE: A Propos du Cas d'un Acte pris sous l'Apparence d'un Réglement' [1976] *CDE* 73.

KUYPER, J. P., 'Some Reflections on the Legal Position of Private Complainants in Various Procedures Relating to Commercial Policy' [1983–5] *LIEI* 115.

LABAUDÉRE, A. DE, 'Traités Généraux du Contentieux Administratif des Communautés Européennes' (1964) 111 *Recueil des Cours, Académie de Droit International* 531.

MANCINI, F., 'Access to Justice. Individual Undertakings and EEC Anti-Trust Law: Problems and Pitfalls' (1988) 12 *Fordham. Int.LJ* 189.

MATARASO, A. M., 'The Independent Importer's Right of Review of Anti-dumping Regulations before the European Court of Justice' (1988) 12 *Fordham. Int. LJ* 682.

NERI, S., 'Le Recours en Annulation dans les Communautés Européennes; Rôle et Limites' [1967] *RMC* 452.

NORALL, C., 'Judicial Review of Anti-dumping Measures: Further Developments' (1984) 9 *ELRev.* 46.

ÖPHULS, C. F., 'Les Réglements et les Directives dans les Traités de Rome' [1966] *CDE* 3.

PARKINSON, K. A., 'Admissibility of Direct Actions by Natural or Legal Persons in the European Court of Justice: Judicial Distinctions between Decisions and Regulations' (1989) 24 *Texas. Int.LJ* 433.

PETERS, J., 'Annotations on *Alfred Toepfer* v. *Commission*' (1965–6) 3 *CMLRev.* 233.

QUINLEY, C., 'The Notion of State Aid in the EEC' (1988) 13 *ELRev.* 242.

RASMUSSEN, H., 'Why is Article 173 Interpreted against Private Plaintiffs?' (1980) 5 *ELRev.* 112.

—— 'The Court of Justice of the European Communities' in *Thirty Years of Community Law* (Office for Official Publications of the European Communities, Brussels, 1981).

RASQUIN, G., and CHEVALLIER, R. M., 'L'Article 173, Alinéa 2 du Traité CEE' [1966] *RTDE* 31.

ST. CLAIR BRADLEY, K., 'The Variable Evolution of the Standing of the European Parliament in Proceedings before the European Court of Justice' (1988) 8 *YEL* 27.

SLYNN, SIR G., Text of the Exeter Lecture in European Community Law, Centre for European Legal Studies, University of Exeter, Friday, 10 May 1985.

STEIN, E., and VINING, J. V., 'Citizen Access to Judicial Review of Administrative Action in a Transnational and Federal Context' in F. G. Jacobs (ed.), *European Law and the Individual* (Amsterdam, New York, and Oxford, 1976), 113.

TEMPLE LANG, J., 'The Position of Third Parties in EEC Competition Law' (1978) 3 *ELRev.* 177.

TOTH, A. G., 'The Individual and European Law' (1975) 24 *ICLQ* 659.

USHER, J. A., 'Regulations, General and Individual at the Same Time?' (1984) 9 *ELRev.* 263.

VAJDA, C., 'Some Aspects of Judicial Review within the Common Agricultural Policy' (1979) 4 *ELRev.* 244 (Part 1), 341 (Part 2).

VERMULST, E. A., and HOOIJER, J. J., 'Note on *Extramet* v. *Council*' (1992) 29 *CMLRev.* 385.

WAELBROECK, M., 'Le Recours en Annulation' [1971] *RCJB* 513.

—— 'Examen de Jurisprudence 1955 à 1971. Communautés Européennes' [1971] *RCJB* 541.

WEILER, J., 'Pride and Prejudice: *European Parliament* v. *Council*' (1989) 14 *ELRev.* 334.

WELTER, F., 'La Protection Juridictionelle du Particulier contre le Pouvoir Exécutif au Luxembourg' in H. Mosler (ed.), *Gerichtsschutz gegen die Exekutive* (2 vols., Köln and Dobbs Ferry, 1970), ii, 679.

OTHER MATERIALS

ANONYMOUS, 'The Proposal for a European Court of First Instance' (1987) 12 *ELRev.* 77.

COMMISSION OF THE EUROPEAN COMMUNITIES: *IX Report on Competition Policy* (Office for Official Publications of the European Communities, Luxembourg, 1980).

—— *Opinion of the Commission of 20 July 1988 on the proposal for a Council Decision establishing a Court of First Instance*, Commission Document Series SEC(88)366 final.

—— *XXII Report on Competition Policy* (Office for Official Publications of the European Communities, Luxembourg, 1993).

EUROPEAN COURT OF JUSTICE AND COURT OF FIRST INSTANCE, 'Suggestions on European Union', Bull. EC 9/75 (Office for Official Publications of the European Communities, Luxembourg, 1975).

EUROPEAN COURT OF JUSTICE AND COURT OF FIRST INSTANCE,, 'Synopsis of the work of the Court of Justice and Court of First Instance of the European Communities in 1988 and 1989' (Office for Official Publications of the European Communities, Luxembourg, 1990).

—— 'Les Activités de la Cour de Justice et du Tribunal de Première Instance des Communautés Européennes en 1993', Service de l'informatique Juridique des Communautés Européennes, Luxembourg, 1994.

—— Report on certain aspects of the application of the Treaty of European Union ('Les Activités de la Cour et du Tribunal de Première Instance des Communautés Européennes', Week of 22 to 26 May 1995).

COURT OF FIRST INSTANCE, Paper Presented by the Court of First Instance on 3 April 1990, 'Reflections on the Future Development of the Community Judicial Systems' (1991) 16 *ELRev.* 175.

EUROPEAN PARLIAMENT, Report of 1 September 1981 drafted by the Committee on External Economic Relations of the EEC, *Anti-dumping Activities*, Doc. 1–422/81, 'The Welsh Report'.

—— *Report drawn up on behalf of the Committee on Legal Affairs and Citizens' Rights on the Proposal for a Council Decision Establishing a Court of First Instance submitted by the European Court of Justice*, Session Documents, Series A, Doc. A2—107/88.

OTHER: 'XXIV General Report on the Activities of the European Communities' (Office for Official Publications of the European Communities, Luxembourg, 1991.

'The Concept of Interest in Administrative Litigation', Eighth Colloquium of the Councils of State and the Supreme Courts of Justice of the Member States of the European Community (Copenhagen, 1982).

GENERAL WORKS

BELLAMY, C., and CHILD, G., *Common Market Law of Competition* (4th edn., London, 1993).

COLLIN, J. R., *Le Gouvernement des Juges dans les Communautés Européennes* (Paris, 1966).

COLLINS, L., *EEC Law in the United Kingdom* (London, 1990).

CUNNANE, J., and STANBROOK, C., *Dumping and Subsidies, the Law and Procedures Governing the Imposition of Anti-dumping Duties and Countervailing Duties in the EEC* (London and Brussels, 1983).

GARCÍA DE ENTERRÍA, E., and FERNANDEZ, T. F., *Curso de Derecho Administrativo* (2 vols., Madrid, 1990).

LASOK, D., and BRIDGE, J. W., *Law & Institutions of the European Communities* (5th edn., London, 1991).

LASOK, K. P. E., *The European Court of Justice: Practice and Procedure* (London, 1984).

LIPSTEIN, K., *The Law of the European Economic Community* (London, 1974).

PESCATORE, P., *L'Ordre Juridique des Communautés Européennes* (2nd edn., Liège, 1973).

POIDEVIN, R., *Histoire des Débuts de la Construction Européenne*, Actes du Colloque de Strasbourg, 18–30 Novembre 1984 sous la direction de Raymond Poidevin

(Brussels, Milan, Paris, Baden-Baden, 1985).

SCHERMERS, H. G., TIMMERMANS, C. W. A., KELLERMAN, A. C., and WATSON, J. S., *Article 177 EEC Treaty. Experiences and Problems* (Amsterdam, 1987).

SCHWARZE, J., *European Administrative Law* (London, 1992).

STEIN, E., HAY, P., and WAELBROECK, M., *European Community Law and Institutions in Perspective* (Indianapolis, New York, 1963).

ARTICLES

ALLENDE SALAZAR, R., 'Participación de los Particulares en el Control de la Legalidad de los Actos de las Instituciones: El Recurso de Anulación,. Evolución Jurisprudencial' (1986) 13 *Revista de las Instituciones Europeas* 655.

BAEL, I. VAN, 'Ten Years of EEC Anti-Dumping Enforcement' (1979) 13 *JWTL* 395.

BEBR, G., 'Preliminary Rulings of the European Court of Justice: Their Authority and Temporal Effect' (21981) 18 *CMLRev.* 475.

CAPELLETTI, M., 'The Mighty Problem of Judicial Review and the Contribution of Comparative Analysis' [1979] *LIEI* 1.

—— 'Is the European Court Running Wild?' (1987) 12 *ELRev.* 3.

CARRO MARINA, M., 'El Artículo 173.2 TCEE y la Legitimación para Recurrir Reglamentos de la CEE' [1987] *Revista Española de Derecho Administrativo* 287.

CATALANO, N., 'La Protection Juridictionelle Indirecte dans le Système des Traités de Rome' [1966] 2 *RTDE* 371.

CHEVALLIER, R. M., 'Methods of Reasoning of the European Court of Justice in its Interpretation of Community Law' (1964–5) 2 *CMLRev.* 21.

CHURCHILL, R., 'Fisheries: A Review of Recent Cases' (1988) 13 *ELRev.* 352.

CROSSLAND, H. G., 'Rights of the Individual to Challenge Administrative Action before Administrative Courts in France and Germany' (1975) 24 *ICLQ* 707.

DAVIS, K. C., 'Standing' (1977–8) 72 *Northwestern ULR* 69.

DE LA TORRE MUNMANY, J., 'Illegalidad de las Normas Comunitarias y Vias de Recurso de los Particulares' (1991) 4 *Cuadernos Europeos de Deusto* 133.

HARDING, C., 'The Impact of Article 177 of the EEC Treaty on the Review of Community Action' [1981] 1 *YEL* 93.

KOVAR, R., 'Le Droit des Personnes Privées a obtenir devant la Cour des Communautés Européennes le Respect du Droit Communautaire par les Etats Membres' [1966] *XII Annuaire Français de Droit International* 707.

LOUIS, J. V., 'Le Droit pour les Particuliers d'agir en Annulation selon le Traité du Marché Commun' [1964] *Revista de Derecho, Jurisprudencia y Administración* 232.

PESCATORE, P., 'The Doctrine of Direct Effect, an Infant Disease of European Community Law' (1983) 8 *ELRev.* 155.

PLENDER, R., 'The European Court of Justice as an International Tribunal' (1983) 42 *CLJ* 279.

RABE, H. J., and SCHÜTTE, M., 'EC Anti-dumping Law: Current Issues in the Light of the Jurisdiction of the Court' (1989) 26 *CMLRev.* 643.

USHER, J. A., 'General Course of EEC Law. The Continuing Development of Law and Institutions' in the *Collected Courses of the Academy of European Law*, Florence

(Deventer, 1992) Book I, vol. II, 37.

VALENTINE, D. G., 'The Jurisdiction of the Court of Justice of the European Communities to Obtain the Annulment of Executive Action' (1960) 36 *BYIL* 174.

VAN RIJN, T., 'L'Exception d'Illegalité' (1980) 16 *CDE* 177.

VEROUGSTRAETE, I., 'Recevabilité du Recours en Annulation et Respect du Principe de Proportionalité de l'Action de l'Administration' [1972] *CDE* 666.

VIGNES, D., and SACCHETINI, A., 'La Protection Juridictionelle des Particuliers à l'Egard de la Réglementation Communautaire en Matière Agricole' [1971] 1 *RDR* 1.

WINTER, J. A., 'Direct Applicability and Direct Effect: Two Distinct Concepts in EEC Law' (1972) 9 *CMLRev.* 425.

WOLTERS, A., 'Le Recours en Annulation devant la CJCEE' [1960] *RDIDC* 165.

Index